PEARSON EDUCATION
SECONDARY GROUP

1 Lake Street
Upper Saddle River, NJ 07458
201-236-5401...781-455-1309
Fax: 201-236-5553...781-433-8425
E-Mail: marty.smith@phschool.com

Martha G. Smith
President
Pearson Education
Secondary Group

To the Teacher:

As a former social studies teacher, I cannot imagine a more important time to be a social studies educator.

Since the terrorist attacks on New York City and Washington, D.C., on September 11, 2001, you have served at the front line of efforts to understand the causes and effects of those momentous events. In the social studies classroom, you have helped your students understand our nation's heritage of unity and determination in times of crisis. You have had the opportunity to instill in your students the core values of democracy, free enterprise, and the rule of law. Your students have probably explored concepts of freedom and justice, through primary sources from the Declaration of Independence to the "I Have a Dream" speech, and the rights and responsibilities of citizenship, through the Constitution of the United States. They may be learning and applying critical thinking skills as well—debating, for example, the benefits and challenges of living in an open and tolerant society.

As a social studies educator, you can help your students master the fundamentals of history, geography, civics, and economics, providing a context within which to analyze current events. With your guidance, this knowledge can inform and encourage young people's participation in the democratic process.

Today more than ever, you play a crucial role in the maturing of responsible citizens. You help create tomorrow's leaders—the future defenders of America's freedoms, as defined by one President during another time of great crisis:

> *"In the future days which we seek to make secure, we look forward to a world founded upon four essential human freedoms. The first is freedom of speech and expression—everywhere in the world. The second is freedom of every person to worship God in his own way—everywhere in the world. The third is freedom from want . . . everywhere in the world. The fourth is freedom from fear . . . anywhere in the world."*
>
> —President Franklin Delano Roosevelt
> State of the Union Address, January 6, 1941

Sincerely,

Martha G. Smith

The world studies program that lets you choose.

Prentice
Hall

Needham, Massachusetts
Upper Saddle River, New Jersey
Glenview, Illinois

Acknowledgments appear on page 230, which constitutes an extension of this copyright page.

ISBN 0-13-062973-1

1 2 3 4 5 6 7 8 9 10   06 05 04 03 02

PRENTICE HALL

Social Studies

Reaching Today's Students

T1

But I'm Not a Reading Teacher!

*F*ew people choose to be social studies teachers in order to focus on reading. Yet a significant number of today's students lack reading proficiency. Without it, they cannot access the wealth of social studies content they need to absorb from textbooks, primary sources, literature, and more. When students can't read well, they don't read and won't read.

Best Practices in Reading

Instead of plunging in and plodding through a section, students need a plan of action, a strategy. Best practices for teaching reading in social studies focus on **comprehension strategies**—teaching students what to do *before reading, during reading,* and *after reading.*

Reading Proficiency in Secondary Students

Source: NAEP Reading Report Card

Here are some ways to implement these strategies with struggling readers:

Before Reading Both teacher and student preparations precede reading.

- Use an anecdote, photo, artifact, or audio to set the scene.
- Display a map or other visual aid to encourage students to identify what they already know and to make predictions by applying this knowledge to a new situation.
- Model for students how to look at pictures, captions, and headings in order to predict what they will be learning.

During Reading Student-directed, individual activities take place during reading. Providing guided practice will help students develop these habits.

- Show students how to take notes, using graphic organizers that match the type of information they are reading. For example, use a Venn diagram for comparing and contrasting, a flow chart for sequencing, and a concept web for finding main ideas and supporting details.
- Teach students to ask themselves questions as they read.
- Demonstrate for students how to make connections between what they read and what they already know.

After Reading Both student-directed and teacher-directed activities can follow reading.

- Conduct a sample self-check for students—"What have I learned?"
- Teach students to ask themselves, "How does this relate to what I already know?"
- Demonstrate both formal and informal assessments that students will encounter.

Comprehension Strategies

Before Reading

- Activate prior knowledge
- Build needed prior knowledge
- Focus attention
- Set purpose for reading
- Make predictions

During Reading

- Confirm predictions
- Read and self-monitor
- Take notes and ask questions

After Reading

- Recall information
- Respond to new learning
- Extend and transfer new learning
- Assess reading success

Reading success happens when students can construct meaning from information.

Prentice Hall Support Throughout the Program

The structure of each Prentice Hall program embeds the development of solid reading skills in the Student Edition. Each section of the text starts with suggestions to the student for *before reading* and *during reading.*

At the end of each section, students will find opportunities to recall and apply information and construct meaning from it.

Notice that the *Before You Read* and *Read Actively* boxes support reading skills throughout each section.

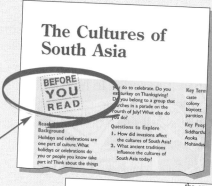

Teacher's Edition

Additional reading strategies as well as ways to customize instruction for English language learners and nontraditional students give you focused strategies to improve students' comprehension.

Section Reading Support Transparency System

Every section of the text has a companion reading support transparency that answers the Questions to Explore and delivers the main points through a graphic organizer.

Student Edition on Audio

Auditory learners, less proficient readers, and English language learners can benefit from listening to the book on CD as they read the text.

Why Should I Teach Skills?

"Give a man a fish, and he eats for a day. Teach a man to fish and he eats for a lifetime."

— Anonymous

*F*ollowing this advice, if we present our students with only content, we are, in essence, giving them the fish. If we are to prepare students for life, we need to teach the skills needed to make sense out of the increasing volume of information in the world. To help students become lifelong learners, we need to develop their abilities to question, read, analyze, interpret, and evaluate information, as well as to communicate their ideas to others.

Best Practices in Skills Integration

These guidelines will help you to embed skills development within content instruction.

1. **Plan each book or chapter around an enduring understanding or big idea. The Guiding Questions in each Book Opener can help you.** For example, if you are beginning study of the United States and Canada, you might stress the question "How have historical events affected the cultures of the United States and Canada?"

Topic: Colonization		
	Example	**Skill**
Facts	Location of colonies	Map reading
Concepts	Migration	Cause and effect
Big Ideas	People make choices to meet needs	Problem solving

2. **Develop each lesson around the facts, concepts, the big idea, and the skills students need to be able to connect the content to the big idea.** For part of a lesson on the geography of North Africa, you might want to focus on desertification and its impact.

3. **Teach skills that are new or that add another level of complexity to a previously mastered skill.** Follow the elements of good skill instruction:
   • Set a purpose for using the skill.
   • Present the steps to follow.
   • Model the process for using the skill.
   • Guide practice and provide feedback.
   • Apply a prompt such as a picture, map, or reading passage.

Elements of Skill Instruction

Teach the skill

Model applying the skill often

Guide practice of the skill

Give feedback and correction

Have students apply the skill independently

4. **Reinforce skills whenever possible.** Ask critical thinking questions about maps, photos, graphs, charts, and primary sources.

5. **Assess both content and skills mastery regularly.** It is important to determine whether students are remembering important information, but equally important to determine whether they are internalizing skills as lifelong learners.

Prentice Hall Support for Skills

Skills mastery means developing habits of mind that enable us to turn information into meaning. Every Prentice Hall social studies program contains a wealth of resources to build skills for life.

Skills pages in the Student Edition provide a three-step instruction strategy.

Skills reinforcement appears in all caption questions.

Social Studies Skills Tutor CD-ROM provides two levels of interactive instruction and practice in 20 core social studies skills.

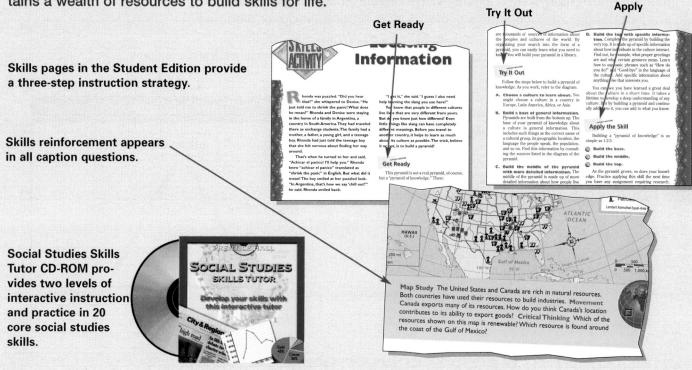

Get Ready   Try It Out   Apply

Map Study The United States and Canada are rich in natural resources. Both countries have used their resources to build industries. Movement Canada exports many of its resources. How do you think Canada's location contributes to its ability to export goods? Critical Thinking Which of the resources shown on this map is renewable? Which resource is found around the coast of the Gulf of Mexico?

Prentice Hall Vertical Alignment System

Mastery also requires that students learn skills at increasing levels of complexity as they progress through school. Prentice Hall programs take the guesswork out of aligning skills instruction by developing 20 core social studies skills with increasing difficulty from grade to grade.

The 20 Core Social Studies Skills

1. Using the Cartographer's Tools	**11.** Comparing and Contrasting
2. Using Special Purpose Maps	**12.** Analyzing Primary Sources
3. Analyzing Graphic Data	**13.** Recognizing Bias and Propaganda
4. Analyzing Images	**14.** Identifying Frame of Reference and Point of View
5. Identifying Main Ideas/Summarizing	**15.** Decision-making
6. Sequencing	**16.** Problem-solving
7. Identifying Cause & Effect/ Making Predictions	**17.** Using Reliable Information
8. Drawing Inferences and Conclusions	**18.** Transferring Information from One Medium to Another
9. Making Valid Generalizations	**19.** Synthesizing Information
10. Distinguishing Fact & Opinion	**20.** Supporting a Position

Should I Teach To The Test?

*T*he increasing importance of state standards and student accountability leads many teachers to wonder whether they must limit their classes to the content of high-stakes exams. While based on state standards and student needs, a truly effective social studies program requires **alignment of curriculum, instruction, and assessment.** When each of these elements dovetails with the others, *all* instruction prepares students for assessment based on curriculum objectives.

In an aligned system, both teacher and student know what is expected. There are no secrets or surprises. To ensure alignment:

- Teach the objectives in your standards to the specified level of understanding.
- Make sure that students know what they should learn before you teach.
- Test those same objectives as precisely as possible to the same depth of understanding that the standards require.

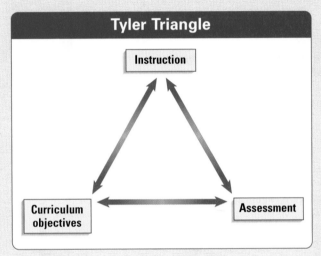

Best Practices in Assessment

Here are some ways to integrate ongoing assessment with instruction:

Assessment Techniques	
Diagnose and Prescribe	Evaluate student abilities at the beginning of the year.
Plan and Align Plan instruction to align with assessment.	• Examine objectives carefully and choose activities where more than a knowledge level (or memorized level) is expected of students. • Test students on all of the objectives, omitting none. • Test skill development at the same time you assess content.
Review and Reteach Weave ongoing review into aligned instruction and assessment.	Connect instruction to prior learning and include review questions on each test.
Practice and Assess Apply assessment results to improve teaching and learning.	• Use individual student information for tutoring and devising individualized plans. • Use whole-class data to determine if your teaching was aligned to the assessment.

Prentice Hall Assessment System

The Prentice Hall Assessment System provides comprehensive support for both program content assessment and preparation for high-stakes standardized tests.

Program Assessment

Use the Chapter Tests to assess core content for every chapter.

💿 Develop your own customized tests and practice worksheets with the ExamView Test Bank CD-ROM, selecting from hundreds of test questions and using the word-processing and editing capabilities. Create online tests and study guides and receive instant feedback on student progress.

Standardized Test Preparation

Prentice Hall Assessment System gives you the tools to help your students succeed on standardized tests, from the beginning of the year to the culminating high-stakes exam.

Diagnose and Prescribe

📖 Profile student skills with Diagnostic Tests A & B.

📖 Address student needs with program resources correlated to diagnostic test questions.

Review and Reteach

📖 Provide cumulative content review with unit-level questions and study sheets.

Practice and Assess

📖 Build assessment skills using Test-Taking Strategies with Transparencies.

Reinforce assessment skills with Test-taking Posters.

📖 Practice taking tests and improve scores on standardized tests with the Test Preparation Workbook.

The world studies program that lets you choose.

Program Components
Student Editions
Teacher's Editions

Classroom Resources
Teaching Resources
  Chapter and Section Support
  Activities and Projects
  Tests
  Social Studies and Geography Skills
  Section Reading Support Transparencies
Program Resources
  Primary Sources and Literature Readings
  Long-Term Integrated Projects
  Outline Maps
  Environmental and Global Issues
  Writing Process Handbook
  Assessment Handbook
  Technology in the Classroom
  Using the Internet
  Block Scheduling
  The Middle Grades Experience
  Pacing Charts
  Glossary of Geographic Terms Poster
  Read Actively Poster
  Nystrom Desk Atlas
Guided Reading and Review Workbook (English)
Guided Reading and Review Workbook (Spanish)
Color Transparencies
Section Reading Support Transparency System
Humanities Pack for Middle Grades
Literature Library for Middle Grades World Studies

Assessment
Prentice Hall Assessment System
  Chapter Tests with ExamView® Test Bank CD-ROM
  Alternative Assessment
  Diagnostic Tests for Middle Grades
    Social Studies Skills
  Review Book for Middle Grades World Studies
  Test Prep Book for Middle Grades World Studies
  Test-Taking Strategies with Transparencies
    for Middle School
  Test-Taking Strategies Posters
ExamView® Test Bank CD-ROM

Technology
Guided Reading Audiotapes (English)
Guided Reading Audiotapes (Spanish)
Student Editions on Audio CD
World Video Explorer
Passport to the World CD-ROM
Social Studies Skills Tutor CD-ROM
Resource Pro® CD-ROM
Prentice Hall Presentation Pro CD-ROM
Companion Web Site

PH SuccessNet

LATIN AMERICA

Prentice Hall

Needham, Massachusetts
Upper Saddle River, New Jersey
Glenview, Illinois

Program Consultants

Heidi Hayes Jacobs

Heidi Hayes Jacobs has served as an educational consultant to more than 1,000 schools across the nation and abroad. Dr. Jacobs served as an adjunct professor in the Department of Curriculum on Teaching at Teachers College, Columbia University. She has written a best-selling book and numerous articles on curriculum reform. She completed her undergraduate studies at the University of Utah in her hometown of Salt Lake City. She received an M.A. from the University of Massachusetts, Amherst, and completed her doctoral work at Columbia University's Teachers College in 1981.

The backbone of Dr. Jacobs' experience comes from her years as a teacher of high school, middle school, and elementary school students. As an educational consultant, she works with K–12 schools and districts on curriculum reform and strategic planning.

Brenda Randolph

Brenda Randolph is the former Director of the Outreach Resource Center at the African Studies Program at Howard University, Washington, D.C. She is the Founder and Director of Africa Access, a bibliographic service on Africa for schools. She received her B.A. in history with high honors from North Carolina Central University, Durham, and her M.A. in African studies with honors from Howard University. She completed further graduate studies at the University of Maryland, College Park, where she was awarded a Graduate Fellowship.

Brenda Randolph has published numerous articles in professional journals and bulletins. She currently serves as library media specialist in Montgomery County Public Schools, Maryland.

Michal L. LeVasseur

Michal LeVasseur is an educational consultant in the field of geography. She is an adjunct professor of geography at the University of Alabama, Birmingham, and serves with the Alabama Geographic Alliance. Her undergraduate and graduate work is in the fields of anthropology (B.A.), geography (M.A.), and science education (Ph.D.).

Dr. LeVasseur's specialization has moved increasingly into the area of geography education. In 1996, she served as Director of the National Geographic Society's Summer Geography Workshop. As an educational consultant, she has worked with the National Geographic Society as well as with schools to develop programs and curricula for geography.

Special Program Consultant

Yvonne S. Gentzler, Ph.D.
Iowa State University
College of Family and Consumer Sciences
Ames, Iowa

Content Consultant on Latin America

Daniel Mugan
Center for Latin American Studies
University of Florida
Gainesville, Florida

ISBN 0-13-062972-3

1 2 3 4 5 6 7 8 9 10   06 05 04 03 02

Prentice
Hall

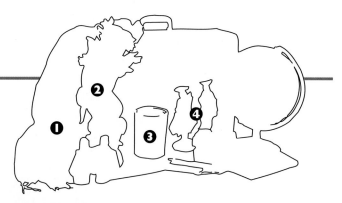

On the Cover

❶ Woven blanket from Mexico

❷ Mexican wood carving of an ancient Mayan snake god

❸ Reproduction of Mayan pottery

❹ Family of dolls from Peru dressed in traditional clothing

Content Consultants for the World Explorer Program

Africa
Barbara Brown
African Studies Center
Boston University
Boston, Massachusetts

Ancient World
Maud Gleason
Department of Classics
Stanford University
Stanford, California

East Asia
Leslie Swartz
Vice President for Program
    Development and Harvard East
    Asian Outreach Program at The
    Children's Museum, Boston
Boston, Massachusetts

Latin America
Daniel Mugan
Center for Latin American Studies
University of Florida
Gainesville, Florida

Middle East
Elizabeth Barlow
Center for Middle Eastern and
    North African Studies
University of Michigan
Ann Arbor, Michigan

North Africa
Laurence Michalak
Center for Middle East Studies
University of California
Berkeley, California

Religion
Michael Sells
Department of Religion
Haverford College
Haverford, Pennsylvania

**Russia, Eastern Europe,
Central Asia**
Janet Vaillant
Davis Center for Russian Studies
Harvard University
Cambridge, Massachusetts

South Asia
Robert Young
Department of History
West Chester University
West Chester, Pennsylvania

Western Europe
Ruth Mitchell-Pitts
Center for West European Studies
University of North Carolina
Chapel Hill, North Carolina

Teacher Advisory Board

Jerome Balin
Lincoln Junior High School
Naperville, Illinois

Elizabeth Barrett
Tates Creek Middle School
Lexington, Kentucky

Tricia Creasey
Brown Middle School
Thomasville, North Carolina

Patricia H. Guillory
Fulton County Schools
Atlanta, Georgia

Stephanie Hawkins
Oklahoma City Public Schools
Oklahoma City, Oklahoma

Fred Hitz
Wilson Middle School
Muncie, Indiana

Kristi Karis
West Ottawa Public Schools
Holland, Michigan

Peggy Lehman
Carmel Junior High/Carmel-Clay
    Schools
Carmel, Indiana

Peggy McCarthy
Beulah School
Beulah, Colorado

Cindy McCurdy
Hefner Middle School
Oklahoma City, Oklahoma

Deborah J. Miller
Detroit Public Schools
Detroit, Michigan

Lawrence Peglow
Pittsburgh Public Schools
Pittsburgh, Pennsylvania

Paula Rardin
Riverview Gardens Schools
St. Louis, Missouri

Kent E. Riley
Perry Meridian Middle School
Indianapolis, Indiana

Christy Sarver
Brown Middle School
Thomasville, North Carolina

Lyn Shiver
Northwestern Middle School
Alpharetta, Georgia

Mark Stahl
Longfellow Middle School
Norman, Oklahoma

TABLE OF CONTENTS

LATIN AMERICA   1

Readable, accessible content to motivate your students (see pp. 8–9)

O F S P E C I A L I N T E R E S T

Maps and charts providing a closer look at countries, regions, and provinces.

A hands-on approach to learning and applying social studies skills

Step-by-step activities for exploring important topics in Latin America

Literature selections by Latin American authors

Profiles of people who made a difference in their country

Detailed drawings show how the use of technology makes a country unique

Maps and statistics for every nation in Latin America

A view of a country through the eyes of a student artist

Active learning approaches to involve and engage students (see pp. 2–7)

READ ACTIVELY

How can I get the most out of my social studies book? How does my reading relate to my world? Answering questions like these means that you are an active reader, an involved reader. As an active reader, you are in charge of the reading situation!

The following strategies tell how to think and read as an active reader. You don't need to use all of these strategies all the time. Feel free to choose the ones that work best in each reading situation. You might use several at a time, or you might go back and forth among them. They can be used in any order.

BEFORE YOU READ

Give yourself a purpose

The sections in this book begin with a list called "Questions to Explore." These questions focus on key ideas presented in the section. They give you a purpose for reading. You can create your own purpose by asking questions like these: How does the topic relate to your life? How might you use what you learn at school or at home?

Preview

To preview a reading selection, first read its title. Then look at the pictures and read the captions. Also read any headings in the selection. Then ask yourself: What is the reading selection about? What do the pictures and headings tell about the selection?

Reach into your background

What do you already know about the topic of the selection? How can you use what you know to help you understand what you are going to read?

Ask questions

Suppose you are reading about the continent of South America. Some questions you might ask are: Where is South America? What countries are found there? Why are some of the countries large and others small? Asking questions like these can help you gather evidence and gain knowledge.

Predict

As you read, make a prediction about what will happen and why. Or predict how one fact might affect another fact. Suppose you are reading about South America's climate. You might make a prediction about how the climate affects where people live. You can change your mind as you gain new information.

Connect

Connect your reading to your own life. Are the people discussed in the selection like you or someone you know? What would you do in similar situations? Connect your reading to something you have already read. Suppose you have already read about the ancient Greeks. Now you are reading about the ancient Romans. How are they alike? How are they different?

Visualize

What would places, people, and events look like in a movie or a picture? As you read about India, you could visualize the country's heavy rains. What do they look like? How do they sound? As you read about geography, you could visualize a volcanic eruption.

Respond

Talk about what you have read. What did you think? Share your ideas with your classmates.

Assess yourself

What did you find out? Were your predictions on target? Did you find answers to your questions?

Follow up

Show what you know. Use what you have learned to do a project. When you do projects, you continue to learn.

Introducing the Guiding Questions

This book was developed around five Guiding Questions about Latin America. They appear on the reduced Student Edition page to the right. The Guiding Questions are intended as an organizational focus for the book. All of the chapter content, activities, questions, and assessments relate to the Guiding Questions, which act as a kind of umbrella under which all of the material falls. You may wish to add your own Guiding Questions to the list in order to tailor them to your particular course. Or, as a group activity, you may want to ask your class to develop its own Guiding Questions.

Ask a volunteer to read the Guiding Questions out loud to the class. These questions will guide students as they learn about Latin America's geography, history, and culture.

Introducing the Project Preview

The projects for this book are designed to provide students with hands-on involvement in the content area. Students are introduced to the projects on pages 160–161. You may assign projects as cooperative activities, whole-class projects, or individual projects. Each project relates to one of the Guiding Questions.

LATIN AMERICA

The ancient peoples of Latin America built great civilizations from the riches of their land. Their descendants have mixed with newcomers from around the world to create a modern society with new and old traditions.

GUIDING QUESTIONS

The readings and activities in this book will help you discover answers to these Guiding Questions.

1 **GEOGRAPHY** What are the main physical features of Latin America?

2 **HISTORY** How has Latin America been shaped by its history?

3 **CULTURE** What factors have affected cultures in Latin America?

4 **GOVERNMENT** What types of government exist in Latin America today?

5 **ECONOMICS** How has geography influenced the ways in which Latin Americans make a living?

PROJECT PREVIEW

You can also discover answers to the Guiding Questions by working on projects. You can find several project possibilities on pages 160–161 at the back of this book.

Resource Directory

Teaching Resources

📁 **Book Projects,** in the Activities and Projects booklet, provide students with directions on how to complete one of the projects described on pages 160–161. You may wish to assign or have students choose a project at the beginning of the course.

Program Resources

📁 **Long-Term Integrated Projects** booklet, in the Program Resources Binder, provide opportunities for students to make comparisons across regions through a variety of long-term projects. You may wish to assign or have students choose a project at the beginning of the course.

1 What are the main physical features of Latin America?

2 How has Latin America been shaped by its history?

3 What factors have affected cultures in Latin America?

5 How has geography influenced the ways in which Latin Americans make a living?

4 What types of government exist in Latin America today?

A journal can be your personal book of discovery. As you explore Latin America, you can use your journal to keep track of things you learn and do. You can also record your thoughts about your journey. For your first entry, write your thoughts on where in Latin America you would like to go and what you would want to see there.

EXPLORER'S JOURNAL

Have students begin their Explorer's Journal as the paragraph on the student book page suggests. If at all possible, encourage students to use a separate small notebook for their Explorer's Journal entries. They can add to this Journal as they learn more about Latin America.

Using the Pictures

Invite students to discuss the five photographs. Use them as a prompt for discussion of what students know about Latin America. You may want to begin a K-W-L chart on the board with the headings What We **K**now About Latin America, What We **W**ant to Know About Latin America, and What We **L**earned About Latin America. Have students fill in the first column with several things they agree they already know. Then ask them to brainstorm what they would like to know about Latin America to add to the second column. Students can fill in the third column as they work through the text.

Using the Explorer's Journal

Have students begin their Explorer's Journal as the paragraph on the student book page suggests. If at all possible, encourage students to use a separate small notebook for their Explorer's Journal entries. They can add to this Journal as they learn more about Latin America.

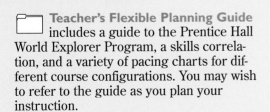 **Teacher's Flexible Planning Guide** includes a guide to the Prentice Hall World Explorer Program, a skills correlation, and a variety of pacing charts for different course configurations. You may wish to refer to the guide as you plan your instruction.

Resource Pro® CD-ROM allows you to create customized lesson plans and print all Teaching Resources and Program Resources, plus the Computer Test Bank, directly from the CD-ROM.

 eTeach

Be sure to check out this month's online discussion with a Master Teacher. Go to **www.phschool.com**

Lesson Objectives

DISCOVERY ACTIVITIES ABOUT

Latin America

Learning about Latin America means being an explorer and a geographer. No explorer would start out without first checking some facts. Begin by exploring the maps of Latin America on the following pages.

Lesson Objectives

❶ Describe the relative location and size of Latin America.

❷ Analyze how Portuguese and Spanish became the major languages of Latin America.

❸ Name the major physical features of Latin America.

❹ Explain the effects of hydroelectric dams on the environment.

Lesson Plan

1 Engage

Warm-Up Activity

Ask students to define the word *neighbor.* Ask them to list the qualities of a good neighbor.

Activating Prior Knowledge

Ask students why they think the United States wishes to have good relations with the countries of Latin America.

Answers to...

LOCATION

Students should note that Panama and Bogotá are located north of the Equator, so birthday seasons here would match those in the United States.

REGIONS

The Pacific Coast of Latin America is almost four times as long as the Pacific Coast of the continental United States.

Relative Location

LOCATION

1. Explore Latin America's Location Notice where the United States and Latin America are located relative to the Equator. On the other side of the Equator, seasons come at the opposite time of year. For example, when it's summer here, it's winter there. Think about the season your birthday falls in. In what season would it fall if you lived in Argentina? What if you lived in Panama? How about in Bogotá, the capital city of Colombia? Or in Brasília, the capital of Brazil?

Relative Size

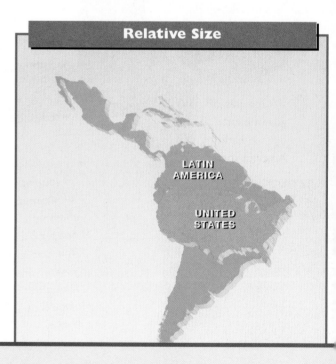

REGIONS

2. Estimate Latin America's Size How long is Latin America's west coast? To get an idea, curve a piece of string along the edge of the continental United States' west coast on the map above. Cut the string the same length as the coast. Now see how many string-lengths fit along the west coast of Latin America. Begin at the edge of the Pacific Ocean where Mexico borders California. Finish at the southern tip of South America. About how many times longer is Latin America's Pacific Coast than that of the United States?

Resource Directory

Teaching Resources

📁 **Activity Atlas** in the Activities and Projects booklet, pp. 3–5, provides a structure that helps students complete the activities in the Latin America Activity Atlas and encourages discovery learning.

LOCATION

3. Compare the Size of Countries The map below shows the countries that make up Latin America. Which two countries are the biggest in land area? Study the map to make your estimates. Check your answers in the Regional Database at the back of your textbook.

MOVEMENT

4. Investigate the Languages of Latin America The languages people speak give us clues about their history. Long ago, settlers from other countries took control of Latin America. Where were they from? Here are your clues: Portuguese is the official language of Brazil, and Spanish is spoken in most other Latin American countries.

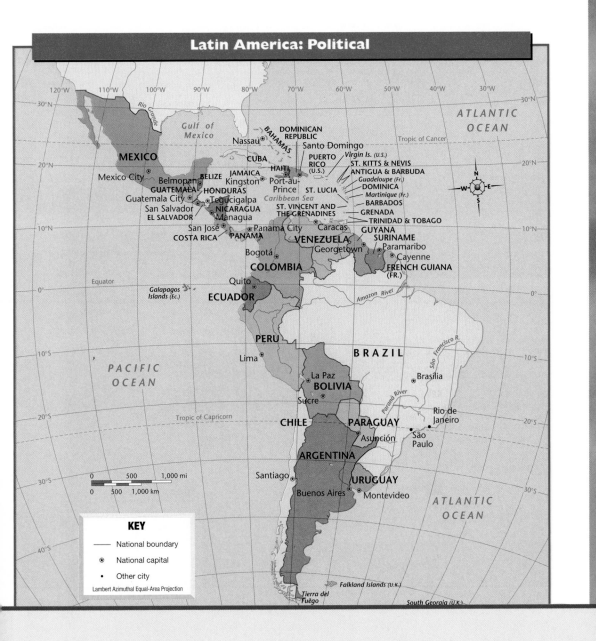

Latin America: Political

KEY

— National boundary

⊛ National capital

• Other city

Lambert Azimuthal Equal-Area Projection

Activity

Interdisciplinary Connections

Mathematics Ask students to use an atlas or an almanac to find the heights of the six highest mountains in South America (Aconcagua, Argentina, 22,831 ft. [6,959 m]; Ojos del Salado, Argentina-Chile, 22,572 ft. [6,880 m]; Bonete, Argentina, 22,546 ft. [6,872 m]; Tupungato, Argentina-Chile, 22,310 ft. [6,800 m]; Pissis, Argentina, 22,242 ft. [6,779 m]; Mercedario, Argentina, 22,211 ft. [6,769 m]. Ask students to create a bar graph comparing the heights of these mountains to the height of Mt. McKinley, the highest peak in the United States at 20,320 ft. (6,194 m).

PLACE

5. Examine the Physical Features of Latin America Volcanoes created many of Latin America's dramatic features. Long ago, volcanoes erupting along the west coast of South America formed the Andes Mountains. Volcanoes that exploded under the Caribbean Sea became a chain of islands called the Lesser Antilles. Central America has volcanic mountains, too. Some are still active! Trace the Andes Mountains, the Lesser Antilles, and the mountains in Central America with your finger. Which of these areas has the highest altitude?

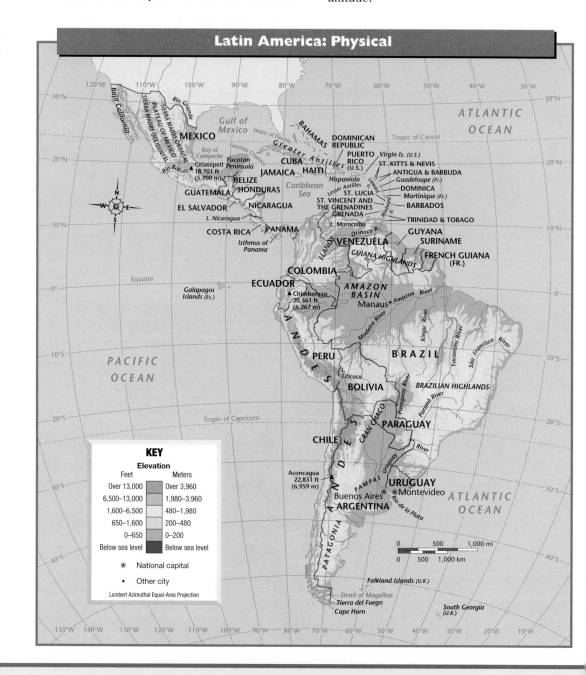

Latin America: Physical

KEY

Elevation

Feet	Meters
Over 13,000	Over 3,960
6,500–13,000	1,980–3,960
1,600–6,500	480–1,980
650–1,600	200–480
0–650	0–200
Below sea level	Below sea level

⊛ National capital

• Other city

Lambert Azimuthal Equal-Area Projection

REGIONS

6. Guide Geo Leo Geo Leo is exploring Latin America by boat, and he's taking you along to navigate. Read the passages below. To answer Geo Leo's questions, use the map below and the map on the opposite page.

A. We board our ship on the south side of the island of Hispaniola. A dense rain forest covers the island's mountain slopes. Which way to the Panama Canal?

B. We are sailing south past one of the Earth's driest deserts. It is in a long, skinny South American country that extends north and south along the continent's west coast. Steep mountains rise to the east. Where are we?

C. From the Falkland Islands, we travel north. For days we sail past desert scrub. Finally, we see tropical rain forest along the coast. What two major cities will we come to next?

D. We continue sailing north, past tropical savanna. We reach more rain forest and sail down a river through a low-lying area. Just ahead the Madeira River joins the one we are traveling on. Which way to the city of Manaus, our final destination?

Latin America: Natural Vegetation

KEY
- Tropical rain forest
- Mixed forest
- Coniferous forest
- Mediterranean vegetation
- Tropical savanna
- Temperate grassland
- Desert scrub
- Desert (little or no vegetation)
- Highlands (vegetation varies with elevation)

Lambert Azimuthal Equal-Area Projection

GEO LEO

BONUS
List each body of water you and Geo Leo traveled over.

Background

Links Across Place

Elevation is an important factor in everyday life in Latin America because elevation helps govern climate. Assuming that air is not moving, air is 3.5°F (1.9°C) cooler for every 1,000 feet (305 meters) one climbs. Thus, while the city of Guayaquil on the coast of Ecuador may be very hot and sticky, at the same time in the city of Quito it is almost cold. That is because Quito is located high in the Andes Mountains.

Answers to...

REGIONS

A. You are in the Dominican Republic. The Panama Canal is southwest.
B. You are passing Chile.
C. Buenos Aires and Montevideo
D. Continue west on the Amazon River.
Bonus Caribbean Sea, Pacific Ocean, Atlantic Ocean, Amazon River

ACTIVITY ATLAS
continued

Practice in the Themes of Geography

Place Ask students to use the Latin America physical map to find the Amazon Basin and the Brazilian Highlands. In which country are they located? (Brazil)

Regions Ask students what region is along the north border of Latin America. (North America)

Movement Ask students which of the following cities they could reach by boat: Manaus, Brazil; Buenos Aires, Argentina; La Paz, Bolivia; Santiago, Chile. (Manaus, Buenos Aires) Which map did they use? (Latin America political map)

Interaction Ask students where in Latin America they think most people live—along the coasts or in the interior? (along the coasts)

Answers to...

LOCATION

Students should identify unpopulated locations along swift moving rivers or coastal cities as good spots for hydroelectric power plants.

LOCATION

7. Investigate Latin America's Use of Hydroelectricity Hydroelectricity is electric power that is made by harnessing the power of water. One way to build a hydroelectric power plant is to build a dam across a river. The dam creates a large lake of water. To make electricity, the plant releases water from the lake into the river. As the water moves into the river, it turns a wheel. In some places, hydroelectric plants harness the power of ocean tides. Some of the largest hydroelectric plants are in Latin America. The world's largest is located on the border of Brazil and Paraguay. Look at the map below. What places in Latin America do you think would be good spots to build new hydroelectric power plants?

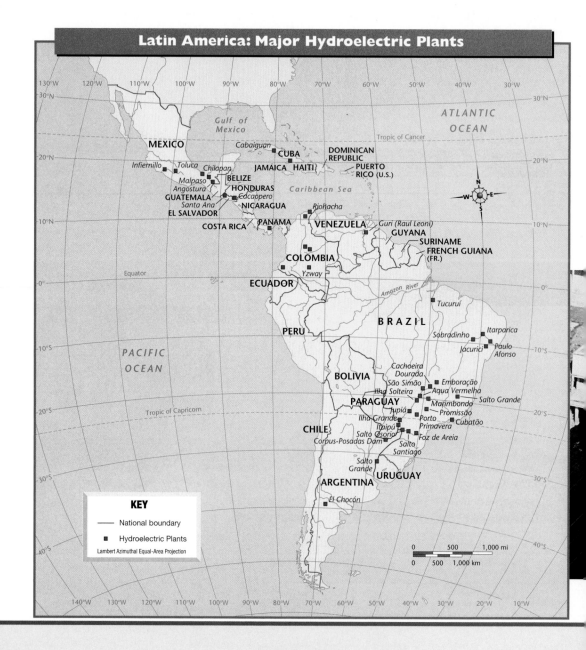

Latin America: Major Hydroelectric Plants

KEY

— National boundary

■ Hydroelectric Plants

Lambert Azimuthal Equal-Area Projection

Biggest Hydroelectric Dams

Name of Dam	Location
1. Itaipú	Brazil/Paraguay
2. Grand Coulee	United States
3. Guri (Raul Leoni)	Venezuela
4. Tucuruí	Brazil
5. Sayano-Shushensk	Russia
6. Corpus-Posadas	Argentina/Paraguay
7. Krasnoyarsk	Russia
8. LaGrande 2	Canada
9. Churchill Falls	Canada
10. Xingo	Brazil

Source: The World Almanac 2001

INTERACTION

8. Explore the Effects of a River Dam Unlike coal and petroleum, water power cannot be used up. It also does not cause air pollution. But building a dam does affect the environment of a river. It creates a large, artificial lake. It also reduces the amount of water that is in the river below the dam. What do you think are some advantages of building a dam across a river? What are some disadvantages?

◀▼ What percentage of its energy does Latin America get from hydroelectricity? How does this compare to energy use around the world?

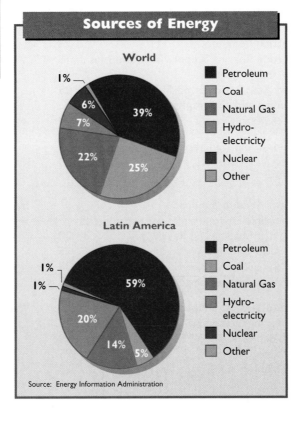

Sources of Energy

World

- 39% Petroleum
- 25% Coal
- 22% Natural Gas
- 7% Hydro-electricity
- 6% Nuclear
- 1% Other

Latin America

- 59% Petroleum
- 20% Coal
- 14% Natural Gas
- 5% Hydro-electricity
- 1% Nuclear
- 1% Other

Source: Energy Information Administration

◀ **Guri Dam** Only two other hydroelectric dams produce more electricity than Venezuela's Guri Dam, on the Caroni River.

Activity

Discovery Learning

What Country Am I? Ask students to write three or four "Who Am I?" questions about countries in Latin America. For example, *My capital is Lima. What country am I?* (Peru) Put a large map of Latin America on display and have students work in pairs. One member of a pair reads a question to an opposing pair. The designated "runner" in that pair goes to the map and points out the correct country. Continue until each pair has asked one question and answered one question. *Kinesthetic*

Answers to...

INTERACTION

Some advantages of dams include power, recreation, and jobs. Disadvantages include loss of habitat for plants and animals, loss of homes, and changes in ecosystems.

SOURCES OF ENERGY

20; about three times world hydroelectric use

Physical Geography

To help you plan instruction, the chart below shows how teaching resources correspond to chapter content. Use the resources to vary instruction, add activities, or plan block schedules. Where appropriate, resources have **suggested time allotments** for students. Time allotments are approximate.

Managing Time and Instruction

	Latin America Teaching Resources Booklet		World Explorer Program Resources Binder	
	Resource	**mins.**	**Resource**	**mins.**
1 SECTION 1 **Land and Water**	**Chapter and Section Support** Reproducible Lesson Plan, p. 3		**Outline Maps** Latin America: Physical, p. 6	20
	S Guided Reading and Review, p. 4	20	**Nystrom Desk Atlas**	**20**
	S Section Quiz, p. 5	25	T **Primary Sources and Literature Readings**	40
	▭ Section Reading Support Transparencies	15	We Live in Mexico, p. 14; Message from the	
	Activities and Projects		Rain Forest Amerindians, p. 15	
	Activity Atlas Activities, pp. 3–5	25		
	Social Studies and Geography Skills, Using the Map Key, p. 3	30		
SKILLS ACTIVITY **Using Regional Maps to Show Climate**	**Social Studies and Geography Skills,** Reading a Climate Map, p. 26	30		
2 SECTION 2 **Climate and Vegetation**	**Chapter and Section Support** Reproducible Lesson Plan, p. 6		**Interdisciplinary Explorations** T *Fate of the Rain Forest*	
	S Guided Reading and Review, p. 7	20		
	S Section Quiz, p. 8	25		
	Critical Thinking Activity, p. 16	30		
	▭ Section Reading Support Transparencies	15		
3 SECTION 3 **Natural Resources**	**Chapter and Section Support** Reproducible Lesson Plan, p. 9		**Writing Process Handbook** Writing Effective Paragraphs, pp. 27–28	25
	S Guided Reading and Review, p. 10	20		
	S Section Quiz, p. 11	25		
	S Vocabulary, p. 13	20		
	Reteaching, p. 14	25		
	Enrichment, p. 15	25		
	S Chapter Summary, p. 12	15		
	▭ Section Reading Support Transparencies	15		
	Tests Form A and B Chapter Tests, pp. 2–7	40		
LITERATURE *The Surveyor* by Alma Flor Ada			T **Primary Sources and Literature Readings**	40

Block Scheduling Program Support

- Block Scheduling Booklet
  PROGRAM RESOURCES BINDER
- Activities and Projects
- Interdisciplinary Links
- Resource Pro® CD-ROM
- Media and Technology
- Pacing Charts Booklet
  PROGRAM RESOURCES BINDER

Assessment Opportunities

From Guiding Questions to Assessment   A series of Guiding Questions serves as an organizing framework for this book. The Guiding Questions that relate to this chapter are listed below. Section Reviews and Section Quizzes provide opportunities for assessing students' insights into these Guiding Questions. Additional assessments are listed below.

Media and Technology

Resource	mins.
World Video Explorer	20
Color Transparencies 4, 34	20
Resource Pro® CD-ROM	30
Presentation Pro CD-ROM	20
Social Studies Skills Tutor CD-ROM	30
Color Transparencies 6, 7	20
Color Transparencies 4, 34, 90, 91	20
Guided Reading Audiotapes	20
Color Transparency 174 (Graphic organizer table template)	20
Computer Test Bank CD-ROM	30
Student Edition on Audio CD	30
Passport to the World CD-ROM	30

- **T** Teaming Opportunity well-suited for teaching teams
- **S** Spanish This resource is also in Spanish support.
- **CD-ROM**
- **Laserdisc**
- **Transparency**
- **Videotape**
- **Audiotape/CD**

GUIDING QUESTIONS

- *What are the main physical features of Latin America?*
- *How has geography influenced the ways in which Latin Americans make a living?*

ASSESSMENTS

Section 1

Students should be able to make a graphic organizer that shows the major landforms and water bodies of Latin America.

▶ **RUBRIC**   See the Assessment booklet for a rubric on assessing graphic organizers.

Section 2

Students should be able to describe how Latin America's landforms affect its climate.

▶ **RUBRIC**   See the Assessment booklet for a rubric on assessing cause-and-effect statements.

Section 3

Students should be able to create a chart of natural resources and list how people use them.

▶ **RUBRIC**   See the Assessment booklet for a rubric on assessing charts.

Prentice Hall Assessment System allows you to:

- Diagnose and Prescribe
- Review and Reteach
- Practice and Assess

Activities and Projects

Mental Mapping

Facing Latin America In the classroom, orient students so that they are facing north. If you wish, use a compass to verify the direction.

Have students extend their right arms and point. Tell them that they are pointing east to the Atlantic Ocean. Next have students extend their left arms and point. They are now pointing west to the Pacific Ocean. Have students point straight ahead. Now they are pointing north to Canada.

Have students carefully turn and face the opposite direction. Ask students what directions they are facing. (south). Tell students they are facing toward Mexico, one of the countries in Latin America. Now have students turn one small step to the left. Tell students they are facing southeast, in the general direction of South America.

Links to Current Events

Latin America News Coverage As you teach this chapter, you might want to have students keep a log of Latin American countries covered in the news media. Establish a period of time for students to keep the log. For example, you might want to choose the same number of days as for teaching the chapter. When students see coverage of a Latin American country, they write the name of that country in their logs.

Encourage students to look for Latin American coverage on television, radio, newspapers, and magazines. At the end of the time period, have students bring in their logs. As a class activity, review with students which countries appeared in their logs most often. Have students speculate on why some Latin American countries appeared in news coverage more than others.

Hands-On Activities

Developing a Sense of Location Have students use a globe to locate Latin America. Point out that Latin America is made up of Mexico, Central America, South America, and the Caribbean islands.

Have students find the Tropic of Cancer and the Tropic of Capricorn. Help students see that most of Latin America lies in the tropical latitudes, while northern Mexico and southern South America are within the middle latitudes. (Refer to the Map and Globe handbook at the back of the textbook if you need to review low and middle latitudes.)

Ask students to note how far east South America extends. Have them determine whether Latin America is closer to Africa or Asia. This activity will help students develop a sense of Latin America's location.

Cut-Out Map Hang a large sheet of poster board on the wall. Use an overhead projector to project an outline map of Latin America on the poster board. Have students trace the outline of Latin America and make a cut-out map. The cut-out can serve as the base for an illustrated map of the physical geography of Latin America. Students can illustrate the map with original drawings. *English Language Learners*

Position Paper The building of Tenochtitlán, the Aztec capital, and the growth of the Incan empire are examples of the ways ancient people changed the physical environment to meet human needs. Have students write a position

paper explaining how the theme of human-environment interaction applies to these topics. *Challenging*

Fantastic Food Fair Have the class hold a Fantastic Food Fair about corn and potatoes, both domesticated in Latin America thousands of years ago. Ask students to use encyclopedias and other library resources to trace the origin of these two important foods. Students' research findings can be presented as captions for an exhibit of corn, potatoes, and products made from these foods such as tortillas, corn flakes, corn oil, corn syrup, corn meal, mashed potatoes, and French fries. *Average*

Geography Chart Work with students to develop a large Geography chart for the bulletin board. Make three columns: Physical Geography, Latin America, and Where We Live. As students read through the chapter, have volunteers insert into the first column elements of physical geography they read about such as examples of landforms, climate, or natural resources. Then they can fill in the other two columns with examples that exist in Latin America and comparable features of your area. *Basic*

This page can help you extend your own and students' understanding of the concepts in this chapter. You may want to browse through some of the suggestions in the **Bibliography**. **Interdisciplinary Links** can connect social studies understandings to areas elsewhere in the curriculum through the use of other Prentice Hall products. **National Geography Standards** reflected specifically in this chapter are listed for your convenience. Some hints about appropriate Internet access are also provided in **Take It to the Net**. **School to Careers** provides insights into the practical uses of some of the concepts in this chapter as they might pertain to various careers.

BIBLIOGRAPHY

FOR THE TEACHER

The Eyewitness Atlas of the World. Dorling, 1994.

National Geographic Picture Atlas of Our World. National Geographic, 1993.

Schlessinger, Andrew. *The Rainforest*. Schlessinger, 1993. Video

South America. National Geographic 51441, 1991. Video

FOR THE STUDENT

Easy
Zak, Monica. *Save My Rainforest*. Volcano, 1992.

Average
Brusca, Maria Cristina. *On the Pampas*. Holt, 1991.

Blue, Rose and Corinne Naden. *Andes Mountains*. Raintree, 1995.

Challenging
Bernhard, Brendan. *Pizarro, Orellana, and the Exploration of the Amazon*. Chelsea, 1991.

LITERATURE CONNECTION

Cherry, Lynne. *The Great Kapok Tree: A Tale of the Amazon Rain Forest*. Harcourt, 1990.

Clark, Ann Nolan. *Secret of the Andes*. Viking, 1952.

George, Jean Craighead. *Shark Beneath the Reef*. HarperCollins, 1989.

INTERDISCIPLINARY LINKS

Subject	Theme: Discovery
MATH	Middle Grades Math: Tools for Success *Course 1*, Lesson 10-7, **Graphing on the Coordinate Plane** *Course 2*, Lesson 3-4, **Subtracting Integers**
SCIENCE	Science Explorer *From Bacteria to Plants*, Lesson 1-1, **What is Life?** *Cells and Heredity*, Lesson 1-1, **Discovering Cells**

NATIONAL GEOGRAPHY STANDARDS

Students explore the 18 National Geography Standards throughout Latin America. Chapter 1, however, concentrates on investigating the following: standards 1, 3, 4, 5, 7, 8, 15, 16, 18. For a complete list of the standards, see the *Teacher's Flexible Planning Guide*.

SCHOOL TO CAREERS

In Chapter 1, Latin America: Physical Geography, students learn about the land, water, climate, vegetation, and natural resources of Latin America. Additionally, they address the skill of using regional maps. Understanding physical geography can help students prepare for careers in many fields such as economics, politics, architecture, geology, mining, and so on. Map reading skills are particularly useful for travel agents, weather forecasters, salespeople, and others. The curriculum presented in this book, as in all eight titles of Prentice Hall's *World Explorer* program, is designed to prepare students not only for careers but also for good citizenship—of the world as well as of this country.

Take It to the NET

Many social studies teachers and students use Internet browsers, or search engines, to investigate particular topics. For the best results, use narrow rather than broad topics. Try these for Chapter 1: Andes Mountains, Amazon River, Mexico City, Caribbean islands. Finding age-appropriate sites is an important consideration when using the Internet. For links to age-appropriate sites in world studies and geography, visit the *World Explorer* companion Web site at:

http://www.phschool.com

CHAPTER 1

LATIN AMERICA

Physical Geography

Connecting to the Guiding Questions

As students complete this chapter, they will focus on the regions that make up Latin America, examining physical features, climate and vegetation, and natural resources. Content in this chapter thus relates to these Guiding Questions:

● What are the main physical features of Latin America?

● How has geography influenced the ways in which Latin Americans make a living?

Using the Picture Activities

Lead a class discussion of the picture, focusing on significant details.

• Encourage students to consider how mountains might affect travel, clothing, farming, and settlement patterns.

• Students should respond that the climate is colder near the peaks of the Andes and warmer at the foot of the mountains.

Heterogeneous Groups

The following Teacher's Edition strategies are suitable for heterogeneous groups.
Cooperative Learning
Making a Puzzle Map   p. 12
Critical Thinking
Expressing Problems
Clearly   p. 26
Interdisciplinary
Connections
Science   p. 17

PICTURE ACTIVITIES

These rugged mountains are the Andes (AN deez). They run the length of South America. To help you get to know this part of Latin America, do the following.

Study the picture
What do you think it would be like to live in or near the Andes? Based on what you see in the photograph, where would be the best area to live?

Think about the climate
Have you ever climbed in the mountains? How did the temperature change as you climbed higher? Based on your experience, do you think the climate is the same at the top of the Andes as at the bottom? Where would it be colder? Where would it be warmer?

Resource Directory

Media and Technology

Opener: Journey Over Latin America, from the World Video Explorer, introduces students to the varied landforms of the regions.

Geography: The Gauchos of Argentina, from the World Video Explorer, enhances students' understanding of how the physical geography of the Pampas of Argentina contributes to the region's economy and way of life.

Chapter 2

Chapter 3

Land and Water

Reach Into Your Background

No two places in the world are exactly the same. Think about the state in which you live. What features set it apart from other states? List some features that make your state special.

Questions to Explore

1. What are the main geographic regions of Latin America?

2. How do Latin America's geographic features affect the lives of the people?

Key Terms

plateau   pampas
isthmus   tributary
coral

Key Places

Mexico
Central America
Caribbean
South America

Lesson Objectives

1. Identify Latin America's main geographic regions.

2. Describe how the physical features of Latin America affect people's lives.

Lesson Plan

1 Engage

Warm-Up Activity

Ask students to describe the physical features of the area in which they live. Prompt students by asking whether the land is flat or hilly. Are there lakes or wooded areas? Are there open areas of land, such as parks, or do buildings and roads take up nearly all the space? List features on the chalkboard. Then discuss with students how these features affect their lives and the lives of other people living in the area.

Activating Prior Knowledge

Have students read Reach Into Your Background in the Before You Read box. Point out that every place in the world has unique features. In addition, explain that people adjust to the physical features around them in various ways. For example, people living near a river may build a bridge across it; people living near a lake may use boats to travel from one place to another. Ask for other examples of how people interact with their surroundings.

igh in the Andes Mountains, planes take off and land at El Alto airport. *El Alto* (ehl AHL toh) is Spanish for "the high one." It is an accurate name, for El Alto is the highest airport in the world. El Alto is the airport for La Paz, Bolivia.

Shortly after leaving the plane, tourists may get mountain sickness. The "thin" air of the Andes contains less oxygen than most people are used to. Oxygen starvation makes visitors' hearts beat faster and leaves them short of breath. Later on in the day, they may get terrible headaches. It takes a few days for visitors' bodies to get used to the mountain air. But the people who live in the Andes do not have these problems. Their bodies are used to the mountain environment.

The Andes mountain range is one of Latin America's major landforms. In this section, you will learn about Latin America's other landforms and about the people who live there.

Where Is Latin America?

Latin America is located in the Western Hemisphere south of the United States. Look at the map in the Activity Atlas. You will see that Latin America includes all the nations from Mexico to the tip of South America. It also includes the islands that dot the Caribbean (ka ruh BEE un) Sea.

Geographic features divide Latin America into three smaller regions. They are (1) Mexico and Central America, (2) the Caribbean, and (3) South America. South America is so large that geographers classify it as a continent. Look at the physical map in the Activity Atlas. Can you identify the geographic features that separate these three areas?

Teaching Resources

📁 **Reproducible Lesson Plan** in the Chapter and Section Resources booklet, p. 3, provides a summary of the section lesson.

📁 **Guided Reading and Review** in the Chapter and Section Resources booklet, p. 4, provides a structure for mastering key concepts and reviewing key terms in the section. Available in Spanish in the Spanish Chapter and Section Resources booklet, p. 3.

📖 **Section Reading Support Transparencies** provide answers to the Questions to Explore in a graphic organizer format.

Program Resources

📁 Material in the **Primary Sources and Literature Readings** booklet extends content with a selection from the region under study.

📁 **Outline Maps** Latin America: Physical, p. 6

2 Explore

Direct students to read the section. Have them locate on a world map and then briefly describe the three regions that make up Latin America: the Caribbean, Mexico and Central America, and South America. Ask how mountains and rivers in Latin America affect travel in the area. Have students find South America's Pampas and the U.S. Great Plains on physical maps. Ask how the two regions are alike.

3 Teach

Have students draw three boxes. Label the boxes *The Caribbean, Mexico and Central America,* and *South America.* Tell students to list one or more physical features of the area in each box. Then ask them to describe ways in which the feature or features affect people's lives. Use students' work as the basis for a discussion of Latin America's regions and features. This activity should take about 20 minutes.

Answers to...
MAP STUDY

• North America and South America; North America

The Regions of Latin America

Map Study Mexico and Central America are also called Middle America because they are located between two continents. **Location** Which two continents does Middle America lie between? Middle America is actually the southern part of a continent. In what continent does all of Middle America lie?

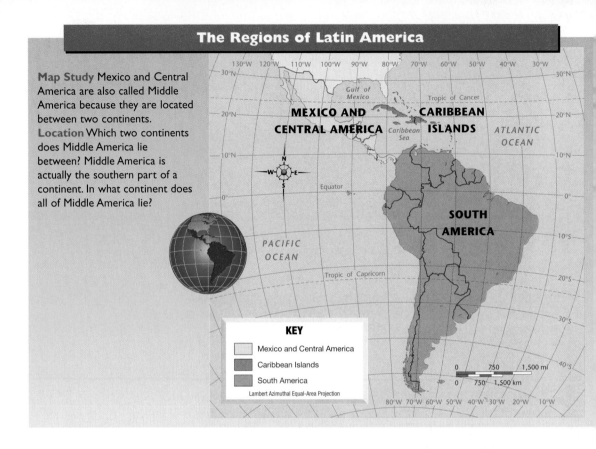

KEY
☐ Mexico and Central America
☐ Caribbean Islands
☐ South America
Lambert Azimuthal Equal-Area Projection

READ ACTIVELY

Predict How do you think the physical features of Latin America might be like those of the United States?

Perhaps you are wondering how Latin America got its name. About 500 years ago, Europeans sailed to Latin America. Most came from Spain and Portugal. European colonists brought their own languages and ways of life with them. Today, most Latin Americans speak Spanish, Portuguese, or French. These languages have their roots in the ancient language of Latin. As a result, the region is known as Latin America.

Landforms of Latin America

Imagine mountains that pierce the clouds and grassy plains that never seem to end. Picture wet rain forests and sunbaked deserts. This is Latin America, a region of variety and contrast.

Mexico and Central America   Mexico and Central America stretch 2,500 miles (4,023 km) from the U.S. border to South America. It is a distance that is almost equal to the width of the mainland United States. Mountains dominate this region. These mountains are part of a long system of mountain ranges. This huge system extends from Canada through the United States all the way to the tip of South America.

Resource Directory

Teaching Resources

📁 **Using the Map Key** in the Social Studies and Geography Skills booklet, p. 3, provides additional skill practice.

Program Resources

Nystrom Desk Atlas

Media and Technology

 Color Transparencies 4, 34

Between the mountains in Mexico lies Mexico's Central Plateau. A **plateau** (pla TOH) is a large raised area of mostly level land. Mexico's Central Plateau makes up more than half of the country's area. Most of Mexico's people live here. However, the surrounding mountains make it hard for people to travel to and from the Central Plateau. Another major landform in Mexico is the narrow coastal plains.

Central America, located south of Mexico, is an isthmus. An **isthmus** is a narrow strip of land that has water on both sides and joins two larger bodies of land. Find Central America on the map in the Activity Atlas. What two large bodies of land does the isthmus of Central America connect? As in Mexico, narrow plains run along Central America's coasts. Between these coastal plains are rugged, steep mountains. More than 40 of these mountains are active volcanoes. Volcanic ash has made the soil fertile. As a result, many people tend farms in the region.

The Caribbean Imagine islands made of skeletons. Imagine other islands that are the tops of underwater mountains. The Caribbean is made up of these two types of islands. The smaller islands are made up of the skeletons of tiny sea animals. Over hundreds of years, the skeletons meld together to form a rocklike substance called **coral**.

The larger islands of the Caribbean are the tops of huge underwater mountains. These include Cuba, Jamaica (juh MAY kuh), Hispaniola (his pun YOH luh), and Puerto Rico. Most people on the islands make a living farming.

LINKS
TO SCIENCE

The Tlaloques According to Aztec religion, a group of rain gods lived on the tops of mountains. They were called the Tlaloques. Tlaloc, the leader of the Tlaloques, was responsible for rain and lightning. Modern science has shown that mountains do affect rainfall. Clouds cool off and drop rain when they rise over the mountains.

4 Assess

See answers to the Section Review. You may also use the students' completed boxes of physical features for assessment purposes.

Acceptable responses include three factually correct entries in each box.

Commendable responses include statements of cause and effect, relating geography and people's lives.

Outstanding responses show an understanding of how the effect of one cause can, in turn, be the cause of other effects.

Background

Global Perspectives

Asia's Mighty Himalaya Mountains Only the Himalaya Mountains, a mountain system in Asia, stand taller than the Andes. The Himalaya Mountains make up the tallest range in the world. They extend along the India-Tibet border and through Pakistan, Nepal, China, and Bhutan. Have students find the Himalaya Mountains on a relief map. The tallest peak of this range is the well known—and often climbed—Mount Everest. At 29,035 feet (8,850 m) above sea level, Everest stands more than a mile higher than the tallest peak in the Andes.

Harvesting Alfalfa in Mexico

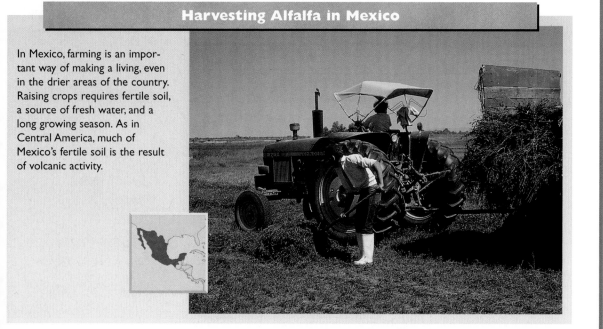

In Mexico, farming is an important way of making a living, even in the drier areas of the country. Raising crops requires fertile soil, a source of fresh water, and a long growing season. As in Central America, much of Mexico's fertile soil is the result of volcanic activity.

Making a Puzzle Map
Students can work in groups of four to create a puzzle map of one or more regions of Latin America. Remind students to include and label important places and physical features mentioned in the text.

One student can be responsible for researching the information, another for drawing the map on construction paper. You may wish to refer students to the physical map of Latin America in the Activity Atlas. Students may trace this map. A third student can mount the map onto cardboard, and the fourth can cut the map into jigsaw pieces. Have groups exchange puzzles and try to reassemble one another's puzzles.
Kinesthetic

South America   South America contains many types of landforms. Perhaps the most impressive landform is the Andes Mountains. The Andes run some 5,500 miles (8,900 km) along the western coast of South America. In some places, the Andes rise to heights of more than 20,000 feet (6,100 m). That's about the same height as twenty 100-story buildings stacked one on top of another. Except for the Himalaya Mountains in Asia, the Andes are the highest mountains in the world.

The Andes are steep and difficult to cross. But their rich soil has drawn farmers to the region. East of the Andes are rolling highlands. These highlands spread across parts of Brazil, Venezuela (ven uh ZWAY luh), Guyana (gy AN uh), and other South American countries. Farther south are the Pampas (PAHM puz), a large plains area that stretches through Argentina (ar jun TEE nuh) and Uruguay (YOOR uh gway). **Pampas** are flat grassland regions that are very similar to the Great Plains in the United States.

The eastern highlands and the Andes frame the Amazon River Basin. The Amazon River Basin contains the largest tropical rain forest in the world. This dense forest covers more than a third of the continent.

The Rivers of Latin America

Latin America is famous for its rivers and lakes. They are some of the longest and largest bodies of water in the world. Latin America's waters are important to the people of the region. Rivers serve as natural

Herding Cattle on the Pampas

Grasslands known as the Pampas can also be found in Brazil. These grasslands are perfect for raising cattle. **Critical Thinking** How are these grasslands similar to the Great Plains in the United States?

Answers to...
HERDING CATTLE ON THE PAMPAS

They both have relatively flat expanses of grassland suitable for raising livestock.

12   CHAPTER 1

highways in places where it is hard to build roads. The fish that swim the waters of Latin America provide food. Rushing water from large rivers provides power for electricity.

Amazon: The Ocean River

Latin America's Amazon (AM uh zahn) River is the second-longest river in the world. Only the Nile in Africa is longer. The Amazon flows 4,000 miles (6,437 km) from Peru across Brazil into the Atlantic Ocean.

How large is the Amazon? The Amazon River carries more water than any other river in the world. It contains about 20 percent of all the fresh river water on Earth. The Amazon River gathers power from the more than 1,000 tributaries (TRIB yoo tehr eez) that spill into it. **Tributaries** are the rivers and streams that flow into a larger river. With its tributaries, the Amazon drains an area of more than two million square miles. No wonder people call the Amazon the "Ocean River."

Other Rivers and Lakes Latin America has many other bodies of water besides the Amazon. The Paraná (pah rah NAH), Paraguay, and Uruguay rivers form the Río de la Plata system. The Río de la Plata separates Argentina and Uruguay. In Venezuela, people travel on the Orinoco River and Lake Maracaibo (mar uh KY boh). Lake Titicaca is the highest lake in the world on which ships can travel. It lies high in the Andes Mountains.

An Amazon Scene

The people who live near the Amazon River in Brazil rely on it for transportation, fish, and water. Families also wash their laundry right at the river bank.

READ ACTIVELY

Visualize How could a ship sail on a lake? What would the lake have to be like?

SECTION 1 REVIEW

1. **Define** (a) plateau, (b) isthmus, (c) coral, (d) pampas, (e) tributary.
2. **Identify** (a) Mexico, (b) Central America, (c) Caribbean, (d) South America.
3. Describe the main landforms of the three regions that make up Latin America.
4. Give one example of how the physical features of Latin America affect the people who live there.

Critical Thinking
5. **Making Comparisons** Explain two ways in which the three regions of Latin America

are alike. Explain two differences.

Activity
6. **Writing to Learn** Suppose your family was planning to move to Latin America. If you had your choice, in which of the three regions of Latin America would you live? Explain why.

Climate and Vegetation

Lesson Objectives

❶ List the climates and vegetation of Latin America.

❷ Explain ways in which climate and vegetation affect how and where the people of Latin America live.

Lesson Plan

1 Engage

Warm-Up Activity

Ask students how climate affects their daily life. For example, how do seasonal weather changes affect the clothing they wear, the activities they do, and the amount of time they spend outdoors? Ask how their lives might be different if they lived in a colder or warmer climate.

Activating Prior Knowledge

Have students read Reach Into Your Background in the Before You Read box. Point out that climate affects vegetation as well as people. For example, plants need water and suitable temperatures and soil to grow. Ask students for examples of places that are too dry or too cold for most plant life to survive.

BEFORE YOU READ

Reach Into Your Background

Suppose the temperature outside is 90°F (32°C). Would you feel more comfortable lying on a sandy beach or sitting under a tree in the woods? In what type of climate would you want to vacation someday?

Questions to Explore

1. What kinds of climate and vegetation does Latin America have?
2. In what ways do climate and vegetation affect how Latin Americans live?

Key Terms
El Niño
elevation

Key Places
Andes
Atacama Desert
Patagonia
Amazonian rain forest

▼ Mexico's Sonoran Desert shows that even a hot, dry desert can be full of plant life.

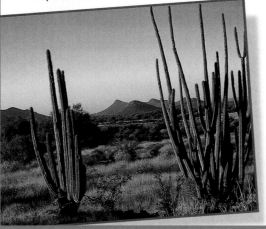

Every few years, a warm ocean current flows along the western coast of South America. This warm current drives away fish that thrive in the cold waters of the Pacific Ocean. The current brings other changes to Latin America, too. Instead of dry weather, heavy rains pour down and low-lying regions are flooded. In other places, drought plagues the land and the people.

Just what is this strange ocean current that brings disaster? It is **El Niño** (el NEEN yoh). Because it usually strikes near Christmas time, Latin Americans named the phenomena El Niño, Spanish for "the Christ child." El Niño is one of many factors that affect climate in Latin America.

Climate: Hot, Cold, and Mild

What's the climate like where you live? Is it hot? Cold? Rainy? If you lived in Latin America, the climate might be any of these. Climate in Latin America can vary greatly even within the same country.

In parts of the Andes, below-zero temperatures would set your teeth chattering. Travel down to the Amazon Basin, and you may be sweating in 80°F (27°C) heat. Don't forget your umbrella: This part of Latin America receives more than 80 inches (203 cm) of rain each year. If you prefer dry weather, visit the Atacama (ah tah KAH mah) Desert in Chile or the Sonoran Desert in Mexico. These are two of the driest places on Earth.

Resource Directory

Teaching Resources

📁 **Reproducible Lesson Plan** in the Chapter and Section Resources booklet, p. 6, provides a summary of the section lesson.

📁 **Guided Reading and Review** in the Chapter and Section Resources booklet, p. 7, provides a structure for mastering key concepts and reviewing key terms in the section. Available in Spanish in the Spanish Chapter and Section Resources booklet, p. 5.

 Section Reading Support Transparencies provide answers to the Questions to Explore in a graphic organizer format.

Program Resources

Interdisciplinary Explorations
Fate of the Rainforest

Media and Technology

🖥 **Color Transparencies 6, 7**

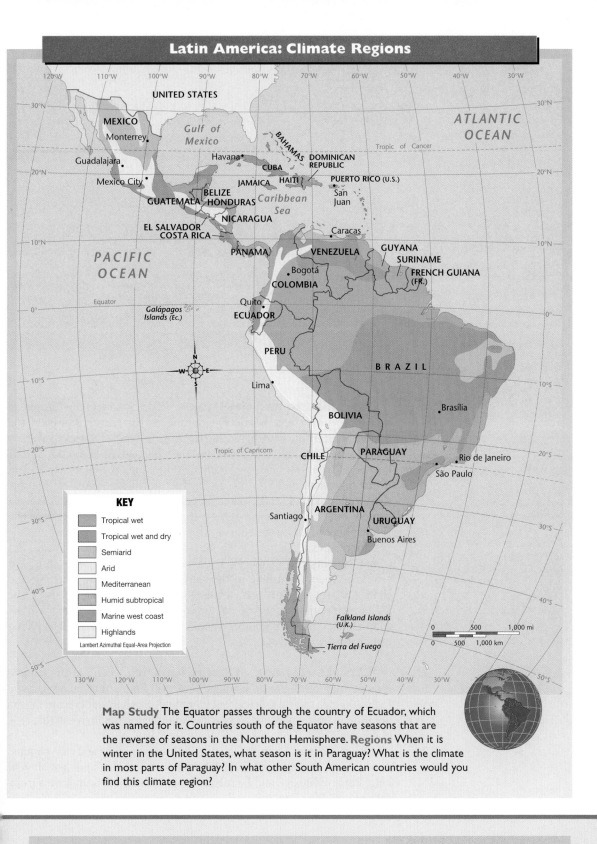

Latin America: Climate Regions

KEY

- Tropical wet
- Tropical wet and dry
- Semiarid
- Arid
- Mediterranean
- Humid subtropical
- Marine west coast
- Highlands

Lambert Azimuthal Equal-Area Projection

0   500   1,000 mi
0   500 1,000 km

Map Study The Equator passes through the country of Ecuador, which was named for it. Countries south of the Equator have seasons that are the reverse of seasons in the Northern Hemisphere. **Regions** When it is winter in the United States, what season is it in Paraguay? What is the climate in most parts of Paraguay? In what other South American countries would you find this climate region?

2 Explore

Direct students to read the section. Have them describe how Latin American climates vary. Then ask why the climates vary so much. Have students compare the climates in Latin America with the climate in their own state. Is there as much climate variation in their region? Why or why not?

3 Teach

Using the climate regions map, discuss Latin America's climate regions. Have students describe the different climates. Next use the vegetation map to discuss Latin America's vegetation. Help students recognize links between climate and vegetation. Then have students write a description that tells how climate and vegetation affect Latin Americans' lives and livelihood. Total discussion time should be about 40 minutes.

Answers to...
MAP STUDY

- summer; humid subtropical; Bolivia, Brazil, Argentina, Uruguay

4 Assess

See answers to the Section Review. You may also use students' classroom discussion to gauge their understanding.

Acceptable responses include two factually correct descriptions of climate and vegetation, their relationship, and their effects on people's lives and livelihood.

Commendable responses include three factually correct descriptions of climate and vegetation, their relationship, and their effects on people's lives and livelihood.

Outstanding responses compare and contrast climate, vegetation, and livelihood in at least three areas of Latin America.

Activity

Journal Writing

Island Living Ask students to imagine life on a Caribbean island. Discuss possible pros and cons of the climate. For example, the island trees and flowers are beautiful, but job opportunities may be limited to farming, tourism, and small industry.

Ask students to write two paragraphs expressing some of the feelings of island residents toward the climate. One paragraph should express advantages of island living; the second should express disadvantages.

Answers to...

SUGAR CANE FARMING

• Responses may vary. Possible answer: Warm weather and adequate rainfall are good for crops while hurricanes and tropical storms can be dangerous for farms and farming.

Sugar Cane Farming

People in the Dominican Republic grow much of their own food, but they also grow sugar cane to export. **Regions** How does the climate in the Caribbean make the area good for farming? How is the climate in the Caribbean dangerous for farms?

The Climate and the People The climate in the Caribbean is usually sunny and warm. From June to November, however, the region is often hit with fierce hurricanes. In 1988, Hurricane Gilbert shattered the sunny Caribbean weather like an atom bomb. Winds howled at over 180 miles per hour (300 km/hr). Waves nearly 20 feet (6 m) high smashed into the coast. The storm tore roofs off houses, shattered windows, and yanked huge trees from the ground. Gilbert turned out to be the strongest hurricane to strike the Western Hemisphere in the twentieth century.

Hurricanes are a part of life for people living in the Caribbean. But climate affects the people of Latin America in other ways, too. For example, people who live in the mountains need warm clothing and shelter to protect them against falling temperatures. That's because the higher up the mountains you go, the cooler it gets. Those who live in the sunny, warm tropics think more about cooling sea breezes than chilling winter winds.

Climate Regions of Latin America Look at the climate regions map on the previous page. You will notice that many parts of Latin America have a tropical wet climate. A tropical wet climate means hot, humid, rainy weather all year round. Rain forests thrive in this type of climate.

Other parts of Latin America have a tropical wet and dry climate. These areas are equally hot, but the rainy season does not last all year long. Parts of Mexico and Brazil and most of the Caribbean have a tropical wet and dry climate.

Resource Directory

Teaching Resources

Critical Thinking Activity in the Chapter and Section Resources booklet, p. 16, helps students apply the skill of drawing conclusions.

Much of Argentina, Uruguay, and Paraguay has a humid subtropical climate, similar to that of parts of the southern United States. People living in this climate usually have hot, wet summers and cool winters. Farmers in these areas can raise such crops as wheat and apples, which need a cold season to grow well. Farther south, the climate turns arid. Farmers raise sheep on the plains of this colder, drier area, called Patagonia (pat uh GOH nee uh).

What Factors Affect Climate?   Have you ever hiked in the mountains? If you have, you probably noticed that as you climbed higher the temperature dropped. At some point during your hike, you may have stopped to put on a sweatshirt or jacket.

Elevation, the height of land above sea level, is a key factor in the climate of mountainous Latin America. Look at the diagram below. It shows how elevation affects climate. The higher the elevation, the colder the temperature. Suppose it is a warm 80°F (27°C) at sea level. At 3,000 feet (914 m), the temperature may be 72°F (25°C). Continue up to 6,000 feet (1,829 m), and the temperature may now be only about 65°F (13°C). Above 10,000 feet (3,048 m), the temperature may remain below freezing—too cold for people to live. Temperature also affects what crops people can grow in each region.

Other factors also affect Latin America's climate. Regions close to the Equator are generally warmer than those farther away. Look at the Latin America: Climate Regions map. Find the Equator. Which parts of Latin America are closest to the Equator? Which are farthest away?

READ ACTIVELY

Visualize Suppose that you were climbing a mountain. How would the vegetation you see change as you climb higher?

Vertical Climate Zones

Diagram Study If you climb high enough on a mountain, you will reach a place where the temperature never warms up. This chart shows how the temperature near the Equator can vary with elevation. **Critical Thinking** Based on this chart, above what elevation will snow not melt?

below 20°F
14,000 feet (4,267 m)
Snow Line

20°–55°F
10,000 feet (3,048 m)
Grazing
Tree Line

Potatoes   Barley
Wheat   Apples

55°–65°F
6,000 feet (1,829 m)

Coffee
Corn
Citrus Fruit

65°–75°F
3,000 feet (914 m)

Bananas   Sugar Cane
Cacao   Rice

75°–80°F
Sea Level

SKILLS MINI LESSON

Drawing Conclusions You may want to **introduce** the skill by telling students that they can combine what they already know with new knowledge to draw conclusions. To help students **practice** drawing conclusions, pose the following question: *The tropical rain forest is large and beautiful. Yet few people live there. Why?* (Vegetation is dense, and farming is difficult in both cleared and uncleared areas. The climate is hot and very humid.) Help students choose sound reasons to support their conclusions. Students can **apply** the skill to explain why desert plant growth is widely scattered. (There is not enough water to support many plants in one place.)

Global Perspectives

Vegetation Affects Climate
For hundreds of years, humans have understood that climate affects how crops and other plants grow. Early farmers chose crops that grew best in the local conditions, cool and dry or warm and wet. Now we understand that plants themselves can affect the climate, not just locally but worldwide. Trees, specifically the great numbers of trees in the tropical rain forest, are capable of removing huge amounts of carbon dioxide from the air and replacing it with oxygen. As a result, trees help keep the climatic temperature relatively constant. If huge stands of rain forest are removed from the Earth, it is likely that temperatures will rise over time.

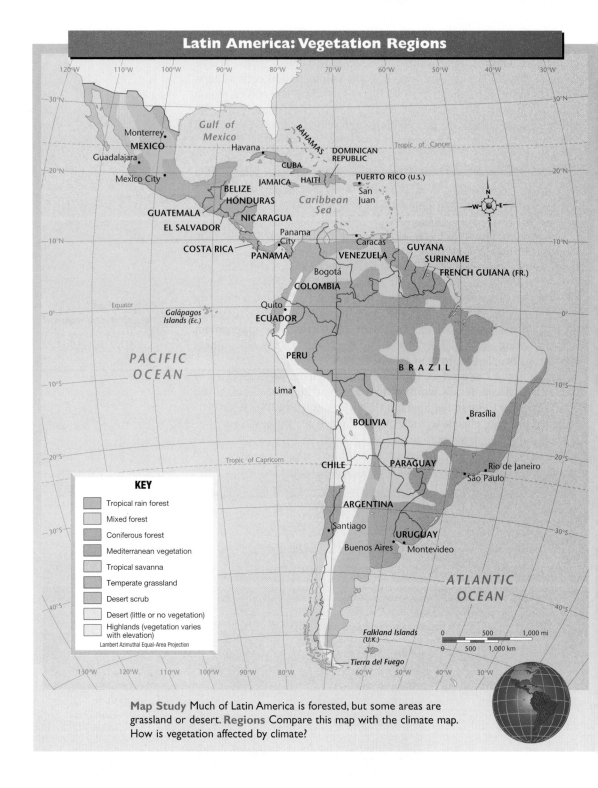

Latin America: Vegetation Regions

KEY
- Tropical rain forest
- Mixed forest
- Coniferous forest
- Mediterranean vegetation
- Tropical savanna
- Temperate grassland
- Desert scrub
- Desert (little or no vegetation)
- Highlands (vegetation varies with elevation)

Lambert Azimuthal Equal-Area Projection

Map Study Much of Latin America is forested, but some areas are grassland or desert. **Regions** Compare this map with the climate map. How is vegetation affected by climate?

Answers to...

MAP STUDY

- Responses should indicate that there is generally more vegetation in areas with warm, wet climates and less vegetation in areas with cold, dry climates.

Resource Directory

Teaching Resources

Section Quiz in the Chapter and Section Resources booklet, p. 8, covers the main ideas and key terms in the section. Available in Spanish in the Spanish Chapter and Section Resources booklet, p. 6.

Wind patterns affect the climate too. Winds move cold air from the North and South Poles toward the Equator. They also move warm air from the Equator toward the Poles. In the Caribbean, sea breezes blowing toward shore help to keep temperatures moderate. Winds also affect rainfall in the Caribbean. More rain falls on the sides of islands facing the wind than on sides facing away.

Natural Vegetation and Climate

Imagine a forest so dense and lush that almost no sunlight reaches the ground. Broad green leaves, tangled vines, and thousands of species of trees and plants surround you. The air is hot and heavy with moisture. Welcome to the Amazonian rain forest.

Now, suppose you have traveled to the coast of northern Chile. You're in the Atacama Desert. Winds carry no moisture to this barren land, and there is little sign of life. The Andes shield this parched region from rain. Parts of the desert have never felt a single raindrop.

Latin America's varied climate and physical features make such extremes possible. Look at the natural vegetation map on the previous page. How many different kinds of vegetation does the map show? Note which countries in Latin America have areas of tropical rain forest. Now, find these countries on the climate map. How do the tropical climate and heavy rainfall in these countries contribute to the vegetation that grows there?

Find Uruguay on the vegetation map and on the climate map. Uruguay's climate and vegetation have helped make sheep and cattle raising a key part of the country's economy.

Elevation also affects vegetation. For example, palm trees and fruit trees that grow well in the coastal plains of Mexico and Central America would not survive high in the Andes. To grow at higher elevations, plants must be able to withstand cooler temperatures, chill winds, and irregular rainfall.

Ask Questions What would you like to know about living in the rain forest?

▲ Tree sloths live in the rain forest trees. They rarely descend from the trees.

SECTION 2 REVIEW

1. **Define** (a) El Niño, (b) elevation.

2. **Identify** (a) Andes, (b) Atacama Desert, (c) Patagonia, (d) Amazonian rain forest.

3. Describe two climates in Latin America. Then explain how climate affects the vegetation that grows in those regions.

4. How do Latin America's climate and vegetation affect how and where the people live?

Critical Thinking

5. **Drawing Conclusions** In what ways would the life of a family living on a Caribbean island be different from a family living high in the Andes?

Activity

6. **Writing to Learn** Latin America has been called a land of extremes. Do you agree or disagree? Write a paragraph or more telling why. Begin with the following sentences: "Many people have called Latin America a land of extremes. I believe that . . ." Support your opinion with examples.

Section 2 Review

1. (a) warm ocean current that flows along the western coast of South America and affects weather patterns (b) the height of land above sea level

2. (a) mountain system extending along the western coast of South America (b) desert in Chile (c) plains region in southern South America (d) tropical rain forest in South America

3. Answers may vary. Sample answers: Tropical wet climates have tropical rain forest vegetation. Arid climates tend to have desert or desert scrub vegetation.

4. Accept reasonable responses. Possibilities may include the following: people living in cool mountain areas need warm clothes and shelter; climate and vegetation help determine whether an area is suitable for farming or ranching. Climate helps determine what types of crops can be raised.

5. Answers will vary. Responses should focus on how location, climate, and vegetation would affect the way families in two different locations live.

6. Answers will vary, but most students will agree. Students may contrast the barren desert with the lush rain forest, or the warm and steamy coastal lowlands with the cold and dry high mountains. Be sure students use specific examples.

Organizing Information

To **introduce** the skill, suggest that students organize information by summarizing what they read. Point out that headings, pictures, maps, and charts can help them focus on important ideas and facts. To **practice** the skill, have students work in pairs to develop written summaries of Section 2. Indicate to students that (1) the summaries should incorporate the headings—rewritten using the students' own words—to present the most important ideas of each part of the text, and that (2) students should support these ideas with facts, details, and examples. Encourage students to **apply** the skill of organizing information as they read the next section.

SKILLS ACTIVITY

Using Regional Maps to Show Climate

If you could follow the Earth's weather for many years, no two years would look exactly alike. Think how the weather in your own location varies. Some years are colder, warmer, wetter, or drier than others. The same is true for every place on the planet.

Still, you could notice patterns in the weather. For example, one place may tend to have hot, rainy summers and cold, dry winters. Another place might be hot and dry all year round. The typical weather patterns in a location are called its climate.

Traveling across the Earth, you would find that no two places have exactly the same climate. Even the next town might be a degree cooler than your own. Still, you would find some similarities. Places in a large area that have similar weather make up a climate region.

Latin America: Climates

KEY

Tropical wet
Tropical wet and dry
Semiarid
Arid
Mediterranean
Humid subtropical
Marine west coast
Highlands

Lambert Azimuthal Equal-Area Projection

Get Ready

A region's climate affects how its inhabitants live. Learning to read a climate map can help you understand what life is like in different regions of the world.

Try It Out

Climates in Latin America fall into four general categories: *tropical, dry, mild,* and *highland*. Read about the climates described below. Use the map to answer each question.

A. Find a tropical climate zone. Tropical climates are hot year round. There are two types. Tropical wet zones have rain nearly every day. Tropical wet and dry zones have a wet season and a dry season. Where are tropical wet and dry zones usually located in relation to tropical wet zones?

B. Find a dry climate. Dry climates have little rain. There are two types. Arid zones may go years without rain. Semiarid zones receive enough rain for short grasses to grow. Where are semiarid zones usually located in relation to arid zones?

C. Find a mild climate. Mild climates are more comfortable than tropical or dry climates. There are three types. Marine climates are wet and have only moderate changes in temperature during the year. Humid subtropical areas are also wet but warmer than marine climates. Mediterranean climates are warm, too, but only rainy in the winter. Where are mild climate regions usually located in relation to large bodies of water?

D. Find a highland climate. Highland climates are found in mountainous regions. In a highland climate, temperatures vary. The higher you climb up a mountain, the colder it gets. Where is South America's highland climate located?

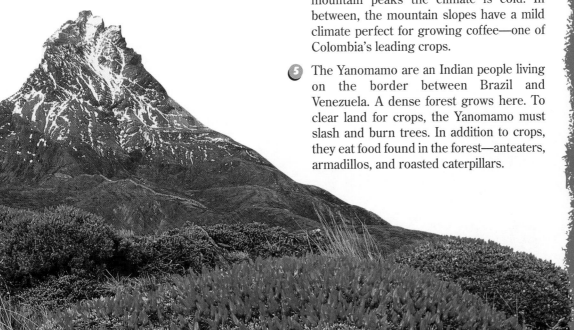

Apply the Skill

A region's climate can affect the kind of homes people build, the jobs they do, and the food they eat. Read the descriptions that follow. Then match each description with a letter on the map.

1 Few trees grow in Mexico's dry central region. Instead of building homes from wood, farmers often use sun-dried brick called adobe. Flat roofs are sometimes made of tile, straw, or sheet metal.

2 In the south of Mexico, more rain falls. The rain would eventually wash away an adobe home. So instead, some farmers build with wooden poles coated with a lime and clay mixture that keeps out the rain. Roofs are slanted so that rain water runs off.

3 Peru's west coast has one of the Earth's driest climates. To raise crops, farmers channel mountain streams to bring water to their fields.

4 Near the base of the Andes Mountains in Colombia, the weather is hot. High in the mountain peaks the climate is cold. In between, the mountain slopes have a mild climate perfect for growing coffee—one of Colombia's leading crops.

5 The Yanomamo are an Indian people living on the border between Brazil and Venezuela. A dense forest grows here. To clear land for crops, the Yanomamo must slash and burn trees. In addition to crops, they eat food found in the forest—anteaters, armadillos, and roasted caterpillars.

SECTION 3

Natural Resources

Reach Into Your Background

Do you know what natural resources are? They are things found in nature that people can use to meet their needs. For example, trees are a natural resource. List two other natural resources. Describe how people use each one.

Questions to Explore

1. What are Latin America's important natural resources?

2. Why is it important for Latin American nations to have more than one source of income?

Key Terms
hydroelectricity
diversify

Key Places
Jamaica
Venezuela
Brazil
Colombia
Chile

Bolivia has always depended on mineral resources for wealth. At first, silver helped to bring money into Bolivia's treasury. Soon, however, another metal became even more important than silver. That metal was tin.

For many years, Bolivia enjoyed the good times that wealth from tin brought. Then, in the 1920s and 1930s, a world-wide economic crisis hit. Industries stopped buying tin, as well as other natural resources. Bolivia suffered as its main resource failed to bring money into the economy. This economic crisis hit all of Latin America hard. It brought home a problem many Latin American nations have: They rely too much on one resource.

▼ Latin America has about 12 percent of the world's petroleum.

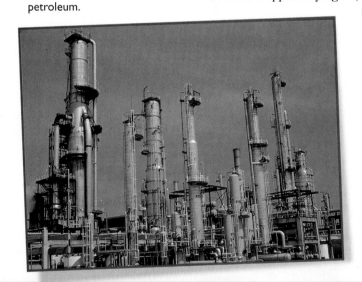

Latin America's Resources

What do the following items have in common? Fish, petroleum, water, silver, and forests. You have probably guessed that all these items are natural resources of Latin America. Latin America's resources are as varied as its physical features and climate.

Mexico and Central America: Riches of Land and Sea

Mexico is a treasure chest of minerals. The country has deposits of silver, gold, copper, coal, iron ore, and just about any other mineral you can name. How many of these mineral resources can you find on the map on the next page? Mexico also has huge amounts of oil and natural gas. In addition, trees cover nearly a quarter of Mexico's land. Wood from these trees is turned into lumber and paper products.

Central America's climate and rich soil are good for farming. The people grow coffee, cotton, sugar cane, and bananas. They also plant cacao trees. Cacao seeds are made into chocolate and cocoa.

Not all of Central America's resources are on land. People catch fish and shellfish in the region's waters. Central Americans use the power of rushing water to produce electricity. This type of power is called **hydroelectricity** (hy droh ee lek TRIS ih tee). Countries build huge dams to harness and control the energy that rushing water produces.

The Caribbean: Sugar, Coffee, and More

Caribbean countries also have rich soil and a good climate for farming. Farmers grow sugar cane, coffee, bananas, cacao, citrus fruits, and other crops on the islands.

The Caribbean has other resources as well. For example, Jamaica is one of the world's main producers of bauxite—a mineral used to make aluminum. Cuba and the Dominican Republic have nickel deposits. Trinidad is rich in oil.

Drilling for Oil

Some of Mexico's petroleum reserves can only be reached through offshore drilling, or drilling into the ocean floor. **Interaction** What special precautions do you think that offshore drillers might have to take to avoid harming the environment?

2 Explore

Direct students to read the section. Have them list Latin America's natural resources on the chalkboard. Ask students which of the resources are most important and why. Stress that a nation's people may consume and export a resource. For example, people in Latin American raise cattle for their own consumption as well as for export.

3 Teach

Have students draw three distinct circles, one for each region of Latin America. Tell them to label the circles *The Caribbean, Mexico and Central America,* and *South America.* Direct students to write, in each circle, the region's major natural resources. Use students' diagrams as the basis for a discussion of Latin America's resources. Then focus on the nations that make up each region. Ask students why it is important for these nations to depend on a variety of resources. This activity should take about 20 minutes.

4 Assess

See answers to the Section Review. For assessment purposes, you may also check students' circles showing Latin America's major natural resources. You may also evaluate students' grasp of concepts by their responses during the classroom discussion.

Answers to...
DRILLING FOR OIL

• Responses should address the possibility of an oil spill occurring at an offshore drilling site.

Biography

Juan Domingo Perón One of South America's most famous leaders was Juan Domingo Perón (1895–1974). Perón served as president of Argentina from 1946 to 1955 and again from 1973 to 1974. Perón's goal was for Argentina to capitalize on its mineral resources, develop its industry, and increase its agricultural output. He also hoped to spread wealth more evenly among the people. Perón instituted reforms that benefited many workers. However, many of Perón's drastic reforms hurt Argentina economically.

Latin America: Natural Resources

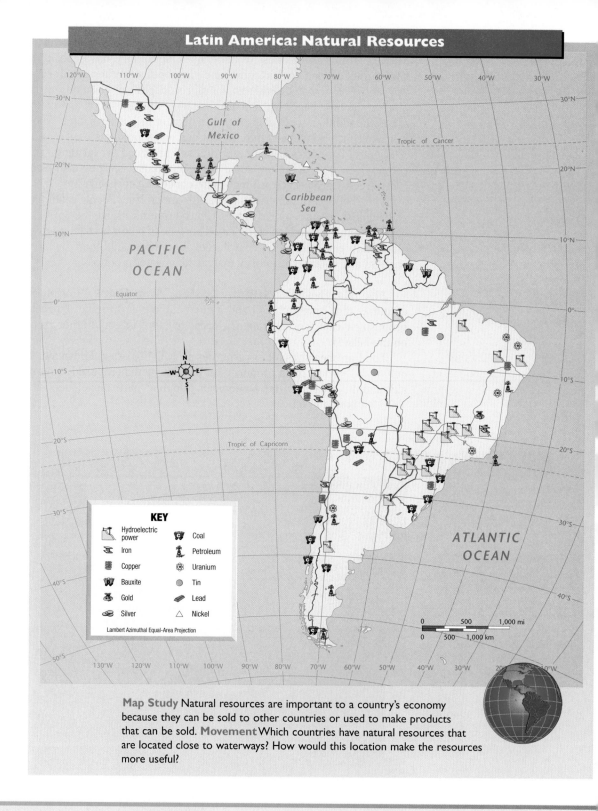

KEY

Hydroelectric power	Coal
Iron	Petroleum
Copper	Uranium
Bauxite	Tin
Gold	Lead
Silver	Nickel

Lambert Azimuthal Equal-Area Projection

Map Study Natural resources are important to a country's economy because they can be sold to other countries or used to make products that can be sold. **Movement** Which countries have natural resources that are located close to waterways? How would this location make the resources more useful?

Answers to...
MAP STUDY

- Brazil, Cuba, Jamaica, Mexico, Peru, Chile, Paraguay, Uruguay, Venezuela, Colombia, Ecuador; Location close to waterways makes transporting resources easier. It is also easier to bring workers and equipment to the resources.

Resource Directory

Teaching Resources

Section Quiz in the Chapter and Section Resources booklet, p. 11, covers the main ideas and key terms in the section. Available in Spanish in the Spanish Chapter and Section Resources booklet, p. 8.

Vocabulary in the Chapter and Section Resources booklet, p. 13, provides a review of key terms in the chapter. Available in Spanish in the Spanish Chapter and Section Resources booklet, p. 10.

Reteaching in the Chapter and Section Resources booklet, p. 14, provides a structure for students who may need additional help in mastering chapter content.

Enrichment in the Chapter and Section Resources booklet, p. 15, extends chapter content and enriches students' understanding.

The hydroelectric power plant at Itaipú Dam is one of the largest in the world. It harnesses the energy of the Paraná River to provide electric power to Paraguay and Brazil. **Critical Thinking** What detail in this picture is a clue that the dam is used to produce electricity?

Daily Life

Living With Few Resources Although most of South America is rich in resources, little of the resource wealth reaches farmers in the Andes. Farmers sell some crops in city markets, but their main concern is to produce food for their families for the whole year. In many villages, people must hike to mountain streams to get drinking water. Houses are made entirely by hand of adobe or stone. They have thatched roofs. Families own few pieces of furniture and few possessions other than farming tools, cooking and eating utensils, and perhaps a single "luxury"—a battery-operated radio.

South America: A Wealth of Resources Like Mexico, South America is rich in minerals. It contains gold, copper, tin, bauxite, and iron ore. Businesses drill for oil in many South American countries. Much of South America's oil is found in Venezuela.

South America's plants and fish are natural resources, too. Forests cover about half the continent. Trees from these forests provide everything from wood for building to coconuts for eating. People harvest many rain forest plants to make medicines. Tuna, anchovies, and other fish are plentiful in the waters off the Pacific Coast.

Like other parts of Latin America, South America has rich soil. Farmers grow many different crops there. For example, coffee is a key crop in Brazil and Colombia. Wheat is important in Argentina. Many South American economies rely on the production of sugar cane, cotton, and rice.

Natural Resources and Latin America's Economy

Not every country shares in the wealth of Latin America's resources. Some Latin American countries have many resources, while others have few. Some countries do not have the money they need to develop all of their resources. Other countries rely too much on one resource or crop.

LINKS

ACROSS TIME

Sailors of the Seventh Century South Americans have been trading with the people of Mexico since at least A.D. 600. They sailed north from Ecuador, Colombia, and Peru on rafts. These adventurers traded not only goods, such as tweezers and bells, but also skills and ideas. For example, they taught people of Mexico how to make metal objects such as needles.

SKILLS MINI LESSON

Reading Actively
You may **introduce** the skill by informing students that they can be active readers by asking themselves questions as they read. Looking for answers to the questions will help them focus on important points. Help students **practice** the skill by suggesting questions that they might ask themselves as they read: *What are the natural resources of the Caribbean? Why are these resources important? What role do people play in developing these resources?* Help students **apply** this skill by directing them to choose two pages of text and then write questions they might ask themselves while reading the information.

Critical Thinking

Expressing Problems Clearly *Suitable as an individual activity.* Encourage students to imagine that they are running for office in a Latin American nation. As a candidate, each must warn the nation of the possible dangers of depending on a single resource for money. Direct students to write a campaign speech on this topic. The speech should describe briefly and clearly the importance of having more than one source of income. Encourage students to use specific examples to make their point. *English Language Learners*

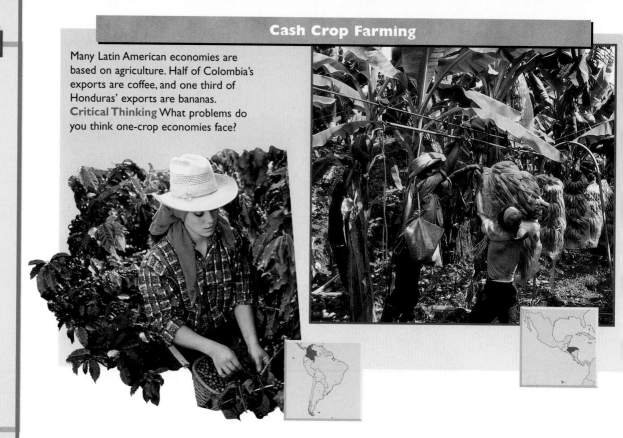

Many Latin American economies are based on agriculture. Half of Colombia's exports are coffee, and one third of Honduras' exports are bananas. **Critical Thinking** What problems do you think one-crop economies face?

READ ACTIVELY

Visualize How would the crops in a field look after a hurricane? How would they look after a drought?

Prices, Weather, and Other Factors Depending on one resource or crop can lead to problems. For example, when world copper prices are high, the copper mining industry is very successful. But suppose copper prices drop sharply. Then copper exports are not worth as much. When this happens, the mining industry loses money. Mining workers may lose their jobs. Chile is the leading producer of copper in the world. When prices plunge, Chile's economy suffers.

Many people in Latin America make their living by farming. Some Latin American countries depend on one or two crops, such as coffee, bananas, or sugar. When the price of a crop goes down, exports of that crop bring less money into the country. As a result, workers' wages may drop, and some workers may lose their jobs.

Weather and disease also cause people and businesses to lose money. Hurricanes, droughts, and plant disease can damage crops. Weather sometimes hurts the fishing industry. The warm ocean current El Niño affects the fish that live in South America's coastal waters. Usually, the cold water of the Pacific supports a large number of small water plants on which the fish feed. When El Niño strikes, the warm water kills the plants and the fish die or move to other areas. Peru is among the countries affected by El Niño. Peruvian fishers have suffered great economic losses due to El Niño effects.

Answers to...

CASH CROP FARMING

- Responses should indicate that dependence on one crop makes the economies vulnerable to disasters such as drought or hurricanes. If the crop is an export crop, it is vulnerable to falling prices.

Resource Directory

Teaching Resources

📁 **Spanish Glossary** in the Spanish Chapter and Section Resources, pp. 62–66, provides key terms translated from English to Spanish as well as definitions in Spanish.

📁 **Chapter Summary** in the Chapter and Section Resources booklet, p. 12, provides a summary of chapter content. Available in Spanish in the Spanish Chapter and Section Resources booklet, p. 9.

📁 **Cooperative Learning Activity** in the Activities and Projects booklet, pp. 20–23, provides two student handouts, one page of teacher's directions, and a scoring rubric for a cooperative learning activity on making a relief map.

Media and Technology

🎧 **Guided Reading Audiotapes** (English and Spanish)

🎧 **Student Edition on Audio CD** The entire text of the Student Edition is available in a series of audio CDs.

Depending on Oil   Oil is one of Latin America's most valuable resources. But it is risky to depend on oil. Oil prices increase and decrease. Sometimes they change suddenly. Mexico, like Venezuela, is a major oil producer. In the mid-1980s, oil companies produced more oil than the world needed. As a result, prices dropped. Mexico earned much less income than it had expected. The same thing happened to Trinidad.

There are other problems as well. In the 1960s, people discovered oil in Ecuador. Soon, oil became the country's main export. But in 1987, earthquakes destroyed Ecuador's major oil pipeline. The country's income was slashed.

Avoiding the Problems of a One-Resource Country
Latin American nations know the risks of depending on one resource or crop. They are trying to diversify their economies. To **diversify** is to add variety. When Latin American nations try to diversify their economies, it means that they are looking for other ways to make money. Many are building factories. Factories make products that can be sold to bring more money into the economy. Factories also provide jobs for people.

Venezuela has been trying to set up more factories and farms. Venezuela is also improving its bauxite and iron mines. Ecuador passed a law to encourage industry. Businesses there built factories to make cloth, electrical appliances, and other products.

Brazil has also been building up its industries. That way Brazil does not have to depend on agriculture. Brazil now exports machinery, steel, and chemicals. Brazil has also encouraged cotton farming. As a result, cotton weaving has become a successful industry.

El Salvador used to depend too heavily on its coffee crop. Now, cotton, sugar, corn, and other crops play an important role in the nation's economy. Trinidad has also encouraged its farmers to raise more kinds of crops. The government realizes that the country depends too much on oil and sugar.

SECTION 3 REVIEW

1. **Define**   (a) hydroelectricity, (b) diversify.

2. **Identify**   (a) Jamaica, (b) Venezuela, (c) Brazil, (d) Colombia, (e) Chile.

3. Describe the important natural resources of Latin America.

4. Why is it important for Latin American nations to diversify their economies?

Critical Thinking

5. **Recognizing Cause and Effect**   Suppose a disease destroyed Colombia's coffee crop. How would this loss affect coffee-plantation workers and their families? How would it affect Colombia's economy?

Activity

6. **Writing to Learn**   Imagine that you are the president of a Latin American country. Your nation depends on bananas for nearly all of its income. What arguments would you use to persuade people to diversify?

Section 3 Review

1. (a) electricity generated by moving water (b) to add variety

2. (a) island country in the Caribbean (b) country in northern South America (c) largest country in South America (d) country in north-western South America (e) country on the southwestern coast of South America

3. Important natural resources include oil and natural gas; fertile soil; fish; forests; and minerals such as copper, gold, bauxite, nickel, and iron.

4. Answers may vary but should reflect students' understanding of the danger of depending on only one resource. Sample answer: If that one resource is damaged or decreases in value, the country's economy would be severely hurt.

5. Answers may vary. Students may respond that workers would be unemployed and their families might not have enough money to live on. The coffee industry workers could no longer buy goods. Coffee shippers would have no coffee to ship, and the country would not have coffee to sell to other nations.

6. Answers will vary. Students' arguments should include mention of the danger of losing the banana crop to bad weather or disease or of the fact that another country might produce so many bananas that the price would drop.

Review and Activities

Reviewing Main Ideas

1. The Caribbean, Mexico and Central America, and South America. Sample answers: The Caribbean is mostly islands; Mexico and Central America are mostly mountains and plateaus; South America is mostly mountains, plains, and forests.

2. Accept reasonable answers. For example, students may mention that mountains make travel difficult or that many islanders in the Caribbean rely on fishing for a living.

3. Climates are colder at higher elevations.

4. Accept reasonable answers. (a) Possibilities include: the warm, rainy weather near the equator helps create the lush vegetation of the rain forest. The dry, hot climate is responsible for the dry and barren deserts of Chile. (b) People within the rain forests can hunt or gather their food. Few people live in the desert regions of Latin America.

5. Resources provide a source of income for the nation and its people. The income allows both the nation and its people to purchase items they may need or want.

6. If the one source of income is reduced or lost, the country's economy would be severely hurt. Examples will vary.

7. Latin American nations are expanding their numbers of export crops and exploring and mining several sources of mineral wealth.

Reviewing Key Terms

1. e   4. d   6. c
2. b   5. g   7. a
3. f

Critical Thinking

1. Accept reasonable answers. Students may mention that ample sun and rain help farmers grow crops, but hurricanes cause great destruction.

2. Most students will agree. Students' answers should reflect sound reasoning. For example, by encouraging cotton farming, Brazil has helped make cotton-weaving a successful industry. This means more jobs and more income for the nation.

Reviewing Main Ideas

1. List the three main regions of Latin America. Then choose two and describe their features.
2. In what ways do the physical features of Latin America affect the people and their way of life?
3. How does elevation affect climate?
4. (a) Give an example of how climate in one region of Latin America affects the vegetation that grows there.
   (b) How does this affect the way in which people live?
5. How are a country's natural resources tied to its economy?
6. What problems arise when a country depends too heavily on a single source of income? Support your answer with one or two examples.
7. How are the nations of Latin America trying to avoid the problems of relying on a single source of income?

Reviewing Key Terms

Match the definitions in Column I with the key terms in Column II

Column I	Column II
1. height of land above sea level	a. isthmus
2. plains in Argentina and Uruguay	b. pampas
3. to add variety	c. plateau
4. river or stream that flows into a larger body of water	d. tributary
5. electricity generated by the power of moving water	e. elevation
6. large raised area of mostly level land	f. diversify
7. narrow strip of land that has water on both sides and joins two larger bodies of land	g. hydro-electricity

Critical Thinking

1. **Identifying Central Issues** Explain the meaning of this statement, and give examples: "The weather in Latin America is a great friend to the people, but also a terrible enemy."
2. **Drawing Conclusions** "How a country uses its natural resources affects the well-being of its people." Do you agree or disagree with this statement? Explain your answer.

Graphic Organizer

Copy the chart to the right onto a separate sheet of paper. Then fill in the empty boxes to complete the chart. Use the maps in this chapter to help you.

	Physical Features	Climate	Vegetation	Natural Resources
Mexico and Central America				
The Caribbean				
South America				

Graphic Organizer

Answers will vary. Some possible answers:

	Physical Features	Climate	Vegetation	Natural Resources
Mexico and Central America	mountains, lowlands, volcanoes	tropical wet and dry, semiarid	mixed forest, rain forest, Mediterranean	minerals, oil, trees
The Caribbean	mountains, volcanoes	tropical wet and dry	rain forest, temperate grassland	rich soil, bauxite
South America	Andes, Amazon River, pampas	tropical wet, tropical wet and dry, humid subtropical, highland, arid	rain forest, temperate grassland, arid, Mediterranean	minerals, oil, fish

Map Activity

Latin America: Place Location

For each place listed below, write the letter from the map that shows its location.

1. Colombia
2. Brazil
3. Jamaica
4. Mexico
5. Venezuela

Writing Activity

Writing a Letter
Imagine that you are a visitor to Latin America. You are touring the whole region: Mexico, Central America, the Caribbean, and South America. Write a letter home, describing your trip. Write about such items as these: impressive sights, the weather, interesting facts you've learned, places you liked or didn't like.

Take It to the NET

Activity Learn more about El Salvador, a country on the west coast of Central America. Write a paragraph on the information you find most interesting. For help in completing this activity, visit www.phschool.com.

Chapter 1 Self-Test To review what you have learned, take the Chapter 1 Self-Test and get instant feedback on your answers. Go to www.phschool.com to take the test.

How Am I Doing?

Answer these questions to help you check your progress.

1. Can I identify and describe the main regions of Latin America?
2. Do I understand how Latin America's physical features, climate, and vegetation affect the people who live in the region?
3. Can I identify important natural resources of Latin America?
4. Can I explain why Latin American countries want to diversify their economies?
5. What information from this chapter can I include in my journal?

Skills Review

Turn to the Skill Activity.
Review the steps for reading a regional map. Then complete the following: (a) In your own words, describe two factors that vary from climate to climate. (b) What types of climates can be found in Latin America?

Take It to the NET

Students may wish to use the Internet to search for similar topics or activities. Suggest possible search terms, such as "El Salvador" or "Central America."

Guide students to a search engine. Four of the most useful are Infoseek, AltaVista, Lycos, and Yahoo. For additional suggestions on using the Internet, refer to the Prentice Hall Social Studies' Educator's Handbook "Using the Internet," in the *Prentice Hall World Explorer* Program Resources.

For chapter-by-chapter links to age-appropriate sites in world studies and geography, including Self-Tests, visit the *World Explorer* companion Web site at:
http://www.phschool.com

How Am I Doing?

Point out to students that this checklist is just a quick reminder for them of what they learned in the chapter. If their answer to any of the questions is *no* or if they are unsure, they may need to review the topic.

Map Activity

1. D	3. A	5. C
2. E	4. B	

Writing Activity

Students should write about various places visited during their imaginary tour of Latin America. Letters should contain specific, descriptive details about the region. Students should support their opinions with reasons.

Skills Review

Answers will vary. Sample answer: Places at different distances from the Equator and at different elevations have different climates. These include tropical wet, tropical wet and dry, semiarid, arid, Mediterranean, humid subtropical, marine west coast, and highlands.

Resource Directory

Teaching Resources
Chapter Tests Forms A and B are in the Tests booklet, pp. 2–7.

Program Resources
Writing Process Handbook includes Writing Effective Paragraphs, pp. 27–28, to help students with the Writing Activity.

Media and Technology
 Color Transparencies Color Transparency 174 (Graphic organizer table template)

Computer Test Bank CD-ROM

Resource Pro® CD-ROM

 Prentice Hall Assessment System

The Surveyor

BY ALMA FLOR ADA

LITERATURE

Lesson Objectives

1 Summarize a short story.

2 Relate a literary work to information about the country of its origin.

Lesson Plan

1 Engage

Building Vocabulary

Point out that notes in the margin can help students understand certain words and can give helpful hints as students read. Vocabulary defined in the margin include *surveyor* and *recruit*.

Ask students to read the title of the story and the definition of *surveyor* in the margin. Invite them to predict what the story will be about and where it might take place.

Activating Prior Knowledge

Read the paragraphs under the heading Before You Read with students. Discuss the value of family stories.

Reach Into Your Background

Do people in your family tell you stories about interesting or exciting events that have happened to them? What stories do you remember the best? What do you learn from these stories?

The stories that family members tell each other become part of the family history. Family stories are important because they teach people about their cultural heritage. Alma Flor Ada grew up in Cuba. The following story shows what Ada learned from one of the stories her father used to tell her.

Questions to Explore

1. What can you learn from this story about family life in Cuba?

2. What does this story tell you about how geography affects people's lives in Cuba?

surveyor (sir VAY ur) *n.:* a person who measures land and geographic features

M y father, named Modesto after my grandfather, was a surveyor. Some of the happiest times of my childhood were spent on horseback, on trips where he would allow me to accompany him as he plotted the boundaries of small farms in the Cuban countryside. Sometimes we slept out under the stars, stringing our hammocks between the trees, and drank fresh water from springs. We always stopped for a warm greeting at the simple huts of the neighboring peasants, and my eyes would drink in the lush green forest crowned by the swaying leaves of the palm trees.

Since many surveying jobs called for dividing up land that a family had inherited from a deceased parent or relative, my father's greatest concern was that justice be achieved. It was not enough just to divide the land into equal portions. He also had to ensure that all parties would have access to roads, to water sources, to the most fertile soil. While I was able to join him in some trips, other surveying work involved large areas of land. On these jobs, my father was part of a team, and I would stay home, eagerly awaiting to hear the stories from his trip on his return.

◄ The equipment that surveyors use must be strong and lightweight.

Latin American families tend not to limit their family boundaries to those who are born or have married into it. Any good friend who spends time with the family and shares in its daily experiences is welcomed as a member. The following story from one of my father's surveying trips is not about a member of my blood family, but instead concerns a member of our extended family.

Félix Caballero, a man my father always liked to recruit whenever he needed a team, was rather different from the other surveyors. He was somewhat older, unmarried, and he kept his thoughts to himself. He came to visit our house daily. Once there, he would sit silently in one of the living room's four rocking chairs, listening to the lively conversations all around him. An occasional nod or a single word were his only contributions to those conversations. My mother and her sisters sometimes made fun of him behind his back. Even though they never said so, I had the impression that they questioned why my father held him in such high regard.

Then one day my father shared this story.

"We had been working on foot in mountainous country for most of the day. Night was approaching. We still had a long way to go to return to where we had left the horses, so we decided to cut across to the other side of the mountain, and soon found ourselves facing a deep gorge. The gorge was spanned by a railroad bridge, long and narrow, built for the sugarcane trains. There were no side rails or walkways, only a set of tracks resting on thick, heavy crossties suspended high in the air.

"We were all upset about having to climb down the steep gorge and up the other side, but

Predict Why do you think that Ada's father admires Félix so much?

recruit (ree KROOT) *v.:* to enlist or hire to join a group

gorge (gorj) *n.:* a narrow canyon with steep walls

span (span) *v.:* to extend across a space

3 Assess

Work through the Exploring Your Reading with students.

1. The author learns to admire Felix for his courage and calmness.

2. Land is very valuable.

3. He came to the house daily; the father valued him.

4. A person's actions reveal character.

5. He survived because he was brave and thought calmly.

6. Acceptable stories will have an introduction and a conclusion explaining the story's importance. Outstanding stories will describe events vividly.

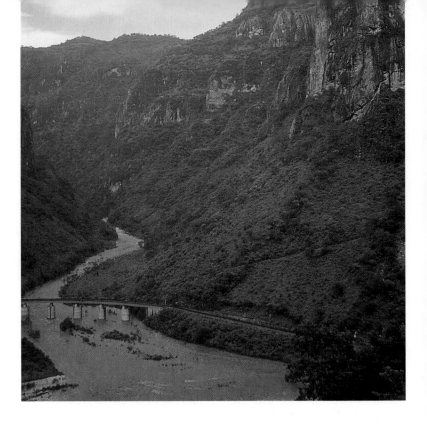

▶ Walking across a railroad bridge is dangerous, because most are just wide enough for a train to pass.

dissuade (dis SWAYD) *v.*: to persuade not to do something
ominous (OM ih nus) *adj.*: threatening

the simpler solution, walking across the bridge, seemed too dangerous. What if a cane train should appear? There would be nowhere to go. So we all began the long descent . . . all except for Félix. He decided to risk walking across the railroad bridge. We all tried to dissuade him, but to no avail. Using an old method, he put one ear to the tracks to listen for vibrations. Since he heard none, he decided that no train was approaching. So he began to cross the long bridge, stepping from crosstie to crosstie between the rails, balancing his long red-and-white surveyor's poles on his shoulder.

"He was about halfway across the bridge when we heard the ominous sound of a steam engine. All eyes rose to Félix. Unquestionably he had heard it, too, because he had stopped in the middle of the bridge and was looking back.

"As the train drew closer, and thinking there was no other solution, we all shouted, 'Jump! Jump!', not even sure our voices would carry to where he stood, so high above us. Félix did look down at the rocky riverbed, which, as it was the dry season, held little water. We tried to encourage him with gestures and more shouts, but he had stopped looking down. We could not imagine what he was doing next, squatting down on the tracks, with the engine of the train already visible. And then, we understood. . . .

"Knowing that he could not manage to hold onto the thick wooden crossties, Félix laid his thin but resilient surveyor's poles across the ties, parallel to the rails. Then he let his body slip down between two of the ties, as he held onto the poles. And there he hung, below the bridge, suspended over the gorge but safely out of the train's path.

"The cane train was, as they frequently are, a very long train. To us, it seemed interminable. . . . One of the younger men said he counted two hundred and twenty cars. With the approaching darkness, and the smoke and shadows of the train, it was often difficult to see our friend. We had heard no human sounds, no screams, but could we have heard anything at all, with the racket of the train crossing overhead?

"When the last car began to curve around the mountain, we could just make out Félix's lonely figure still hanging beneath the bridge. We all watched in relief and amazement as he pulled himself up and at last finished walking, slowly and calmly, along the tracks to the other side of the gorge."

After I heard that story, I saw Félix Caballero in a whole new light. He still remained as quiet as ever, prompting a smile from my mother and her sisters as he sat silently in his rocking chair. But in my mind's eye, I saw him crossing that treacherous bridge, stopping to think calmly of what to do to save his life, emerging all covered with soot and smoke but triumphantly alive—a lonely man, hanging under a railroad bridge at dusk, suspended from his surveyor's poles over a rocky gorge.

If there was so much courage, such an ability to calmly confront danger in the quiet, aging man who sat rocking in our living room, what other wonders might lie hidden in every human soul?

resilient (rih ZIL yunt) *adj.*: able to withstand shock and bounce back from changes

treacherous (TRECH ur us) *adj.*: dangerous

READ ACTIVELY

Visualize Visualize the team of surveyors as they watch the train go by. How do you think they looked? How might they have acted?

EXPLORING YOUR READING

Look Back

1. How does this story change the way the author feels about Félix Caballero?

Think It Over

2. Why is surveying land important in Cuba?

3. Why do you think that the author's family accepts Félix Caballero as a member of their extended family?

4. What lesson does the author of this story hope to teach?

Go Beyond

5. What does this story tell you about the character traits that help a person to act in an emergency?

Ideas for Writing: A Short Story

6. Choose a story that has been told to you by a family member or friend. Or, choose a story that you have told others about an event that happened to you. Write the story. Include an introduction and conclusion that explain why the story is important to you.

Shaped by Its History

To help you plan instruction, the chart below shows how teaching resources correspond to chapter content. Use the resources to vary instruction, add activities, or plan block schedules. Where appropriate, resources have suggested time allotments for students. Time allotments are approximate.

Managing Time and Instruction

	Latin America Teaching Resources Booklet		World Explorer Program Resources Binder	
	Resource	mins.	Resource	mins.
1 SECTION 1 Early Civilizations of Middle America	**Chapter and Section Support** Reproducible Lesson Plan, p. 18		**Outline Maps** Latin America: Physical, p. 6	20
	Ⓢ Guided Reading and Review, p. 19	20	**Nystrom Desk Atlas**	20
	Ⓢ Section Quiz, p. 20	25	Ⓣ **Primary Sources and Literature Readings**	40
	▯ Section Reading Support Transparencies	15	The Talking Stone, p. 7; Journal Entry, p. 45	
SKILLS ACTIVITY Using a Time Line	**Social Studies and Geography Skills,** Reading a Time Line, p. 61	30		
2 SECTION 2 The Incas People of the Sun	**Chapter and Section Support** Reproducible Lesson Plan, p. 21		**Outline Maps** Latin America: Physical, p. 6	20
	Ⓢ Guided Reading and Review, p. 22	20		
	Ⓢ Section Quiz, p. 23	25		
	▯ Section Reading Support Transparencies	15		
3 SECTION 3 European Conquest	**Chapter and Section Support** Reproducible Lesson Plan, p. 24			
	Ⓢ Guided Reading and Review, p. 25	20		
	Ⓢ Section Quiz, p. 26	25		
	▯ Section Reading Support Transparencies	15		
	Social Studies and Geography Skills, Reading a Historical Map, p. 28	30		
4 SECTION 4 Independence	**Chapter and Section Support** Reproducible Lesson Plan, p. 27			
	Ⓢ Guided Reading and Review, p. 28	20		
	Ⓢ Section Quiz, p. 29	25		
	▯ Section Reading Support Transparencies	15		
5 SECTION 5 Issues in Latin America Today	**Chapter and Section Support** Reproducible Lesson Plan, p. 30		**Outline Maps** Latin America: Political, p. 7	20
	Ⓢ Guided Reading and Review, p. 31	20	**Interdisciplinary Explorations**	
	Ⓢ Section Quiz, p. 32	25	Ⓣ *Fate of the Rain Forest*	
	Critical Thinking Activity, p. 37	30	**Writing Process Handbook**	
	Ⓢ Vocabulary, p. 34	20	Writing Effective Paragraphs, pp. 27–28	25
	Reteaching, p. 35	25		
	Enrichment, p. 36	25		
	Ⓢ Chapter Summary, p. 33	15		
	▯ Section Reading Support Transparencies	15		
	Tests Forms A and B Chapter Tests, pp. 8–13	40		

Block Scheduling Program Support

- Block Scheduling Booklet
  PROGRAM RESOURCES BINDER
- Activities and Projects
- Interdisciplinary Links
- Resource Pro® CD-ROM
- Media and Technology
- Pacing Charts Booklet
  PROGRAM RESOURCES BINDER

Media and Technology

Resource	mins.
World Video Explorer	20
Color Transparency 66	20
Prentice Hall Humanities Pack	20
Resource Pro® CD-ROM	30
Presentation Pro CD-ROM	20
Social Studies Skills Tutor CD-ROM	30
Color Transparencies, Historical Map Set 4	20
Color Transparency 34	20
Guided Reading Audiotapes	20
Color Transparency 172 (Graphic organizer tree map template)	20
Computer Test Bank CD-ROM	30
Student Edition on Audio CD	30
Passport to the World CD-ROM	30

T Teaming Opportunity
well-suited for teaching teams

S Spanish
This resource is also in Spanish support.

CD-ROM

Laserdisc

Transparency

Videotape

Audiotape/CD

Assessment Opportunities

From Guiding Questions to Assessment A series of Guiding Questions serves as an organizing framework for this book. The Guiding Questions that relate to this chapter are listed below. Section Reviews and Section Quizzes provide opportunities for assessing students' insights into these Guiding Questions. Additional assessments are listed below.

GUIDING QUESTIONS

- *How has Latin America been shaped by its history?*
- *What factors have affected cultures in Latin America?*

ASSESSMENTS

Section 1

Students should be able to make a time line showing the development of the Mayan and Aztec civilizations in Middle America.

▶ **RUBRIC** See the Assessment booklet for a rubric on assessing a time line.

Section 2

Students should be able to give an oral presentation on an Incan accomplishment of their choice.

▶ **RUBRIC** See the Assessment booklet for a rubric on assessing an oral presentation.

Section 3

Students should be able to write an explanation of the effects of European rule on Native Americans in Latin America.

▶ **RUBRIC** See the Assessment booklet for a rubric on assessing cause-and-effect statements.

Section 4

Students should be able to make a web that describes the people who led independence movements in Latin America.

▶ **RUBRIC** See the Assessment booklet for a rubric on assessing graphic organizers.

Section 5

Students should be able to write a glossary of the key terms in the section.

▶ **RUBRIC** See the Assessment booklet for a rubric on assessing a glossary.

 PRENTICE HALL ASSESSMENT SYSTEM

Prentice Hall Assessment System allows you to:

- Diagnose and Prescribe
- Review and Reteach
- Practice and Assess

Activities and Projects

Mental Mapping

What's Up? We are used to seeing maps that show North at the top of the map and South at the bottom. Early Arab maps, however, such as those used by Marco Polo to cross Asia, placed North at the bottom of the map. North is not really up, and South is not really down. "Up" is the top of a mountain or a high building.

Ask students to draw a map of the Americas on a sheet of notebook paper. Then ask them to turn their sketch upside down. Encourage discussion of how this map looks. Then ask them to draw the map again, this time placing South at the top of the page as they draw. How does their sense of South America, Central America, and Mexico change as they create this map and look at it? Invite them to speculate on the possible impact of portraying some parts of the world on the top and others on the bottom.

Links to Current Events

Issues in the News Provide one or more issues of major newspapers (such as *The New York Times*, *The Wall Street Journal*, *The Washington Post*, *Los Angeles Times*, or *Chicago Tribune*) and news magazines such as *Time*, *Newsweek*, and *U.S. News and World Report*. Periodicals need not be the current issue, but should be less than a year old. Ask students to look through periodicals to see what kinds of issues are discussed in United States news coverage of Latin America.

Have students create a chart listing the kinds of issues. Ask students whether they think these are the issues that people in Latin America are most likely to read or hear about in their own newspapers and TV news programs. Encourage students to discuss why or why not.

Hands-On Activities

History Speaks The countries of this region are called "Latin America" because most people in this region speak languages that come from Latin, such as Spanish, Portuguese, or French.

Using a large bulletin-board sized map of Latin America, have students use colored pins or tags to mark the countries where each language is spoken. Encourage students to check their knowledge by referring to almanacs, encyclopedias, or other sources. Have students note other languages they find in this region (such as Dutch and English).

Invite students to suggest the reasons for these language differences. You might extend this activity by having students locate European countries or countries in other parts of the world where these languages are spoken.

Illustrated Time Line Hang a long, narrow piece of paper marked with dates from A.D. 100 to 2000 marked at 100 year intervals. Invite students to place illustrations of events or people on the line as they learn about them in this chapter. Students should add and correctly position a specific date or range of dates to the line. Students may make their own illustrations or use illustrations clipped or photocopied from other sources. *Basic*

Pot Luck Have students find recipes that incorporate foods from both sides of the Columbian Exchange (possibilities include wheat, barley, beef, honey from Europe; tomatoes, potatoes, corn, chocolate, oranges from the Americas). Have them prepare a recipe and bring it to class. Invite them to identify the country the recipe came from. *English Language Learners*

Wish You Were Here Each country of Latin America has its own culture and history. Have students create a bulletin board of postcards from as many countries in the region as they can. They may use actual postcards, if they are available. They may also create postcards with their own drawings or clippings. Each postcard should illustrate an historic landmark or physical feature of a country in Latin America. *Average*

Technology Past and Present The peoples of Central and South America did not have the wheel, yet they overcame major physical barriers to build great cities. Suggest that students visit a construction site (from a safe distance) and note the many uses of wheels they observe. Have them do research to find out how the Aztecs, Incas, and other urban peoples of pre-Columbian America constructed cities without the wheel. Students may present their findings in the form of an illustrated report or by building models of some of the technology used. *Challenging*

F.Y.I.

This page can help you extend your own and students' understanding of the concepts in this chapter. You may want to browse through some of the suggestions in the **Bibliography**. **Interdisciplinary Links** can connect social studies understanding to areas elsewhere in the curriculum through the use of other Prentice Hall products. **National Geography Standards** reflected specifically in this chapter are listed for your convenience. Some hints about appropriate Internet access are also provided in **Take It to the Net**. **School to Careers** provides insights into the practical uses of some of the concepts in this chapter as they might pertain to various careers.

BIBLIOGRAPHY

FOR THE TEACHER

Arnold, Caroline. *City of the Gods: Mexico's Ancient City of Teotihuacán.* Clarion, 1994.

Baquedano, Elizabeth. *Aztec, Inca, and Maya.* Dorling, 1993. Eyewitness Series.

Fritz, Jean et al. *The World in 1492.* Holt, 1992.

Stein, R. Conrad. *The Mexican Revolution: 1910–1920.* New Discovery, 1994.

FOR THE STUDENT

Easy
Defrates, Joanna. *What Do We Know About the Aztecs?* Bedrick, 1995.

Average
Garcia, Guy. *Spirit of the Maya: A Boy Explores His People's Mysterious Past.* Walker, 1995.

Wood, Marion. *Growing Up in Aztec Times.* Troll, 1993.

Wood, Tim. *The Aztecs.* Viking, 1992.

Challenging
Meyer, Carolyn and Charles Gallenkamp. *The Mystery of the Ancient Maya.* McElderry, 1995. (New ed.)

LITERATURE CONNECTION

Dorris, Michael. *Morning Girl.* Hyperion, 1992.

DeTreviño, Elizabeth Borton. *El Güero: A True Adventure Story.* Farrar, 1989.

INTERDISCIPLINARY LINKS

Subject	Theme: History
MATH	Middle Grades Math: Tools for Success *Course 2*, Lesson 9-5, **Independent and Dependent Events** *Course 3*, Chapter 4, Math Toolbox, **Graphing Lines**
SCIENCE	Science Explorer *Cells and Heredity*, Lesson 5-2, **The Fossil Record** *Environmental Science*, Lesson 2-5, **Succession**
LANGUAGE ARTS	Prentice Hall Literature *Bronze*, **Popocatepetl and Ixtlaccihuatl**

NATIONAL GEOGRAPHY STANDARDS

Students explore the 18 National Geography Standards throughout Latin America. Chapter 2, however, concentrates on investigating the following: standards 1, 9, 10, 11, 12, 13, 14, 16, 17. For a complete list of the standards, see the *Teacher's Flexible Planning Guide*.

SCHOOL TO CAREERS

In Chapter 2, Latin America: Shaped by Its History, students learn about the early civilizations of Middle America and the European conquest and colonization. Additionally, they address the skill of using a time line. Understanding history can help students prepare for careers in education, publishing, journalism, and so on. Time line reading skills are particularly helpful for teachers, writers, editors, reporters, and others. The curriculum presented in this book, as in all eight titles of Prentice Hall's *World Explorer* program, is designed to prepare students not only for careers but also for good citizenship—of the world as well as of this country.

Take It to the NET

Many social studies teachers and students use Internet browsers, or search engines, to investigate particular topics. For the best results, use narrow rather than broad topics. Try these for Chapter 2: Incan civilization, Tenochtitlán, Mexican revolution, Christopher Columbus. Finding age-appropriate sites is an important consideration when using the Internet. For links to age-appropriate sites in world studies and geography, visit the *World Explorer* companion Web site at:

http://www.phschool.com

CHAPTER 2

Connecting to the Guiding Questions

As students complete this chapter, they will focus on the history of Latin America, tracing highlights of ancient cultures and European conquests. Content in this chapter thus corresponds to the following Guiding Questions:

- How has Latin America been shaped by its history?
- What factors have affected cultures in Latin America?

Using the Map Activities

As students complete the map activities, point out that great civilizations have existed in Latin America.

- Incan, Mayan, and Aztec; Mayan.
- Possible response: Mayan, because it could be attacked by land from two directions and from both seacoasts.

Heterogeneous Groups

The following Teacher's Edition strategies are suitable for heterogeneous groups.

Cooperative Learning
Talking With Liberators p. 53

Interdisciplinary Connections
Science   p. 58

Critical Thinking
Recognizing Cause
and Effect   p. 45
Distinguishing Fact
From Opinion   p. 57

LATIN AMERICA
Shaped by Its History

KEY

Aztec Empire
A.D. 1200s–A.D. 1521

Mayan Empire
A.D. 300–A.D. 900

Incan Empire
A.D. 1400s–A.D. 1535

Lambert Azimuthal Equal-Area Projection

0   600   1,200 mi
0   600 1,200 km

MAP ACTIVITIES

This map shows the location of three civilizations in Latin America that existed before Europeans arrived in the region.

Study the map
What are the names of the civilizations shown on the map? Which civilization is the oldest?

Consider the geography
Which civilization do you think was the most difficult to defend from invaders? Explain your answer.

Resource Directory

Media and Technology

 A Trip to: Ruins of the Maya, from the World Video Explorer, enhances students' understanding of ancient Mayan culture and its contributions to Latin America culture today.

Early Civilizations of Middle America

BEFORE YOU READ

Reach Into Your Background

What does the word *pyramid* bring to mind? Write down three things you know about pyramids. Then, compare what you know about pyramids with the pyramids you will read about in this section.

Questions to Explore

1. What were the chief characteristics and accomplishments of Mayan and Aztec civilizations?
2. How have Latin America's early civilizations affected present-day cultures in Latin America?

Key Terms

maize
hieroglyphics

Key Places

Copán
Tikal
Valley of Mexico
Tenochtitlán

Lesson Objectives

1. Describe the chief characteristics and accomplishments of the Mayan and Aztec civilizations.

2. Explain how Latin America's early civilizations have affected present-day cultures in Latin America.

Lesson Plan

1 Engage

Warm-Up Activity

Write the word *civilization* on the board. Ask students to list all the things that they think of when they hear this word. When students have finished their lists, call on volunteers to write their responses on the chalkboard. Invite discussion.

Activating Prior Knowledge

Have students read Reach Into Your Background in the Before You Read box. Tell students that, generally, a civilization is a culture that has built cities and has developed a writing system, the arts, the sciences, and a system of education. The culture also generally has a government, public buildings, and thriving commerce. Ask students to name some features of American civilization. (Sample responses: airplane, Washington D.C.)

Fans cheered as the players brought the ball down the court. Suddenly, the ball flew into the air and sailed through the hoop. Fans and players shouted and screamed. Although this may sound like a championship basketball game, it is actually a moment of a game played over 1,000 years ago. The game was called pok-ta-tok.

Pok-ta-tok was a game played by the ancient Mayas. Using only their leather-padded hips and elbows, players tried to hit a five-pound (1.9 kg), six-inch (15.2 cm) rubber ball through a stone hoop mounted 30 feet (9.1 m) above the ground.

▼ This pok-ta-tok court is in Copán, Honduras. How is it similar to a basketball court?

Mayan Civilization

How do we know about this ancient game? Crumbling ruins of pok-ta-tok courts and ancient clay statues of players have been found at sites in Central America and southern Mexico. In these areas, Mayan civilization thrived from about A.D. 300 to A.D. 900. By studying ruins, scientists have learned much about Mayan civilization.

Teaching Resources

📁 **Reproducible Lesson Plan** in the Chapter and Section Resources booklet, p. 18, provides a summary of the section lesson.

📁 **Guided Reading and Review** in the Chapter and Section Resources booklet, p. 19, provides a structure for mastering key concepts and reviewing key terms in the section. Available in Spanish in the Spanish Chapter and Section Resources booklet, p. 12.

📖 **Section Reading Support Transparencies** provide answers to the Questions to Explore in a graphic organizer format.

Program Resources

📁 Material in the **Primary Sources and Literature Readings** booklet extends content with a selection from the region under study.

Answers to...

POK-TA-TOK COURT

• Both courts are rectangular and open, each has a space for an audience.

2 Explore

Have students read the section and use the illustrations to investigate the Mayan and Aztec civilizations. Students should find supporting details for the following headings: Major Achievements, Reasons for Decline, Influences on Today.

3 Teach

Have students create two concept maps, one entitled *Mayas,* and the other, *Aztecs.* The maps should include facts for subtopics such as Cities, Achievements, Decline, Influence on Latin American Empire, and Religion. Discuss how the achievements of the two civilizations have influenced students' lives. Activity should take about 30 minutes.

4 Assess

See answers to the Section Review. You may also use students' completed concept maps as an assessment, evaluating the maps on the basis of number of facts and overall organization.

Background

Global Perspectives

Hieroglyphics The term *hieroglyph,* meaning "sacred carving," was used by the Greeks to describe the characters on Egyptian monuments. Eventually, *hieroglyphic* was applied to the picture-writing of other cultures, such as the Mayas. The Mayan writing system is pictorial, but bears no other relation to Egyptian hieroglyphics.

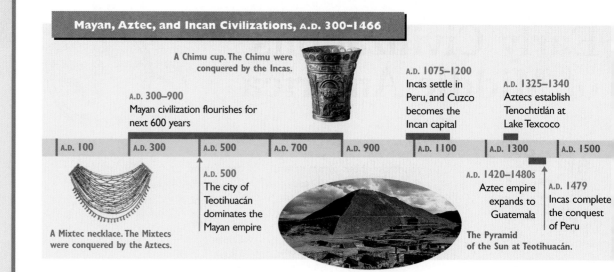

Mayan, Aztec, and Incan Civilizations, A.D. 300–1466

A Chimu cup. The Chimu were conquered by the Incas.

A.D. 300–900 Mayan civilization flourishes for next 600 years

A.D. 1075–1200 Incas settle in Peru, and Cuzco becomes the Incan capital

A.D. 1325–1340 Aztecs establish Tenochtitlán at Lake Texcoco

| A.D. 100 | A.D. 300 | A.D. 500 | A.D. 700 | A.D. 900 | A.D. 1100 | A.D. 1300 | A.D. 1500 |

A Mixtec necklace. The Mixtecs were conquered by the Aztecs.

A.D. 500 The city of Teotihuacán dominates the Mayan empire

A.D. 1420–1480s Aztec empire expands to Guatemala

A.D. 1479 Incas complete the conquest of Peru

The Pyramid of the Sun at Teotihuacán.

The Concept of Zero The Mayas created a numbering system that included the idea of zero. Zero is important in math because it is a symbol that shows that there is none of something. For example, to write the number 308, you need a symbol to show that there are no tens. Mathematicians consider the idea of zero to be one of the world's greatest inventions.

The Mayas built great cities. One such city was Copán (ko PAHN) in the present-day country of Honduras. Another was Tikal (tee KAHL) in present-day Guatemala. Mayan cities were religious centers. A large pyramid-shaped temple stood in the center of the city. The Mayas worshipped their gods there. Farmers worked in fields surrounding the cities. Past the fields lay the dense tropical rain forest.

Mayan Farming and Science The Mayan farmers' most important crop was **maize,** or corn. Maize was the main food of the Mayas. They also grew beans, squash, peppers, avocados, and papayas. Mayan priests studied the stars and planets. They designed an accurate calendar, which they used to decide when to hold religious ceremonies. The Mayan calendar was more accurate than any used in Europe until the 1700s. The Mayas developed a system of writing using signs and symbols called **hieroglyphics** (hy ur oh GLIF iks). They also developed a number system that is similar to the present-day decimal system.

The Great Mystery of the Mayas About A.D. 900, the Mayas suddenly left their cities. No one knows why. Crop failures, war, disease, drought, or famine may have killed many Mayas. Or perhaps people rebelled against the control of the priests and nobles. The Mayas left their cities, but stayed in the region. Millions of Mayas still live in the countries of Mexico, Belize, Guatemala, Honduras, and El Salvador.

Aztec Civilization

Another ancient civilization of Middle America is that of the Aztecs. They arrived in the Valley of Mexico in the 1100s. The Valley of Mexico is in Central Mexico and includes the site of present-day Mexico City.

Resource Directory

Program Resources

Nystrom Desk Atlas

Outline Maps Latin America physical map

Media and Technology

Color Transparency 66

Prentice Hall Humanities Pack Fine art transparencies, posters, audio CDs and a performing arts video help students explore the arts and cultures of all regions of the world. Includes discussion questions and activities. Use Transparency 6 to show how the Aztecs' religious beliefs were reflected in their art.

The Aztecs wandered about the valley looking for a permanent home until 1325. They finally settled on an island in Lake Texcoco. They changed the swampy lake into a magnificent city, which they called Tenochtitlán (tay nawch tee TLAHN). Tenochtitlán stood on the site of present-day Mexico City.

Tenochtitlán

Tenochtitlán, the Aztec capital, was built in the center of a lake. The Aztecs built floating islands by piling rich earth from the bottom of the lake onto rafts made of wood. After a while, the roots of plants and trees grew down to the lake bottom, anchoring the rafts. Some islands were the size of football fields. What do you think it would be like to live on a lake?

Lake Texcoco

Great Temple

Ordinary dwellings were made of reeds and mud.

Upper-class dwellings were made of stone.

Canals, laid out in a grid system, connected all parts of the city.

Causeways, or raised earthen roads, connected the city to the mainland.

SKILLS MINI LESSON

Interpreting Diagrams As a way to **introduce** the skill, tell students that a picture or diagram can help explain a complex idea or process or how something is organized. Direct students' attention to the diagram of Tenochtitlán. Suggest that students **practice** the skill by finger-tracing the wall that defined the heart of the city or locating causeways that connected the islands. Encourage students to **apply** the skill by using the diagram to find out how all parts of the city were connected.

Exploring Technology

Tenochtitlán Use the map at the beginning of this section to locate Tenochtitlán. Remind students that present-day Mexico City is located on the same site. Ask students what the location of Tenochtitlán tells about the city. (The location at an elevation of over 7,000 feet [2,134 m] and at 19.28°N latitude means that the climate of Tenochtitlán was mild.)

Have students compare the drawing to a map. How is it similar to the map? How is it different?

Read the following quotation from Bernal Diaz, one of the first Spaniards to see Tenochtitlán:

> "Some of our soldiers who had been . . . . in Constantinople, in Rome, and all over Italy said they had never seen a market so well laid out, so large, so orderly, and so full of people."

Ask students to explain how the buildings and rules of the city were related to the strict social system of the Aztecs. (Upper-class dwellings were made of stone. Ordinary people lived in small, simple houses made of mud and reeds.)

Answers to...

TENOCHTITLÁN

• Accept any reasonable answer.

Aztec and Mayan Languages Today, Nahuatl, a descendant of the Aztec language, is spoken by more than one million people in Mexico and Central America. The various Mayan languages are spoken by about two million people.

1. (a) corn (b) a kind of writing, using signs and symbols

2. (a) Mayan city in present-day Honduras (b) Mayan city in present-day Guatemala (c) area inhabited by Aztecs in the 1100s (d) central city of the Aztec empire that stood at the site of present-day Mexico City

3. Mayas built great cities, many of which were religious centers. Priests and nobles controlled the city. Mayan farmers grew many crops; the most important was maize. Mayas designed an accurate calendar and wrote using hieroglyphics.

4. The emperor ruled over the people. Nobles and priests helped the emperor; warriors fought battles; traders carried goods; craftpersons created works of art. Most people were farmers.

5. Statement (a) is a fact; (b) is an opinion. Student explanations will vary.

6. Answers will vary. Students should include in their answers that no one knows why the Mayan civilization declined. Crop failures, war, disease, drought, and famine are possibilities.

Aztec Astronomy

The Aztecs observed the stars and planets carefully. They named them after their gods, like Quetzalcoatl, shown at right. The Aztecs used their knowledge of astronomy to make calendars like the one below.

The Aztecs Expand Their Empire In the 1400s, Aztec warriors began conquering the other people in the region. They forced the people they conquered to pay tribute, or taxes. Tribute could be paid in food, cotton, gold, or slaves. The Aztecs grew rich from the tribute.

The Aztecs had an emperor who ruled over all Aztec lands. The rest of Aztec society had several classes. Nobles and priests helped the emperor. Warriors fought battles. Traders carried goods throughout the empire and beyond. Craftworkers created jewelry, garments, pottery, sculptures, and other goods. Most people, however, were farmers.

Other Aztec Accomplishments Tenochtitlán was a center of trade and learning. Aztec doctors made more than 1,000 medicines from plants. They used the medicines to lower fevers, cure stomachaches, and heal wounds. Like the Mayas, Aztec astronomers predicted eclipses and the movements of planets. Aztec priests kept records using hieroglyphics similar to those used by the Mayas.

SECTION 1 REVIEW

1. Define (a) maize, (b) hieroglyphics.

2. Identify (a) Copán, (b) Tikal, (c) Valley of Mexico, (d) Tenochtitlán.

3. What were the main features of Mayan civilization?

4. How was Aztec society organized?

Critical Thinking

5. Distinguishing Fact From Opinion Tell if the following statements are facts or opinions. Explain why. (a) Mayan calendars were very accurate. (b) Aztec civilization was more advanced than Mayan civilization.

Activity

6. Writing to Learn What are some reasons for the decline of Mayan and Aztec civilizations? Does every society decline sooner or later?

Teaching Resources

Section Quiz in the Chapter and Section Resources booklet, p. 20, covers the main ideas and key terms in the section. Available in Spanish in the Spanish Chapter and Section Resources booklet, p. 13.

The Incas

PEOPLE OF THE SUN

BEFORE YOU READ

Reach Into Your Background
The United States has roads that run from state to state. These roads are called inter- state highways. Think about some ways that interstate highways are useful. Then, compare what you know about interstate highways with the roads you will read about in this section.

Questions to Explore
1. What was Incan civilization like?

2. How did the Incas interact with and change their environment to increase farmland and farm production?

Key Terms
aqueduct   quipu

Key People and Places
Pachacuti   Cuzco
Topa Inca

The runner sped along the mountain road. He lifted a horn made from a shell to his lips and blew. A second runner appeared and began running beside him. Without stopping, the first runner relayed to the second runner the message he carried. The second runner took off like the wind. He would not stop until he reached the next runner.

The Incas used runners to spread news from one place in their empire to another. Incan messengers carried news at a rate of 250 miles (402 km) a day. Without these runners, controlling the vast empire would have been very difficult.

The Rise of the Incas

This great and powerful empire had small beginnings. In about 1200, the Incas settled in Cuzco (KOOS koh), a village in the Andes that is now a city in the country of Peru. Most Incas were farmers. They grew maize and other crops. Through wars and conquest, the Incas won control of the entire Cuzco valley, one of many valleys that extend from the Andes to the Pacific Ocean.

In 1438, Pachacuti (PAHTCH an koo tee) became ruler of the Incas. The name Pachacuti means "he who shakes the earth." Pachacuti conquered the people who lived near the Pacific Ocean, from Lake Titicaca north to the city of Quito.

▼ The Incas shaped their stones so well that they did not need cement to hold a wall together.

Teaching Resources

📁 **Reproducible Lesson Plan** in the Chapter and Section Resources book- let, p. 21, provides a summary of the section lesson.

📁 **Guided Reading and Review** in the Chapter and Section Resources book- let, p. 22, provides a structure for mastering key concepts and reviewing key terms in the section. Available in Spanish in the Spanish Chapter and Section Resources booklet, p. 14.

📖 **Section Reading Support Transparencies** provide answers to the Questions to Explore in a graphic organizer format.

Lesson Objectives

1 Identify three main fea- tures of Incan civilization.

2 Explain how the Incas altered their environment to increase farm produc- tion.

Lesson Plan

1 Engage
Warm-Up Activity
Ask students to complete the following: *Americans, People of _____.* Tell them to fill in the blank with a term that they think best tells what is important to people in the United States today. Call on volunteers to share their statements.

Activating Prior Knowledge
Have students read Reach Into Your Background in the Before You Read box. Lead students to the conclusion that interstate highways make travel easier between cities. Bring out the point that goods, information, and peo- ple all use the highways.

2 Explore
Have students read the section to learn about the achievements of the Incas. Ask students why they think the Incas might have been referred to as "People of the Sun." Some students might indicate that the sun was important to the Incas because farming was their main way of making a living. Others might indicate that the sun was important to them as a god.

3 Teach

Provide students with the following topic sentence: *The Incas used their environment wisely.* Have students use the information in the section to write a paragraph that supports the topic sentence. Use volunteers' paragraphs as discussion springboards. This activity should take about 20 minutes.

4 Assess

See answers to the Section Review. You may also use students' paragraphs as an assessment.

Acceptable paragraphs list three achievements of the Incas.

Commendable paragraphs describe four or more achievements, including those in farming.

Outstanding paragraphs show an understanding of how the Incas altered their environment, both to increase farm productivity and to maintain a widespread empire.

Answers to...

MACHU PICCHU, LOST CITY OF THE INCAS

• Students should recognize that like Incan farm land, the city is terraced.

Pachacuti demanded loyalty from the people he conquered. If they proved disloyal, he forced them off their land. He replaced them with people loyal to the Incas.

Pachacuti's son, Topa Inca, expanded the empire. In time, it stretched some 2,500 miles (4,023 km) from what is now Ecuador south along the Pacific coast through Peru, Bolivia, Chile, and Argentina. The 12 million people ruled by the Incas lived mostly in small villages.

Incan Accomplishments

The Incas were excellent farmers, builders, and managers. Their capital, Cuzco, was the center of government, trade, learning, and religion. In the 1500s, one of the first Spaniards to visit Cuzco described it as "large enough and handsome enough to compare to any Spanish city."

The emperor, and the nobles who helped him run the empire, lived in the city near the central plaza. They wore special headbands and earrings that showed their high rank. Most of the farmers and workers outside Cuzco lived in mud huts.

Roads and Aqueducts   The Incas built more than 14,000 miles (22,530 km) of roads. The roads went over some of the most mountainous land in the world. The road system helped the Incas to govern their vast empire. Not only did runners use the roads to deliver messages, but Incan armies and trade caravans also used the roads for speedy travel.

READ ACTIVELY

Connect How do your family and community depend on roads?

▼Pachacuti built many cities. The most famous one is the "lost city" of Machu Picchu. It lies high in the Andes Mountains, 54 miles (87 km) northwest of Cuzco. **Interaction** Look closely at the picture. How did the Incas adapt their city to the mountains?

Resource Directory

Program Resources

Outline Maps Latin America physical map

History on a String

The Incas used quipus to record information about births, deaths, trade, and taxes. **Critical Thinking** Think of some other ways to communicate information without using spoken or written words.

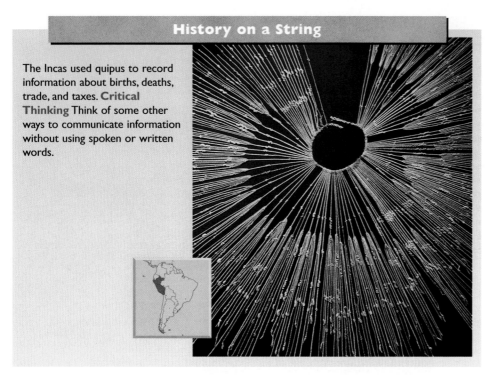

The Incas also built canals and aqueducts to carry water to dry areas. An aqueduct is a pipe or channel designed to carry water from a distant source. One stone aqueduct carried water from a mountain lake almost 500 miles (805 km) to its destination. The system of canals and aqueducts allowed the Incas to irrigate land that was otherwise too dry to grow crops.

Government and Records The Incas organized their government carefully. The emperor chose nobles to govern each province. Each noble conducted a census to count people so they could be taxed. Local officials collected some of each village's crops as a tax. The villagers also had to work on government building projects. However, the government took care of the poor, the sick, and the elderly.

The Incas did not have a written language. Incan government officials and traders recorded information on knotted strings called quipus (KEE poos). Every quipu had a main cord with several colored strings attached to it. Each color represented a different item, and knots of different sizes at certain intervals stood for numbers.

Religion Like the Mayas and the Aztecs, the Incas worshipped many gods. The sun god, Inti, was an important god of the Incas. They believed Inti was their parent. They referred to themselves as "children of the sun." Another important Incan god was Viracocha (vee ra KOCH ah), the creator of all the people of the Andes.

LINKS ACROSS TIME

Earthquake-proof Buildings Incan stone walls were so firmly constructed that even violent earthquakes could not knock them down. The walls swayed but did not crumble the way some modern buildings do. Engineers today are learning to make buildings that can resist an earthquake.

Section 2 Review

1. (a) a pipe or channel designed to carry water from a distant source (b) knotted strings used by the Incas to keep records

2. (a) Incan ruler who demanded loyalty from the people he conquered (b) ruler who expanded the Incan empire (c) Incan capital

3. Roads connected all parts of the empire. This made travel easier for the army, traders, and especially the message runners.

4. Sample answer: The Incas worshipped many gods. The main god, Inti, was the sun god.

5. Sample response: Being in the valley would make it difficult to defend the empire. The mountains would help keep enemies from attacking the empire.

6. Students' lists might include building aqueducts to carry water to dry areas to make farming possible and building terraces in hilly areas. Students might indicate that Incas used their environment wisely.

Answers to...

FARMING IN THE MOUNTAINS

- Responses will vary. Sample answers: plowing terraces might be difficult; there may be less direct sunlight because mountain peaks cast shadows; cold weather may last longer than in non-mountain regions.

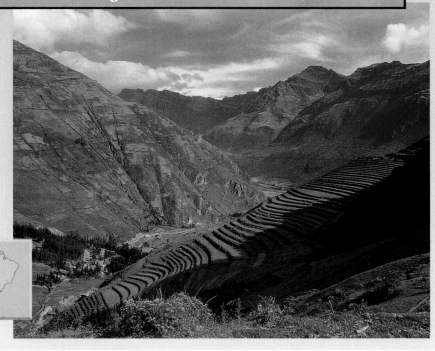

The Incas increased the amount of farmland in hilly areas by building terraces into the sides of steep slopes. The terraces helped keep soil from washing down the mountain. These terraces are at Pasaq, an ancient Incan fortress in Peru. **Interaction** Think of some other reasons why farming in the mountains might be hard.

Quechua Descendants of the Incas The Spanish conquered the Incan empire in the 1500s. However, descendants of the Incas still live in present-day Peru, Ecuador, Bolivia, Chile, and Colombia. They speak Quechua (KECH wah), the Incan language.

They use farming methods that are like those of the ancient Incas. The Incan culture also survives in the poncho and in other clothing styles, as well as in cloth woven into brightly colored complex patterns.

SECTION 2 REVIEW

1. Define (a) aqueduct, (b) quipu.

2. Identify (a) Pachacuti, (b) Topa Inca, (c) Cuzco.

3. Why was a good network of roads important to the Incan empire?

4. Describe a few features of the Incan religion.

Critical Thinking

5. Drawing Conclusions Look at the shape of the Incan empire on the map on the opening page of this chapter. In an attack, what features would make the empire difficult to defend? What features would help defend the empire?

Activity

6. Writing to Learn Make a list of some of the ways the Incas used land for farming. Do you think the Incas made good use of farmland? Why or why not?

Resource Directory

Teaching Resources

Section Quiz in the Chapter and Section Resources booklet, p. 23, covers the main ideas and key terms in the section. Available in Spanish in the Spanish Chapter and Section Resources booklet, p. 15.

European Conquest

BEFORE YOU READ

Reach Into Your Background

How do you decide what is right and what is wrong? Think of a time when you were not sure what was the right thing to do. As you read this section, notice how the people made decisions. Think about whether or not you agree with the decisions they made.

Questions to Explore

1. Why did Europeans sail to the Americas?
2. What were the effects of European rule on Native Americans in the region?

Key Terms

Treaty of Tordesillas
treaty
Line of Demarcation
conquistador
mestizo
hacienda
encomienda

Key People

Hernán Cortés
Malinche
Christopher Columbus
Moctezuma
Francisco Pizarro

Lesson Objectives

1. Summarize the reasons that Europeans sailed to the Americas.

2. Analyze the effects of European rule on Native Americans in the region.

Lesson Plan

1 Engage

Warm-Up Activity

Ask students to list reasons why countries today explore outer space and the ocean floor. Call on volunteers to share their lists and record their responses on the board. Ask students to evaluate the reasons and choose the one that they think is the most important.

Activating Prior Knowledge

Have students read Reach Into Your Background in the Before You Read box. Students may provide a variety of ways to determine whether something is right or wrong: learning from parents, knowing it's against the rules, and realizing "It isn't the way I would like to be treated."

2 Explore

Ask students to skim the section and note the main headings. Have them find answers to the following questions: Why did Europeans come to America? How did Spanish explorers treat the Native Americans living in the Americas? How did Spain and Portugal organize their empires in the Americas?

Hernán Cortés was the Spanish soldier who conquered the Aztecs. He landed in Mexico in 1519 and soon met Malinche (mah LIHN chay). The daughter of an Aztec leader, Malinche had been given to the Mayas as a slave. Malinche, whom Cortés called Doña Marina, spoke several languages. She quickly learned Spanish and became Cortés's main translator. She also kept an eye on Aztec spies. Without Malinche, Cortés could not have conquered the Aztecs. Why did European explorers, like Cortés, want to conquer Native Americans? Why did some Native Americans, like Malinche, help the conquerers?

Europeans Arrive in the Americas

In the 1400s, Spain and Portugal searched for new trade routes to Asia. They knew that in Asia they would find expensive goods such as spices and silks. These goods could be traded for a profit.

Columbus Reaches America Christopher Columbus thought he could reach Asia by sailing west across the Atlantic Ocean. Columbus knew the world was round, as did most educated

▼ Sailors in the 1400s guided their ships using only the stars, a compass, and an astrolabe. Below is a drawing of an astrolabe.

Teaching Resources

📁 **Reproducible Lesson Plan** in the Chapter and Section Resources booklet, p. 24, provides a summary of the section lesson.

📁 **Guided Reading and Review** in the Chapter and Section Resources booklet, p. 25, provides a structure for mastering key concepts and reviewing key terms in the section. Available in Spanish in the Spanish Chapter and Section Resources booklet, p. 16.

📖 **Section Reading Support Transparencies** provide answers to the Questions to Explore in a graphic organizer format.

3 Teach

Have students write an essay that answers the question: How did European rule affect both the Europeans and the Native Americans in the Americas? Encourage students to include specific examples from this section in their essays. This activity should take about 25 minutes.

4 Assess

See answers to the Section Review. You may also use students' completed essays as an assessment.

Acceptable essays include the facts that Europeans gained land and wealth and that the Native Americans lost their empires.

Commendable essays include details about the conquistadors and how they conquered the Native American civilizations.

Outstanding essays provide information about the organization of the Portuguese and Spanish empires and show an understanding of the effects of the cultural interaction between the Native Americans and the Europeans.

Answers to...
MAP STUDY

- Rival or conquered groups helped the conquistadors find their enemies; there was an agreement that Spain could settle land to the west and Portugal land to the east of the Line of Demarcation.

Spanish Conquest and Colonization of the Americas

Map Study Columbus sailed to the Americas in 1492, 1493, 1498, and 1502. His 1502 voyage is shown here. Cortés sailed to the Americas in 1504 and conquered the Aztecs in 1519. Pizarro sailed in 1502 and conquered the Incas in 1533. **Movement** Once they reached the Caribbean, what factors do you think helped the Spanish to find the Aztec and Incan empires so quickly? **Regions** South America has two major language regions: Spanish and Portuguese. How did the Line of Demarcation create these regions?

KEY

→ Christopher Columbus 1502–1504

→ Hernan Cortés 1519–1521

→ Francisco Pizarro 1531

---- Line of Demarcation

Lambert Azimuthal Equal-Area Projection

0   600   1,200 mi
0 600 1,200 km

LINKS TO MATH

Navigating Without Modern Instruments
Explorers like Columbus did not have radar, satellites, and computers to guide their ships. They used the stars as a reference. Sailors imagined a triangle with a straight line from the ship to the horizon, and a line from the horizon to a star. Measuring the angle between the line to the star and the horizon helped them figure out their location.

Europeans. But Columbus believed the distance around the world was shorter than it was. First Columbus asked Portugal to sponsor his voyage. Then he asked Spain. Queen Isabella of Spain finally agreed.

Columbus set sail in early August, 1492. Some 10 weeks later, on October 12, he spotted land. Columbus thought he had reached the East Indies in Asia, so he described the people there as Indians.

Dividing the World   Spain and Portugal soon became fierce rivals. Each country tried to stop the other from claiming land in the Americas. In 1494, Spain and Portugal signed the **Treaty of Tordesillas** (tor day SEE yas). A **treaty** is an agreement in writing made between two or more countries. The treaty set an imaginary line from North Pole to South Pole at about 50° longitude, called the **Line of Demarcation**. It gave Spain the right to settle and trade west of the line. Portugal could do the same east of the line. The only part of South America that is east of the line is roughly the eastern half of present-day Brazil. Because of the Treaty of Tordesillas, the language and background of Brazil are Portuguese.

A Clash of Cultures

Spanish explorers heard stories of wealthy kingdoms in the Americas. They hoped to find gold and other treasures. Spanish rulers did not pay for the trips of the explorers. Instead, they gave the **conquistadors** (kon KEES ta dors), or conquerors, the right to hunt for treasure. The conquistadors could also settle in America. In exchange, conquistadors agreed to give Spain one fifth of any treasures they found. If a conquistador failed, he lost his own fortune. If he succeeded, both he and Spain gained fame, wealth, and glory.

Cortés Conquers the Aztecs In 1519, Hernán Cortés sailed to the coast of Mexico in search of treasure. He brought a small army with him. The Aztec ruler Moctezuma (mahk the ZOOM uh) heard that a strange ship was offshore. He sent spies to find out about it. The spies reported back to Moctezuma:

“ We must tell you that we saw a house in the water, out of which came white men, with white hands and faces, and very long, bushy beards, and clothes of every color: white, yellow, red, green, blue, and purple, and on their heads they wore round hats.”

The Aztecs demanded heavy tribute from the peoples who lived near them, so these groups disliked the Aztecs. Cortés made agreements with these groups. Then he headed for Tenochtitlán with 500 soldiers and 16 horses. Aztec spies told Moctezuma that the Spanish were coming. The Aztecs had never seen horses before. Moctezuma's spies described the Spanish as "supernatural creatures riding on hornless deer, armed in iron, fearless as gods." Moctezuma thought Cortés might be the god Quetzalcoatl (ket sahl koh AHTL). According to Aztec legend, Quetzalcoatl had promised to return to rule the Aztecs.

With a heavy heart, Moctezuma welcomed Cortés and his soldiers. Cortés tried to convince Moctezuma to surrender to Spain. After several months, Moctezuma agreed. But the peace did not last long. Spanish soldiers killed some Aztecs. Then the Aztecs began to fight against the Spanish. The battle was fierce and bloody. Moctezuma was killed, and Cortés and his army barely escaped.

With the help of the Aztecs' enemies, Cortés surrounded and attacked Tenochtitlán. In 1521, the Aztecs finally surrendered. By then, about 240,000 Aztecs had died and 30,000 of Cortés's allies had been killed. Tenochtitlán and the Aztec empire lay in ruins.

Pizarro Conquers the Incas Francisco Pizarro (fran SIS koh pih ZAR oh), like Cortés, was a Spanish conquistador. He heard stories about the rich Incan kingdom. Pizarro planned to attack the Pacific coast of South America. In 1531, Pizarro set sail with a small force of 180 Spanish soldiers. Pizarro captured and killed the Incan

A Court Welcome

This historical painting shows Moctezuma welcoming Cortés to his court. **Critical Thinking** Based on this painting, what conclusions can you draw about Aztec wealth?

READ ACTIVELY

Connect How would you feel if you saw people riding on a large animal that you had never seen before?

Biography

Defender of the Indians
Bartolomé de Las Casas, born in Seville, Spain, in 1474, was a Spanish missionary and historian who spoke out against the Europeans' harsh treatment of Native Americans. He had witnessed the abuses that Native Americans had suffered and worked to improve their conditions. Las Casas' work helped Spain pass the New Laws in 1542, which brought about some improvements in the lives of the Native Americans in the Spanish colonies. Las Casas also contributed to our knowledge of Spanish colonies in America through his writings in *History of the Indies*. He died in Madrid in July 1566.

Ask Questions Suppose that you were a doctor living in South America at the time of the Conquest. What questions would you ask to discover why so many Native Americans were dying of European diseases?

emperor. He also killed many other Incan leaders. By 1535, Pizarro had conquered most of the Incan empire, including the capital, Cuzco.

The conquistadors defeated the two most powerful empires in the Americas. It took them only 15 years. How did they do it? The Spanish had guns and cannons that the Native Americans had never seen. They also rode horses. At first, horses terrified Native Americans. The Europeans also carried diseases such as smallpox, measles, and chicken pox. These diseases wiped out entire villages. And, because of local rivalry, some Native Americans like Malinche helped the Spanish conquistadors.

Colonization

By the 1540s, Spain claimed land throughout much of the Americas. Spain's lands stretched from what today is Kansas all the way south to the tip of South America. Brazil was claimed by Portugal.

Spain Organizes Its Empire Spain divided its territory into provinces. Spain also set up a strong government. The two most important provinces were New Spain and Peru. The capital of New Spain was Mexico City. Lima became the capital city of Peru.

Lima's geographic layout was based on the Spanish social classes. The most powerful citizens lived in the center of Lima. They either came from Spain or had Spanish parents. **Mestizos,** people of mixed Spanish and Native American descent, lived on the outskirts of the city. Many

Spanish and Portuguese Empires in the Americas

Map Study Portuguese sailor Pedro Cabral landed on the coast of Brazil by accident. He was trying to sail around Africa to India and was blown off course. Since Cabral landed east of the Line of Demarcation, Portugal built an empire there. **Location** Where was Portugal's empire relative to Africa? How far did Spain's empire reach into North America?

NORTH AMERICA

ATLANTIC OCEAN

Gulf of Mexico

CENTRAL AMERICA

Caribbean Sea

SOUTH AMERICA

PACIFIC OCEAN

KEY
Spanish Empire
Portuguese Empire
Lambert Azimuthal Equal-Area Projection

0   600   1,200 mi
0   600 1,200 km

Answers to...

MAP STUDY

• Portugal's empire was west of Africa, across the Atlantic; into what is now Texas, New Mexico, and Florida as well as along the Gulf Coast.

Resource Directory

Teaching Resources

📁 **Section Quiz** in the Chapter and Section Resources booklet, p. 26, covers the main ideas and key terms in the section. Available in Spanish in the Spanish Chapter and Section Resources booklet, p. 17.

📁 **Reading a Historical Map** in the Social Studies and Geography Skills booklet, p. 28, provides additional skill practice.

Media and Technology

📺 **Color Transparencies,** Historical Map Set 4

mestizos were poor. But some were middle class or quite wealthy. Native Americans were the least powerful class. Most Native Americans continued to live in the countryside. The Spanish forced them to work on haciendas. A **hacienda** (hah see EN duh) was a plantation owned by Spaniards or the Catholic Church.

The Effect of European Rule Spain gave its settlers **encomiendas** (en KOH mee en dus), which were rights to demand taxes or labor from Native Americans. Native Americans were allowed to stay on their own land, so the Spanish claimed that encomiendas protected Native Americans. In fact, encomiendas forced Native Americans to work for the settlers. At first, the Native Americans worked only on the haciendas. But when silver was discovered in Mexico and Peru, the Spanish forced Native Americans to also work in the mines. Some died from overwork and malnutrition. Many died from European diseases. In 1519, New Spain had a Native American population of 25 million. Only 3 million survived the first 50 years of Spanish rule. In 1532, 12 million Native Americans lived in Peru. Fifty years later, there were fewer than 2 million.

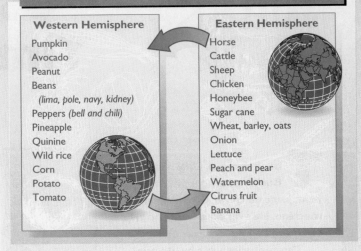

The Columbian Exchange

Western Hemisphere	Eastern Hemisphere
Pumpkin	Horse
Avocado	Cattle
Peanut	Sheep
Beans	Chicken
(lima, pole, navy, kidney)	Honeybee
Peppers (bell and chili)	Sugar cane
Pineapple	Wheat, barley, oats
Quinine	Onion
Wild rice	Lettuce
Corn	Peach and pear
Potato	Watermelon
Tomato	Citrus fruit
	Banana

Chart Study Goods, as well as people, crossed the Atlantic in the years after the conquest. Do you think that the Eastern and Western hemispheres benefitted equally from the Columbian Exchange? Why or why not?

SECTION 3 REVIEW

1. **Define** (a) Treaty of Tordesillas, (b) treaty, (c) Line of Demarcation, (d) conquistador, (e) mestizo, (f) hacienda, (g) encomienda.

2. **Identify** (a) Hernán Cortés, (b) Malinche, (c) Christopher Columbus, (d) Moctezuma, (e) Francisco Pizarro.

3. What was the effect of the Treaty of Tordesillas on the European settlement of the Americas?

4. How did the Spanish conquest affect Native Americans?

Critical Thinking

5. **Recognizing Bias** The Treaty of Tordesillas affected the lives of millions of Native Americans. However, Native Americans were not asked about the treaty. What do you think this says about European attitudes toward Native Americans?

Activity

6. **Writing to Learn** Write two paragraphs: one by a Native American who has just seen a European for the first time and another by a European who has just seen a Native American for the first time.

Section 3 Review

1. (a) treaty between Spain and Portugal that gave Spain the right to settle and trade west of the line. Portugal could do the same east of the line. (b) an agreement in writing between two or more countries (c) imaginary line from the North Pole to the South Pole at about 50° longitude (d) conqueror (e) people of Spanish and Native American descent (f) plantation owned by Spaniards or the Catholic Church (g) rights to demand taxes or labor from Native Americans

2. (a) Spanish soldier who conquered the Aztecs (b) Cortés's main translator (c) explorer who reached the Americas in 1492 (d) Aztec ruler (e) Spanish conquistador who conquered the Incas

3. Sample answer: Lands in the western Americas were settled by Spain; eastern lands were settled by the Portuguese.

4. Native Americans were forced to farm for the settlers and to work in dangerous mines. Native Americans also died from diseases brought by the Europeans.

5. Sample answer: Europeans believed that Native Americans were inferior to them.

6. Answers may vary. Paragraphs should reflect the two perspectives.

SKILLS MINI LESSON

Recognizing Bias
As a way to **introduce** the skill, tell students that bias, or prejudice, involves judging what a person is like based on assumptions or a stereotype, rather than on that person's individual qualities. Help students **practice** this skill by discussing how European actions, such as demanding taxes or labor from Native Americans, shows that the Europeans prejudged the Native Americans. Ask students what kinds of biases or opinions the Spanish might have had concerning the Native Americans that would have led to this treatment.

Answers to...

CHART STUDY

• Responses will vary. Students should support their responses with details from the chart.

SKILLS ACTIVITY

Using a Time Line

Lesson Objectives

1 Identify the purpose of a time line.

2 Construct and use a time line to relate events to each other.

Lesson Plan

1 Engage

Warm-Up Activity

To **introduce** the skill, have students read the opening paragraphs. Ask students to describe the mistake Biff made. Did he go too far back in time or did he not go back far enough? (He didn't go back far enough.) Discuss with students how a time line that placed dates and events in sequence might have helped Biff land in the right place at the right time.

Activating Prior Knowledge

Ask students to think of time lines they have seen. Have they encountered time lines in other textbooks? In magazines or on television? Discuss with students why time lines are useful in a variety of contexts.

The year is A.D. 2098. Biff Bucko, a star geography student, jumps into his shiny new time machine. He's off on a weekend trip to ancient Mayan civilization.

The centuries whiz by. As our hero approaches the year A.D. 1000, he slows to a stop. "When was Mayan culture at its height?" he wonders. Biff looks to the left and right. "Hmm . . . I think it's this way." Biff should have checked the time line in his glove compartment. If he had, he would have known that Mayan civilization declined after A.D. 900. Instead, he's landed in the 1400s where the Aztecs are busy conquering Middle America. "Oops," thinks Biff as a band of Aztec warriors descends upon him.

Studying the past makes you a kind of time traveler, too. Still, it's always best to know where you're going. Creating a time line can help.

Get Ready

A time line is like a map of the past. It keeps important dates in order so you don't get lost in time. Keep yours handy while you study for a test, research a report, or read for fun.

To make a time line you'll need:
- two sheets of paper
- thirteen paper clips

Try It Out

A. **Make a paper ruler.** Fold one sheet of paper in half the long way. Now fold it over again. You'll use this paper as a ruler to measure your time line.

B. **Mark the divisions of time periods.** Attach three paper clips along the top edge of your paper ruler. Slide one to the left corner, one to the right corner, and one to the exact center.

Resource Directory

Teaching Resources

📁 **Social Studies and Geography Skills** Reading a Time Line, p. 61

Media and Technology

💿 **Social Studies Skills Tutor CD-ROM** builds core social studies skills through interactive lessons and provides skill assessment.

C. **Look at dates for your time line.** Your time line will cover a span of about 1,200 years. Label the left paper clip on your ruler with the year 300. Label the right paper clip 1500 and the middle one 900.

D. **Figure out time intervals.** Space your other paper clips evenly across the top of the ruler. The space between each will stand for 100 years. Label your clips with the years 400, 500, and so on.

E. **Locate the dates on your time line.** Turn your other paper so the long side is on top. Draw a straight line across it. Using your ruler, mark the 100-year intervals. Then mark where each of the four time line dates belongs on the line. (Estimate for the dates 1345 and 1438.) Label each mark with its date and event.

Dates for Your Time Line			
300	**900**	**1385**	**1438**
Mayan civilization rises	Mayas leave their cities	Aztecs found the city of Tenochtitlán	Pachacuti founds the Incan Empire

Apply the Skill

Now choose some other dates in Latin American history that you want to remember. Follow the steps below to create a time line.

1 **Design a time line ruler.** First look at the dates you've selected. What time span will your time line cover? For a long span, each paper clip could mark 100 years. For a shorter span, you could mark every 50 years, 10 years, or 1 year. Choose a measurement that makes sense.

2 **Find a date to start your ruler.** Take the earliest date you chose for your time line. Round it to a lower number. For example, if you are measuring every 50 years, round the date 1492 down to 1450.

3 **Find a date to end your ruler.** Take your last date. Round it up.

4 **Count the paper clips you'll need.** Say your ruler starts at 1450, ends at 1650, and marks every 50 years. Count: 1450, 1500, 1550, 1600, 1650. That's five clips.

5 **Put a clip at each end of the ruler.** Space the others evenly. Label each with its year. Now use the ruler to mark points on your time line. Label each point with its date and event.

2 Explore

Have students read the text under the heading Get Ready. Provide materials for students and call attention to the boxed dates and events they will use to make their time lines. Then ask them to read the rest of the skills activity.

3 Teach

Students may **practice** making a time line by carrying out the instructions listed under the heading Try It Out. Before students begin, point out the photograph so students can see how the time line should look. You might monitor students' progress and allow students who finish early to assist any students who are having difficulties.

For additional reinforcement, have students calculate how many years passed between successive events on their time lines.

4 Assess

Have students **apply** the skill by completing the rest of the activity. Suggest that students review Chapter 2 to select dates and events they would like to include on their time lines. To **assess**, evaluate students' time lines on the basis of accuracy and the suitability of the time scale.

Section 4

Lesson Objectives

1. Describe how Latin American nations won independence from their European rulers.

2. Analyze the ways in which the American and French Revolutions influenced events in Latin America.

Lesson Plan

1 Engage

Warm-Up Activity

Write *Fourth of July* on the board. Ask students what they think of when they see these words. Students might indicate fireworks, parades, and picnics. Then ask students what the Fourth of July commemorates. Ask them why they think Americans continue to celebrate this day.

Activating Prior Knowledge

Have students read Reach Into Your Background in the Before You Read box. Students' responses might include bravery, courage, perseverance.

SECTION 4
Independence

BEFORE YOU READ

Reach Into Your Background
What qualities do you think make a hero? What about bravery, or doing the right thing no matter what the personal cost? Jot down at least three qualities that you think a hero should have.

Questions to Explore
1. How did Latin American nations win independence from their European rulers?
2. How did the American and French revolutions influence events in Latin America?

Key Terms
revolution
criollo
caudillo

Key People
Miguel Hidalgo
Agustín de Iturbide
Simón Bolívar
José de San Martín
Dom Pedro

▼ Toussaint L'Ouverture was captured by the French, but his followers won Haiti's independence.

On August 24, 1791, the night sky over Saint-Domingue (san duh MANG) glowed red and gold. The French Caribbean colony was on fire. The slaves were sick of being mistreated by their white masters. They finally had rebelled. Now they were burning every piece of white-owned property they could find. This Night of Fire was the beginning of the first great fight for freedom in Latin America. Toussaint L'Ouverture (too SAN loo vur TOOR), a former slave, led the people of Saint-Domingue in this fight for more than 10 years. Eventually they won. They founded the independent country of Haiti (HAY tee) in 1804.

The flame of liberty lit in Haiti soon spread across Latin America. By 1825, most of the region was independent. Latin Americans would no longer be ruled by Europe.

Independence in Mexico

Haiti's leaders drew encouragement from two famous revolutions. A **revolution** is a political movement in which the people overthrow the government and set up another. During the 1770s and early 1780s, the 13 British colonies in North America fought a war to free themselves from Britain's rule. In 1789, the ordinary people of France staged a violent uprising against their royal rulers. These actions inspired not only the people of Haiti, but also people across Latin America.

Criollos (kree OH yohz) paid particular attention to these events. A **criollo** had Spanish parents, but had been born in Latin America.

Resource Directory

Teaching Resources

 Reproducible Lesson Plan in the Chapter and Section Resources booklet, p. 27, provides a summary of the section lesson.

Guided Reading and Review in the Chapter and Section Resources booklet, p. 28, provides a structure for mastering key concepts and reviewing key terms in the section. Available in Spanish in the Spanish Chapter and Section Resources booklet, p. 18.

Section Reading Support Transparencies provide answers to the Questions to Explore in a graphic organizer format.

Media and Technology

Color Transparency 34

Criollos often were the wealthiest and best-educated people in the Spanish colonies. Few criollos had any political power, however. Only people born in Spain could hold government office. Many criollos attended school in Europe. There, they learned about the ideas that inspired revolution in France and the United States. The criollos especially liked the idea that people had the right to govern themselves.

The "Cry of Dolores" Mexico began its struggle for self-government in 1810. Miguel Hidalgo (mee GEHL ee DAHL goh) led the way. He was a criollo priest in the town of Dolores. With other criollos in Dolores, he planned to begin a revolution.

In September 1810, the Spanish government discovered Hidalgo's plot. But before the authorities could arrest him, Hidalgo took action. He wildly rang the church bells. A huge crowd gathered. "Recover from the hated Spaniards the land stolen from your forefathers," he shouted. "Long live America, and death to the bad government!"

Hidalgo's call for revolution became known as the "Cry of Dolores." It attracted some 80,000 fighters in a matter of weeks. This army consisted mostly of mestizos and Native Americans. They were angry. They wanted revenge against anybody connected with the Spanish government. The rebels won some victories. Their luck, however, soon changed. By the beginning of 1811, they were in full retreat. Hidalgo tried to flee the country. However, government soldiers soon captured him. He was put on trial and convicted of treason. Hidalgo was executed by firing squad in July 1811.

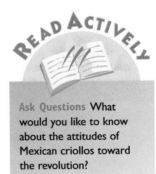

READ ACTIVELY

Ask Questions What would you like to know about the attitudes of Mexican criollos toward the revolution?

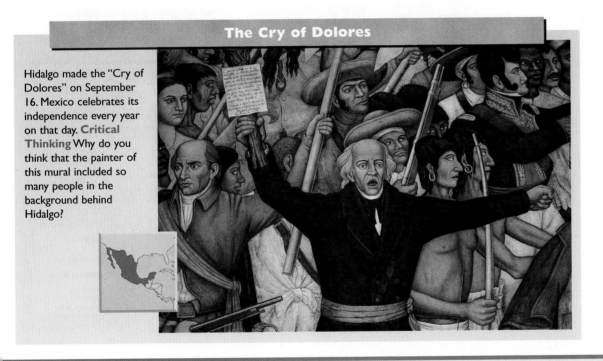

The Cry of Dolores

Hidalgo made the "Cry of Dolores" on September 16. Mexico celebrates its independence every year on that day. **Critical Thinking** Why do you think that the painter of this mural included so many people in the background behind Hidalgo?

2 Explore

Have students read the section and examine the pictures, maps, charts, and diagrams. Ask students to focus on the significance of the following people to the independence movement in Latin America: Toussaint L'Ouverture, Miguel Hidalgo, Simón Bolívar, and José de San Martín.

3 Teach

Ask students to create an illustrated poster entitled *Independence in Latin America* using the information in this section. Suggest that students work with a partner. Encourage them to include information about the people who worked for independence, the locations of battles, the countries that gained their independence as a result of the movement, and the years in which they became independent. Display and discuss completed posters. This activity should take about 90 minutes.

Answers to...

THE CRY OF DOLORES

• Accept any reasonable answer. Sample answer: The artist is trying to show that Hidalgo had the support of the people.

4 Assess

See answers to the Section Review. You might also use students' completed posters as an assessment.

Acceptable posters include basic information about three of the major figures involved.

Commendable posters include basic information concerning the people involved and illustrate the locations of battles.

Outstanding posters present the basic information as well as information about the influences of the American and French revolutions on the Latin American revolutions.

African Independence
Although Africa is closer to Europe than to Latin America, Europeans began to colonize Africa later. Europeans began claiming parts of Africa in the 1880s. Like the people of Latin America, many people in Africa later were inspired by the ideas of self-government and independence. African countries began to achieve independence in the 1950s and 1960s.

Independence Finally Comes The Spanish could execute the revolution's leaders, but they could not kill its spirit. Small rebel groups kept fighting. Then Agustín de Iturbide (ee toor BEE day) joined the rebels. He was a high-ranking officer in the Spanish army. Many people who had opposed the rebellion changed their minds. They had viewed Hidalgo as a dangerous hothead. But Iturbide was different. He was a criollo and an army officer. They could trust Iturbide to protect their interests. They decided to support the rebellion. In 1821, Iturbide declared Mexico independent.

South American Independence

Simón Bolívar (see MOHN boh LEE vahr) was not the first Latin American revolutionary leader. Almost certainly, however, he was the greatest. He was born in the country of Venezuela in 1783. His family was one of the richest and most important families in Latin America. Like most wealthy Latin Americans, he went to school in Spain. There, he met Prince Ferdinand, the heir to the Spanish throne. They decided to play a game similar to present-day badminton. Custom required that Bolívar show respect for the prince by losing. Instead, Bolívar played hard and tried to win. He even knocked the prince's hat off with his racquet! The angry prince demanded an apology. Bolívar refused. He claimed it was an accident. Furious, the prince insisted that they fight a duel. He soon calmed down, however.

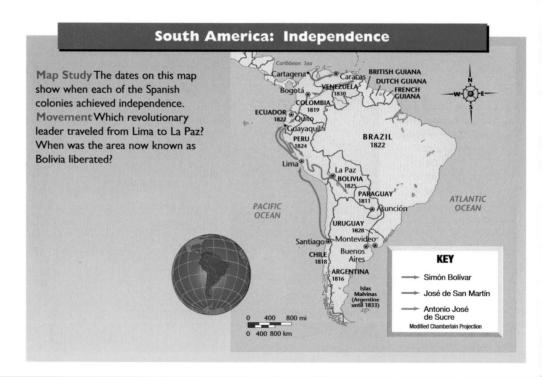

South America: Independence

Map Study The dates on this map show when each of the Spanish colonies achieved independence. **Movement** Which revolutionary leader traveled from Lima to La Paz? When was the area now known as Bolivia liberated?

KEY
→ Simón Bolívar
→ José de San Martín
→ Antonio José de Sucre
Modified Chamberlain Projection

Answers to...
MAP STUDY
• Antonio José de Sucre; 1825

Many years later, these two faced off again. This time, Bolívar knocked Spanish America from under Ferdinand's feet.

Bolívar and San Martín: The Liberators Bolívar joined the fight for Venezuelan independence in 1804. Six years later he became its leader. Bolívar was completely certain that he would win. His confidence, courage, and daring inspired his soldiers. They enjoyed victory after victory. By 1822, Bolívar's troops had freed a large area from Spanish rule (the future countries of Colombia, Venezuela, Ecuador, and Panama). This newly liberated region formed Gran Colombia. Bolívar became its president. Even though his country was free, Bolívar did not give up the cause of independence. "The Liberator," as he was now known, turned south toward Peru.

José de San Martín (san mahr TEEN), an Argentine, had lived in Spain and served in the Spanish army. When Argentina began its fight for freedom, he quickly offered to help. San Martín took good care of his troops. He shared each hardship they had to suffer. They loved him for it. Many said they would follow San Martín anywhere—even over the snow-capped Andes Mountains. In 1817, his soldiers had to do just that. He led them through high passes in the Andes into Chile. This bold action took the Spanish completely by surprise. In a matter of months, Spain was defeated. San Martín declared Chile's independence. Then he turned his attention to Peru.

Again, San Martín took an unexpected action. This time, he attacked from the sea. The Spanish were not prepared for San Martín's tactics. Spanish defenses quickly collapsed. In July 1821, San Martín pushed inland and seized Lima, the capital of Peru.

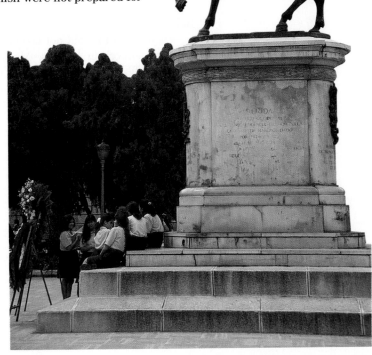

▶ Nearly every town or city in South America has a central square with a statue of Bolívar or San Martín. These high school girls are visiting the statue of Bolívar in Meridá, Venezuela.

Activity

Cooperative Learning

Talking With Liberators
Organize students into groups of six or seven. Have each group prepare a talk show featuring the heroes of the Latin American independence movement as guests. Individual group members should work on the following tasks: preparing questions to ask the heroes, creating props, writing the script, assigning roles for heroes and talk-show host, rehearsing the show. Call on groups to present their shows to the class. Activity should take about 40 minutes. *Auditory*

Activity

Journal Writing

Ask students to imagine that they are soldiers in San Martín's army. Have students write a journal entry describing their experiences and their feelings about fighting for independence. Invite volunteers to share their journal entries with the class.

Take It to the NET

Prentice Hall's *World Explorer* companion Web site offers activities for exploring geographical, historical, and cultural resources on the Internet. It also provides online links for key content, data updates, and all chapter review activities.

The **Teacher site** provides teachers with ideas for student research and activities. It also presents *eTeach*, a monthly discussion with Master Teachers.

Students can use the **Student site** to find chapter-by-chapter Internet resource links, data updates, and Self-Tests.

http://www.phschool.com

A year later, San Martín met with Bolívar to discuss the fight for independence. Historians do not know what happened in that meeting. But afterward, San Martín suddenly gave up his command. He left Bolívar to continue the fight alone. This Bolívar did. Eventually, he drove the remaining Spanish forces out of South America altogether. By 1825, only Cuba and Puerto Rico were still ruled by Spain.

Brazil Takes a Different Route to Freedom   Portugal's colony, Brazil, became independent without fighting a war. In the early 1800s, French armies invaded Spain and Portugal. Portugal's royal family fled to Brazil for safety. The king returned to Portugal in 1821. However, he left his son, Dom Pedro, to rule the colony. Dom Pedro used more power than the king expected. He declared Brazil independent in 1822. Three years later, Portugal quietly admitted that Brazil was independent.

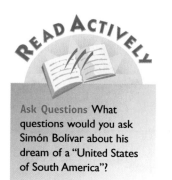

Ask Questions What questions would you ask Simón Bolívar about his dream of a "United States of South America"?

Challenges of Independence

After winning independence, Latin American leaders faced hard challenges. They had to decide how to govern their nations. Also, after years of fighting, Latin American nations were very poor.

Simón Bolívar dreamed of uniting South America as one country. Gran Colombia was the first step. Bolívar hoped it would become the "United States of South America." In trying to govern Gran Colombia, however, Bolívar found that his dream was impossible. Latin America was a huge area, divided by the Andes and dense rain forests. Also, the leaders of the countries in Gran Columbia wanted little to do with Bolívar. In poor health, he retired from politics.

Even though he did not last long in office, Bolívar set the standard for Latin American leaders. Most were **caudillos** (kow DEE yohs), military officers who ruled very strictly. Bolívar cared about the people he governed. Many other caudillos did not. These others just wanted to stay in power and get rich.

SECTION 4 REVIEW

1. Define (a) revolution, (b) criollo, (c) caudillo.

2. Identify (a) Miguel Hidalgo, (b) Agustín de Iturbide, (c) Simón Bolívar, (d) José de San Martín, (e) Dom Pedro.

3. What world events influenced the independence movement in Latin America?

4. How was Brazil's path to independence different from that of the rest of South America?

Critical Thinking

5. Identifying Central Issues What do you think Simón Bolívar had in mind when he wanted South America to become the "United States of South America"?

Activity

6. Writing to Learn Imagine you are a journalist with Bolívar's or San Martín's army. Describe the army's main actions.

Issues in Latin America Today

BEFORE YOU READ

Reach Into Your Background
Most people like the feeling of being able to take care of themselves. What could you do now to prepare for your own independence?

Questions to Explore
1. How are Latin American nations trying to improve their economies?
2. What issues has the move to the cities created in Latin America?

Key Terms
invest
economy
campesino
rural
urban

Key Places
Brazil

Samuel Zemurray came from Russia to the United States in 1892. He worked for his aunt and uncle, who owned a store in Alabama. As part of his job, Zemurray sometimes traveled to the port city of Mobile. He noticed that fruit and vegetable traders there often threw away ripe bananas. They knew the bananas would spoil before reaching stores. Zemurray bought the ripe bananas and delivered them to stores overnight. The quick delivery meant that the fruit was still fit to be sold. Zemurray's business was so successful that he decided to expand. He did this by buying land in the country of Honduras, where bananas were grown. Zemurray soon became a leading banana grower.

▼ Many large-scale farming operations in Latin America are still foreign-owned.

Foreign Investment

In the 1900s, many companies like Zemurray's invested in Latin America. To **invest** means to spend money to earn more money. Some companies owned farms and grew crops such as sugar and bananas. Other foreign companies ran mines. By the mid-1900s, most businesses in Latin America were owned by or did work for foreign companies. As a result, foreign companies became powerful in Latin American economies. A country's **economy** is made up of the ways that goods and services are produced and made available to people. When money from the sale of goods and services comes into or goes out of a country, it affects the country's economy.

Lesson Objectives
1. Describe how Latin American nations are trying to achieve economic independence.
2. Identify the issues that land use and the move to the cities have created in Latin America.

Lesson Plan

1 Engage
Warm-Up Activity
Write the following statement on the chalkboard for students to complete: *After independence, the biggest problems facing Latin American nations were _____*. When students have completed the statement, call on volunteers to read their versions. Have students explain their responses.

Activating Prior Knowledge
Have students read Reach Into Your Background in the Before You Read box. Students' answers will vary. Allow students to express their plans and how they might prepare to carry out those plans.

Teaching Resources

📁 **Reproducible Lesson Plan** in the Chapter and Section Resources booklet, p. 30, provides a summary of the section lesson.

📁 **Guided Reading and Review** in the Chapter and Section Resources booklet, p. 31, provides a structure for mastering key concepts and reviewing key terms in the section. Available in Spanish in the Spanish Chapter and Section Resources booklet, p. 20.

📖 **Section Reading Support Transparencies** provide answers to the Questions to Explore in a graphic organizer format.

Program Resources

📁 **Outline Maps** Latin America: Political, p. 7

2 Explore

Write the four main headings of Section 5 on the board. At the same time, have students write the headings on a sheet of paper, leaving space after each for notes. As students read the section, have them jot down the main ideas in the space following each heading. Record some of their ideas on the chalkboard.

3 Teach

Ask students to construct a diorama that illustrates some of the issues facing Latin America today. Issues might include the problem of foreign investment, improving the Latin American economy, distributing and conserving land, and urbanization. Have students use the completed dioramas to explore possible ways that Latin America might deal with the issues.

Predict What steps do you think Latin American countries took to balance their economies?

Foreign companies made huge profits from their businesses in Latin America. However, these companies did little to help Latin American countries build their economies. Many Latin Americans realized that it was important to improve their economies. They needed to build factories so that they could make their own manufactured goods. They also needed to grow many different kinds of crops and to develop a wide range of resources.

Some Latin American countries soon took steps to carry out these economic building plans. And they proved successful. During the 1960s and early 1970s, the economies of many Latin American countries grew. However, in the early 1980s, oil prices went up. Latin American countries needed oil to run their factories—and they had to pay higher and higher prices for it. At the same time, the prices of Latin American products fell. Latin American countries had to spend more money, but they were making less and less. To make up the difference, they borrowed money from wealthy countries such as the United States. By the 1980s, many Latin American countries had huge foreign debts.

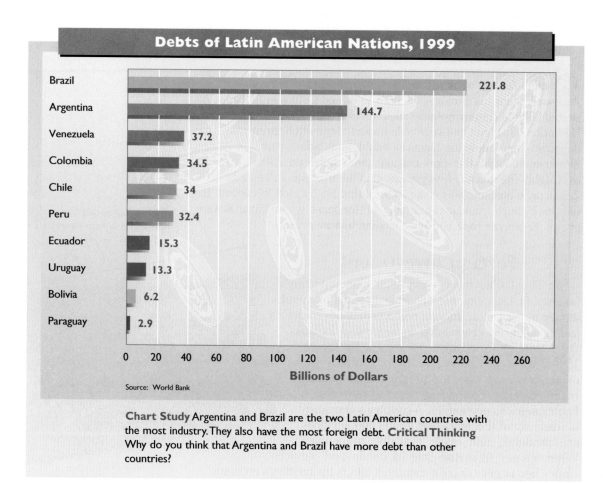

Debts of Latin American Nations, 1999

Country	Billions of Dollars
Brazil	221.8
Argentina	144.7
Venezuela	37.2
Colombia	34.5
Chile	34
Peru	32.4
Ecuador	15.3
Uruguay	13.3
Bolivia	6.2
Paraguay	2.9

Source: World Bank

Chart Study Argentina and Brazil are the two Latin American countries with the most industry. They also have the most foreign debt. **Critical Thinking** Why do you think that Argentina and Brazil have more debt than other countries?

Answers to...

CHART STUDY

• Responses will vary but may indicate that the greater debt is a result of borrowing money to build factories.

Facing Economic Challenges

People in Latin American countries have expanded their economies by building more factories and growing different kinds of crops. And they have taken other steps to improve their economies.

Foreign companies still invest in Latin America. But most Latin American countries limit how investments can be made. They want to prevent foreign countries from having too much control over important parts of their economies. Some countries, for instance, have tried to stop foreign companies from acquiring too much land.

Latin American countries have tried to improve their economies by cooperating with one another. For a long time, most Latin American countries did not trade with one another. They did not need to because, for the most part, they all produced the same kinds of goods. Recently, however, some countries have developed new industries. The products these countries make can be traded to other countries in the region. This kind of trade has increased in the last few years. Latin American countries also have formed several organizations that encourage cooperation in the region.

Land Distribution

The issue of how land is used greatly affects the future of Latin America's economies. Land is one of Latin America's most important resources. Some people and companies own great amounts of land in

LINKS ACROSS THE WORLD

African Economies Many African countries are also trying to improve their economies with less foreign investment. Africans are trying to earn more money by growing more types of cash crops. They are also working to build their own industries and mine their own resources without help from foreign companies.

Building Televisions on an Assembly Line

In the last 50 years, Latin American countries have begun to produce many more products in factories like this one in Brazil. **Critical Thinking** What skills do you think these factory workers need?

4 Assess

See answers to the Section Review. You may also use students' completed dioramas as an assessment.

Acceptable dioramas illustrate at least two of the issues listed.

Commendable dioramas illustrate all four issues listed and present some relationships between the issues.

Outstanding dioramas illustrate the four issues listed, indicate how the issues are related, and show a clear understanding of the issues facing Latin America today.

Activity

Critical Thinking

Distinguishing Fact From Opinion *Suitable as a whole class activity.* Write the following sentences on the board. Ask students to identify which ones are facts and which are opinions. Have them explain why.

1. Before the wars for independence, most Latin American countries traded with Spain. (fact)
2. Latin American countries would have been better off had they not traded with Spain. (opinion) *English Language Learners*

Answers to...

BUILDING TELEVISIONS ON AN ASSEMBLY LINE

• Responses may vary. Sample answer: attention to detail, manual dexterity, mechanical aptitude.

Activity

Interdisciplinary Connections

Science Tell students that there is much concern about conserving the Amazon Rain Forest. One reason for the concern is the great number of species that live in the forest. It contains several million species of plants, fish, birds, insects, and other forms of life.

Ask students to find out about the Amazon Rain Forest and report on 10 kinds of plants or animals found there. Indicate to students that their reports should include some information about the animals' habits and food. Information about plants might include the possible economic benefits of protecting the plants. Have students present their findings in the form of a two-minute newscast. Encourage students to accompany their newscasts with photos or drawings of some of the plants and animals found in the Amazon Rain Forest. Activity should take about 60 minutes.

In El Salvador, many farmers do not have modern farming equipment. They use traditional wooden plows and oxen. **Critical Thinking** What would it cost a farmer to own oxen? How would this cost compare to the cost of owning a tractor?

Latin America but most people in the region do not own any land. In Brazil, for example, 45 percent of the land is owned by only 1 percent of the population.

Dividing the Land Much of the farmland in Latin America is owned by a few wealthy families. This land is occupied by haciendas where crops are grown to sell abroad. In contrast, many poor farmers—known as **campesinos** (kahm peh SEE nohs)—own only small tracts of land. They often grow enough only to meet their own needs.

Starting in the 1930s, many Latin American countries tried to help the campesinos by dividing the land more equally. These programs have met with mixed success. In some cases, the land given to the campesinos was of poor quality. No matter how hard they tried, they could not make a living from it. In other cases, the campesinos struggled because they had neither the money to buy seeds and equipment nor the skills necessary for success. Many Latin American countries have begun to see that taking land from one person and giving it to another does not necessarily improve people's lives or the economy.

Using and Protecting the Land Dividing up the land has raised other issues. Brazil gave land to landless peasants by moving them to the Amazonian rain forest. The peasants burned down trees to clear the land for farming. After a few years, however, the soil in the rain forest became unfit for farming.

Answers to...

A FARM IN EL SALVADOR

- Responses should indicate that farmers would have to provide food and water for the oxen, but would have to spend money for fuel for a tractor.

Resource Directory

Teaching Resources

📁 **Section Quiz** in the Chapter and Section Resources booklet, p. 32, covers the main ideas and key terms in the section. Available in Spanish in the Spanish Chapter and Section Resources booklet, p. 21.

📁 **Vocabulary** in the Chapter and Section Resources booklet, p. 34, provides a review of key terms in the chapter. Available in Spanish in the Spanish Chapter and Section Resources booklet, p. 23.

📁 **Reteaching** in the Chapter and Section Resources booklet, p. 35, provides a structure for students who may need additional help in mastering chapter content.

📁 **Enrichment** in the Chapter and Section Resources booklet, p. 36, extends chapter content and enriches students' understanding.

📁 **Spanish Glossary** in the Spanish Chapter and Section Resources, pp. 62–65, provides key terms translated from English to Spanish as well as definitions in Spanish.

Many people around the world expressed worries about the clearing of the rain forest. Some believed that this would hurt the environment. Others said that it would change the way of life of the Native Americans who live there. Some people, however, have challenged this view. Economic progress, they say, will come only if Brazil uses all its resources. Brazilian leaders are looking for a balance. They want to find ways to help the economy and the campesinos without destroying the rain forest.

The Move to the City

Many campesinos have decided that making a living from the land is just too difficult. They have left the land and gone to the cities in search of different economic opportunities. This move has resulted in the rapid growth of the populations of large cities. Since the 1950s, many Latin American countries have had a population explosion. The population has increased dramatically in both the **rural,** or countryside, and the **urban,** or city, areas of Latin America. The population of urban areas, however, has gone up the most.

Many Latin Americans who move to the cities are looking for better jobs. They also want to improve the quality of their lives. They hope to find comfortable homes, better medical care, and good schools for their children. However, they do not always realize their hopes. As Latin American countries strive to build their economies, there will be greater opportunities for people to have a better life.

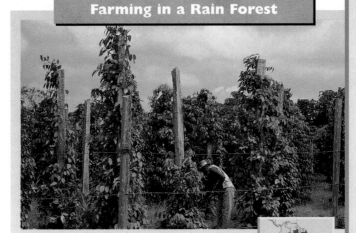

Farming in a Rain Forest

This pepper farmer has cleared land on an island in the Amazon River, in northern Brazil. **Critical Thinking** How does pepper farming contribute to Brazil's economy?

SECTION 5 REVIEW

1. **Define** (a) invest, (b) economy, (c) campesino, (d) rural, (e) urban.

2. **Identify** Brazil.

3. What steps have Latin American countries taken to improve their economies?

4. How have Latin American countries tried to change the landowning system in the region?

Critical Thinking

5. **Recognizing Cause and Effect** How has the increase in population contributed to the growth of cities in Latin America?

Activity

6. **Writing to Learn** You have read that many people oppose Brazil's plans to move poor farmers to the rain forest. Write a paper that explores both the pro and the con sides of the following statement: "A country has the right to use its resources as it sees fit."

CHAPTER 2

Review and Activities

Reviewing Main Ideas

1. They needed it to decide when to hold ceremonies.

2. by conquering other people in the region, forcing them to pay taxes, and ruling them

3. They built canals and aqueducts to water their crops.

4. Answers will vary, but might include the facts that many people in Mexico today eat foods similar to those eaten by the Aztecs and that Mayan and Incan languages are still spoken.

5. These Native Americans disliked the Aztecs because they had to pay the Aztecs tribute.

6. (a) and (b) the Line of Demarcation divided the land such a way that Spain received most of Latin America and Portugal received Brazil.

7. They supported the fight for independence. A criollo priest named Miguel Hidalgo began the fight for independence by assembling an army made up of 80,000 fighters.

8. In Chile, San Martín invaded from the high passes in the Andes. In Peru, he attacked from the sea.

9. They have built more factories, diversified their crops, not allowed foreign companies to own too much land, and cooperated among each other.

Reviewing Key Terms

Students' sentences will vary but should show the correct meanings of words through context.

Critical Thinking

1. Possible causes: killing the leader and taking over the capital. Possible effects: The Native Americans were forced to work for the Spanish settlers; they died from European diseases.

2. Mexico's bid for independence was led, at first, by two priests. Other South American countries were freed by the actions of military men.

Reviewing Main Ideas

1. Why was an accurate calendar important to Mayan priests?
2. How did the Aztecs expand their empire?
3. How were the Incas able to change their environment in order to grow more food?
4. Give two examples of how the Mayan, Aztec, or Incan empires affect culture in Latin America today.
5. Why was Hernán Cortés able to persuade many Native Americans in the region to fight the Aztecs?
6. (a) Why did Spain gain control over most of Latin America?
   (b) How did Portugal come to control Brazil?
7. What role did the criollos play in the fight for Latin American independence?
8. How did José de San Martín surprise the Spanish in Chile and Peru?
9. How have many Latin American countries been trying to improve their economies in recent years?

Reviewing Key Terms

Use each key term below in a sentence that shows the meaning of the term.

1. maize
2. hieroglyphics
3. aqueduct
4. quipu
5. Line of Demarcation
6. conquistador
7. mestizo
8. hacienda
9. encomienda
10. criollo
11. caudillo
12. invest
13. economy
14. campesino
15. rural
16. urban

Critical Thinking

1. **Recognizing Cause and Effect** What were two causes of the fall of the Aztec and Incan empires? What were two effects on the Native American people of the region?
2. **Making Comparisons** Compare the way in which Mexico gained its independence with the way in which the countries of South America gained theirs.

Graphic Organizer

Copy this tree map onto a separate sheet of paper. Then use the empty boxes to outline Latin American history from Mayan civilization through the Spanish conquest.

Latin American History

Graphic Organizer

Students' graphic organizers should contain information similar to that shown in this sample.

Latin American History			
Maya	**Aztec**	**Inca**	**European Conquest**
• great cities like Copán, Tikal • present-day Honduras, Guatemala • priest and nobles controlled the cities • most people were farmers or artisans • achievements: calendar, corn	• built city on a lake • present-day Mexico • expanded empire • one ruler over all • religion central to life • medicine and astronomy	• empire started in Peru • built cities and roads • constructed aqueducts to irrigate crops • farmers, builders • religion important in everyday life	• Spain and Portugal decide to divide up Latin America • Cortés conquers Aztecs, looking for gold • Pizarro conquers Incas, looking for gold • Spain and Portugal force Native Americans to work on haciendas

Map Activity

For each place listed below, write the letter from the map that shows its location.

1. Brazil
2. Guatemala
3. Mexico
4. Chile
5. Peru
6. Andes
7. Mexico City

Latin America: Place Location

Writing Activity

Writing a Story

The Mayas, Aztecs, and Incas had spoken histories. Information was passed from generation to generation in stories and songs. Suppose that you lived at the time of the Spanish conquest. Write a story or a song that tells about the conquest.

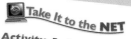

Take It to the NET

Activity Explore the culture of the ancient Mayan civilization and play Mayan games. For help in completing this activity, visit www.phschool.com.

Chapter 2 Self-Test To review what you have learned, take the Chapter 2 Self-Test and get instant feedback on your answers. Go to www.phschool.com to take the test.

Skills Review

Turn to the Skill Activity.

Review the steps for using a time line. Then: (a) Explain in your own words how using a time line can help you to understand history. (b) What kinds of events should you list on a time line?

How Am I Doing?

Answer these questions to help you check your progress.

1. Can I identify and describe characteristics of the Mayan, Aztec, and Incan civilizations?
2. Can I explain how European rule affected Native Americans?
3. Can I explain how Latin American countries achieved independence?
4. Can I explain how foreign investment has affected Latin America?
5. What information from this chapter can I include in my journal?

How Am I Doing?

Point out to students that this checklist is just a quick reminder for them of what they learned in the chapter. If their answer to any of the questions is *no* or if they are unsure, they may need to review the topic.

Map Activity

1. G	4. F	6. E
2. C	5. D	7. B
3. A		

Skills Review

Student responses will vary but should indicate (a) that a time line is a useful way of keeping events in the correct sequence, and (b) that important events that change the course of a culture or nation should be listed.

Writing Activity

Students' stories or songs should include the names of the conquistadors and the time of the conquest. Songs or stories should contain specific descriptive details about the conquest. Encourage volunteers to perform their songs or tell their stories to the class.

Resource Directory

Teaching Resources

Chapter Tests Forms A and B are in the Tests booklet, pp. 8–13.

Media and Technology

Computer Test Bank CD-ROM

Resource Pro® CD-ROM

Prentice Hall Assessment System

Cultures of Latin America

To help you plan instruction, the chart below shows how teaching resources correspond to chapter content. Use the resources to vary instruction, add activities, or plan block schedules. Where appropriate, resources have suggested time allotments for students. Time allotments are approximate.

Managing Time and Instruction

	Latin America Teaching Resources Booklet		World Explorer Program Resources Binder	
	Resource	**mins.**	**Resource**	**mins.**
SECTION 1 The Cultures of Mexico and Central America	**Chapter and Section Support** Reproducible Lesson Plan, p. 39 Ⓢ Guided Reading and Review, p. 40 Ⓢ Section Quiz, p. 41 ▢ Section Reading Support Transparencies	 20 25 15	**Outline Maps** Mexico: Political, p. 8 Central America and the Caribbean: Political, p. 9 **Nystrom Desk Atlas** Ⓣ **Primary Sources and Literature Readings** Morning Girl, p. 42	 20 20 20 40
SKILLS ACTIVITY Distinguishing Facts From Opinions	**Social Studies and Geography Skills,** Distinguishing Facts From Opinions, p. 43	30		
2 SECTION 2 The Cultures of the Caribbean	**Chapter and Section Support** Reproducible Lesson Plan, p. 42 Ⓢ Guided Reading and Review, p. 43 Ⓢ Section Quiz, p. 44 ▢ Section Reading Support Transparencies	 20 25 15	**Outline Maps** Central America and the Caribbean: Political, p. 9	 20
3 SECTION 3 The Cultures of South America	**Chapter and Section Support** Reproducible Lesson Plan, p. 45 Ⓢ Guided Reading and Review, p. 46 Ⓢ Section Quiz, p. 47 Critical Thinking Activity, p. 52 Ⓢ Vocabulary, p. 49 Reteaching, p. 50 Enrichment, p. 51 Ⓢ Chapter Summary, p. 48 ▢ Section Reading Support Transparencies **Social Studies and Geography Skills,** Analyzing a Photograph, p. 58 **Tests** Forms A and B Chapter Tests, pp. 14–19	 20 25 30 20 25 25 15 15 30 40	**Outline Maps** South America: Political, p. 11 **Writing Process Handbook** Outlining Your Material, p. 25	 20 25

Block Scheduling Program Support

- Block Scheduling Booklet
  PROGRAM RESOURCES BINDER
- Activities and Projects
- Interdisciplinary Links
- **Block Scheduling Program Support**
- Resource Pro® CD-ROM
- Media and Technology
- Pacing Charts Booklet
  PROGRAM RESOURCES BINDER

Media and Technology

Resource	mins.
🎬📀 Ⓢ World Video Explorer	20
⬛ Color Transparencies 63, 64, 65	20
📀 Resource Pro® CD-ROM	30
📀 Presentation Pro CD-ROM	20
📀 Social Studies Skills Tutor CD-ROM	30
⬛ Color Transparency 64	20
⬛ Color Transparency 69	20
🎧 Ⓢ Guided Reading Audiotapes	20
⬛ Color Transparency 174 (Graphic organizer table template)	20
📀 Computer Test Bank CD-ROM	30
🎧 Student Edition on Audio CD	30
📀 Passport to the World CD-ROM	30

- **T** Teaming Opportunity
  well-suited for teaching teams
- Ⓢ Spanish
  This resource is also in Spanish support.
- 📀 CD-ROM
- 📀 Laserdisc
- ⬛ Transparency
- 🎬 Videotape
- 🎧 Audiotape/CD

Assessment Opportunities

From Guiding Questions to Assessment A series of Guiding Questions serves as an organizing framework for this book. The Guiding Question that relates to this chapter is listed below. Section Reviews and Section Quizzes provide opportunities for assessing students' insights into this Guiding Question. Additional assessments are listed below.

GUIDING QUESTION

- *What factors have affected cultures in Latin America?*

ASSESSMENTS

Section 1

Students should be able to make a web that describes the causes of Mexican and Central American immigration to the United States.
▶ **RUBRIC** See the Assessment booklet for a rubric on assessing graphic organizers.

Section 2

Students should be able to give an oral presentation outlining the key characteristics of Caribbean cultures.
▶ **RUBRIC** See the Assessment booklet for a rubric on assessing an oral presentation.

Section 3

Students should be able to describe how geography has created cultural diversity in South America.
▶ **RUBRIC** See the Assessment booklet for a rubric on assessing cause-and-effect statements.

Prentice Hall Assessment System allows you to:
- Diagnose and Prescribe
- Review and Reteach
- Practice and Assess

Activities and Projects

Mental Mapping	Links to Current Events	Hands-On Activities

Everything in Its Place List the names of some Central American, South American, and Caribbean countries on the chalkboard. Include Mexico, Panama, Haiti, Brazil, Puerto Rico, Peru, Guatemala, Cuba, Chile, and Venezuela.

Have students draw three columns on a sheet of notebook paper. The columns should have the following heads: "North and Central America," "The Caribbean," and "South America." Ask students to sort the countries into the appropriate columns.

Distribute outline maps of Latin America and ask students to locate as many countries on the maps as they can. Tell them to write the names of the countries they cannot locate on the water area of the map near the correct landmass. Ask them to keep their lists and outline maps. They may add, correct, or update information as they work through these chapters.

Many Cultures, Many Songs Provide recent recordings of music from Brazil, Peru, Cuba, and Mexico. You can look, in a library with a good music collection, for recordings by artists such as Willy Chirino (Cuba), Elis Regina (Brazil), Beth Carvalho (Brazil), Trina Medina (Venezuela), and Willy Rosario (Puerto Rico). Play selections, giving students a chance to compare and contrast the tempos and rhythms, instrumentation, and vocal arrangements. Ask students whether they think the Latin American recordings influenced U.S. recording artists.

What's For Dinner? Provide phone book yellow pages (or photocopies of pages) that show listings of restaurants in your own city or a large city with a diverse population. Have students go through listings and find restaurants that offer food from Latin America. Ask them to make a chart showing the countries and cultures for which they find restaurants. If possible, have them find out the names of dishes or characteristic ingredients of that culture's cuisine. They may do this by examining display ads for restaurants, by calling restaurants in the local area, or by researching library cookbooks.

If practical, invite students to extend this activity by visiting local restaurants to examine menus.

A Tropical Christmas Christmas is a very important holiday in Latin America because of the importance of the Roman Catholic religion. Contrast the evergreen and yule logs used to celebrate Christmas in the northern United States with the ripe fruit and fresh flowers used in Latin America's Christmas. Invite students to find pictures of Christmas ornaments in Mexico, Brazil, or another part of Latin America by looking through travel magazines, *National Geographic,* or illustrated books about different countries. Have them make versions of these ornaments with construction paper, clay, or other materials. *English Language Learners*

Culture Map Tell students that Latin American traditions are practiced in many parts of the United States. Just as the different countries of Latin America have their own cultures and traditions, however, parts of the United States that have been settled by people from different parts of Latin America have distinctive traditions. For example, there are many people of Mexican ancestry in Texas, New Mexico, and California. Many people from Cuba live in Florida, while there are many people from Puerto Rico in New York City. Have students locate these parts of the United States and Latin America on a map. Ask students of Cuban, Mexican, or Puerto Rican ancestry to offer some examples of

traditions unique to their culture. Alternatively, have volunteers research to find some examples. *Basic*

Natural Resources Have students refer back to Chapter 1, where they learned about the climate, vegetation, and natural resources of Latin America. Remind them that the geography of a country influences its culture. As students explore the cultures of Latin America, have them make a poster showing how some aspect of culture is linked to the geography of different countries. Suggest they create a poster showing two countries from each region of Latin America (two from Mexico and Central America, two from the Caribbean, and two from South America). *Challenging*

F.Y.I.

This page can help you extend your own and students' understanding of the concepts in this chapter. You may want to browse through some of the suggestions in the **Bibliography**. **Interdisciplinary Links** can connect social studies understandings to areas elsewhere in the curriculum through the use of other Prentice Hall products. **National Geography Standards** reflected specifically in this chapter are listed for your convenience. Some hints about appropriate Internet access are also provided in **Take It to the Net. School to Careers** provides insights into the practical uses of some of the concepts in this chapter as they might pertain to various careers.

BIBLIOGRAPHY

FOR THE TEACHER

Moss, Joyce. *People of the World: The Culture, Geographical Setting, and Historical Background of 42 Latin American Peoples.* Gale Research, 1989.

Machado, Ana Maria. *Exploration into Latin America.* New Discovery, 1995.

Ortiz Cofer, Judith. *Silent Dancing: A Partial Remembrance of a Puerto Rican Childhood.* Arte Publicao, 1990.

FOR THE STUDENT

Easy
Dorros, Arthur. *Tonight Is Carnaval.* Dutton, 1992.

Average
Lehtinen, Ritva and Kari E. Nurmi. *The Grandchildren of the Incas.* Carolrhoda, 1991.

Challenging
Peterson, Marge. *Argentina: A Wild West Heritage.* Dillon, 1990.

LITERATURE CONNECTION

Joseph, Lynn. *Coconut Kind of Day: Island Poems.* Lothrop, 1990.

O'Dell, Scott. *The Black Pearl.* Houghton, 1967.

Wisniewski, David. *Rain Player.* Clarion, 1991.

INTERDISCIPLINARY LINKS

Subject	Theme: Customs
MATH	Middle Grades Math: Tools for Success *Course 1*, Lesson 1-3, **Mean, Median, and Mode** *Course 1*, Lesson 11-4, **Theoretical Probability**
SCIENCE	Science Explorer *Cells and Heredity*, Lesson 4-1, **Human Inheritance** *From Bacteria to Plants*, Lesson 1-3, **Classifying Organisms**
LANGUAGE ARTS	Prentice Hall Literature *Bronze*, **Mi Amigo Mark** *Copper*, **The Circuit**

NATIONAL GEOGRAPHY STANDARDS

Students explore the 18 National Geography Standards throughout Latin America. Chapter 3, however, concentrates on investigating the following: standards 6, 9, 10, 11, 12, 15, 17, 18. For a complete list of the standards, see the *Teacher's Flexible Planning Guide*.

SCHOOL TO CAREERS

In Chapter 3, Cultures of Latin America, students learn about the cultures of Mexico and Central America, the Caribbean, and South America. They also learn the skill of distinguishing fact from opinion. These understandings can help prepare students for careers in economics, politics, education, and the arts. Distinguishing fact from opinion is useful for attorneys, customer service representatives, journalists, and police officers. The curriculum presented in this book, as in all eight titles of Prentice Hall's *World Explorer* program, is designed to prepare students not only for careers but also for good citizenship—of the world as well as of this country.

Many social studies teachers and students use Internet browsers, or search engines, to investigate particular topics. For the best results, use narrow rather than broad topics. Try these for Chapter 3: maquiladora, Carnival, Caribs, Brasília. Finding age-appropriate sites is an important consideration when using the Internet. For links to age-appropriate sites in world studies and geography, visit the *World Explorer* companion Web site at:
http://www.phschool.com

Connecting to the Guiding Questions

As students complete this chapter, they will focus on the cultures of Latin America. By linking history and culture, students will compare and contrast the unique cultural influences found throughout Latin America. Content in this chapter thus corresponds to the following Guiding Question:

● What factors have affected culture in Latin America?

Using the Picture Activities

Invite members of the class to describe several cultural characteristics of their own town or city. List the characteristics on the chalkboard. In a positive manner, help students compare these characteristics with those represented in the picture.

● Answers will vary.
● Student responses should indicate that successive waves of people coming to Latin America helped make the diversity shown.

Heterogeneous Groups

The following Teacher's Edition strategies are suitable for heterogeneous groups:

Cooperative Learning
Creating a Culture
Mural   p. 71

Interdisciplinary Connections
Language Arts   p. 66

Critical Thinking
Distinguishing Fact
From Opinion   p. 71

CHAPTER 3

Cultures of Latin America

SECTION 1
The Cultures of Mexico and Central America

SECTION 2
The Cultures of the Caribbean

SECTION 3
The Cultures of South America

PICTURE ACTIVITIES

These people are attending a festival in Peru. Get to know more about the people of Latin America by completing the following.

Link culture and history
Look at the people in this scene. Based on what you know about the history of Latin America, what do you think is the ethnic background of the people in the picture?

Compare regions
The cultures of Latin America are a unique blend of Native American, African, and European influences. How do you think the variety of peoples found in Latin America compares with that in the United States?

Resource Directory

Media and Technology

Cultures of Latin America, from the World Video Explorer, provides students with a visual overview of the region's many cultures.

Chapter 5

The Cultures of Mexico and Central America

BEFORE YOU READ

Reach Into Your Background

What are your hopes and dreams for the future? Do you hope to work in a particular profession? Do you plan to go to college? Many Mexicans and

Central Americans have the same kinds of dreams.

Questions to Explore

1. What is the ethnic heritage of the people of Mexico and Central America?
2. Why have many people in this region been moving from the country to the city?
3. What are the causes of Mexican and Central American immigration to the United States?

Key Terms

diversity
indigenous
injustice
maquiladora
emigrate
immigrant

Key Places

Mexico City

Lesson Objectives

1 Describe the heritage of the people of Mexico and Central America.

2 Explain why people in this region have been moving from the country to the city.

3 Identify the causes of Mexican and Central American immigration to the United States.

Lesson Plan

1 Engage

Warm-Up Activity

Ask students to list three things that come to mind when they think of Mexico and Central America. Ask students to share their ideas. Then extract key words or terms to make a list of geographical features, clothing, food items, and so on. Allow students to create a master list on a colorful piece of poster board. Add to the master list as students progress through the chapter.

Activating Prior Knowledge

Have students read Reach Into Your Background in the Before You Read box. Student responses may vary. Allow students to express their hopes and dreams without judgment.

Elvia Alvarado (el VEE ah ahl vah RAH doh) walks the back roads of rural Honduras. She helps poor campesinos make a living. Honduran campesinos are like rural people in all of Central America. Many have little land of their own. It is hard for them to make enough money to support their families.

Alvarado is a mother and grandmother. She works for an organization of campesinos. She helps people get loans to buy seeds and farm machinery. Alvarado also helps them get more land. She works with community groups.

Alvarado's work is not easy. "The communities we work in are hard to get to," she says. "Sometimes I don't eat all day, and in the summertime the streams dry up and there's often no water to drink." Sometimes Alvarado does not get paid. "But I couldn't be happy if my belly was full while my neighbors didn't have a plate of beans and tortillas to put on the table," she says. "My struggle is for a better life for all Hondurans."

Cultural Heritage

Alvarado lives and works in Honduras, in Central America. It is one of seven nations in this area. Together they form a crooked, skinny isthmus. The isthmus links Mexico and South America.

Teaching Resources

📁 **Reproducible Lesson Plan** in the Chapter and Section Resources booklet, p. 39, provides a summary of the section lesson.

📁 **Guided Reading and Review** in the Chapter and Section Resources booklet, p. 40, provides a structure for mastering key concepts and reviewing key terms in the section. Available in Spanish in the Spanish Chapter and Section Resources booklet, p. 25.

📖 **Section Reading Support Transparencies** provide answers to the Questions to Explore in a graphic organizer format.

Program Resources

📁 Material in the **Primary Sources and Literature Readings** booklet extends content with a selection from the region under study.

---

2 Explore

Have students read the section. Then have them identify some of the major characteristics of Central American and Mexican culture. The following questions may provide prompts: *What groups of people live in these countries? What is the main language in most Central American countries? Which religion is common in all the countries?*

3 Teach

Work with students as they create a chart similar to the "Increased Urbanization and Emigration" chart below:

Increased Urbanization and Emigration	
Conditions/ Problems in Mexico	Results/ Solutions

Work with the class to put one or two items in each column. Then suggest that students complete the chart with facts from the section. Indicate to students that case histories can help support their entries. Use the completed chart as the basis for discussion about the future of Central America and Mexico. This activity should take about 20 minutes.

Answers to...

SALVADORAN PAINTING

• the Plaza and the style of the church

LINKS TO ART

Huipiles Huipiles, or Mayan blouses, are works of art as well as clothing. The beautiful designs in a huipile have existed for thousands of years. Diamond-shaped designs stand for the universe. Other designs identify the weaver.

▶ The people of El Salvador are mostly mestizo, and their mixed heritage is reflected in their paintings. **Critical Thinking** What in this painting illustrates the Salvadorans' Spanish heritage?

One Region, Many Faces There is much **diversity**, or variety, among the people of Central America. Hondurans, like Alvarado, are mostly mestizo. They have both Spanish and indigenous ancestors. **Indigenous** (in DIJ uh nus) people are descendants of the people who first lived in a region. In Latin America, indigenous people are also called Native Americans or Indians. About half of Guatemala's people are mestizo. The other half are indigenous. Many Costa Ricans are direct descendants of Spaniards. And more than 40 percent of the people of Belize are of African or mixed African and European descent.

These countries have many languages, too. Guatemala is home to more than 20 languages. Spanish is the language of government and business. But the indigenous people in Guatemala speak their own languages. So do indigenous people in Panama, El Salvador, and Nicaragua. Spanish is the main language in six of the seven countries. People in Belize speak English.

Mexico's Heritage Mexico blends Native American and Spanish influences. Spanish is the first language for most Mexicans, and Mexico is the largest Spanish-speaking country. Some Mexicans speak Native American languages. About 20 percent of the people of Mexico are indigenous, and about 55 percent are mestizos.

The Church Religion is important to the people of Mexico and Central America. In the 1500s and 1600s, Spanish missionaries converted many Native Americans to Christianity. The Roman Catholic Church has been important to this region ever since. Most of the people are Catholic. Native Americans have blended many elements of their religions with Christianity.

Resource Directory

Media and Technology

 Color Tranparencies 63, 64, 65

Program Resources

Nystrom Desk Atlas

Outline Maps Mexico political map, and Central America and Caribbean political map

A Growing Population

United States

| Ages | Males | | Females | Ages |

Percentage of Total Male/Female Population

Mexico

| Ages | Males | | Females | Ages |

Percentage of Total Male/Female Population

Source: Dorling Kindersley World Desk Reference

Chart Study Unlike the United States, Mexico is a nation of young people. **Critical Thinking** Think about what different skills and needs people have at different ages. What challenges do you think Mexico faces because so many of its people are very young?

Often, the Roman Catholic Church has fought injustice. **Injustice** is the unfair treatment of people. There are many examples of injustice. Injustice occurs when people have their property taken from them unfairly. It also occurs when people are imprisoned without first having a trial. Injustice often happens in countries that have undemocratic governments. Priests and bishops have called for all people to be treated fairly.

Following the Church's lead, many citizens have taken their own steps to end poverty and injustice. People have started their own health clinics, farms, and organizations. Like Elvia Alvarado and her campesino families, they hope that by working together they will be able to create a better way of life.

Looking for Work

The population of Mexico and Central America is growing rapidly. If it continues at the current rate, it will double in 20 to 30 years. Rapid population growth has made it hard for young people in rural areas to

A Voice of Protest In the late 1600s, Mexican nun Sor Juana Inez de la Cruz was punished by her bishop for writing a letter defending women's right to learn. Sor Juana was a published poet, but the bishop took away her books and writing materials. However, Sor Juana's essay inspired later generations of women to stand up for their rights.

Activity

Interdisciplinary Connections

Language Arts Have students reread the stories of Elvia Alvarado and Fermin Carrillo. Organize students into two groups and assign one of the stories to each. Have students write their own dialogue for a short play about either Alvarado or Carrillo. Be sure students identify the main characters in the story, as well as the supporting roles. Students may wish to present their playlets to other classes. *English Language Learners, Kinesthetic*

Background

Daily Life

Learning English as a Second Language Many immigrants who come to the United States from Mexico and Central America have limited knowledge of the English language. While some may speak English adequately, they may need to learn how to read and write the language. Immigrants who migrate to large cities such as New York, Los Angeles, and Chicago can usually find free adult-education classes at a local community college. Often these people work long hours and then fit English classes into their evening or Saturday hours. They continue their studies, spurred on by the hope of gaining a better-paying job, adapting to their new home in the United States, and helping their family.

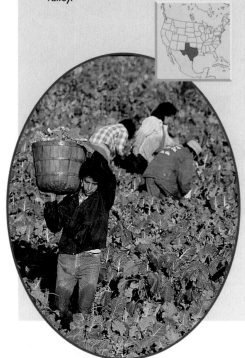

Many Mexican and Central American immigrants to the United States find jobs on farms, picking crops. The farm workers on the right are picking strawberries near Salinas, California. The worker below is harvesting broccoli in Texas' Rio Grande Valley.

READ ACTIVELY

Ask Questions What questions about maquiladoras would you like answered?

find jobs. Many have left their homes to look for work in the city. Today, most people in Mexico and Central America live in cities.

In Mexico, some people move to towns along the border with the United States. There, they can work in factories owned by American companies. These companies place their factories in Mexico because wages are lower there. Border factories are called **maquiladoras** (ma kee la DOR as).

Life in the City In many cities in the region, there are big contrasts between the lives of the wealthy and the lives of the poor. Wealthy people live in big houses on wide streets. They go to good schools and can afford to pay for medical care. Many of them have a lifestyle similar to that of wealthy people in the United States.

For the poor, however, life in the city can be hard. There is a shortage of housing. It is not easy to find work. Sometimes, the only job available is selling fruit or soda on street corners. It is hard to feed a family

Resource Directory

Teaching Resources

Section Quiz in the Chapter and Section Resources booklet, p. 41, covers the main ideas and key terms in the section. Available in Spanish in the Spanish Chapter and Section Resources booklet, p. 26.

on the wages such work commands. Yet people are willing to live with hardships they find in the city. Cecilia Cruz can explain why. She moved with her husband and their two sons to Mexico City from the southern state of Oaxaca (wah HAH kah). They live in a two-room house made of cinder blocks. It is on the outermost boundary of the city. "We came here for the schools," says Cruz. "There are more choices here. The level of education is much higher." Most newcomers to the city would agree.

Moving to the United States Most people in Mexico and Central America move somewhere else within their own country if they cannot find work. Some move to cities or border towns. In addition, however, thousands of people emigrate. To **emigrate** means to move out of one country into another. Most leave because they cannot find work at home. Also, rising prices have made living more expensive. Many people emigrate to the United States.

Fermin Carrillo (fair MEEN kah REE yoh) is one worker who did just that. He left his home town of Huaynamota, Mexico. There were no more jobs at home, and his parents needed food and medical care. Carrillo moved to a town in Oregon. Now he works in a fish processing plant. He sends most of the money he earns home to his parents. Carrillo hopes one day to become a U.S. citizen. Other immigrants are different. They want to return home after earning some money to help their families. An **immigrant** is a person who has moved into one country from another.

Many Mexicans and Central Americans, like Fermin Carrillo, have left the region in search of a better life. Many more have followed Elvia Alvarado's example. They have stayed and begun to build a better life for themselves at home.

READ ACTIVELY

Visualize What would a house made of cinder blocks look like? What problems might you notice if you went inside a cinder block house?

1. (a) variety (b) descendants of a region's first inhabitants (c) unfair treatment of people (d) border factory (e) to move out of one country to another (f) a person who has moved into one country from another

2. the capital city of the country of Mexico

3. (a) Spanish, Roman Catholic (b) Sample answer: The language and religion were brought by the Spanish when they explored the area and conquered the indigenous people.

4. It is extremely difficult to find jobs in the countryside, so thousands of people are moving to the cities.

5. Students' answers should reflect the idea that most Mexicans and Central Americans emigrate because they cannot find work in their home countries and because rising prices there have made life more and more expensive.

6. Student responses will vary. Students should compare and contrast their own dreams and desires with those of the person writing the journal.

SECTION 1 REVIEW

1. **Define** (a) diversity, (b) indigenous, (c) injustice, (d) maquiladora, (e) emigrate, (f) immigrant.

2. **Identify** Mexico City.

3. (a) What is the main language and religion of the people of Mexico and Central America? (b) How do the languages and religions of the region reflect its history?

4. What is one reason that rural people in Mexico and Central America are moving to the cities?

Critical Thinking

5. **Recognizing Cause and Effect** Explain several reasons for Mexican and Central American immigration to the United States.

Activity

6. **Writing to Learn** Write a journal entry from the point of view of one of the people mentioned in this section. Write about that person's hopes and dreams. How are they like your own? How are they different?

SKILLS MINI LESSON

Recognizing Cause and Effect
A novel way to **introduce** the skill is to drop a book on the floor. Indicate that the noise is an effect caused by the book hitting the floor. Explain that many conditions are the results, or *effects,* of other actions. The things that create the effects are called *causes.* Help students **practice** the skill by reading the following pair of sen-tences. Ask students to determine which is the cause and which is the effect.

• *Thousands of young people in the countryside are unable to find jobs.* (cause)
• *Thousands move to cities to find work.* (effect)

Encourage students to **apply** the skill by writing a pair of sentences about Fermin Carrillo. Have students describe a cause in one sentence and an effect in the other.

SECTION 2

The Cultures of the Caribbean

Lesson Objectives

1. Describe how European, African, and Native American cultures blended to create unique Caribbean cultures.

2. Identify the key characteristics of Caribbean cultures.

Lesson Plan

1 Engage

Warm-Up Activity

Ask students to think how they would feel if they had to travel by boat to a neighboring city rather than by car or bus. Encourage students to imagine living on an island. Prompt their imagination with questions about how they might make a living. How would they visit friends on another island? Discuss responses.

Activating Prior Knowledge

Have students read Reach Into Your Background in the Before You Read box. If any students have experienced island living, allow them to describe their views of island life. If no students have had the experience, encourage the class to discuss their thoughts on what island life might be like.

BEFORE YOU READ

Reach Into Your Background

Have you ever been on an island? Have you ever read a story about someone who lived on an island? What was the island like? What do you remember most about life there?

Questions to Explore

1. How did European, African, and Native American cultures blend to create unique Caribbean cultures?

2. What are the key characteristics of Caribbean cultures?

Key Terms

ethnic group
Carnival

Key Places

Jamaica
Cuba
Hispaniola
Trinidad and Tobago

▼ Many Jamaican women carry goods on their heads. This practice came to the Caribbean from Africa.

Dorothy Samuels is a ten-year-old from Jamaica, a tropical island in the Caribbean Sea. She lives in a village near the ocean and goes to a village school. Dorothy is a good student. She hopes one day to go to college in Kingston, Jamaica's capital city. Jamaican laws require that women have as much opportunity to educate themselves as men do. Equality for women is important to Jamaican culture because many Jamaican women are independent farmers and business owners.

Dorothy's family are farmers. They plant yams and other vegetables and fruits. They also plant cocoa beans. Every Saturday, Dorothy's mother and grandmother take their fruits and vegetables to the market to sell. All the traders at the market are women.

The People of the Caribbean

People in the Caribbean can make a living farming because most Caribbean islands have very fertile soil. These islands stretch over 2,000 miles (3,219 km) from Florida to the northeast coast of South America. As you might expect, a variety of peoples and cultures live within this large area.

Resource Directory

Teaching Resources

📁 **Reproducible Lesson Plan** in the Chapter and Section Resources booklet, p. 42, provides a summary of the section lesson.

📁 **Guided Reading and Review** in the Chapter and Section Resources booklet, p. 43, provides a structure for mastering key concepts and reviewing key terms in the section. Available in Spanish in the Spanish Chapter and Section Resources booklet, p. 27.

📺 **Section Reading Support Transparencies** provide answers to the Questions to Explore in a graphic organizer format.

The First People of the Caribbean The Caribbean islands are also called the West Indies because when Christopher Columbus arrived there, he thought he had reached the Indies in Asia.

The first people to live in the Caribbean were Native Americans, the Ciboney (SEE boh nay). The Ciboney lived on the islands for thousands of years. In about 300 B.C., they were joined by another indigenous group, the Arawaks (AR ah wahks), who came from South America. In about 1000, the Caribs (KA ribz), another South American group, arrived.

The Caribs gave the region its name. They lived there for more than 400 years before the first Europeans came to the area. Christopher Columbus and other Spaniards enslaved the Native Americans. Almost all of the Caribs, Arawaks, and other groups died of overwork and of diseases the Spanish brought with them. Today, just a few hundred Caribs still live on the island of Dominica.

Other Europeans followed the Spanish. They hoped to make money from the region's wealth of natural resources. Dutch, French, and English colonists began claiming territory in the 1600s. They built large sugar plantations and brought many enslaved Africans to work on them.

READ ACTIVELY

Predict What ethnic groups do you think live in the Caribbean today?

Caribbean Customs

	Jamaica	Puerto Rico	Dominican Republic
Greetings	A handshake; "Good morning/ afternoon/evening"; use Mr., Mrs., Miss.	A handshake. Women kiss each other on the cheek.	Shake hands. Greet everyone when you enter a room. Ask about people's families.
Gestures	Show approval of an idea by touching fists. Suck air through your teeth to mean "Give me a break."	Wiggle your nose to mean, "What's going on?" Point with puckered lips.	Point with puckered lips. Clap hands to request your check in a restaurant.
Table Manners	Keep the fork in the left hand. If you buy food from a street cart, eat it on the spot.	Keep both hands above the table. Stay at the table after the meal to relax and chat.	Guests are served first and sometimes separately. They often are given more elaborate food than the hosts.
Clothing	Women wear colorful skirts and matching headdresses. Many people have tailors make their clothes. Jewelry is common.	Casual clothing is worn for everyday occasions. Parties and social events require formal clothing.	Dressing well is considered important. Clothing is always clean and well-pressed. Men have a traditional suit called a chacabana, which is a white shirt over dark trousers.

Chart Study When you visit another culture, knowing the local customs can help you understand what you see. **Critical Thinking** Name some customs that are unique to the United States.

Media and Technology

 Color Transparency 64

Program Resources

Outline Maps Central America and the Caribbean political map

2 Explore

Have students read the section. Then ask them to describe the unique blend of cultures on the Caribbean islands. Lead the discussion so that students address the following characteristics: many islands; first inhabitants were Native Americans called the Ciboney; most natives died from overwork and disease once Spain established rule over the islands; Caribbean culture today is a blend of Native American, African, European, Asian, and Middle Eastern cultures.

3 Teach

Provide the following topic sentence for a paragraph: *Caribbean culture is known for its liveliness.* Direct students to write a paragraph that supports the sentence using details from the section to identify the rich traditions in food, music, art, and entertainment from the Caribbean region. This activity should take from 20 to 30 minutes.

Answers to...

CHART STUDY

• Accept any reasonable answer such as saying "hello" or waving good-bye.

4 Assess

See answers to the Section Review. You may also use students' completed paragraphs as an assessment.

Acceptable paragraphs include at least four factually correct supporting details, one for each cultural element listed.

Commendable paragraphs include some specific examples from countries mentioned in the text.

Outstanding paragraphs mention the origins of some of these cultural traditions.

Background

Global Perspectives

Cultural Comparison
Also known for its Caribbean culture is the northern part of South America, including Colombia, Venezuela, Guyana, and parts of Brazil. Largely Roman Catholic, the people here also celebrate Carnival in the days before the beginning of Lent. Brazil's diverse African, Native American, and European cultures result in its cities' lively celebrations, featuring people in dramatic costumes playing traditional rhythms and improvising dances. The many cultures are represented in different forms of celebration.

Most of the Caribbean people today are descended from these Africans. Immigrants from China, India, and the Middle East also came to the region to work.

People in the Caribbean Today   Since slavery was legally ended in the Caribbean, its population has grown to about 32 million. Nearly one third of these people live on the region's largest island, Cuba.

Because so many people came to the Caribbean as colonists, slaves, or immigrants, the area has great ethnic variety. An **ethnic group** is a group of people who share race, language, religion, or cultural traditions. The ethnic groups of the Caribbean are Native American, African, European, Asian, and Middle Eastern.

Depending on their island's history, the people of a Caribbean island may speak one of several European languages. Their language may also be a mixture of European and African languages. For example, two countries and two cultures exist on the island of Hispaniola. On the eastern half is one country, the Dominican Republic. Its population is Spanish-speaking and mostly mestizo. West of the Dominican Republic is the country of Haiti. Nearly all of Haiti's people are descended from Africans. They speak French and Creole, which is a blend of French and African languages.

Most West Indians are Christians, but there are also small groups of Hindus, Muslims, and Jews. Some people practice traditional African religions.

A Caribbean Family

Family life is very important to people in the Caribbean. This family, from Montserrat, British West Indies, is made up of parents and their children. Many people in the Caribbean live in family groups that also include grandparents, uncles, aunts, and cousins.

Take It to the **NET**

Prentice Hall's *World Explorer* companion Web site offers activities for exploring geographical, historical, and cultural resources on the Internet. It also provides online links for key content, data updates, and all chapter review activities.

The **Teacher site** provides teachers with ideas for student research and activities. It also presents *eTeach*, a monthly discussion with Master Teachers.

Students can use the **Student site** to find chapter-by-chapter Internet resource links, data updates, and Self-Tests.

http://www.phschool.com

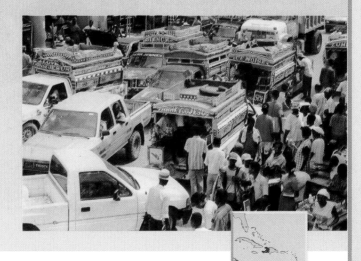

Haiti was one of the first places where the work of folk artists was recognized as real art. Large, colorful murals comment on religious and political themes. Bus drivers gain prestige by painting public buses, called taptaps.

Food, Music, Art, and Fun

Caribbean culture is known for its liveliness. People play music, dance, and tell stories. People also play many sports. Baseball, soccer, and track and field are popular. On some islands, people also play cricket, which is a British game similar to baseball. Dominoes is a popular game throughout the region.

Food Caribbean food is a mixture from all the cultures of the islands. Caribbean people can enjoy many types of seafood that are not found in U.S. waters. For instance, the people of Barbados love to eat flying fish and sea urchin eggs. Bammy—a bread made from the cassava plant—is still made the way the African slaves made it. People also cook spicy curries from India, sausages from England, and Chinese dishes. Many tropical fruits grow on the islands. West Indians use the fruit to make many juices and other drinks that are not readily available in the United States.

Music Caribbean music is famous around the world. Calypso is a form of song that uses humor in its lyrics. You may have heard reggae (REG ay) music. It is from Jamaica. Steel drums are Caribbean musical instruments. They are made from recycled oil drums. A steel drum can be "tuned" so that different parts of it play different notes. Players strike the instruments with rubberized drumsticks. The rubber hitting the drum makes an almost liquid sound.

LINKS TO MUSIC

Soca—Calypso with Soul
In the 1970s, a new form of Caribbean music evolved. It blended calypso with two other styles— funk and ska. Funk is an earthy, blues music. Ska is similar to reggae. The first song to use this music was Lord Shorty's "Soul Calypso." The name of the new musical form comes from the title "Soul Calypso." It is called *soca*.

SKILLS MINI LESSON

Using the Writing Process
You may **introduce** the skill by reviewing the basic steps of the writing process: prewriting, writing, editing, and presenting. Have students **practice** by following the steps to write a paragraph about Caribbean culture. Help students **apply** the skill by following the writing process as they develop writing assignments throughout this book.

1. (a) groups of people distinguished by race, language, religion, or cultural traditions (b) a celebration held throughout the Caribbean just before the beginning of Lent

2. (a) large tropical island in the Caribbean (b) the largest island in the Caribbean region (c) Caribbean island that is home to the Dominican Republic and Haiti (d) where a large Carnival celebration takes place

3. the Ciboney

4. Native American, African, European, Asian, and Middle Eastern cultural traditions

5. Answers may vary, but should include elements such as these: All the region's islands have fertile soil. The native populations of the islands were enslaved by the Spanish. Enslaved Africans were brought from Africa to work in the islands. The Caribbean culture is known for its liveliness.

6. Responses will vary, but students should compare and contrast an aspect of Caribbean culture with their own.

Carnival at Port of Spain, Trinidad

Many people in Caribbean countries dress in lavish, colorful costumes to celebrate before Lent. **Critical Thinking** What similar celebration takes place in the United States?

Carnival   Many islanders observe the Roman Catholic tradition of Lent, which is the period of 40 days before Easter Sunday. People consider Lent to be a very solemn time, so just before Lent they throw a huge party. The party is called **Carnival.**

Different countries celebrate Carnival in different ways. Carnival is an important event in Trinidad and Tobago. People spend all year making costumes and floats. Lent always starts on a Wednesday. At 5 A.M. the Monday before, people go into the streets in their costumes. Calypso bands play. Thousands of fans follow the bands through the streets, dancing and celebrating. At the stroke of midnight Tuesday, the party stops. Lent has begun.

SECTION 2 REVIEW

1. Define   (a) ethnic group, (b) Carnival.

2. Identify   (a) Jamaica, (b) Cuba, (c) Hispaniola, (d) Trinidad and Tobago.

3. Who were the first inhabitants of the Caribbean islands?

4. Which traditions does modern Caribbean culture blend?

Critical Thinking

5. Making Comparisons What common elements in their histories have shaped the cultures of the various Caribbean islands?

Activity

6. Writing to Learn Select one aspect of Caribbean culture (food, music, celebrations, and so on) and jot down what you have learned about it in this section. Then, write ways in which it is similar to and different from your own culture.

Resource Directory

Teaching Resources

Section Quiz in the Chapter and Section Resources booklet, p. 44, covers the main ideas and key terms in the section. Available in Spanish in the Spanish Chapter and Section Resources booklet, p. 28.

The Cultures of South America

BEFORE YOU READ

Reach Into Your Background

Think about the books you read, the music you like to listen to, and the clothes you wear. These things are all part of your culture. How is your culture related to the history of your family and your region? How does the geography in your region affect your culture?

Questions to Explore

1. What major cultural groups live in South America?

2. How has geography created diversity in this region?

Key Terms

subsistence farming
import

Key Places

Andes
Chile
Argentina
Brazil

Lesson Objectives

1. Identify the major cultural groups living in South America.

2. Explain how geography has created diversity in this region.

Lesson Plan

1 Engage

Warm-Up Activity

Ask students to recall the major ethnic groups that live in the Latin American regions of Mexico, Central America, and the Caribbean. Then have students compare the picture of the reed boat and its builder to the picture of Peru in the chapter opener. Ask students to predict which photo better represents the present-day cultures of South America.

Activating Prior Knowledge

Have students read Reach Into Your Background in the Before You Read box. Students may mention that their culture is a result of their families or the part of the country they are from. Some students might mention that different kinds of music are favored in different regions.

Between Peru and Bolivia is the deep lake called Lake Titicaca. It lies high in the Andes Mountains. This area is bitterly cold. There are few trees. Native Americans here make their living from totora reeds, a kind of thick, hollow grass that grows on the lakeshore. They use these reeds to make houses, mats, hats, ropes, sails, toys, roofs, and floors. They eat the reeds, feed them to livestock, and brew them into tea. Totora reeds can even be made into medicine. Long ago, some Native American groups built floating islands with totora reeds. They used the islands to hide from the Incas. Today, some Native Americans live on floating islands.

The People of South America

Most South Americans today are descended from Native Americans, Africans, or Europeans. In this way, they are like the people of Mexico and Central America. South America's history is also like that of its neighbors to the north. It was colonized mainly by Spain. Most South Americans speak Spanish and are Catholic. Each nation has its own unique culture, however.

▼ The Native Americans who live on Lake Titicaca use totora reeds to make boats.

Teaching Resources

📁 **Reproducible Lesson Plan** in the Chapter and Section Resources booklet, p. 45, provides a summary of the section lesson.

📁 **Guided Reading and Review** in the Chapter and Section Resources booklet, p. 46, provides a structure for mastering key concepts and reviewing key terms in the section. Available in Spanish in the Spanish Chapter and Section Resources booklet, p. 29.

📖 **Section Reading Support Transparencies** provide answers to the Questions to Explore in a graphic organizer format.

2 Explore

Have students read the section. Then ask them to identify the major cultural groups living in South America. Lead the discussion to elicit the following information from students: Many Native Americans live high in the Andes. People have lived in South America since prehistoric times. Most South Americans are descended from Native Americans, Africans, Europeans, or a blend of these.

3 Teach

Compose a chart on the chalkboard. Allow one column for each of the four regions discussed in the section. Place two categories along the side of the chart: *Geographic Characteristics* and *Cultural Characteristics*. Work with students to fill in the first cell on the chart. Suggest that students complete their own charts by using the information from the section. Use the charts to discuss the features of each region. This activity will take about 20 minutes.

Answers to...

HERDING LLAMAS IN PERU

Students' responses may vary. Sample response: for their wool, to carry loads.

READ ACTIVELY

Connect How are the Pampas of Argentina like the plains of the United States?

Regions Within South America There are four cultural regions in South America. The first region includes Colombia, Venezuela, Guyana, Suriname, and French Guiana, which are in the northern part of South America. They each border the Caribbean Sea. The cultures of these countries are like those of the Caribbean islands.

To the south and west, the culture is very different. Peru, Ecuador, and Bolivia are Andean countries. Many Native Americans live high in the Andes. In Bolivia, there are more indigenous people than mestizos. The Quechua and Aymara (eye muh RAH) people each speak their own languages.

The third cultural region consists of Chile, Argentina, Paraguay, and Uruguay. The long, thin country of Chile has mountains, beaches, deserts, forests, and polar regions. Although its geography is diverse, its people are not. Most people in Chile are mestizos. The big cities of Argentina and Uruguay, however, are very diverse. Many different ethnic groups live there. Another culture exists on Argentina's Pampas, or plains. On the Pampas, gauchos (GOW chohz), or cowhands, herd cattle.

Brazil is South America's largest country. Brazil was a colony of Portugal. Its people speak Portuguese. However, Brazil is culturally diverse. Many Native Americans live in Brazil. So do people of African and European descent. Some Brazilians are of mixed descent. Many people have moved to Brazil from other countries. Brazil's largest city, São Paulo (sow PAW loh), is home to more Japanese than any other place in the world except Japan!

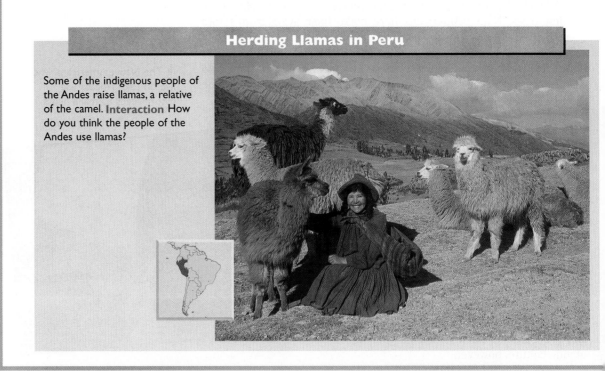

Herding Llamas in Peru

Some of the indigenous people of the Andes raise llamas, a relative of the camel. **Interaction** How do you think the people of the Andes use llamas?

Resource Directory

Teaching Resources

Analyzing a photograph in the **Social Studies and Geography Skills** booklet, p. 58, provides additional skill practice.

Media and Technology

Color Transparency 64

Program Resources

Outline Maps South America political map

Yhaninc Puelles Enriquez
age 12
Cuzco, Peru

The scene shown by this student artist is similar to the photograph on the previous page. **Critical Thinking** How are the scenes in the art and the photograph alike and different?

4 Assess

See answers to the Section Review. You may also use students' completed charts as an assessment.

Acceptable charts include at least one characteristic for each country and category.

Commendable charts include two or three facts for each.

Outstanding charts include some cause and effect relationships linking culture and unique features.

Journal Writing

Travel Diary Ask students to write a travel diary or journal entry about one of the regions mentioned in the section. Explain that they should describe physical and human characteristics. Students might include illustrations from travel magazines to illustrate their entries.

Art and Literature in South America South America has produced many famous artists, novelists, filmmakers, and poets. Chilean poets Pablo Neruda (PAH bloh nay ROO duh) and Gabriela Mistral (gah bree AY lah mees TRAHL) both were awarded the Nobel Prize for their work. Neruda wrote about everyday objects, including rain, tomatoes, and socks. Mistral wrote for and about children. Colombian Gabriel García Márquez (gah bree EL gar SEE uh MAR kays) and Chilean Isabel Allende (EES uh bel ah YEN day) both are famous for writing novels telling about several generations of life in one family. García Márquez was awarded the Nobel Prize.

Country and City Life

South America contains cities with millions of people, but it also has vast areas with hardly any people at all. Many people still live in the countryside. Others are leaving farms and moving to cities.

Farming in South America Outside of Chile, Argentina, and Uruguay, most rural people with land of their own do **subsistence farming.** That means they grow only enough food for their families to eat. They only have small plots of land. Farmers plant corn, beans, potatoes, and rice.

LINKS TO LANGUAGE ARTS

Gabriela Mistral Chilean poet Gabriela Mistral was awarded the Nobel Prize for Literature in 1945. But Mistral considered herself to be more a teacher than a writer. Mistral taught school in rural Chile in the early 1900s, but she was frustrated by the low quality of the textbooks that were available. In response, Mistral began to write poetry and prose for children.

SKILLS MINI LESSON

Assessing Your Understanding

To **introduce** the skill to students, point out that building knowledge of a subject is much like building a house. What students learn today forms the foundation for what they learn next week or next year. Point out that one way to ensure that their foundation is strong is to check their learning as they go. Help students **practice** assessing their under-standing by asking them to read each of the paragraphs following "Regions Within South America." Tell students to read one paragraph and then stop and restate the ideas from the paragraph in their own words. After reading another paragraph, students might list the paragraph's important points. Tell students that if they have trouble restating or summarizing a paragraph they should reread it and try again.

Answers to...
A PERUVIAN SCENE

• Responses should indicate that each shows an aspect of life in the Andes.

Brasília Point out that this capital city is in the interior of the country, far from the crowded, noisy cities of the Atlantic Coast.

Read the following quotation from Oscar Neimeyer, the chief architect of the city:

"[Those who live there] can enjoy tree-lined avenues. The light from the sky seems to bring with it kindlier ways of living. . . ."

Tell students that as early as 1789, Brazilians thought of building a new capital city in the interior of the country. The idea came up again when Brazil won its independence from Portugal. Have students speculate on why the people might have wanted to build a new capital. (crowded settlements along the ocean, desire to build a capital that had no influence of European conquerors) Ask students to point out features of the capital that indicate that the country is no longer under European rule. (Presidential Palace, the Plaza of the Three Powers)

Have students use the diagram to explain why the Presidential Palace is called the Palace of the Dawn. (It faces east, the direction of the sunrise.)

Very large farms grow crops to export to other countries. The main export crops of South America are coffee, sugar, cocoa, and bananas. Export farming uses so much land for cash crops that South America has to import food to eat. To **import** means to buy from another country.

Brasília

Brasília is a planned city. Some people think it looks like a bow and arrow. Others think it looks like a jet plane. Government offices and shopping areas are located in the middle of the city, where the two "wings" meet. The wings contain superblocks, or residential neighborhoods. Each includes 10 to 16 apartment buildings, a school, and shops. What would you like about living in a completely new city? What would you dislike?

The **Plaza of the Three Powers** is the center of government.

Residential Superblocks

Presidential Palace

Lake Paranoa

Resource Directory

Teaching Resources

Section Quiz in the Chapter and Section Resources booklet, p. 47, covers the main ideas and key terms in the section. Available in Spanish in the Spanish Chapter and Section Resources booklet, p. 30.

Vocabulary in the Chapter and Section Resources booklet, p. 49, provides a review of key terms in the chapter. Available in Spanish in the Spanish Chapter and Section Resources booklet, p. 32.

Reteaching in the Chapter and Section Resources booklet, p. 50, provides a structure for students who may need additional help in mastering chapter content.

Enrichment in the Chapter and Section Resources booklet, p. 51, extends chapter content and enriches students' understanding.

Spanish Glossary in the Spanish Chapter and Section Resources, pp. 62–66, provides key terms translated from

The population of South America is booming. Latin America is one of the fastest-growing regions in the world. Like Mexicans and Central Americans, South Americans cannot find enough jobs in rural areas. Every day, thousands of rural South Americans move to the cities looking for work.

South America's Cities   The cities of South America illustrate the region's mix of cultures. Many major cities—Lima, Peru, and Buenos Aires, Argentina, for example—were built by Spanish colonists more than 400 years ago. Some of the buildings in these older cities follow Native American designs. In contrast, modern office blocks and apartment buildings of concrete, steel, and glass tower above the downtown areas. One or two cities were built quite recently. Brasília, the Brazilian capital, was constructed in the 1950s. It was a completely planned city, designed to draw people to the country's interior.

By contrast, one of the unplanned things about many South American cities is the slums. They are called *favelas* (fuh VEH luz) in Brazil and *barrios* (BAR ee ohs) in Venezuela. More and more people have migrated into the cities in recent years. Usually they have ended up in poor neighborhoods. City governments try to provide electricity and running water to everyone. But people move into cities so quickly that it is hard for city governments to keep up.

The Role of Women   In some ways, women do not yet play a role equal to that of men in South America. Women in South America are more likely than men to be poor. They also do not attend school for as many years as men do.

More and more women in South America today are fighting to make a living for themselves and their children. They are demanding equal rights. Women are struggling for the rights to go to school, to get into different types of jobs, to have good health care, and to have a voice in government. Some women are getting bank loans to start small businesses. These businesses are sometimes based on traditional skills such as sewing, weaving, or preparing food.

Working Together From 1976 to 1983, Argentina had a military government. The government took thousands of people prisoner. Many were never seen again. The mothers and grandmothers of the "disappeared" marched in protest every week for six years in Buenos Aires. Their actions forced the government to explain what happened to the missing people.

SECTION 3 REVIEW

1. **Define** (a) subsistence farming, (b) import.
2. **Identify** (a) Andes, (b) Chile, (c) Argentina, (d) Brazil.
3. What pressures does rapid population growth place on the countries of South America?
4. Name two ways in which the geography of South America has shaped how people live.

Critical Thinking
5. **Recognizing Cause and Effect** What is one cause of rapid population growth in the cities? What is one effect?

Activity
6. **Writing to Learn** Choose one region of South America you'd like to visit, and write a paragraph explaining why.

English to Spanish as well as definitions in Spanish.

 Chapter Summary in the Chapter and Section Resources booklet, p. 48, provides a summary of chapter content. Available in Spanish in the Spanish Chapter and Section Resources booklet, p. 31.

 Cooperative Learning Activity in the Activities and Projects booklet, pp. 28–31, provides two student handouts, one page of teacher's directions, and a scoring rubric for a cooperative learning activity on sharing the music.

 Critical Thinking Activity in the Chapter and Section Resources booklet, p. 52, helps students apply the skill of identifying central issues.

Media and Technology

 Guided Reading Audiotapes (English and Spanish)

 Student Edition on Audio CD The entire text of the Student Edition is available in a series of audio CDs.

Section 3 Review

1. (a) growing enough food for the farmers' own families (b) to buy goods from another country

2. (a) huge mountain range that runs almost the whole length of the west coast of South America (b) long, thin country in South America that has many different geographic regions (c) a country in southern South America with vast plains called pampas (d) South America's largest country

3. Answers will vary. Possible answer: Rapid population growth makes it difficult for South American countries to maintain their large cities. City governments try to provide electricity and running water to everyone, but it is hard to keep up. Many people end up in poor neighborhoods.

4. Answers may vary, but might include the comparison between northern South America, which is close to the Caribbean and shares its diverse island culture, and countries lying partly in the Andes, which have a cold, high-altitude environment that has helped preserve the culture of the indigenous people.

5. Answers will vary. One cause is the huge migration of people from the farm areas into the cities to find work. One effect is that the newcomers often have difficulty finding places to live.

6. Students' responses will vary but should be supported with reasons and illustrative facts.

Distinguishing Facts From Opinions

Lesson Objectives

❶ Define the terms *fact* and *opinion*.

❷ Identify facts and opinions in context.

Lesson Plan

1 Engage

Warm-Up Activity

To **introduce** the skill, invite a volunteer to read the introduction to the class. Write the terms *fact* and *opinion* on the chalkboard.

Activating Prior Knowledge

Ask students if they can define the terms *fact* and *opinion*. Have them write their definitions on a piece of paper.

Kate was nervous, but excited. This was her first trip out of the United States. For two weeks, she had seen more fantastic things in Mexico than she could have dreamed of: beautiful countryside, ancient ruins ... the list was endless. Now, she was about to start a new adventure.

Today, she would travel from Mexico City to Paplanta, a small town near the coast to the east. A fellow traveler had discouraged her. "The train trip is very long," she had said.

"And boring. There's nothing to look at out the windows. The town is not interesting, either. You should skip that trip altogether."

"Hmmm," Kate thought as she pulled out her guidebook and train schedule. The guidebook said that the ruins of an old Spanish mission were located at Paplanta. The El Tajin ruins were also there. On Sundays, the town hosted an open-air market. The train schedule said it was only a three-hour train ride away, through mountainous country. "A long trip? Nothing to look at? Ha!" More determined than ever, Kate headed to the train station.

The train trip is very long and boring!

GUIDE BOOK

The train ride to Paplanta is three hours long.

Get Ready

Kate decided to go to Paplanta because she relied on facts instead of opinions. Facts are statements that can be proved true. Opinions are beliefs. That the train ride was three hours long is a fact. The traveler's statement that the train ride "is very long" is an opinion. Distinguishing facts from opinions, as Kate found out, is a valuable skill.

Distinguishing facts from opinions is something you will need to do almost every day of your life. You will do it as you watch television, read books and magazines, and—like Kate—as you reach your own decisions.

Resource Directory

Teaching Resources

📁 **Social Studies and Geography Skills** Distinguishing Facts From Opinions, p. 43

Media and Technology

💿 **Social Studies Skills Tutor CD-ROM** builds core social studies skills through interactive lessons and provides skill assessment.

How can you distinguish, or tell the difference between, facts and opinions? It's as simple as A-B-C:

A. Facts can be proved true.

B. Opinions cannot be proved true.

C. Opinions are often indicated by words and phrases like "I think," "I believe," "should," and "ought to," and by adjectives like "beautiful" or "ugly."

Ladinos make up about 50 percent of the population of Guatemala.

Guatemala is the most beautiful country in Latin America.

F

O

Try It Out

Learn to distinguish facts from opinions by playing a simple game. All you need are some note cards, a couple of pens, and a partner.

A. Deal the cards. Deal ten note cards to your partner and ten to yourself. Each of you should then write one fact or one opinion about Latin America on each of your note cards. You can get the facts from your textbook. The opinions should be your own beliefs. On the back of each note card, write an F if you wrote a fact and an O if you wrote an opinion. Don't let your partner see these!

B. Shuffle the cards. Shuffle your cards, and give them to your partner. Challenge him or her to identify each sentence as a fact or an opinion. Award one point for each correct answer. Give a bonus point if your partner can explain how the statement could be proved true if it is a fact or how your partner knew it was an opinion. Total your partner's score, and write it down.

C. Switch cards. Now try your hand at your partner's note cards. Compare scores. Which of you won? The winner should help the loser learn more about distinguishing fact from opinion.

Apply the Skill

Now distinguish facts from opinions in a real case.

1 Read for understanding. Read the paragraph in the box below once or twice, until you are sure you understand its meaning.

2 Read for facts and opinions. Now reread *one sentence at a time.* For each sentence, apply the A-B-C method of distinguishing facts from opinions. Ask yourself: A) Is this a fact that *can* be proved true? B) Is this an opinion that *cannot* be proved true? C) Are there words in the sentence that identify it as an opinion? Which sentences are facts and which are opinions? How could you prove the facts true? How do you know the other sentences express opinions?

Urbanization takes place when people move from rural areas to urban areas. I believe that urbanization in Mexico is a bad thing. First, the cities are already too crowded. There are thousands of homeless people in urban areas. Lots of people can't find jobs. Second, the city streets were not designed for so many cars. Traffic jams are a huge headache. Finally, the water and electric systems do not have the capacity to serve more people. I think the time has come for the government to try to stop urbanization.

2 Explore

Read the material under the heading Get Ready with students. Ask volunteers to write the definitions for fact (a statement that can be proved true) and opinion (a belief) on the board under the terms. Tell students to compare these definitions with the ones they wrote down earlier. Then have them read the rest of the skills activity.

3 Teach

Pair students and allow them to **practice** by playing the game described in Try It Out. Monitor their discussions and share interesting examples of facts and opinions with the entire class.

For additional reinforcement, ask students to write three facts and three opinions on a topic of their own choice.

4 Assess

Have students **apply** the skill by completing the final part of the activity. To **assess,** evaluate students' contributions to a sentence-by-sentence judgment of the facts and opinions in the paragraph. You might want to display the paragraph on an overhead projector and identify each sentence as a class. Highlight opinion words such as "believe" and "think."

Reviewing Main Ideas

1. (a) Mexican border factories that are owned by United States companies (b) they provide jobs

2. the United States

3. (a) Native Americans called the Ciboney (b) They were joined by another indigenous group from South America. Once the Europeans enslaved them, nearly all native groups died of overwork and disease.

4. Sample answer: Calypso is a form of song that features humor in its lyrics. Reggae music is from Jamaica.

5. Communities of Native Americans make their living harvesting reeds used for housing, mats, ropes, sails, toys, roofs, and floors. Totora reeds can also be eaten or made into medicine.

6. (a) Chile has mountains, beaches, deserts, forests, and polar regions. (b) The people include members of many Native American groups, as well as descendants of Africans, Europeans, and people of mixed descent. Immigrants to Brazil include large numbers of Japanese.

Reviewing Key Terms

1. F		**4.** F		**6.** F	
2. T		**5.** T		**7.** F	
3. T					

Critical Thinking

1. Answers may differ, but possibilities may include the facts that the cultures and history of Latin America were influenced by Native Americans, Africans, and Europeans, especially Spaniards. Geographically, these regions are quite diverse, and their living conditions may vary accordingly.

2. Thousands of Latin Americans emigrate each year because they cannot find work in their own countries.

Reviewing Main Ideas

1. (a) What are maquiladoras? (b) Why are they important to the economy of Mexico?

2. To which country are some Mexicans and Central Americans emigrating to find jobs?

3. (a) Who were the first people on the Caribbean islands? (b) What happened to those people?

4. What are some of the musical styles that began in the Caribbean?

5. How do some of the people of the Andes make a living?

6. (a) How is the country of Chile geographically diverse? (b) How is Brazil culturally diverse?

Reviewing Key Terms

Decide whether each statement is true or false. If it is true, write "true." If it is false, change the underlined term to make the statement true.

1. Border factories are called mestizos.

2. Indigenous people are descendants of a region's first inhabitants.

3. To emigrate is to move from one's home country to another country.

4. Many Mexicans become pampas in the United States because they cannot find jobs in their home countries.

5. Ethnic diversity refers to people with a variety of cultures, customs, religions, or languages.

6. Imports occur when a government does not respect people's human rights.

7. To immigrate means to buy from another country.

Critical Thinking

1. **Making Comparisons** Consider these three regions: Mexico and Central America; the Caribbean; South America. What do the cultures of these regions have in common? How are they different?

2. **Recognizing Cause and Effect** What is the main reason that many Latin Americans move from one region or one country to another?

Graphic Organizer

Copy the chart to the right onto a separate sheet of paper. Then fill in the empty boxes to complete the chart.

	Mexico and Central America	The Caribbean	South America
Languages			
Religions			
Ethnic Background			
Special Features			

Graphic Organizer

	Mexico and Central America	The Caribbean	South America
Languages	many indigenous, Spanish, English	European, Creole	mostly Spanish
Religions	Roman Catholic and blend of Christianity and traditional religions	Christian and small groups of Hindu, Muslim, and Jewish	mostly Catholic and traditional
Ethnic Background	mestizo, indigenous, Spanish, African, and European	African, indigenous, and European	indigenous, African, and European
Special Features	Central Plateau Panama Canal	rich soil, musical traditions	Andes Mountains, Amazon River, rain forest

Map Activity

For each place listed below, write the letter from the map that shows its location.

1. Andes
2. Argentina
3. Brazil
4. Honduras
5. Jamaica
6. Mexico City
7. Trinidad and Tobago

Latin America: Place Location

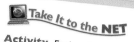

Map Activity

1. E	4. B	6. A
2. G	5. C	7. D
3. F		

Writing Activity

Writing a Magazine Article
In this chapter, you've taken a guided tour of the cultures of Latin America. Write an article for a travel magazine

describing the "high points" of your tour. As you write, consider how historical events and geography influenced the region's culture.

Skills Review

Turn to the Skill Activity.
Review the steps for distinguishing facts from opinions. Then, write a brief paragraph about the cultures of Latin America that includes both facts and opinions.

Take It to the NET

Activity Explore Mexican culture and create a portfolio highlighting some of your favorite findings. For help in completing this activity, visit www.phschool.com.

Chapter 3 Self-Test To review what you have learned, take the Chapter 3 Self-Test and get instant feedback on your answers. Go to www.phschool.com to take the test.

How Am I Doing?

Answer these questions to help you check your progress.

1. Can I explain how the cultures in a region reflect its history?
2. Can I explain how most people make a living in the countryside?
3. Can I identify the reasons why many people in Latin America are moving from rural to urban areas?
4. What information from this chapter can I include in my journal?

Take It to the NET

Students may wish to use the Internet to search for similar topics or activities. Suggest possible search terms, such as "Mexican culture" or "Mexican literature."

Guide students to a search engine. Four of the most useful are Infoseek, AltaVista, Lycos, and Yahoo. For additional suggestions on using the Internet, refer to the Prentice Hall Social Studies' Educator's Handbook "Using the Internet," in the *Prentice Hall World Explorer* Program Resources.

For chapter-by-chapter links to age-appropriate sites in world studies and geography, including Self-Tests, visit the *World Explorer* companion Web site at:
http://www.phschool.com

How Am I Doing?

Point out to students that this checklist is just a quick reminder for them of what they learned in the chapter. If their answer to any of the questions is *no* or if they are unsure, they may need to review the topic.

Writing Activity

Students should write about the various places mentioned in the chapter. Magazine articles should include specific descriptive details about the region, where it is located, the cultures that exist today, and the roots of those cultures.

Skills Review

Answers will vary. Students should write a paragraph with facts from the chapter as well as opinions. Encourage students with questions or those who are unsure whether any specific statement is fact or opinion to present their questions to the class.

Resource Directory

Teaching Resources

 Chapter Tests Forms A and B are in the Tests booklet, pp. 14–19.

Media and Technology

 Computer Test Bank CD-ROM

 Resource Pro® CD-ROM

Prentice Hall Assessment System

Exploring Mexico and Central America

To help you plan instruction, the chart below shows how teaching resources correspond to chapter content. Use the resources to vary instruction, add activities, or plan block schedules. Where appropriate, resources have **suggested time allotments** for students. Time allotments are approximate.

Managing Time and Instruction

	Latin America Teaching Resources Booklet		World Explorer Program Resources Binder	
	Resource	**mins.**	**Resource**	**mins.**
SECTION 1 Mexico One Family's Move to the City	**Chapter and Section Support** Reproducible Lesson Plan, p. 54 ⑤ Guided Reading and Review, p. 55 ⑤ Section Quiz, p. 56 ▭ Section Reading Support Transparencies	 20 25 15	**Outline Maps** Mexico: Political, p. 8 **Nystrom Desk Atlas** Ⓣ **Primary Sources and Literature Readings** Locks, Crocs, & Skeeters, p. 19; Beyond the Chagres, p. 21	20 40
SKILLS ACTIVITY Previewing a Reading Selection	**Social Studies and Geography Skills,** Previewing the Headings and the Pictures, p. 68	 30		
SECTION 2 Guatemala Descendants of an Ancient People	**Chapter and Section Support** Reproducible Lesson Plan, p. 57 ⑤ Guided Reading and Review, p. 58 ⑤ Section Quiz, p. 59 Critical Thinking Activity, p. 67 ▭ Section Reading Support Transparencies **Social Studies and Geography Skills,** Reading a Circle Graph, p. 55	 20 25 30 15 30	**Outline Maps** Central America and the Caribbean: Political, p. 9	 20
SECTION 3 Panama Where Two Oceans Meet	**Chapter and Section Support** Reproducible Lesson Plan, p. 60 ⑤ Guided Reading and Review, p. 61 ⑤ Section Quiz, p. 62 ⑤ Vocabulary, p. 64 Reteaching, p. 65 Enrichment, p. 66 ⑤ Chapter Summary, p. 63 ▭ Section Reading Support Transparencies **Tests** Forms A and B Chapter Tests, pp. 20–25	 20 25 20 25 25 15 15 40	**Outline Maps** Central America and the Caribbean: Political, p. 9 **Writing Process Handbook** Limiting a Topic, p. 15	 20 25
ACTIVITY SHOP: Lab Making A Model Canal	**Activities and Projects** Activity Shop: Lab, p. 6	 30		

Block Scheduling Program Support

Block Scheduling Booklet
PROGRAM RESOURCES BINDER

Activities and Projects

Interdisciplinary Links

Resource Pro® CD-ROM

Media and Technology

Pacing Charts Booklet
PROGRAM RESOURCES BINDER

Assessment Opportunities

From Guiding Questions to Assessment A series of Guiding Questions serves as an organizing framework for this book. The Guiding Questions that relate to this chapter are listed below. Section Reviews and Section Quizzes provide opportunities for assessing students' insights into these Guiding Questions. Additional assessments are listed below.

Media and Technology

Resource	mins.
🔲🎞️ Ⓢ World Video Explorer	20
⬜ Color Transparencies 19, 24, 65	20
💿 Resource Pro® CD-ROM	30
💿 Presentation Pro CD-ROM	20
💿 Social Studies Skills Tutor CD-ROM	30
🔲 World Video Explorer	10
⬜ Color Transparency 66	20
⬜ Color Transparency 66	20
🎧 Ⓢ Guided Reading Audiotapes	20
⬜ Color Transparency 172 (Graphic organizer tree map template)	20
💿 Computer Test Bank CD-ROM	30
🎧 Student Edition on Audio CD	30
💿 Passport to the World CD-ROM	30

Key

🅣 **Teaming Opportunity** well-suited for teaching teams	💿 **CD-ROM**
	💿 **Laserdisc**
	⬜ **Transparency**
Ⓢ **Spanish** This resource is also in Spanish support.	🔲 **Videotape**
	🎧 **Audiotape/CD**

GUIDING QUESTIONS

- *How has Latin America been shaped by its history?*
- *How has geography influenced the ways in which Latin Americans make a living?*

ASSESSMENTS

Section 1

Students should be able to write a report outlining the challenges Mexicans from the country face when they move to cities.

▶ **RUBRIC** See the Assessment booklet for a rubric on assessing a report.

Section 2

Students should be able to explain why Mayan political movements began in Guatemala, and describe their impact.

▶ **RUBRIC** See the Assessment booklet for a rubric on assessing cause-and-effect statements.

Section 3

Students should be able to create a map of Panama showing the location of the Panama Canal.

▶ **RUBRIC** See the Assessment booklet for a rubric on assessing a map produced by a student.

Prentice Hall Assessment System allows you to:
- Diagnose and Prescribe
- Review and Reteach
- Practice and Assess

Activities and Projects

Mental Mapping

Centrally Located Display a map of Latin America. Ask students a series of location questions about Mexico and Central America, such as:

• What U.S. states share a border with Mexico? [Texas, New Mexico, Arizona, California]

• Which bodies of water lie on either side of Central America? [Pacific Ocean; Gulf of Mexico or Atlantic Ocean]

• Traveling from the border of Mexico, in what direction does Central America extend? [southeast]

• What Central American country lies closest to South America? [Panama]

• If you took a bus or train in a direct route from the border of Mexico to the border of South America, approximately how far would you travel? [1,500 miles]

Links to Current Events

Prepare for an Interview If possible, invite a first- or second-generation immigrant from Mexico or Central America to come to the class to speak and be interviewed. Tell the visitor that students will be interested in hearing about both the achievements and appealing aspects of that country as well as about some of the challenges faced by people there.

Before the visitor arrives, ask students to prepare questions they would like to have answered. Have students review Chapters 1, 2, and 3 to prepare one question about geography, one question about history, and one question about the culture of the visitor's country of origin.

If it is not possible to invite someone from this region to visit the class, have students prepare questions and then try to research the answers themselves.

Hands-On Activities

Short Cut Using a wall map, let students compare the length of sea journeys from San Francisco to New York; from Los Angeles to São Paulo, Brazil; and from Philadelphia to Santiago, Chile, with and without the Panama Canal.

Suggest that they do this by making model ships out of construction paper or lightweight cardboard. These ships need not be to scale, but the same ship should be used to measure the distance for each journey with and without the canal. Have students count the number of ship lengths for each journey using both routes.

Encourage students to discuss some of the reasons why people would want to decrease the length of time required for such voyages.

Mexico City Sights Have students look at newspaper or magazine travel articles or at travel books about Mexico City. Ask them to identify three "sights" they would want to visit on a trip to Mexico City. Each student may describe the three things they would want to see in writing or in an oral presentation. *Basic*

Labels Tell students that trade with Mexico and Central America is very important to the United States. Ask students to look at labels of clothing, toys, and other objects at home, as well as at the labels on produce in a supermarket or grocery store. Have them list the things they find that come from Mexico or Central America. *Average*

Make a Map Give students an outline map of Mexico and Central America. As they work through this chapter, have them locate and label countries, cities, and natural features of this region on their maps. They may also create icons to show natural resources or principal products of the countries on the map. Direct students to provide a key to information shown on the map. *English Language Learners*

Canal Diary Have students write several diary entries that might have been written by someone involved in the building of the Panama Canal. Diary entries might be written by a worker, by a director of the project, by a politician involved with the project, or by someone living in Panama at the time. Students should do additional research into the building of the canal and the controversies surrounding it so that they can include historically accurate concerns and details in their diary entries. *Challenging*

F.Y.I.

This page can help you extend your own and students' understanding of the concepts in this chapter. You may want to browse through some of the suggestions in the **Bibliography**. **Interdisciplinary Links** can connect social studies understandings to areas elsewhere in the curriculum through the use of other Prentice Hall products. **National Geography Standards** reflected specifically in this chapter are listed for your convenience. Some hints about appropriate Internet access are also provided in **Take It to the Net**. **School to Careers** provides insights into the practical uses of some of the concepts in this chapter as they might pertain to various careers.

BIBLIOGRAPHY

FOR THE TEACHER

Ancona, George. *The Piñata Maker: El Piñatero.* Harcourt, 1994.

Nye, Naomi Shihab, ed. *The Tree Is Older Than You Are: A Bilingual Gathering of Poems and Stories from Mexico with Paintings by Mexican Artists.* Simon, 1995.

St. George Judith. *Panama Canal: Gateway to the World.* Putnam, 1989.

Silverthorne, Elizabeth. *Fiesta!: Mexico's Great Celebrations.* Millbrook, 1992.

FOR THE STUDENT

Easy
Herrera, Juan Felipe. *Calling the Doves/El canto de las palomas.* Children's Book Press, 1995.

Average
Lazo, Caroline. *Rigoberta Menchú.* Dillon, 1994.

Challenging
Dolan, Edward F. *Panama and the United States: Their Canal, Their Stormy Years.* Watts, 1990.

Rummel, Jack. *Mexico.* Chelsea, 1990.

LITERATURE CONNECTION

Casteñada, Omar S. *Among the Volcanoes.* Lodestar, 1992.

Moeri, Louise. *The Forty-Third War.* Houghton, 1989.

Strasser, Todd. *The Diving Bell.* Scholastic, 1992.

INTERDISCIPLINARY LINKS

Subject	Theme: Transitions
MATH	Middle Grades Math: Tools for Success *Course 1*, Lesson 9-8, **Proportions and Changing Dimensions**
SCIENCE	Science Explorer *Cells and Heredity*, Lesson 5-1, **Darwin's Voyage**
LANGUAGE ARTS	Prentice Hall Literature *Bronze*, **Tenochtitlán, Barrio Boy** *Copper*, **Señor Coyote and the Tricked Trickster**

NATIONAL GEOGRAPHY STANDARDS

Students explore the 18 National Geography Standards throughout Latin America. Chapter 4, however, concentrates on investigating the following: standards 1, 2, 3, 4, 5, 6, 8, 9, 10, 11, 12, 13, 14, 18. For a complete list of the standards, see the *Teacher's Flexible Planning Guide.*

SCHOOL TO CAREERS

In Chapter 4, Exploring Mexico and Central America, students learn about issues important to the peoples of Mexico, Guatemala, and Panama. Additionally, they address the skill of previewing. Understanding issues of other countries can help students prepare for careers in economics, politics, education, and business.

Previewing is particularly useful for actors, human resource workers, researchers, secretaries, and others. The curriculum presented in this book, as in all eight titles of Prentice Hall's *World Explorer* program, is designed to prepare students not only for careers but also for good citizenship—of the world as well as of this country.

Take It to the NET

Many social studies teachers and students use Internet browsers, or search engines, to investigate particular topics. For the best results, use narrow rather than broad topics. Try these for Chapter 4: ladinos, Panama Canal, Quiché Maya. Finding age-appropriate sites is an important consideration when using the Internet. For links to age-appropriate sites in world studies and geography, visit the *World Explorer* companion Web site at:
http://www.phschool.com

Connecting to the Guiding Questions

As students complete this chapter, they will focus on the countries of Mexico, Guatemala, and Panama. A compelling issue—migration to cities, the status of the indigenous people, or the operation of the Panama Canal—provides a starting point for study. Content in this chapter corresponds to two Guiding Questions:

● How has Latin America been shaped by its history?

● How has geography influenced the ways in which Latin Americans make a living?

Using the Map Activities

Point out to students the shape of Mexico and Central America. Encourage students to trace the outline of the region, while describing its funnel shape.

• seven; the Pacific Ocean and the Caribbean Sea

• Mountain ranges and rivers helped divide Central America.

Heterogeneous Groups

The following Teacher's Edition strategies are suitable for heterogeneous groups.

Critical Thinking
Recognizing Cause and Effect   p. 87

Interdisciplinary Connections
Math   p. 100

Exploring Mexico and Central America

SECTION 1
Mexico
ONE FAMILY'S MOVE TO THE CITY

SECTION 2
Guatemala
DESCENDANTS OF AN ANCIENT PEOPLE

SECTION 3
Panama
WHERE TWO OCEANS MEET

Look at the map above. Notice that the shape of Mexico and Central America is like a funnel, wide at the top and narrowing to a point. To learn more about this region, complete the following activities.

Study the map
How many countries are there in Central America? What bodies of water do they border?

Consider the geography
Mexico is a large country, while the countries of Central America are small. How do you think geography helped divide Central America into small countries?

Resource Directory

Media and Technology

Case Study: Cleaning up the Air in Mexico City, from the World Video Explorer, enhances students' understanding of one of the major consequences of urbanization and what Mexico City is doing to meet this challenge.

Chapter 6

Mexico

ONE FAMILY'S MOVE TO THE CITY

BEFORE YOU READ

Reach Into Your Background

Have you ever moved from one house to another or from one city to another? Did you have to change schools? Think about what the move was like and make a few notes about how you felt at the time.

Questions to Explore

1. Why have many Mexicans been moving from the countryside to the city?

2. What challenges do Mexicans from the country face when they build new lives in the city?

Key Terms

squatter
plaza
migrant farmworker

Key Places

Mexico City

Ramiro Avila (rah MEE roh ah VEE lah) is one of seven children. He grew up in the state of Guanajuato (gwah nuh HWAH toh), in central Mexico. In his small village, Ramiro knew everyone and everyone knew him.

Ramiro's family were campesinos who owned no land. Even as a young child, Ramiro had to work to help support the family. He and his father had jobs as farm laborers. They worked on someone else's farm. They made less than a dollar a day.

The Move to Mexico City

Ramiro's village is located in the southern part of the Mexican Plateau. This area has Mexico's best farmland. It also is home to more than half of the country's people. Not surprisingly, it is the location of Mexico's largest city—Mexico City. Find Mexico City on the map on the previous page.

When Ramiro was 13, his parents decided to move the family to Mexico City. They hoped to find better work. The city was far away and their lives would be completely different. But moving offered them a chance to make a decent living.

Mexico's Urban and Rural Population

More and more people are moving to cities in Mexico. **Chart Study** Turn to the Regional Database at the back of this book to find Mexico's total population. About how many Mexicans live in urban areas? About how many live in rural areas?

25%

75%

☐ Rural
☐ Urban

Source: Dorling Kindersley World Desk Reference

---

2 Explore

Have students read the section. Then discuss with them life in rural Mexico, identifying characteristics of that life that lead people to move to cities. Point out that new problems arose when Ramiro's family moved. Ask students to list things Ramiro might like about living in the country and things he might like about living in the city.

3 Teach

Have students create a cause-effect chart based on information in the section. Direct students to list causes such as the following: family cannot earn enough in the country; family could not afford house in the city; Mexico's population rising dramatically; Mexico's cities growing quickly. For each cause, ask students to write at least one effect. Use their completed charts as a springboard for a discussion of possible solutions to the problems of Mexico's cities. This activity should take about 20 minutes.

Answers to...

MAP AND CHART STUDY

(a) central
(b) 14.5 percent
(c) Mestizo

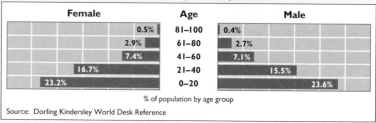

COUNTRY · PROFILE

Mexico: Population

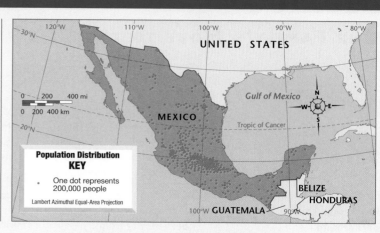

Ethnic Groups

- Other 9%
- European 16%
- Mestizo 55%
- Indigenous Indian 20%

Source: Dorling Kindersley World Desk Reference

Population Distribution KEY
One dot represents 200,000 people
Lambert Azimuthal Equal-Area Projection

Population by Age Group and Sex

Female	Age	Male
0.5%	81–100	0.4%
2.9%	61–80	2.7%
7.4%	41–60	7.1%
16.7%	21–40	15.5%
23.2%	0–20	23.6%

% of population by age group

Source: Dorling Kindersley World Desk Reference

Take It to the NET
Data Update For the most recent data on Mexico, visit **www.phschool.com**.

Culture The map and charts above present information about the population of Mexico. **Map and Chart Study** (a) Which area in Mexico is the most densely populated? (b) What percentage of the population is between the ages of 41 and 60? (c) What is the largest ethnic group in Mexico?

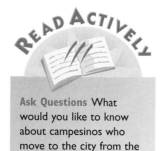

READ ACTIVELY

Ask Questions What would you like to know about campesinos who move to the city from the countryside?

Housing in the City Like thousands of other campesino families coming to the city, Ramiro's family did not have much money. When they arrived in Mexico City, they could not afford a house. They went to live in Colonia Zapata, which is one of many neighborhoods where poor people become **squatters.** That means they settle on someone else's land without permission. Many small houses of squatters cling to the sides of a steep hill in the Colonia. The older houses near the bottom of the hill are built of concrete. However, most people cannot afford to make sturdy houses when they first arrive. Therefore, many of the newer houses higher up the hill are constructed of scrap metal.

Ramiro's family made a rough, one-room house of rock. Ramiro felt that his new house was ugly. He and his family hoped that soon they would be able to buy land from the government. Then they could build a real house with a garden and a patio.

Resource Directory

Program Resources

Nystrom Desk Atlas

Media and Technology

Social Studies Skills Tutor CD-ROM builds core social studies skills through interactive lessons and provides skill assessment.

World Video Explorer See the Mexico case study for an overview of Mexico's history, economy, government, and culture. Discussion questions are included.

Passport to the World CD-ROM This interactive CD-ROM allows students to explore each region of the world. Students view regional videos, take a photo tour, and explore a historical time line. Students record their travels in an Explorer's Journal, and receive passport stamps when they pass regional tests.

Work and School Ramiro went to school in Mexico City, but he also worked as a cook in a tiny restaurant. He started work at 7 A.M. and worked until 2 P.M., preparing scrambled eggs and sausage. For these seven hours of work he earned about $3. His mother and some of his brothers and sisters worked, too. Ramiro went to a school that held night classes, attending classes until 9:30 at night.

Ramiro's father could not get a job in Mexico City. He decided to go to Texas in the United States. He found work as a farm laborer there. He sent money home every month. The move to Mexico City brought a lot of responsibilities for Ramiro. It became his job to look after his younger brothers and sisters while his father was gone. Ramiro's life was very different from how it had been in his village.

Life in Rural Mexico

Before Ramiro's family moved, they lived in a village where life has changed little over the years. Every village has a church and a market. At the center of most villages is a public square called a **plaza.** Farm families grow their own food. If they have extra food, they sell it at the market. Rural people buy nearly everything they need—clothing, food, toys, housewares—at the market rather than in stores.

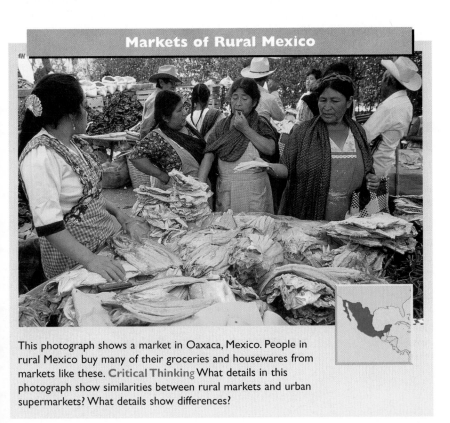

Markets of Rural Mexico

This photograph shows a market in Oaxaca, Mexico. People in rural Mexico buy many of their groceries and housewares from markets like these. **Critical Thinking** What details in this photograph show similarities between rural markets and urban supermarkets? What details show differences?

4 Assess

See answers to the Section Review. You may also use students' completed charts as an assessment.

Acceptable charts include one factually correct effect for each cause.

Commendable charts include two additional effects for last two causes.

Outstanding charts show that an effect can, in turn, become a cause for another effect.

Background

Links Across Place

Economics and Migration When money and jobs are scarce, people often move in search of work. Thousands of Irish immigrants came to the United States in the 1840s and 1850s because the Great Potato Famine in Ireland left potato farmers and others with no food and no money. In this century, thousands of black Americans moved from the South to the North in the 1910s and 1920s in search of jobs.

Answers to...

MARKETS OF RURAL MEXICO

• Responses may vary. Possible answer: Food is being sold at each location. The management of rural stalls is similar to the produce section of a grocery store. Differences include the rural markets are open-air and different products are sold by different vendors.

SKILLS MINI LESSON

Using Distribution Maps
To **introduce** the skill, point out to students that if they walk two miles through a crowded city, they are likely to see more people than if they walk two miles through farmland. Tell students that a distribution map is a special-purpose map that presents this kind of information.

Direct students' attention to the population distribution map in the Country Profile. Help students **practice** the skill by asking them to describe the dot pattern they see on the map. Have them discuss how the dot pattern helps them visualize how many more people live in central Mexico than live farther south. Ask students to explain how they could use the map to locate Mexico City.

Global Perspectives

Earthquakes in Urban Centers Although the volcanoes that ring Mexico City are dormant, the land is still seismically active. One of Mexico's most destructive earthquakes occured in Mexico City in 1985. Other cities that lie on earthquake faults include San Francisco; Tokyo, Japan; and Katmandu, Nepal.

Daily Life

Cooking Mexican Food A popular Mexican dish, *chiles en nogada,* consists of breaded chili peppers stuffed with ground meat and pine nuts and covered by a sweet walnut sauce. This dish combines both Aztec and Spanish influences.

Farm Work Most farm families in Mexico and Central America are poor. Many campesinos work their own small farms. They often plow the land and harvest their crops by hand because they cannot afford expensive equipment. **Migrant farmworkers** do not own land. Like Ramiro and his father, they work on large farms owned by rich landowners. Migrants travel from one area to another, picking the crops that are in season.

Lack of Jobs Mexico's population has risen dramatically over the last 20 years. The country's population is growing at a rate of more than two percent each year—one of the highest rates in the world. There is not enough farm work for so many people. A large family cannot support itself on a small farm. And there are not enough jobs for all the migrant workers. Many people move to the cities because they cannot find work in the countryside.

Much of Mexico's urban population lives in Mexico City. If you count the people in the outlying areas, Mexico City has nearly 20 million people. It is one of the largest cities in the world.

Mexico City: A Megacity

Mexico City is huge. Its population sprawls over a large area. It is a megacity, an urban center where many of Mexico's people live. Unlike most big cities, Mexico City does not have many skyscrapers and major streets. Two- and three-story buildings still form its downtown. Only a

READ ACTIVELY

Predict What problems might occur as more people move into a city?

Mexico: Volcanoes and Earthquake Faults

Map Study Earth's crust is made up of many large plates. Usually, earthquakes occur and volcanoes erupt along earthquake faults, places where two plates collide or pull apart. Many parts of Mexico have had earthquakes and volcanic eruptions. Volcanic ash makes much of Mexico's soil rich and fertile. **Movement** Compare this map with the one in the Country Profile. Do many Mexicans live near volcanoes? Name one reason why someone might want to live near a volcano.

KEY
— Earthquake fault
● Earthquake
▲ Volcano

Lambert Conformal Conic Projection

The Growth of Mexico City

Map Study Mexico City covers more than twice the land that it did in 1945. **Interaction** How do you think the challenges of living in a city might be different from the challenges of living in a rural area?

KEY

City limits, 1945

City limits, 1995

Lambert Azimuthal Equal-Area Projection

0   5   10 mi
0   5   10 km

Lake Zumpango

Lake Texcoco (dry)

Activity

Critical Thinking

Recognizing Cause and Effect *Suitable as a whole class activity.* Discuss with students the causes of air pollution in Mexico City and the geographic features that contribute to it. Have students create a diagram that shows the process. Diagrams should start with causes and show how they lead to effects. Diagrams should also show how effects can then become causes. *Visual*

few streets are wide enough for the city's traffic. The subway, the underground railroad system, carries thousands of people each day.

Small neighborhoods of very wealthy people are tucked away from the rest. But most of Mexico City's residents are not wealthy. They live in all areas of the city. The poorest, like Ramiro and his family, live on the outskirts. Some must travel several hours a day to get to their jobs and back.

Pollution and Geography   Because the cities have grown so large, Mexico's capital and other large cities in the region are facing problems of pollution and traffic jams. Four million cars and trucks jam Mexico City's narrow streets. They compete with taxis, trolleys, and buses. Mexico City's location traps pollution close to the city. The city spreads across a bowl-shaped valley. The mountains surrounding the valley stop winds from carrying away factory smoke, automobile exhaust fumes, and other pollution. The pollution creates smog. It hangs over the city like a black cloud.

Making a Living   Large cities offer many ways to make a living. Factories and offices employ millions of people. Thousands more sell goods from stalls in the street. Ramiro's sister, Carmela, is a street vendor. She sells juice at a stand in the bus station near their neighborhood.

LINKS ACROSS TIME

Tenochtitlán—A Clean City Tenochtitlán, the Aztec capital, did not have a pollution problem. In fact, the first Europeans to visit Tenochtitlán were amazed at how clean the city was. At least 1,000 workers cleaned and swept the city's streets. Clean water was piped in from springs. At the time, European cities did not have fresh, clean water.

SKILLS MINI LESSON

Writing for a Purpose To **introduce** this skill, point out to students that we use different kinds of writing for different purposes. Indicate that songs and poems are ideal for expressing feelings. Encourage students to **practice** the skill by writing a poem or song lyrics that explain how Ramiro might have felt about moving to Mexico City. Encourage students to rely on facts from the text to support the imagined feelings. Invite volunteers to read their poems or lyrics to the class.

Answers to...

MAP STUDY

• Accept any reasonable answer. Students should support their answer with evidence given in the photograph.

1. (a) people who settle on someone else's land without permission (b) a public square in the center of a Mexican village (c) farmworkers who travel with the seasons and the crops to work on large farms

2. megacity in Mexico, where many Mexicans live.

3. to find jobs

4. Answers may vary. Possible answers: People have to find or create housing when they move to the city. They may live without running water or electricity. Some children work part of the day. It may take hours to get to and from jobs.

5. Answers may vary. Possible answer: The lives of rural Mexicans improve because they may find some work and can support themselves and their families. Their lives are difficult in that they must work very hard. They live in poor housing and spend many hours a day getting to and from work.

6. Students' journal entries will vary but should contrast their own lives with that of Ramiro.

Answers to...

SMOG OVER MEXICO CITY

- Pollutants from traffic and industry are part of smog. These pollutants are trapped by the air inversion caused by the city's valley location. Accept any reasonable discussion of how smog might affect how people live.

Smog Over Mexico City

Even on a sunny day, buildings a few blocks away appear dim and blurry in Mexico City because of smog. **Interaction** Why do you think Mexico City has so much smog? How do you think the smog affects the way people in Mexico City live?

Every morning, she gets up at 5:30 to make juice from oranges and carrots. People on their way to work buy her juice for their long trip into the city.

Mexico City is not the only city that is growing. All of Mexico's major cities are becoming more crowded. City life is not easy for most Mexicans. Hard work and hope are what keep people going.

SECTION 1 REVIEW

1. Define (a) squatter, (b) plaza, (c) migrant farmworker.

2. Identify Mexico City.

3. What is the main reason that rural people from all over Mexico have been moving to the cities?

4. What difficulties do rural people face when they move to Mexico City?

Critical Thinking

5. Expressing Problems Clearly How do the lives of rural Mexicans improve when they move to the city? How do their lives continue to be difficult?

Activity

6. Writing to Learn Write an entry in your journal comparing and contrasting Ramiro's life with your own. How are your lives different? What similarities do you notice?

Resource Directory

Teaching Resources

Section Quiz in the Chapter and Section Resources booklet, p. 56, covers the main ideas and key terms in the section. Available in Spanish in the Spanish Chapter and Section Resources booklet, p. 35.

Guatemala

DESCENDANTS OF AN ANCIENT PEOPLE

Lesson Objectives

1. Describe the indigenous people of Guatemala.

2. Discuss how Guatemala's indigenous people have been mistreated.

3. Describe how indigenous people in Guatemala survived civil war and gained a voice in their government.

BEFORE YOU READ

Reach Into Your Background

Have you ever felt that you had an important opinion about something, but no one was listening to it? What are some ways that people can voice their opinions?

Questions to Explore

1. How are the indigenous people of Guatemala a unique culture?

2. What are the main issues that indigenous people face?

3. What kinds of changes have been taking place in Guatemala recently?

Key Terms

ladino
ethnic group
political movement
strike

Key Places

Guatemala

Lesson Plan

1 Engage

Warm-Up Activity

Ask students to imagine that one day soldiers come to all the houses in their neighborhood and order the people to leave. Prompt the discussion by asking, *How would you feel? What would you do?* Have students try to imagine what life is like in a country where such actions really happen.

Activating Prior Knowledge

Have students read Reach Into Your Background in the Before You Read box. Student responses will vary. Ask students to share their ideas with the class.

Juanita Batzibal (wahn EE tah baht zee BAHL) had a childhood "like all Indian girls, at the side of my mother, making tortillas and learning to weave and embroider." Juanita is Guatemalan, and was born in the town of Patzun (paht ZOON). She is also Cakchiquel (kahkt chee KAHL), which is one of many Mayan groups in Guatemala. The mountains of Juanita's homeland are beautiful. But Juanita's family was poor. Though her family raised corn on a tiny plot of land, they could not earn enough money to survive. Juanita had to weave throughout her childhood to bring in extra money. She hoped to go to school one day. She remembered, "My big dream was to study economics or literature…."

▼ Most Mayas who live in the highlands of Guatemala have only small plots of land to farm.

The Struggle for Land

Juanita's childhood home was in the mountains of Guatemala. This southern neighbor of Mexico is "first" in Central America in many categories. For example, it has the largest population among Central American countries. To learn more about Guatemala, study the Country Profile on the next page.

Teaching Resources

📁 **Reproducible Lesson Plan** in the Chapter and Section Resources booklet, p. 57, provides a summary of the section lesson.

📁 **Guided Reading and Review** in the Chapter and Section Resources booklet, p. 58, provides a structure for mastering key concepts and reviewing key terms in the section. Available in Spanish in the Spanish Chapter and Section Resources booklet, p. 36.

Media and Technology

💿 📼 **Making a Living: Farming in Central America,** from the World Video Explorer, enhances understanding of how the region's physical geography combines with unique farming methods to contribute to the success of farming.

Chapter 7

2 Explore

Direct students to read the section. Next, ask them to explain who the indigenous people of Guatemala are and what happened to them. Review how various people and groups became involved in fighting for rights for campesinos and other indigenous people in Guatemala. How have different groups tried to bring about peace? Conclude the discussion by reviewing students' ideas about how groups can make sure that all opinions are heard and considered. Have students identify people from the text who found ways to express their ideas and concerns.

3 Teach

Have students create posters showing who the indigenous people of Guatemala are and how they are trying to reshape their lives after civil war. Remind students to use facts from the section to support their work. Use completed posters as the basis for a discussion on the future of Guatemala. This activity should take about 20 minutes.

Answers to ...
MAP AND CHART STUDY

(a) The land in southern Guatemala is used mostly for raising livestock.
(b) almost $550 million

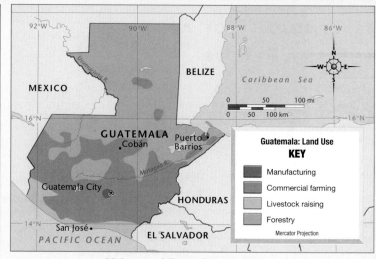

COUNTRY · PROFILE

Guatemala: Land Use and the Economy

Guatemala City

Urban and Rural Population

41%   59%

Source: Dorling Kindersley World Desk Reference

Culture The map and charts show information about land use, population, and economics in Guatemala. **Map and Chart Study** (a) What is the land in southern Guatemala used for? (b) How much money does Guatemala earn from the exporting of coffee?

Income from Exports, 1999

Exports	Income
Coffee	
Sugar	
Bananas	

Source: Food and Agriculture Organization of the United Nations   ⬭ $50 million

Take It to the NET
Data Update For the most recent data on Guatemala, visit **www.phschool.com**.

Most Mayas lived in the mountains because it was the only land available to Native Americans. Most land in Guatemala belongs to a few rich families. The rich landowners of Guatemala are **ladinos** (luh DEE nohs), mestizos who are descended from Native Americans and Spaniards. Native Americans who follow European ways are also considered to be ladinos.

Though families like Juanita's worked hard to make their land produce crops, they often failed. The soil of the Guatemalan highlands is not very good, and soil erosion is a serious problem there. The Mayas have had many challenges to overcome.

Resource Directory

Teaching Resources

📁 Reading a Circle Graph in the **Social Studies and Geography Skills** booklet, p. 55, provides additional skill practice.

📖 **Section Reading Support Transparencies** provide answers to the Questions to Explore in a graphic organizer format.

Media and Technology

💿 **Social Studies Skills Tutor CD-ROM** builds core social studies skills through interactive lessons and provides skill assessment.

Losing Their Homes During most of Juanita's childhood, there was a civil war going on in Guatemala. The Mayas were caught in the middle. Indigenous people do not always think of themselves as citizens of the country in which they live. A Mayan woman is more likely to think of herself as a Maya than as a Guatemalan.

Also, most Native Americans in Guatemala cannot read or write. Most Mayas have not filed any papers with the government showing that they own land. The Mayas often have no way to prove that their land belongs to them. Mayan people worked hard for many years to grow crops. But then the civil war and landowners caught up with them.

In hundreds of villages throughout Guatemala, soldiers came to challenge the Mayas. Sometimes the landowners sent them to claim the Mayas' land for themselves. Other times, they just wanted to exert control over the Mayas by taking away their land and possessions from them.

Mayan survivors from these villages have similar stories to tell. Most of them lost all of their belongings and were forced out of their villages. Many Mayas had to move to other countries to live. Juanita, for example, had to start her life over again in Costa Rica.

LINKS ACROSS THE WORLD

The Sami The Sami live in the far north of Norway, Sweden, Finland, and Russia. The governments of these countries consider the Sami their citizens. Most Sami, however, look upon themselves as part of a separate nation. In recent years, the Sami have won some degree of self-government. The Sami of Norway, for example, have their own elected assembly.

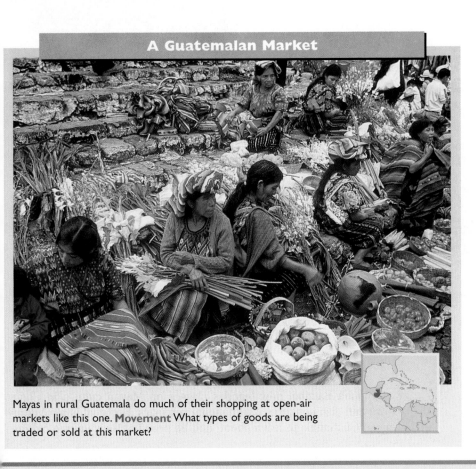

A Guatemalan Market

Mayas in rural Guatemala do much of their shopping at open-air markets like this one. **Movement** What types of goods are being traded or sold at this market?

Program Resources

📁 **Outline Maps** Central America and the Caribbean political map

Another Guatemalan Hero
Justo Rufino Barrios (1835–1885) served as president of Guatemala from 1873 to 1885. Barrios strengthened local government. Under his administration, education improved, roads were built, and employment figures rose. Barrios hoped that someday the countries of Central America would unite to form a strong political force.

Colorful Clothing

Mayan communities each have their own hand-woven style of clothing. **Critical Thinking** What skills do you think are needed to weave cloth into a certain pattern?

CITIZEN HEROES

Overcoming Obstacles
Justina Tzoc travels through rural Guatemala, teaching Quiché Maya women about their rights and teaching them to read. Her work is dangerous, because she sometimes travels through areas that are torn by civil war. But Tzoc is determined to help every woman she can reach.

A 500-Year-Old Struggle Juanita's story is a common one. The indigenous people of Guatemala have fought against injustice for 500 years. They started when the Spanish first arrived.

The Spanish conquered Native Americans by force. Many were killed. Others died of hunger or the hardships of slavery. Still others died from European diseases. In many Latin American countries, there are few indigenous people left.

But in Guatemala, Native Americans are the majority of the population. They form 23 ethnic groups. An **ethnic group** is a group of people who share the same language, ancestors, culture, or religion. The indigenous groups of Guatemala are related to each other. However, each group is different. Each has its own language and customs. Juanita is Cakchiquel Maya; the largest group is the Quiché Maya.

The Peace Process in Guatemala

Juanita Batzibal now teaches classes on Mayan culture in Costa Rica, and also conducts international seminars. Her goal is for Mayas inside Guatemala to learn about and be proud of their unique culture

Take It to the NET

Prentice Hall's *World Explorer* companion Web site offers activities for exploring geographical, historical, and cultural resources on the Internet. It also provides online links for key content, data updates, and all chapter review activities.

The **Teacher site** provides teachers with ideas for student research and activities. It also presents *eTeach*, a monthly discussion with Master Teachers.

Students can use the **Student site** to find chapter-by-chapter Internet resource links, data updates, and Self-Tests.

http://www.phschool.com

and traditions. In her words, "We want to write with our own hands and speak with our own mouths what we feel."

Other Mayas have started **political movements**, which are large groups of people who work together to defend their rights or to change the leaders in power. One such movement, called Nukuj Akpop (noh KOOHJ ahk POHP), is striving to fight poverty and bring human rights to Mayas. Their Founding Declaration states, "Our cries, pain, and woe from the last several hundred years have begun to end, and now we can begin to listen to our own voices."

Some Mayan political movements seek to defend campesino rights. People involved in these movements help villages plan ways to protect themselves. They teach people the history of their land and how to read. They also help organize meetings, protests, and **strikes**, or work stoppages. Above all, they are determined to defend Native American land rights.

All of these efforts have brought about change in Guatemala. For the first time, Mayas have gained a voice in their own government. For example, Guatemala's government appointed 21 Mayan priests to advise officials about Mayan culture. New Mayan organizations are being formed every day. In addition, Mayan languages are being used in books, newspapers, and radio programs.

In 1996, a number of agreements were signed in Guatemala, paving the way for peace. Among these was a promise that indigenous communities would be rebuilt. However, the agreements are only one step toward real peace. It is up to the people of Guatemala—both ladino and Mayan—to make sure that equality and justice are carried out. As one Guatemalan points out, "The war was difficult. But I think the next phase, the building of the peace, will be even harder."

READ ACTIVELY

Ask Questions What questions would you like to ask a member of a Mayan political organization about his or her activities?

SECTION 2 REVIEW

1. **Define** (a) ladino, (b) ethnic group, (c) political movement, (d) strike.

2. **Identify** Guatemala.

3. How does Juanita Batzibal describe her childhood?

4. How do most indigenous people in Guatemala make a living? What difficulties do they face?

Critical Thinking

5. **Identifying Cause and Effect** Explain the main reason that Guatemala's indigenous people and other farmers have formed a political movement.

Activity

6. **Writing to Learn** Write a short essay explaining what you would have done if you were a Mayan villager during the civil war. Then, explain what you would do if you were the president of Guatemala.

Previewing a Reading Selection

Lesson Objectives

❶ Explain the process of previewing.

❷ Apply previewing to a reading selection.

Lesson Plan

1 Engage

Warm-Up Activity

To **introduce** the skill, write the word *preview* on the chalkboard. Ask students to name the prefix and the word that form the word *preview*. (pre-, view) Have a volunteer suggest a meaning for the word based on the root word.

Activating Prior Knowledge

Ask students how they decide which television program to watch, which CD to buy, or what to order at a restaurant. Have them discuss how previewing might help them make a decision.

Sean asked his mom if he could go for a bike ride before it got dark. His mom said, "Sure, if you finish your homework first." Sean didn't have much homework. "If I can finish it in an hour," Sean thought to himself, "I'll have a whole hour for a killer mountain bike adventure."

He settled down to study. His assignment was to answer ten questions about the Panama Canal using two books he had checked out from the school library. He read the first question: "What are three obstacles workers faced when building the Panama Canal?" He picked up the first book and began reading on page 1. Five pages and 10 minutes later he didn't have his answer. He tried the other book. Ten pages and 20 minutes later he still hadn't found what he was looking for. "Half an hour gone and not one question answered!" he thought, disgustedly. "No bike ride tonight!"

Sean missed out on his bike ride because he forgot to apply an important skill: previewing. Previewing means looking over a book or chapter before you read it or try to find information in it. Previewing is a valuable study skill that will help you read more efficiently.

Get Ready

How do you preview? You might be surprised to learn that this is one skill you already know! If you've ever seen a preview for a movie, you've "previewed" that movie. You have a gen-

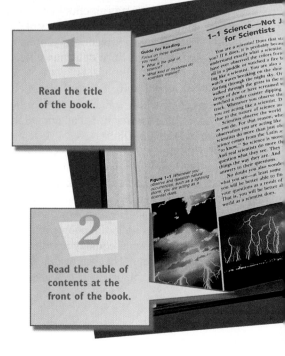

1
Read the title of the book.

2
Read the table of contents at the front of the book.

eral idea what the movie is about. If you've ever looked over a menu, you've "previewed" your meal. You have a general idea of what the food will be like.

Of course, previewing a reading selection is a little different from previewing a movie or meal. Previewing means looking over something you are about to read in a general way to become familiar with it. The idea is to get a "sense" of the material. To get a sense of what a book is about, you can use five things: the title, the table of contents, the illustrations, the index, and sample paragraphs. To do this with a chapter, you can use titles, subtitles, illustrations, and captions.

Resource Directory

Teaching Resources

📁 **Social Studies and Geography Skills** Previewing the Headings and the Pictures, p. 68

Media and Technology

💿 **Social Studies Skills Tutor CD-ROM** builds core social studies skills through interactive lessons and provides skill assessment.

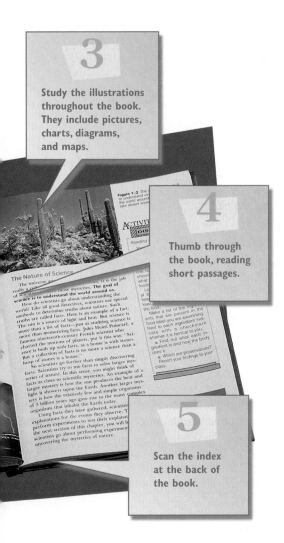

3 Study the illustrations throughout the book. They include pictures, charts, diagrams, and maps.

4 Thumb through the book, reading short passages.

5 Scan the index at the back of the book.

Try It Out

You can practice previewing a book in a fun and easy way by playing a "What Does It Tell Us?" game with a group of six students. Choose your group members, and choose a book. Then sit down and preview it together. Your group will follow the script to the right. After each person reads his or her part to the group, the other group members should work together to answer the question. Group Member 6 is the group secretary, who writes the answers down.

Group Member 1: "The title indicates the main subject of the book. Many books have a subtitle that gives even more information. What does the title of our book tell us?"

Group Member 2: "The table of contents is like a menu at a restaurant. It tells us what general topics are available in the book. What does the table of contents tell us?"

Group Member 3: "The illustrations in a book provide clues to the subjects discussed in the book. What do the illustrations tell us about the book?"

Group Member 4: "The index lists the specific topics in a book and the pages where they are discussed. What does the index tell us about the content of our book?"

Group Member 5: "By thumbing through a book and reading a few paragraphs here and there, you can get an idea of how a book is written. You can see if there are special headings in the book. What does a little reading tell us about our book?"

When you've completed this process, use the secretary's notes to find specific information in the book. If you are going to read the whole book, this process can help you get the most out of your reading.

Apply the Skill

Now that you know how to preview, practice by previewing Chapter 4. What do the titles and subtitles tell you about the chapter? How about the illustrations and captions? Take notes as you preview the chapter. Then, use your notes to write a short description of the chapter. Finally, as you read through the chapter, see how it matches your description.

2 Explore

Direct students to read the text under the heading Get Ready. Then have them read the rest of the skills activity. Ask each of five volunteers to list one part of a book they can use for previewing. (title, table of contents, illustrations, index, and sample paragraphs)

3 Teach

Organize students into groups of six. Have students **practice** the skill by directing groups to play the game What Does It Tell Us? as described in Try It Out. Suggest that student groups pool their answers and then create a class list of them.

4 Assess

Have students **apply** the skill by previewing the chapter. Have students use their notes to write no more than three sentences that they think describe the chapter. To **assess,** evaluate students' sentences, as well as their notes indicating what the titles, subtitles, illustrations, and captions reveal about the chapter.

Section 3

Panama

WHERE TWO OCEANS MEET

BEFORE YOU READ

Reach Into Your Background

Have you ever agreed to a deal or given away something and then wondered if you made the best choice? Think about how you felt. Write down some ways you might try to undo the deal.

Questions to Explore

1. What geographic and political factors made Panama a good site for a canal?

2. How was the Panama Canal built?

3. How did Panama gain control of the Panama Canal?

Key Term
lock

Key Places
Panama Canal
Canal Zone

The Panama Canal is the shortcut of the Western Hemisphere. It's the only way to get from the Pacific Ocean to the Atlantic by ship without going all the way around South America. That's a savings of 7,800 miles (12,553 km).

But be prepared to wait. Traffic jams can leave you bobbing in the ocean for up to 20 hours. Then the trip through the 40-mile (64.4-km) canal takes another eight hours. That's about walking speed. Then there is the toll: as much as $34,000.

Going Through the Canal

Cruising through the Pacific Ocean, a tanker approaches the city of Balboa, in the country of Panama. It is heading for the Panama Canal. The ship is loaded with petroleum. Other ships sailing toward the canal carry lumber, metal ores, and other cargo. Ships pass through the Panama Canal 24 hours a day, 365 days a year. The canal is crowded. The tanker must get in line.

The tanker enters the canal at sea level. But parts of the canal go through mountains and are not at sea level. The tanker will need to be raised and lowered several times as it travels toward the Atlantic Ocean.

Miraflores Lock The ship sails north to Miraflores (mee ruh FLOR uhs) Lock. A **lock** is a section of waterway in which ships are raised or lowered by adjusting the water level. The tanker passes through a set of gates into a lock chamber. The water in the chamber is still at sea level. Then, more water comes pouring into the chamber

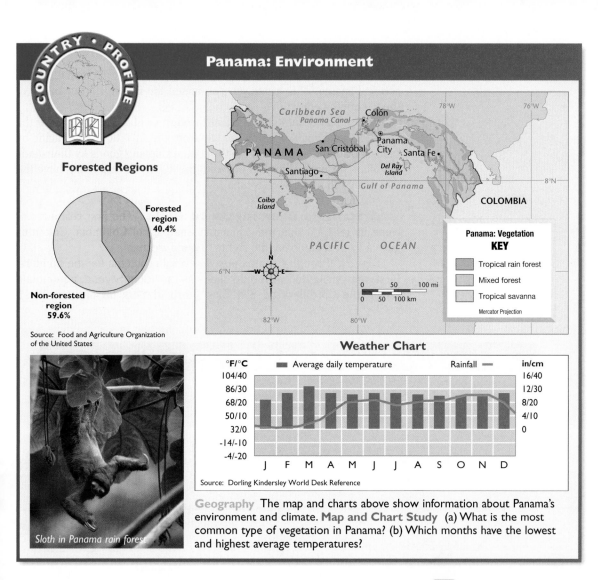

Panama: Environment

Forested Regions

Forested region 40.4%

Non-forested region 59.6%

Source: Food and Agriculture Organization of the United States

Panama: Vegetation
KEY
- Tropical rain forest
- Mixed forest
- Tropical savanna

Mercator Projection

0   50   100 mi
0 50 100 km

Sloth in Panama rain forest

Weather Chart

°F/°C — Average daily temperature — Rainfall — in/cm

°F/°C		in/cm
104/40		16/40
86/30		12/30
68/20		8/20
50/10		4/10
32/0		0
-14/-10		
-4/-20		

J F M A M J J A S O N D

Source: Dorling Kindersley World Desk Reference

Geography The map and charts above show information about Panama's environment and climate. **Map and Chart Study** (a) What is the most common type of vegetation in Panama? (b) Which months have the lowest and highest average temperatures?

---

through valves. The tanker rises like a toy boat in a bathtub filling with water. When the water rises high enough, the ship passes through a second set of gates and enters a small lake. It proceeds to the next lock, and the water level is raised again.

Galliard Cut During the voyage, the tanker will pass through two more sets of locks. It will zigzag through the eight-mile (13-km) Galliard (GAL yurd) Cut. The Galliard Cut was blasted through the hard rock of Panama's mountains. The tanker will sail through a huge artificial lake and past an island that is home to a wild game preserve. Finally, eight hours after entering the canal, the tanker exits at Limón (lih MOHN) Bay in the city of Colón (kuh LOHN). It has traveled only 40 miles (64 km), but it is now in the Atlantic Ocean.

Take It to the NET
Data Update For the most recent data on Panama, visit www.phschool.com.

Program Resources

📁 **Outline Maps** Central America and the Caribbean: Political, p. 9

Media and Technology

💿 **Social Studies Skills Tutor CD-ROM** builds core social studies skills through interactive lessons and provides skill assessment.

4 Assess

See answers to the Section Review. You may also use students' news reports as an assessment.

Acceptable reports include suitable facts from the text.

Commendable reports may include appropriate opinions, supported by facts.

Outstanding reports draw reasonable conclusions about the topic.

Background

Global Perspectives

Canals Change the World
Other canals have significantly changed countries and world travel. For example, the Erie Canal, completed in 1825, changed American history. The canal linked Chicago, Detroit, and Buffalo to the Atlantic Ocean. The resulting industry made the Midwest a magnet for settlement by immigrants. In the Middle East, the Suez Canal—connecting the Mediterranean Sea to the Red Sea and the Indian Ocean—opened in 1869. The canal greatly shortens the distance between Europe and Asia.

Answers to ...
MAP STUDY

- Responses may vary but should indicate that both countries wanted to profit from control of the Canal Zone and the United States wanted a faster route for its ships.

The Idea for a Canal Takes Hold

Look at the map on this page and trace the route the canal follows across Panama. This waterway dominated life in Panama for much of the twentieth century.

Sailors had dreamed of a canal through Central America since the 1500s. A canal could shorten the trip from the Atlantic to the Pacific by thousands of miles. It would cut the cost of shipping goods by thousands of dollars for each ship. But not until the 1900s did engineers have the technology to make such a canal.

A Struggle Over Rights to Build The first real attempt came in 1881. At that time, Panama was part of Colombia. Colombia gave a French company the rights to build a canal.

Digging through Panama posed several problems for the builders. First, they struggled with mud slides as they dug. Second, a mountain range, the Cordillera de San Blas (kord ul YEHR uh day san blas),

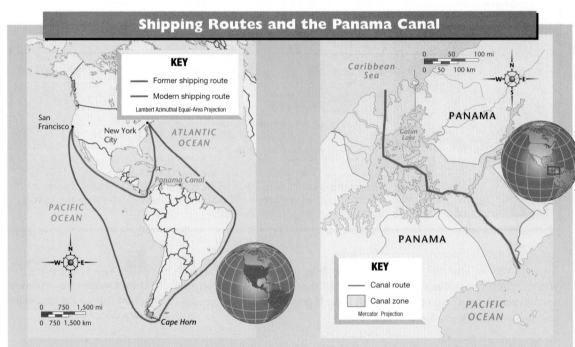

Shipping Routes and the Panama Canal

KEY
—— Former shipping route
—— Modern shipping route
Lambert Azimuthal Equal-Area Projection

San Francisco
New York City
ATLANTIC OCEAN
Panama Canal
PACIFIC OCEAN
Cape Horn
0 750 1,500 mi
0 750 1,500 km

Caribbean Sea
0 50 100 mi
0 50 100 km
PANAMA
Gatún Lake
PANAMA
PACIFIC OCEAN

KEY
—— Canal route
☐ Canal zone
Mercator Projection

Map Study The map on the left shows shipping routes from New York to San Francisco before and after construction of the Panama Canal. The map on the right is a close up of the Panama Canal route. Before the Panama Canal was built, ships had to travel more than 13,000 miles (20,900 km) around South America. After the canal was built, ships only had to travel 5,200 miles (8,370 km). **Movement** Why do you think that Panama and the United States both wanted to control the Canal Zone?

Panama's Tropical Rain Forest

Panama's Barro Colorado rain forest is inside the Canal Zone. **Critical Thinking** This photograph shows a trail through the rain forest. Where is it? Based on this photograph, think of some difficulties that might have faced the Panama Canal workers.

blocked the way. Disease was also a problem. Much of Panama is covered with dense tropical forest. Tropical diseases such as malaria and yellow fever killed many workers. After several years of digging and blasting, the French company went bankrupt. Work on the canal stopped.

In 1902, the United States government bought what was left of the French company. Then, the United States began talks with Colombia about getting the rights to continue building a canal.

Colombia refused to grant the United States rights to build the canal. The businesspeople of Panama were disappointed. They knew that a canal would bring business to Panama. They wanted the canal to be built as soon as possible. Also, many Panamanians wanted to be free of Colombia's rule. They saw the canal as a chance to win independence.

In November 1903, the United States helped Panama revolt against Colombia. Two weeks after Panama declared its independence, the United States received the rights needed to build the canal.

LINKS ACROSS THE WORLD

Not Made in Panama You would assume the "Panama hat," a hand-woven straw hat, is made in Panama. However, you would be wrong—the hats were originally made in Ecuador. They were named for Panama because it was a shipping center for hats in the 1800s. Ecuadorans still make the Panama hat. But today, many hats are made even farther from Panama—in Asia.

The cut through Panama's soft earth hills was the hardest part of the canal to build. Earth still slides into the canal there today. **Movement** Based on the picture on the left, how were workers and supplies moved to and from the canal?

Interdisciplinary Connections

Math Have students use their knowledge of math applications to answer the following questions.

1. If it takes 8 hours for a ship to pass through the canal, how many miles per hour does a ship average? (40 miles in 8 hours = 5 miles per hour)

2. What fraction of the total time it took to build the canal was spent in controlling the mosquito problem? Make a circle graph to show the fraction. (1/8)

READ ACTIVELY

Predict How do you think workers overcame problems to build the Panama Canal?

Building the Canal
The builders of the canal faced numerous problems. They had to scoop out and remove mountains of earth and rock. The hills were made of soft earth. Whenever the diggers carved out a hole, more earth would slide into its place. The project called for a dam to be built to form a lake. There were locks to design and build.

While the work was difficult and slow, by far the biggest problem facing the project was disease. Some 25,000 workers had died of malaria and yellow fever while the French worked on the canal. Scientists did not know what caused these diseases, so they could do little to prevent them.

In the early 1900s, doctors discovered that malaria and yellow fever were both carried by mosquitoes. The mosquitoes bred in swamps and also in people's drinking water. In 1904, the Panama Canal Company hired a doctor and a large crew to deal with the mosquito problem. It took one year, 1,000 tons (907 metric tons) of timber, 200 tons (181 metric tons) of wire mesh, and 4,500 workers to do the job. Workers burned sulfur in every house to kill mosquitoes. They covered

Answers to ...
LIKE DIGGING THROUGH SAND

- railroad

every water vessel with mesh so mosquitoes could not get in. They filled in swampy breeding grounds with dirt. Without this effort, the Panama Canal probably could not have been built.

Modern medicine and machinery were important to the project. So was good planning. Still, it took eight years and the sweat of 45,000 workers, mostly Caribbean islanders, to make the waterway. The Panama Canal remains one of the greatest engineering feats of modern times.

Control of the Canal

When the United States gained rights to build a canal, it signed a treaty with Panama. The treaty gave the United States the right to build the Panama Canal, and to control it forever.

The Canal Zone The United States also controlled an area called the Canal Zone. The Canal Zone included the land on either side of the canal, the ports, the port cities, and the railroad. The treaty allowed the United States to run the Zone according to its laws, and gave the United States the right to invade Panama to protect the canal.

Many Panamanians felt this was too high a price to pay for the privilege of having the canal in their country. The canal gave the United States a great deal of power in Panama. The United States built 14 military bases in the Canal Zone and stationed thousands of soldiers there.

For years, Panama talked with the United States about regaining control of the canal. In the 1960s and 1970s, many Panamanians grew angry. They rioted to protest U.S. control.

A Change of Ownership In 1978, after years of talks, U.S. President Jimmy Carter signed two new treaties with Panama's government. The Panama Canal Neutrality Treaty and the Panama Canal Treaty gave Panama more control over the canal. In 1999, Panama finally gained full control of the Panama Canal.

Ask Questions What would you like to know about life near the Canal Zone?

SECTION 3 REVIEW

1. **Define** lock.

2. **Identify** (a) Panama Canal, (b) Canal Zone.

3. How did a canal come to be built in Panama?

4. What difficulties did the builders of the canal face?

5. How did the United States gain control of rights to build the canal?

6. Two sets of treaties have determined the control of the Panama Canal, the original treaty of 1903 and two in 1978. Describe the terms of these treaties.

Critical Thinking

7. **Identifying Central Issues** It was very important to Panamanians to regain control of the canal. Explain why, in both political and economic terms.

Activity

8. **Writing to Learn** Imagine that you are a newspaper editor in 1900. Decide whether you think Panama or Nicaragua is a better choice for the location of the canal, and write a short editorial defending your position.

SKILLS MINI LESSON

Expressing Problems Clearly
To **introduce** the skill, tell students that expressing a problem clearly can help them find possible solutions to the problem. Help students **practice** the skill by having small groups choose the point of view of either the United States or Panama. Work with them to express clearly what the problems were. Have them list positive and negative effects of relinquishing control of the canal. You may want to have groups debate the issue.

Chapter 4 Review

Reviewing Main Ideas

1. Many Mexicans move from one rural area to another and from rural to urban areas in search of work, so they can earn money to support their families.

2. Many people live in makeshift houses made out of scrap metal or even rock. Transportation and air pollution are major problems, too.

3. The indigenous cultures consist of Native Americans, who try to maintain their traditional ways. Ladinos, many of whom are rich landowners, follow European ways.

4. Indigenous Guatemalans are struggling to hold on to their land and to assure that equal rights are guaranteed in their country.

5. The United States supported and aided the Panamanian revolt against Colombia. The Panamanians signed a treaty with the United States, giving it the right to build and control the canal.

6. (a) important to United States for economic and defense reasons; important to Panamanians to have control in their own country and gain economic benefits (b) Panama gained ownership of the canal in 1999.

Reviewing Key Terms

1. c	3. a	5. b
2. f	4. e	6. d

Critical Thinking

1. Answers may vary. Sample answer: Mayan political movements want to force the government and landowners to change. They want indigenous people to own land and live there peacefully. They seek equal rights for all and an end to racism against indigenous people.

2. Answers may vary. Sample answer: The Panama Canal shows that the United States had nearly unlimited power in Central America; the United States helped Panama become independent, then took part of the country under its own control. The United States seems to be relinquishing its influence in the area, as evidenced by letting go of control of the canal.

Review and Activities

Reviewing Main Ideas

1. Describe the movement of Mexicans from one area to another—rural to rural, rural to urban. Why do many people make these moves?
2. What problems has Mexico City experienced as a result of its rapid population growth?
3. How are the indigenous cultures of Guatemala distinct from the ladino culture?
4. What are the main challenges that indigenous Guatemalans face?
5. How did the United States gain the rights to build a canal in Panama?
6. (a) Why was the canal important to the United States and Panama?
   (b) How did control of the canal recently change?

Reviewing Key Terms

Match the definitions in Column I with the key terms in Column II.

Column I

1. a landless person who travels from one area to another working other people's land
2. a section of a waterway in which ships are raised or lowered by adjusting the water level
3. a person who settles on someone else's land without permission
4. a work stoppage
5. a public square
6. people who share race, language, religion, and cultural traditions

Column II

a. squatter
b. plaza
c. migrant farmworker
d. ethnic group
e. strike
f. lock

Critical Thinking

1. **Identifying Central Issues** What are the main demands that Mayas have made of the government and landowners? How has the government responded?
2. **Drawing Conclusions** Over the years, the United States has exercised a great deal of economic and political influence in Central America. How does the history of the Panama Canal demonstrate U.S. influence in the region? What do you think the changes that took place over the control of the canal say about U.S. influence in the region today?

Graphic Organizer

Copy the tree map onto a piece of paper. In the first set of boxes, note the three kinds of population movement. In the second set, note details about these movements.

Graphic Organizer

Population Movements in Mexico

Poor people move from rural to urban areas.	Some Mexicans move to the United States.	Population movement to cities is increasing.
They make more money but live in substandard housing. Children work to earn money for family. Workers spend hours traveling to and from work.	They work as migrant laborers. They send money home to families.	There is not enough housing. Air pollution is a problem because of cars and factories. Cities are spread out, and transportation can be a problem.

Map Activity

For each place listed below, write the letter from the map that shows its location.

Mexico and Central America: Place Location

1. Guatemala

2. Colón, Panama

3. Panama

4. Mexico City

Writing Activity

Writing News Stories Imagine you are a writer for a radio news program. Write brief news stories on population movements in Mexico, the work of political movements, and the history of the Panama Canal. Be sure that each of your stories can be read in two to three minutes.

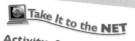

Take It to the NET

Activity Compare what children learned in ancient and modern-day Mexico to what you learn in school. For help in completing this activity, visit www.phschool.com.

Chapter 4 Self-Test To review what you have learned, take the Chapter 4 Self-Test and get instant feedback on your answers. Go to www.phschool.com to take the test.

Skills Review

Turn to the Skill Activity. Review the steps for previewing. Then use these steps to preview Chapter 5. Based on your preview, write a brief paragraph describing what you expect to read in the chapter.

How Am I Doing?

Answer these questions to help you check your progress.

1. Can I explain why a Mexican family might decide to leave the countryside for the city?

2. Do I understand the major challenges that face the indigenous peoples of Guatemala?

3. Can I describe the building of the Panama Canal and its impact on the Panamanian people?

4. What information from this chapter can I include in my journal?

 ### Take It to the NET

Students may wish to use the Internet to search for similar topics or activities. Suggest possible search terms, such as "ancient Mexico" or "Mexico education."

Guide students to a search engine. Four of the most useful are Infoseek, AltaVista, Lycos, and Yahoo. For additional suggestions on using the Internet, refer to the Prentice Hall Social Studies' Educator's Handbook "Using the Internet," in the *Prentice Hall World Explorer* Program Resources.

For chapter-by-chapter links to age-appropriate sites in world studies and geography, including Self-Tests, visit the *World Explorer* companion Web site at: **http://www.phschool.com**

How Am I Doing?

Point out to students that this checklist is just a quick reminder for them of what they learned in the chapter. If their answer to any of the questions is *no* or if they are unsure, they may need to review the topic.

Map Activity

1. B		3. D	
2. C		4. A	

Skills Review

Students' paragraphs will vary. Sample response: The chapter will tell about life in the Caribbean countries of Cuba, Haiti, and Puerto Rico. The chapter will describe communism in Cuba and the people who live there. The country of Haiti has struggled to be a democracy. Puerto Rico, a commonwealth of the United States, has ties to the U.S. mainland and to the Caribbean.

Writing Activity

Students' news stories will vary, but should contain the main ideas of each section.

Resource Directory

Teaching Resources

Chapter Tests Forms A and B are in the Tests booklet, pp. 20–25.

Program Resources

Writing Process Handbook includes Limiting a Topic, p. 15, to help students with the Writing Activity.

Media and Technology

Color Transparency 172 (Graphic organizer tree map template)

Computer Test Bank CD-ROM

Resource Pro® CD-ROM

Prentice Hall Assessment System

Making a Model Canal Lock

The Panama Canal cuts a stunning 7,800 miles (12,553 km) off the distance a ship would have to travel from New York to San Francisco.

The canal could not work without locks. Canal locks are huge chambers filled with water that raise and lower ships.

The Panama Canal needs locks because the sea level at the Atlantic and the Pacific entrances to the canal is not the same. Also, the path of the canal is not level—it goes up one slope to the continental divide and down the other.

Purpose

The best way to understand how canal locks work is to build a model of one. As you complete this activity, you will understand how a real ship travels through a real canal.

Materials

- two half-gallon cardboard juice or milk cartons
- modelling wax
- scissors
- duct tape
- a ballpoint pen
- a cork
- a paper clip
- a pitcher of water

Procedure

STEP ONE

Construct a model canal and lock. Follow the illustrations. Cut the cartons in half lengthwise. Line up three of the four halves lengthwise and connect them on the outside with duct tape. Then carefully cut out the walls of cardboard that separate the boxes and divide your canal. Line three edges of each cut-out wall with modelling wax. Then replace the walls. Use

STEP THREE
both gates in
cork

STEP FOUR
first gate is out
cork

both gates in
cork

cork
second gate is out

both gates in
cork

enough wax to make a watertight seal. These are the gates in the canal lock.

STEP TWO

Use the pen, cork, and paper clip to make a model ship. Look at the picture for an example. Stick the paper clip into the bottom of the ship to make it float upright.

STEP THREE

Fill your canal with water. Fill one end and the middle of the carton with water about one inch deep. Fill the other end with water almost to the top. Float your boat in the end of the canal with the lower water level.

STEP FOUR

Operate the canal lock to raise your ship to the higher water level. Remove the gate that separates your ship from the middle chamber. Sail your ship into the middle chamber and close the gate behind it by carefully replacing it. To raise your ship to the next level, slowly pour water into the middle chamber until the water level matches the level in the last chamber. Remove the second gate, sail your ship into the last chamber, and replace the gate. You have successfully navigated a canal!

Observations

1. How did you raise your ship from one level to a higher level?

2. Why does the canal lock need gates to work?

ANALYSIS AND CONCLUSION

1. How do you think the water level is raised in a real lock?

2. Repeat the activity in reverse. How will you lower your ship?

2 Explore

Have students read through the Activity Shop before they begin to follow its directions. Tell students that many of today's ships are too large to pass through the locks of the Panama Canal. At least one company has investigated the possibility of building a new canal through Nicaragua. Ask students to look at the Latin America political map in the Activity Atlas and speculate on the route of such a canal. Ask students to list some of the problems involved in building such a canal.

3 Teach

You might build and display the model as a class project. Organize the class into groups. Assign one group to collect the materials for the cork boat and to construct it. Tell another group to collect the milk cartons, cut and connect them. A third group can line the cartons with wax and make the gates. Choose students to fill the canal with water and to operate the gates.

Before students fill the model canal, cover the surface and floor with newspaper in case of spills. If there is a leak, ask students what would happen if an actual canal lock sprung a leak.

4 Assess

Ask students to revise their paragraphs explaining how a canal lock operates. Invite several students to read their revisions to the class.

Answers to...

OBSERVATIONS

1. raised the water level
2. to separate different levels of water

ANALYSIS AND CONCLUSION

1. The water is pumped in.
2. Take water out of the lock.

Exploring
the Caribbean

To help you plan instruction, the chart below shows how teaching resources correspond to chapter content. Use the resources to vary instruction, add activities, or plan block schedules. Where appropriate, resources have **suggested time allotments** for students. Time allotments are approximate.

Managing Time and Instruction

	Latin America Teaching Resources Booklet		World Explorer Program Resources Binder	
	Resource	mins.	Resource	mins.
1 SECTION 1 Cuba Clinging to Communism	**Chapter and Section Support** Reproducible Lesson Plan, p. 69		**Outline Maps** Central America and the Caribbean:	
	⑤ Guided Reading and Review, p. 70	20	Political, p. 9	20
	⑤ Section Quiz, p. 71	25	**Nystrom Desk Atlas**	
	⌐ Section Reading Support Transparencies	15	⊤ **Primary Sources and Literature Readings**	40
SKILLS ACTIVITY Locating Information	**Social Studies and Geography Skills,** Using your Textbooks, p. 94	30		
	Using the Library, p. 95	30		
2 SECTION 2 Haiti The Road to Democracy	**Chapter and Section Support** Reproducible Lesson Plan, p. 72		**Outline Maps** Central America and the Caribbean:	
	⑤ Guided Reading and Review, p. 73	20	Political, p. 9	20
	⑤ Section Quiz, p. 74	25		
	⌐ Section Reading Support Transparencies	15		
3 SECTION 3 Puerto Rico Cultural Identity of a People	**Chapter and Section Support** Reproducible Lesson Plan, p. 75		**Outline Maps** Central America and the Caribbean:	
	⑤ Guided Reading and Review, p. 76	20	Political, p. 9	20
	⑤ Section Quiz, p. 77	25	**Writing Process Handbook**	
	Critical Thinking Activity, p. 82	30	Proofreading, p. 37	20
	⑤ Vocabulary, p. 79	20		
	Reteaching, p. 80	25		
	Enrichment, p. 81	25		
	⑤ Chapter Summary, p. 78	15		
	⌐ Section Reading Support Transparencies	15		
	Tests Forms A and B Chapter Tests, pp. 26–31	40		

Block Scheduling Program Support

- Block Scheduling Booklet — PROGRAM RESOURCES BINDER
- Activities and Projects
- Interdisciplinary Links
- Resource Pro® CD-ROM
- Media and Technology
- Pacing Charts Booklet — PROGRAM RESOURCES BINDER

Media and Technology

Resource	mins.
◼️⫶ Ⓢ World Video Explorer	20
⬒ Color Transparency 66	20
⫶ Resource Pro® CD-ROM	30
⫶ Presentation Pro CD-ROM	20
⫶ Social Studies Skills Tutor CD-ROM	30
⬒ Color Transparency 66	20
🎧 Ⓢ Guided Reading Audiotapes	20
⬒ Color Transparency 174 (Graphic organizer table template)	20
⫶ Computer Test Bank CD-ROM	30
🎧 Student Edition on Audio CD	30
⫶ Passport to the World CD-ROM	30

From Guiding Questions to Assessment A series of Guiding Questions serves as an organizing framework for this book. The Guiding Question that relates to this chapter is listed below. Section Reviews and Section Quizzes provide opportunities for assessing students' insights into this Guiding Question. Additional assessments are listed below.

GUIDING QUESTIONS

- *How has Latin America been shaped by its history?*
- *What types of government exist in Latin America today?*

ASSESSMENTS

Section 1

Students should be able to write a paragraph describing what life in Cuba is like today.

▶ **RUBRIC** See the Assessment booklet for a rubric on assessing a writing assignment.

Section 2

Students should be able to describe how Haiti's struggle for democracy affected people's lives.

▶ **RUBRIC** See the Assessment booklet for a rubric on assessing cause-and-effect statements.

Section 3

Students should be able to create a concept web of the factors that have influenced Puerto Rican culture.

▶ **RUBRIC** See the Assessment booklet for a rubric on assessing graphic organizers.

Prentice Hall Assessment System allows you to:
- Diagnose and Prescribe
- Review and Reteach
- Practice and Assess

Key

🅣	Teaming Opportunity well-suited for teaching teams	⫶	CD-ROM
Ⓢ	Spanish This resource is also in Spanish support.	⫶	Laserdisc
		⬒	Transparency
		◼️	Videotape
		🎧	Audiotape/CD

Activities and Projects

Mental Mapping

Sea Cruise Ask students to imagine that they are planning a cruise through the Caribbean. Have them suggest islands they would like to visit.

Then ask students to pair up. One student in each pair will locate islands they would like to visit and work out an itinerary for the order in which they would visit the islands. Then ask them to provide the compass directions for getting from one island to the other.

The other student in each pair will use the directions provided by the first student to navigate through an unlabeled outline map of the Caribbean. Using the itinerary and directions provided by the first student, the second student will label islands on the map. Students may then reverse roles.

At the end of the activity, both students will check their own map against a published map to evaluate the accuracy of the directions and their ability to follow them.

Links to Current Events

Foreign Policies Tell students that although Cuba, Haiti, and Puerto Rico are in the same region and fairly close to each other, the United States has very different relationships with each one.

Divide the class into three large groups. Assign one of the three countries to each group. Have each student in each group use the library to look for some event in the history of the relationship between the United States and their country. They should work together to avoid duplicating the same events.

Each student should write the date and a description of the event on an index card. The groups can then arrange their index cards along a time line.

Hands-On Activities

Sorting Help students distinguish among islands, countries, cities, and continents by writing those categories on the chalkboard.

Invite students to take turns walking to the front of the room to read a label from a wall map. Another student will decide in which category the label belongs.

Every student should have the chance to suggest a name and choose a category. This activity should be performed briskly, with some of the quality of a relay race. You may want to provide time limits for placing names into categories. Emphasis should be placed on cooperative efforts and the performance of the class as a whole, however, rather than on the ability of individual students.

Once everyone has had a chance at each type of action, have students work together to determine whether the names were properly categorized.

Compare and Contrast Have students visit a travel agency or look at travel magazines for information and descriptions of a Caribbean country. Have them list descriptions used in travel literature. Then ask them to compare and contrast those descriptions with information they find in a nonfiction book that describes the geography, history, economy, and culture of the same country. Encourage students to discuss the reasons for the differences and similarities they find. *Average*

Get to Know Someone Ask students to write a letter that could be sent to a potential pen pal in Cuba, Haiti, or Puerto Rico. As they work on their letters,

suggest they think about what they would want to tell a student in one of these countries about themselves. Urge them to list several questions they might have about their pen pal, and the pen pal's country as well. *Basic*

A Nation of Immigrants Tell students that there are communities of immigrants from Cuba, Haiti, and Puerto Rico in different parts of the United States. Ask them to research one of these immigrant groups to answer questions such as: What led (or leads) people to come to the United States from this country? What problems do they encounter in getting here? What problems do they have settling

here? What parts of the country are they most likely to live in? What festivals and customs do they bring with them when they come to the United States? *Challenging*

Make a Collage Have students make a picture collage poster of images they associate with one of the countries in this chapter. Encourage students to include pictures that illustrate the geography, history, culture, and economy of the country they are depicting. Students may clip pictures from old magazines or brochures or create the pictures themselves. *English Language Learners*

F.Y.I.

This page can help you extend your own and students' understanding of the concepts in this chapter. You may want to browse through some of the suggestions in the **Bibliography**. **Interdisciplinary Links** can connect social studies understandings to areas elsewhere in the curriculum through the use of other Prentice Hall products. **National Geography Standards** reflected specifically in this chapter are listed for your convenience. Some hints about appropriate Internet access are also provided in **Take It to the Net**. **School to Careers** provides insights into the practical uses of some of the concepts in this chapter as they might pertain to various careers.

BIBLIOGRAPHY

FOR THE TEACHER

Ada, Alma Flor. *Where the Flame Trees Bloom.* Atheneum, 1994.

Aliotta, Jerome J. *The Puerto Ricans.* Chelsea, 1995. (Immigrant Experience series)

Sheehan, Sean. *Jamaica.* Cavendish, 1993.

FOR THE STUDENT

Easy
Dorros, Arthur. *Isla.* Dutton, 1995

Average
Hoobler, Thomas. *Toussaint L'Ouverture.* Chelsea, 1990.

Challenging
Hauptly, Dennis J. *Puerto Rico: An Unfinished Story.* Atheneum, 1991.

Temple, Frances. *Taste of Salt: A Story of Modern Haiti.* Orchard, 1992.

Temple, Frances. *Tonight, By Sea.* Orchard, 1995.

LITERATURE CONNECTION

Mohr, Nicholasa. *Going Home.* Dial, 1986.

Taylor, Theodore. *The Cay.* Doubleday, 1969.

INTERDISCIPLINARY LINKS

Subject	Theme: Identity
MATH	Middle Grades Math: Tools for Success *Course 1*, Lesson 8-8, **Congruent and Similar Figures** *Course 3*, Lesson 2-11, **Scientific Notation**
SCIENCE	Science Explorer *Chemical Building Blocks*, Lesson 3-1, **Organizing the Elements** *Electricity and Magnetism*, Lesson 1-1, **Nature of Magnetism**
LANGUAGE ARTS	Prentice Hall Literature *Bronze*, **I am a Native of North America, Amigo Brothers**

NATIONAL GEOGRAPHY STANDARDS

Students explore the 18 National Geography Standards throughout Latin America. Chapter 5, however, concentrates on investigating the following: standards 1, 3, 5, 6, 9, 10, 11, 12, 13, 17, 18. For a complete list of the standards, see the *Teacher's Flexible Planning Guide.*

SCHOOL TO CAREERS

In Chapter 5, Exploring the Caribbean, students learn about the different political systems of Cuba, Haiti, and Puerto Rico. Additionally, they address the skill of locating information. Understanding different political systems can help students prepare for careers in politics, economics, business, sociology, and so on. Information locating skills are particularly useful for writers, researchers, real estate agents, employment counselors, teachers, and others. The curriculum presented in this book, as in all eight titles of Prentice Hall's *World Explorer* program, is designed to prepare students not only for careers but also for good citizenship—of the world as well as of this country.

Take It to the NET

Many social studies teachers and students use Internet browsers, or search engines, to investigate particular topics. For the best results, use narrow rather than broad topics. Try these for Chapter 5: Jean-Bertrand Aristide, Cuban exiles, Port-au-Prince, condado. Finding age-appropriate sites is an important consideration when using the Internet. For links to age-appropriate sites in world studies and geography, visit the *World Explorer* companion Web site at:

http://www.phschool.com

CHAPTER 5

Exploring the Caribbean

Connecting to the Guiding Questions

In this chapter, students will read about life in present-day Cuba, Haiti, and Puerto Rico, and identify the reasons behind current changes in economic and political life. Content in this chapter thus corresponds to the Guiding Questions:

● How has Latin America been shaped by its history?

● What types of government exist in Latin America today?

Using the Map Activities

Draw students' attention to the map. Lead a class discussion about how Caribbean nations might get the goods and services their people need.

• Answers should indicate that fishing and shipping would be important.

• Answers should include that islanders traded among themselves, but they did not have boats that could take them to either North or South America.

Heterogeneous Groups

The following Teacher's Edition strategies are suitable for heterogeneous groups.

Cooperative Learning
Create a Play   p. 114
Critical Thinking
Drawing Conclusions   p. 116
Interdisciplinary Connections
Science   p. 115
Language Arts   p. 124

MAP ACTIVITIES

The islands of the Caribbean stretch about 1,500 miles (2,414 km) across blue-green waters. Each island has its own traditions and cultures. To learn more about the Caribbean, complete the following activities.

Understanding geography
How do you think the sea may have affected the economies of the Caribbean islands?

Study the map
Before the Europeans arrived in the region, how do you think the sea may have served as both a highway and a barrier to contact with other people?

Resource Directory

Media and Technology

 Spotlight on: Music of the Caribbean, from the World Video Explorer, enhances students' understanding of how the blending of Indian, European, and African influences have resulted in a unique Caribbean culture.

Chapter 8

Cuba

CLINGING TO COMMUNISM

Lesson Objectives

1 Describe current life in Cuba and relate it to the history of Cuba's governments.

2 Analyze ties of Cuban-Americans to Cuba.

Lesson Plan

1 Engage

Warm-Up Activity

Invite students to imagine that they must leave America and move to another country. Inform them that the new country will have a very different way of life, climate, landscape, language, and set of customs. Direct students to do a quick-write, listing the people and things they would miss most. Have volunteers share their lists. Discuss how they might feel about such changes.

Activating Prior Knowledge

Have students read Reach Into Your Background in the Before You Read box. Students' lists will vary. Record responses on the chalkboard and use them as a springboard for a discussion of feelings about what students would have to leave behind.

Ask students what they know of immigration from their own family histories or from books, movies, or television. Discuss feelings immigrants retain for their place of origin.

BEFORE YOU READ

Reach Into Your Background

Suppose that you had to move tomorrow and you could pack exactly one suitcase. You could never come back for the things you left behind. What would you pack?

Questions to Explore

1. What is life in Cuba like today?

2. What ties do Cuban Americans have to Cuba?

Key Terms

dictator
communist
exile
illiterate

Key People and Places

Fidel Castro
Fulgencio Batista
Miami

Twelve-year-old Venesa Alonso (vuh NEH suh uh LAHN zoh) lives in Miami, Florida. Her home is just a few miles away from the ocean. Venesa hardly ever goes to the beach, however. The blue waves and roaring surf remind her of her trip from Cuba to the United States. The memory still gives her nightmares.

Venesa and her family left Cuba in the summer of 1994. They built a rickety raft and carried it to the ocean. They were among the 35,000 Cubans who took to the sea that summer. They sailed on anything that would float—rubber tires, old boats, and home-made rafts. One hope kept them going. It was the thought of making it to the United States. They planned to apply to enter the United States as immigrants.

Venesa's family and thousands of others left Cuba for two main reasons. The first reason was that Cuba's economy was in bad shape. People often did not have enough food to eat. Clothing, medicine, and other basic necessities were hard to get. A desire for freedom was the second reason why many people left. Cuba's leader, Fidel Castro (fee DEL KAS troh), does not allow Cubans to speak out against government policies they disagree with.

▼ Cubans trying to reach the United States in 1995 took to the sea in boats like this one.

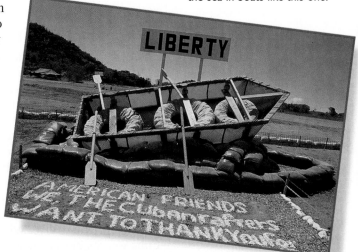

Teaching Resources

📁 **Reproducible Lesson Plan** in the Chapter and Section Resources booklet, p. 69, provides a summary of the section lesson.

📁 **Guided Reading and Review** in the Chapter and Section Resources booklet, p. 70, provides a structure for mastering key concepts and reviewing key terms in the section. Available in Spanish in the Spanish Chapter and Section Resources booklet, p. 43.

🖨 **Section Reading Support Transparencies** provide answers to the Questions to Explore in a graphic organizer format.

Program Resources

📁 Material in the **Primary Resources and Literature Readings** booklet extends content with a selection from the region under study.

📁 **Outline Maps** Central American and the Caribbean: Political, p. 9

2 Explore

Have students read the section. Encourage them to find answers to the following questions as they read: Why did some Cubans leave their country? What ties do they still have to Cuba? Why has it been difficult for them to go back? Direct students to work with partners and draw three waves labeled *1994, 1970,* and *1960*. Inside each wave, have them list the reasons Cubans left their homeland during that time.

3 Teach

Have students create a chart about Cuba with the following column headings: *Before Castro, Under Castro Until 1991,* and *Recent Changes.* Have students fill in the chart with facts from the section. Students may include opinions, but the opinions must be backed by facts. Invite students to use the completed charts as the basis for predictions about the future of Cuba. This activity should take about 20 minutes.

COUNTRY · PROFILE

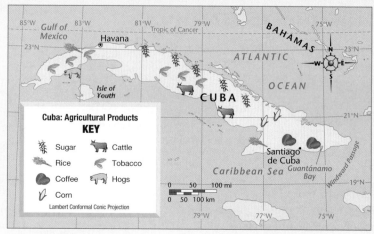

Cuba: Agriculture and the Economy

Cuba: Agricultural Products
KEY

Sugar		Cattle	
Rice		Tobacco	
Coffee		Hogs	
Corn			

Lambert Conformal Conic Projection

Workers cutting down sugar cane plants

Economics The map and charts show information about agriculture and the economy in Cuba. **Map and Chart Study** (a) In which areas of Cuba is sugar cane grown? (b) In what area does more than half of the labor force work? (c) What percentage of Cuba's exports is shipped to Russia?

Major Export Destinations

Japan 6%
Spain 6%
Netherlands 14%
Canada 15%
Russia 17%
Other 42%

Source: Dorling Kindersley World Desk Reference

Labor Force

Agriculture 23%
Industry 24%
Services 53%

Source: CIA World Factbook 2000

Take It to the NET
Data Update For the most recent data on Cuba, visit **www.phschool.com.**

Cuba's History

Cuba is a small country. It is about the size of the state of Pennsylvania. Cuba's farmland is fertile, and Cuba is the third largest sugar producer in the world. Look at the political map in the Activity Atlas in the front of your book. Cuba is located between the two entrances to the Gulf of Mexico. It also has excellent harbors. This makes it a good place to trade with the United States and other parts of the Caribbean. But Cuba's relationship with the United States and many of its neighbors has not been friendly since the 1960s.

Cuban Independence Cuba's government and economy were not always like they are now. Cuba was a Spanish colony. In 1898, the United States defeated Spain in the Spanish-American War, and Cuba won its independence. In the years that followed, Cuba became the richest country in the Caribbean. Sugar planters made money

Resource Directory

Program Resources

Nystrom Desk Atlas

Media and Technology

Social Studies Skills Tutor CD-ROM builds core social studies skills through interactive lessons and provides skill assessment.

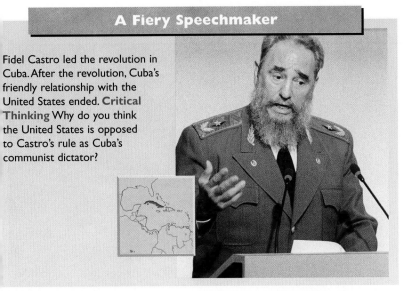

Fidel Castro led the revolution in Cuba. After the revolution, Cuba's friendly relationship with the United States ended. **Critical Thinking** Why do you think the United States is opposed to Castro's rule as Cuba's communist dictator?

READ ACTIVELY

Ask Questions If you could interview Fidel Castro, what questions would you ask him?

4 Assess

See answers to the Section Review. You may also use students' completed charts as assessment.

Acceptable charts include at least four factually correct entries in each column.

Commendable charts show changes in the economy, government, and U.S.-Cuba relations.

Outstanding charts explore the causes for changes in the economy and government.

---

selling to people in the United States. Hotels were built, and tourists came to Cuba to enjoy its beautiful beaches and great climate. Many Cubans became businesspeople, teachers, doctors, and lawyers.

Not all Cubans shared the country's wealth, however. Most farm and factory workers earned low wages. Cuba also had many harsh leaders who ruled as dictators. A **dictator** is a ruler who has complete power. In the 1950s, Fulgencio Batista (fool HEN see yoh bah TEE stah) was Cuba's leader. During his rule, some people formed rebel groups to remove Batista and change the country.

Communism in Cuba A young lawyer named Fidel Castro led one of these small rebel groups. He tried three times to overthrow the government during the 1950s. By his third attempt, he had gained many supporters. Finally, Batista gave up and left the country in 1959.

When Batista left, Fidel Castro took control of Cuba. He still holds power today. Castro's government is **communist.** In a communist country, the government owns all large businesses and most of the country's land. Under Castro, the Cuban government took over private businesses and land. Further, Castro said that newspapers and books could print only information supporting his government. Anyone who disagreed with government policy was put in jail. Huge numbers of Cubans fled the island. Many settled in Miami, Florida.

Cuba became a communist country in the early 1960s. At the same time, it became friendly with the Soviet Union. The Soviet Union was then the most powerful communist nation in the world. It sent money and supplies to Cuba. The United States and the Soviet Union, however, were not friendly. As a result, Cuba's relationship with the United States became tense. Relations grew worse when the United States openly welcomed the people who fled from Cuba.

CITIZEN HEROES

To Be a Leader When José Martí grew up in Cuba in the 1800s, it was still a colony of Spain. At age 16, he started a newspaper dedicated to Cuban independence. Martí later became famous for his poems and essays. In 1895, he led the revolution that eventually liberated Cuba. By the time independence was achieved, however, Martí had died in a battle with the Spanish.

Biography

Fidel Castro (1926–) As a young lawyer in the 1950s, Castro gathered supporters who wanted to end the rule of dictator Fulgencio (Juan) Batista. On July 26, 1953, Castro led a small group in an attack on the Moncada Army barracks in the city of Santiago de Cuba. Castro was captured and spent two years in prison, followed by exile to Mexico. There he organized a small group of revolutionaries who invaded Cuba in 1956. When Batista fled on January 1, 1959, Castro became the head of the new government.

SKILLS MINI LESSON

Reading Tables and Analyzing Statistics As a way to **introduce** the skill, tell students that many important facts about a country can be presented in table form. Help students **practice** the skill by assisting them in finding the following information about Cuba in the Database at the back of the book: Cuba's main agricultural product (sugar); most common ethnic group (white); most common religion (Roman Catholic). Have students **apply** the skill by forming questions whose answers can be found in the table. Direct students to share and answer one another's questions.

Answers to . . .

A FIERY SPEECHMAKER

- Accept any reasonable answer, for example, a communist dictatorship is not democratic.

Journal Writing

Discuss with students how young refugees probably felt as they fled to the United States. What hopes for the future might they have had? Challenge students to write in their journals as if they were one of these young people. If students are keeping an Explorer's Journal as described in the Book Opener, you may wish to do this writing activity as part of that journal.

Cuban Americans Relax in Miami

There is a large Cuban American community in Miami, Florida. These men are playing dominoes in a Miami park. Behind them is a mural showing the presidents of many countries in the Western Hemisphere.

Cubans Leaving Cuba

Lydia Martin left Cuba in 1970. She was only six years old. Her mother had grown tired of the limits on freedom and lack of opportunity in communist Cuba. She wanted to take Lydia to the United States with her. Lydia's father begged her to stay.

"For years [my mother] had been anxious to leave Cuba . . . to take me to a place where I could learn about freedom. Her exit papers had finally arrived, but my father wouldn't let me go. . . . There was no talking sense into a man who feared losing his little girl forever. . . . While my mother was away at the church, I called him.

"I'm leaving with my mother," I told him with all the bravery a six-year-old could muster. . . .

"Have you stopped to think you may never see me again?" my father asked. . . ."

Cuban Exiles Many Cuban exiles tell stories like Lydia's. An **exile** is a person who leaves his or her homeland for another country because of political problems. From the 1960s onwards, large numbers of people left Cuba. Many families were torn apart.

Dreams of Returning to Cuba Some Cubans never got over the loss of their home. In the 1970s, relations between the United States and Cuba grew worse. Even if she wanted to, Lydia Martin could not write to her father. The government might punish him if he got a letter from the United States. Still, Lydia hoped to reunite with him one day. Lydia's mother now spoke of Cuba with longing. She said that in Cuba, the sky was bluer, the sand whiter, and the palm trees greener.

In 1991, the government of the Soviet Union collapsed and could no longer help Cuba. Food, medicine, tools, and other necessities became more scarce. Lydia began worrying about her father and her other relatives. In 1995, she flew back to the island for the first time. Visitors from the United States are not always welcome in Cuba, especially if they once fled the island. Lydia was nervous.

Cuba: Today and Tomorrow

When Lydia stood on the beach in Cuba, she thought of her mother. Her mother had been right. The sky did seem bluer here, the sand whiter, and the palm trees greener.

Lydia had heard about the food shortages in Cuba, but she had not known how bad they were. Her father's new family sometimes had little more than rice to eat. When Lydia unpacked the shoes, soap, powdered milk, and underwear she had brought, her father and his new family took them with joy. They cooked her a delicious meal of lobster and rice on her first night. They had been saving money for it for months.

Livan Hernandez At 21 years old, Livan Hernandez was close to becoming a star pitcher in the Cuban Baseball League. He left Cuba for a chance to make millions of dollars pitching for a major league team in the United States. If that decision sounds easy, consider that Hernandez left behind everyone who is dear to him in Cuba. Hernandez hopes his family can one day enjoy the same freedom he has found.

Background

Links Across Place

Breakup of the Soviet Union Between 1988 and 1991, the Eastern European countries of East Germany, Poland, Hungary, Czechoslovakia, Romania, and Bulgaria broke away from the Soviet Union. The countries shook off their communist political and economic systems. In 1991, the Soviet Union itself began to break up. By 1992, Russia and 10 other former Soviet republics became a commonwealth of independent states.

◀ After Lydia Martin (left) departed from Cuba, she did not see or talk to her father (right) again for 25 years.

Section Review

1. (a) a ruler with complete power (b) government that owns all large businesses and most of the land (c) a person who leaves his or her homeland for another country because of political problems (d) a person unable to read or write

2. (a) present dictator of Cuba (b) Cuban dictator during 1950s (c) place where great numbers of Cuban exiles have settled

3. The lack of Soviet aid to Cuba created shortages of food and other necessities.

4. Answers will vary. Possible answers: dictatorship, no freedom of press or speech, lack of economic opportunity, tense relations with the United States.

5. Student answers should show understanding of how exiles usually maintain strong feelings for their homeland and its language and customs, while the first generation born in the new country is more assimilated.

6. Student letters should be written from the appropriate point of view. Possible content might include family news, life in each country, and a perspective on changes in Cuba and in U.S.–Cuba relations.

Answers to ...
A CUBAN HIGH SCHOOL

- Responses should address similarities or differences, such as school uniforms or desks for two.

A Cuban High School

At many of Cuba's rural schools, students spend four hours in the classroom and four hours doing manual labor. **Critical Thinking** How is this school similar to yours? How is it different?

One thing that Cubans do not need to save money for is education. In the 1960s and 1970s, Castro overhauled Cuba's schools. At the time, many Cubans were **illiterate,** or unable to read and write. Castro sent students and teachers into the countryside to teach. Soon, more Cubans could read and write than ever before. Today, about 96 percent of Cubans can read and write.

Schools in Cuba may have helped many Cubans to learn how to read. However, they teach only communist ideas. But because Cuba is close to the United States, Cubans can tune in to American radio stations. Cuban teenagers listen to popular American dance music. They wear jeans from the United States whenever they can get them. Castro has allowed some businesses to be privately owned. The tourist industry is growing.

No one knows what Cuba's future will bring. Many think the time is near when those who left Cuba will be able to return home to visit or live there in freedom.

SECTION 1 REVIEW

1. Define (a) dictator, (b) communist, (c) exile, (d) illiterate.

2. Identify (a) Fidel Castro, (b) Fulgencio Batista, (c) Miami.

3. How did the collapse of the Soviet Union affect Cuba's economy?

4. What problems did communism bring to Cuba?

Critical Thinking

5. Drawing Conclusions Do you think that Cubans born in the United States feel as strongly about Cuba as their Cuban-born parents do? Why or why not?

Activity

6. Writing to Learn Work with a partner. One of you will write a letter to a relative in Cuba from the point of view of a Cuban exile in the United States. The other will write a response from the point of view of a Cuban who has never left Cuba.

Resource Directory

Teaching Resources

Section Quiz in the Chapter and Section Resources booklet, p. 71, covers the main ideas and key terms in the section. Available in Spanish in the Spanish Chapter and Section Resources booklet, p. 44.

Haiti

THE ROAD TO DEMOCRACY

Reach Into Your Background
Is there something in your life that you have had to try many times to achieve? What strate-gies did you use to try to get what you wanted? Did they work? Why or why not?

Questions to Explore
1. How did Haiti's struggle for democracy affect people's lives?
2. How does the history of Haiti affect the culture of its people?

Key Terms
Creole
dialect

Key People and Places
Jean-Bertrand Aristide
Toussaint L'Ouverture
François Duvalier
Jean-Claude Duvalier
Port-au-Prince

The plane dipped toward Port-au-Prince (port oh PRINS), the capital of Haiti. It flew over a spreading slum. The slum was a neighborhood of crumbling cardboard huts with tin roofs. In the streets, people were jammed into a solid mass. All heads turned up toward the sky.

As if in one voice, a cheer of joy rose from the crowd. In the plane, Haiti's president, Jean-Bertrand Aristide (zhan behr TRAHND uh ris TEED), was returning to his country after a three-year exile. He had been elected by the people, but Haiti's military had forced him to leave. Then, a group of generals had taken over the country. The United States and other nations had pressured the military to give power back to Aristide. Many hoped that Aristide's return would also bring back democracy.

▼ After his exile, Haitian President Jean-Bertrand Aristide returned to Haiti amid cheers of support.

Haiti's Struggle for Democracy

Aristide was the first president to be elected democratically in many years. This does not mean that most Haitians did not want democracy. Their country was born out of a desperate struggle for freedom. Haiti is the only nation in the Americas formed from a successful revolt of enslaved Africans.

Teaching Resources

📁 **Reproducible Lesson Plan** in the Chapter and Section Resources booklet, p. 72, provides a summary of the section lesson.

📁 **Guided Reading and Review** in the Chapter and Section Resources booklet, p. 73, provides a structure for mastering key concepts and reviewing key terms in the section. Available in Spanish in the Spanish Chapter and Section Resources booklet, p. 45.

📖 **Section Reading Support Transparencies** provide answers to the Questions to Explore in a graphic organizer format.

Program Resources

📁 **Outline Maps** Central America and the Caribbean: Political, p. 9

Lesson Objectives

1. Summarize the Haitian struggle for freedom and describe the effects of this struggle on the Haitian people.

2. Examine the influence of Haiti's history on its culture.

Lesson Plan

1 Engage

Warm-Up Activity

Have students try to imagine what it must be like to be poor and live in a country where there is no chance for a better life. Then have them imagine that there is an election. A president is elected who promises better living conditions, improved education, and more freedom. Finally, tell students to consider how they might feel if suddenly the army took over, removing the president from power. Discuss with students how they would feel about their hopes and dreams. Have them describe what they and their families might do.

Activating Prior Knowledge

Have students read Reach Into Your Background in the Before You Read box. Students' description of their attempts to achieve a goal may vary. Listen to their descriptions without judgment. Ask students to recall what they learned about dictatorships from the previous section on Cuba. Prompt students with questions such as *What freedoms are absent in a dictatorship?* (freedom of speech, freedom to dissent, sometimes freedom of religion)

2 Explore

Have students read the section. Indicate that as they read, they will find answers to questions like these: Why have Haitians had to fight over and over again for freedom? Why are most Haitians poor? What is Haitian rural life like? Haitian city life? Why did so many Haitians flee after the military took over? Discuss these questions after students have finished reading.

Activity

Cooperative Learning

Create a Play Organize students into small groups and have each find information about Toussaint L'Ouverture in one reference source. Students can then share information and choose events in his life they would like to dramatize. Each group can produce a scene, working cooperatively to cast roles, improvise dialogue, and stage the action. Conclude by having each group present its scene to the rest of the class. *English Language Learners*

Answers to ...

MAP AND CHART STUDY

(a) Most of Haiti's coastline is dominated by forests.
(b) The percentages are almost equal. Most Haitians who live in rural areas probably work in agriculture.

COUNTRY · PROFILE

Haiti: Land Use and the Economy

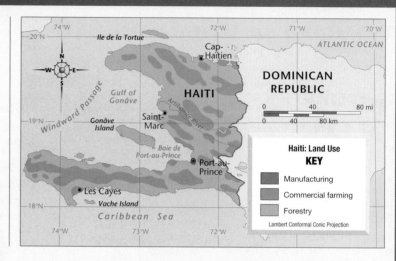

Labor Force

Agriculture 66%
Industry 9%
Services 25%

Source: CIA World Factbook 2000

Haiti: Land Use
KEY
- Manufacturing
- Commercial farming
- Forestry

Lambert Conformal Conic Projection

Urban and Rural Population

32%   68%

Source: Dorling Kindersley World Desk Reference

Economy The map above shows information about land use in Haiti. The charts show information about the economy in Haiti. **Map and Chart Study** (a) How is the land on Haiti's coast primarily used? (b) Compare the percentage of the labor force that works in agriculture with the percentage of the population that lives in rural areas. What conclusions can you draw from this comparison?

Fishermen off the coast of a rural Haitian village

Take It to the NET
Data Update For the most recent data on Haiti, visit **www.phschool.com.**

The Birth of Haiti As you can see on the Country Profile above, Haiti lies on the western third of the island of Hispaniola. Haiti was once a colony of France. Europeans brought enslaved Africans to Haiti to work on sugar cane and coffee plantations. In the 1790s, slave revolts began. A Haitian leader named Toussaint L'Ouverture helped banish slavery from Haiti in 1801. He also offered Haitians a new way of life, based on the idea that all people could live as equals.

Troubled Years In the years that followed, Toussaint L'Ouverture's goal of freedom and equality was never fully realized. Most of Haiti's presidents became dictators once they got into power. One of the worst was François Duvalier (frahn SWAH doo VAHL yay), who took power in 1957. Because Duvalier had been a country doctor, Haitians called him "Papa Doc."

Resource Directory

Media and Technology

Social Studies Skills Tutor CD-ROM builds core social studies skills through interactive lessons and provides skill assessment.

Passport to the World CD-ROM This interactive CD-ROM allows students to explore each region of the world. Students view regional videos, take a photo tour, and explore a historical time line. Students record their travels in an Explorer's Journal, and receive passport stamps when they pass regional tests.

Papa Doc died in 1971. He was followed by his son, Jean-Claude Duvalier (zhan KLAHD doo VAHL yay), or "Baby Doc." Both Papa Doc and Baby Doc were cruel leaders. They stole government funds and used violence to keep power. During their rule, Haiti became the poorest country in the Western Hemisphere.

In 1986, rebels forced Baby Doc to leave the country. Many Haitians thought a period of freedom and prosperity was about to begin. But this was not to be. Haiti was ruled by one military leader after another. And most Haitians still made a living trying to farm small plots of land.

Life on a Farm When farmer Pierre Joseph stands at the top of his land, he can see the calm waters of the Caribbean. When he looks down, he sees the dry, cracked earth of his one acre.

About two thirds of the people in Haiti make their living by farming. The land has been overused. Most trees have been cut. Rains wash the topsoil into the sea. Joseph is thin because he rarely gets enough to eat. "The land just doesn't yield enough," he says. He points to the few rows of corn and beans that he can grow on his one acre.

Farmers like Pierre Joseph can barely make a living, but many feel they are rich in other ways. Haitian culture blends African, French, and West Indian tradition. The blend of traditions gives Haiti a Creole culture. **Creole** is a word referring to people of mixed ancestry.

Creole also refers to the dialect spoken in Haiti. A **dialect** is the different version of a language that is spoken in a particular region. The Creole dialect is based on both French and African languages.

READ ACTIVELY

Connect How do most people in the United States make a living?

Papa Doc and Baby Doc

François (left) and Jean-Claude Duvalier (right) often used violence to rule Haiti. The country also became much poorer during their rule. By the time Baby Doc was forced from power, the average Haitian earned only about $300 a year.

3 Teach

Organize students into four groups of reporters. Each group should cover one of the following topics: (1) what life was like under military rule, (2) reasons why people fled Haiti for the United States, (3) Aristide's plans for a better Haiti. Students should use the information in the text to collaborate on a short report on their topic. This activity should take about 20 minutes.

Activity

Interdisciplinary Connections

Science Have students work in groups to research how land such as Pierre Joseph's can yield larger crops. Have students choose from the following topics: 1) tree-planting to stop erosion, 2) methods of irrigation, 3) improving soil through fertilizers, and 4) help available for farmers from agencies such as the United Nation's UNESCO. Each group should prepare and present a short report. Encourage students to use pictures as well as text to show how farming can be improved.

Take It to the NET

Prentice Hall's *World Explorer* companion Web site offers activities for exploring geographical, historical, and cultural resources on the Internet. It also provides online links for key content, data updates, and all chapter review activities.

The **Teacher site** provides teachers with ideas for student research and activities. It also presents *eTeach*, a monthly discussion with Master Teachers.

Students can use the **Student site** to find chapter-by-chapter Internet resource links, data updates, and Self-Tests.

http://www.phschool.com

4 Assess

See the answers to the Section Review. Assess each group's understanding of the information they presented by the content and clarity of their reports.

Acceptable work covers the main ideas presented in the text.

Commendable work includes further research.

Outstanding work includes some analysis of the causes and effects of events. Save the reports for a "Television News Special."

Activity

Critical Thinking

Drawing Conclusions
Suitable as a whole class activity. Tell students that knowing how to draw conclusions about what they read helps them better understand the text. Explain that to draw a conclusion they must use evidence in the text plus what they already know. Pose the following question: *Why do you think some Haitians tried to come to the United States?* Ask students to draw conclusions about what Haitians hoped to find once they reached the United States. Record their answers on the chalkboard. Then, have them find evidence to support their conclusions in the paragraphs that describe the military takeover.

Answers to ...

A RURAL VILLAGE IN HAITI

• There are only a few houses, but much grass, trees, and dirt roads. Responses should include clues such as palm trees.

Predict Why do you think that Haitians were so glad to see Jean-Bertrand Aristide?

Life in the City Haiti's capital, Port-au-Prince, is a blend not only of cultures, but also of rich and poor. The wealthy live in spacious wooden houses on the hills overlooking the city. There is a small middle class of doctors, lawyers, teachers, and owners of small businesses, that also live fairly well. Many poor people from the country live in tiny homes of crumbling concrete.

Hopes for the Future

In December 1990, Jean-Bertrand Aristide was elected president. Haitians held high hopes for the future. Aristide was a Catholic priest who had long defended the rights of the poor. He took office in February 1991.

A Military Takeover Aristide served as president for seven months. Then Haiti's military forced him to leave the country. The military also attacked his supporters. "We have been in hiding since police shot up our house in October," an Aristide supporter told reporters in 1991. "We got away because people warned us they were coming."

The year after the election, thousands of Aristide supporters fled the capital. They feared for their lives. They squeezed into trucks by the dozen and went to hide in the hills. Others tore their homes apart to make rafts. Then they took to the sea. Many headed for the United States. Some were sent back.

A Rural Village in Haiti

Cange Walthe
age 12
Haiti

This student drawing of rural Haiti contrasts with the urban scene on the next page. **Critical Thinking** What clues does this student provide to show that this village is in a rural area? What clues show that the village is in a place that has a tropical climate?

Dancing in the Streets

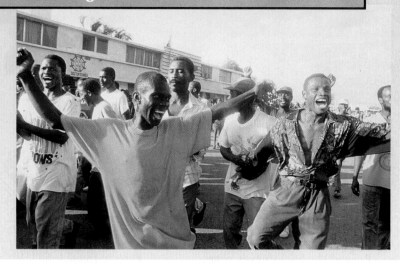

Haiti's people danced in the streets of Port-au-Prince when they heard that Aristide was returning to the country. They hoped that peace would return to Haiti along with Aristide.

Hundreds of children also left Haiti on rafts. Fifteen-year-old Fresenel Pierre (frehz uh NEL pea EHR) was one. He had an older brother waiting for him in Miami, where there is a large Haitian community. The children Fresenel sailed with were the children of Aristide supporters. Many were coming to the United States with no one to take them in.

Good Times and Bad   In 1994, Aristide came back to Haiti, restoring democratic government. Haitians rejoiced, believing that peace and progress would follow. Instead, by 1998, quarreling between Haiti's parliament and its new president, René Préval, had nearly shut down the government. A powerful hurricane struck Haiti that same year, leaving more than 150,000 homeless and destroying precious crops. As a result, Haiti remains the poorest nation in the region. As Aristide took presidential office once again in 2001, the future of Haiti remained uncertain.

SECTION 2 REVIEW

1. Define   (a) Creole, (b) dialect.

2. Identify   (a) Jean-Bertrand Aristide, (b) Toussaint L'Ouverture, (c) François Duvalier, (d) Jean-Claude Duvalier, (e) Port-au-Prince.

3. How did Haiti win its independence?

4. What obstacles to making a living do farmers like Pierre Joseph face?

Critical Thinking

5. Making Comparisons Give an example of how Haitian culture blends African and European traditions.

Activity

6. Writing to Learn   Write a diary entry from the point of view of Pierre Joseph about how economic and political conditions in Haiti affect his life.

Resource Directory

Teaching Resources

Section Quiz in the Chapter and Section Resources booklet, p. 74, covers the main ideas and key terms in the section. Available in Spanish in the Spanish Chapter and Section Resources booklet, p. 46.

Section Review

1. (a) a person of mixed ancestry (b) different version of a language spoken in a particular region

2. (a) president of a democratic Haiti (b) leader who helped banish slavery from Haiti in 1801 (c) and (d) dictators of Haiti (e) capital of Haiti

3. Through a slave revolt in 1790 led by L'Ouverture.

4. Students' responses should identify obstacles such as poor soil, insufficient land, lack of modern machinery, and poverty.

5. Creole, a mix of French and African languages.

6. The diary entry should reflect the point of view of a poor farmer. Students should mention that poverty and environmental disasters keep Joseph from bettering his condition, and previous dictatorships kept him from voting for change. Today, problems in Haiti's government make him unsure about his future.

Lesson Objectives

1 Identify important ways to locate information.

2 Use the skill to seek specific information.

Lesson Plan

1 Engage

To **introduce** the skill, invite a volunteer to read aloud the opening scenario. Ask students what advice they would give Marisol to help her focus and begin her search. Record students' ideas on the board.

Activating Prior Knowledge

Ask each student to write on a sheet of paper a place or resource they have used to successfully find a piece of information. Invite students to share their responses with the class. Use students' responses to compile a class information resource bank.

2 Explore

With students, read the material under the heading Get Ready. Ask students to name some situations in which they have used the skill of locating information. Encourage them to describe both frustrating and rewarding aspects of their search. Then have students read the rest of the skills activity.

Locating Information

Marisol felt like a sailor lost at sea.

She was surrounded by an ocean of information. Shelves overflowing with books towered above her. Beyond the bookshelves, more shelves loomed, filled with magazines. Past the magazines were computer terminals. Enough information to fill millions of pages could be accessed through them. Although she was in her community library, Marisol felt just as lost as if she were adrift in a lifeboat.

Marisol had gone to the library to find information about Toussaint L'Ouverture. Marisol had read in her textbook how L'Ouverture had led the Haitian people to freedom more than 200 years ago. Marisol's assignment was to write a one-page biography, or life story, about L'Ouverture. One question loomed in her mind: Where should she begin?

Get Ready

Locating information is an essential skill. Throughout your school career, you will need to locate information to complete homework assignments and class projects. As an adult, you will need to locate information to help you decide many things such as where to live, what job to do, and how to do it.

The first rule about locating information is *Don't panic!* Marisol felt lost in the library. But libraries and other sources of information are carefully designed to make your search for information as easy as possible. Just like a sailor at sea, it's a matter of choosing your destination, planning your route, and finally sailing to the one little island where the information you need is located.

Try It Out

Locating the information you need can be an exciting adventure. When you locate the information you've been searching for, you will feel

Resource Directory

Teaching Resources

📁 **Social Studies and Geography Skills** Using Your Textbooks, p. 94

Using the Library, p. 95

Media and Technology

💿 **Social Studies Skills Tutor CD-ROM** builds core social studies skills through interactive lessons and provides skill assessment.

the satisfaction and excitement of an explorer who finds the right island. Work with a partner to plan a voyage out into the Sea of Information:

A. Choose your destination. Your destination is the information you need. You and your partner should pick one now, and write it down. It might look like this: *"Destination: Information about how many Cubans live in the United States."*

B. Determine the best way to get there. Just as there are many ways to travel, there are many ways to locate information. Five important routes to information are listed in the box to the right. Discuss each source of information with your partner. Choose the source most likely to have the information you seek.

C. Prepare for your journey. You're about to depart, so pack your bags! You'll need a notebook and a pencil to jot down information. You might need a few coins for the copy machine.

D. Use signposts. Just as signposts can help you find your way on a real journey, different "signposts" can help you on your journey to find information. Read about these "signposts" in the box.

Five Important Routes To Information

Libraries Most of the world's information is stored in libraries. *Signposts:* the card catalog and librarians.

Books There are books about nearly every subject. *Signposts:* book titles and tables of contents.

Periodicals Magazines and newspapers can provide up-to-date information on a huge range of topics. *Signposts:* magazine indexes and newspaper indexes found in libraries.

The Internet The Internet is a worldwide network of computers containing information. *Signposts:* special electronic search indexes on the Internet.

People By interviewing experts, you can learn what they know about their specialties. *Signposts:* the telephone directory to locate appropriate people to interview.

Apply the Skill

Now that you've made an information-seeking journey with a partner, it's time to do it alone. Choose one of the following destinations:

- Destination: Information that identifies the chief agricultural product grown in Cuba.

- Destination: Information that identifies the President of Haiti.

- Destination: Information that identifies three historic sites you could visit in Puerto Rico.

Once you have reached your destination by locating the information, draw a map to show how you found it.

---

3 Teach

Pair students and allow them to carry out the instructions in the Try It Out section. Suggest that students locate additional information about the topics studied in Chapter 5. Review students' choices and help them focus topics that are too broad. Put the class information resource bank at students' disposal.

For additional reinforcement, have students write a question related to Chapter 5 on an index card. Place the cards in a box and allow students to draw a card and locate the information that will answer the question.

4 Assess

Allow students to **apply** the skill by completing the final part of the activity. Suggest that students write down the source or sources they used to find answers. To **assess,** evaluate the accuracy and completeness of students' information.

Answers to...

APPLY THE SKILL

- Cuba's chief agricultural product is sugar. Cuba is the world's largest exporter of sugar. Possible sources: almanacs, encyclopedias, books about Cuba, the Internet
- Students should name the current President of Haiti. Possible sources: almanacs, magazines and newspapers, the Internet
- Answers will vary. Possible answers: El Morro Fortress, Hacienda Buena Vista, Old San Juan historic district. Possible sources: books about Puerto Rico, magazines, the Internet, people

Puerto Rico

CULTURAL IDENTITY OF A PEOPLE

Lesson Objectives

1. Describe Puerto Rican culture and how it has been influenced by American culture.

2. Compare life on the island to life on the mainland for Puerto Ricans.

3. Analyze the benefits and drawbacks of commonwealth, state, and nationhood status for Puerto Rico.

BEFORE YOU READ

Reach Into Your Background

Do you ever feel that you have "two selves"? One that acts a certain way with some people? And another that comes out when you are with other people? Are both of them the real you?

Questions to Explore

1. What factors influenced Puerto Rican culture?

2. What is Puerto Rico's relationship with the United States?

Key Terms

citizen
commonwealth
constitution

Key Places

San Juan
Condado

Lesson Plan

1 Engage

Warm-Up Activity

Write the following names of famous Puerto Ricans on the board. Ask students which of the following people they are familiar with and what they have in common. Raúl Julia (actor), Rita Moreno (singer, dancer), Nicholasa Mohr (author), Geraldo Rivera (television journalist), Roberto Clemente and Orlando Cepeda (baseball players), Angel Cordero (jockey), Juan "Chi Chi" Rodriguez (professional golfer), Antonia Novello (U.S. Surgeon General 1990–1993), Rafael Colón (artist). (They are all native Puerto Ricans.)

Activating Prior Knowledge

Have students read Reach Into Your Background in the Before You Read box. Ask students to explain how they deal with feeling like two people at the same time.

▼ Esmeralda Santiago moved from Puerto Rico to New York City when she was 13 years old.

Puerto Rican Esmeralda Santiago (ez mur EL duh sant ee AHG oh) can never forget the first time she saw the movie *West Side Story*. She was living in New York. It was 1961 and she was 13 years old. The movie was about Puerto Ricans living in New York, but most of the actors who played them were English-speaking whites. To her, they just didn't seem like Puerto Rican people.

Seeing the movie was a turning point in Esmeralda's life. She knew the movie was not about her. But she did not know what the film should have been like. Realizing this made her feel confused.

❝I had no sense of Puerto Rican culture or what it was to me. Where did I come from? Who is this person who calls herself a Puerto Rican and what does that mean? . . . [W]hen I think Puerto Rican, there's this big void, this empty space where my history should be.❞

Puerto Rican and American

Even though Esmeralda felt confused about who she was, she remembered her early days in Puerto Rico vividly. When Esmeralda's mother brought her to New York City, everything changed.

Resource Directory

Teaching Resources

📁 **Reproducible Lesson Plan** in the Chapter and Section Resources booklet, p. 75, provides a summary of the section lesson.

📁 **Guided Reading and Review** in the Chapter and Section Resources booklet, p. 76, provides a structure for mastering key concepts and reviewing key terms in the section. Available in Spanish in the Spanish Chapter and Section Resources booklet, p. 47.

📖 **Section Reading Support Transparencies** provide answers to the Questions to Explore in a graphic organizer format.

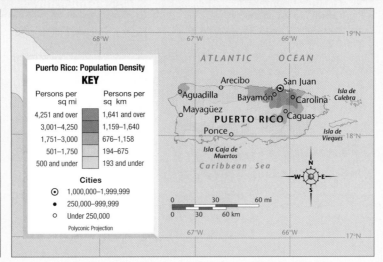

COUNTRY · PROFILE

Puerto Rico: Population

Religious Groups

Protestant and other 15%

Roman Catholic 85%

Source: CIA World Factbook 2000

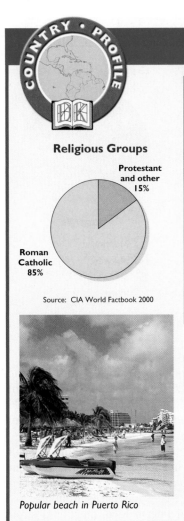

Popular beach in Puerto Rico

Puerto Rico: Population Density
KEY

Persons per sq mi	Persons per sq km
4,251 and over	1,641 and over
3,001–4,250	1,159–1,640
1,751–3,000	676–1,158
501–1,750	194–675
500 and under	193 and under

Cities
- ⊙ 1,000,000–1,999,999
- ● 250,000–999,999
- ○ Under 250,000

Polyconic Projection

ATLANTIC OCEAN

Arecibo   San Juan
Aguadilla   Bayamón   Carolina   Isla de Culebra
Mayagüez
PUERTO RICO   Caguas
Ponce
Isla de Vieques
Isla Caja de Muertos
Caribbean Sea

0   30   60 mi
0   30   60 km

Population by Age Group and Sex

Female	Age	Male
5.9%	65 and over	4.5%
34.1%	15–64	31.5%
11.7%	0–14	12.3%

% of population by age group

Source: Dorling Kindersley World Desk Reference

Culture The map and charts above show information about the population of Puerto Rico. **Map and Chart Study** (a) What are the least populated areas in Puerto Rico? (b) What is the major religious group in Puerto Rico?

It was not that Esmeralda was completely separated from her people. Puerto Ricans are U.S. citizens. **Citizens** are individuals with certain rights and responsibilities under a particular government. However, Puerto Ricans cannot vote in U. S. presidential elections. They do not pay U.S. taxes. And they have only a non-voting representative in the U.S. Congress. Puerto Rico is a commonwealth of the United States. A **commonwealth** is a place that has its own government but also has strong ties to another country. Esmeralda had the right to return to Puerto Rico whenever she chose.

Esmeralda found life on the mainland strange and confusing. One problem was that to succeed in school, she had to improve her English. Esmeralda was also confused by her new group of friends. She found that Puerto Ricans living on the mainland were different from her friends on the island of Puerto Rico. Instead of the salsa and merengue

Take It to the NET
Data Update For the most recent data on Puerto Rico, visit **www.phschool.com**.

Program Resources

📁 **Outline Maps** Central America and the Caribbean: Political, p. 9

Media and Technology

💿 **Social Studies Skills Tutor CD-ROM** builds core social studies skills through interactive lessons and provides skill assessment.

---

2 Explore

Have students read the section. Tell them that after they read, they should be able to describe (a) the differences between life on the island and life on the mainland; (b) the ties mainland Puerto Ricans have to the island; and (c) how island life is influenced by both American and Caribbean cultures.

3 Teach

To explore the issue of Puerto Rico's status, ask students to make a chart with three column headings like the following:

Statehood	
Pro	Con

Commonwealth	
Pro	Con

Nationhood	
Pro	Con

Have students fill in the pro and con columns with arguments from the section. Students' opinions must be backed by facts. (You may want to save students' charts for use in a later activity in this section.) This activity should take about 20 minutes.

4 Assess

See the answers to the Section Review. You may also use students' completed charts as assessment.

Acceptable charts include arguments from the text.

Commendable charts reflect students' thoughts on these issues.

Outstanding charts contain relevant, well-thought-out, original arguments backed by facts.

Background

Daily Life

Baseball Many Caribbean people share America's passion for baseball. In Puerto Rico, *beisbol* has produced such stars as Roberto Clemente and Ruben Sierra. Puerto Rico has a league of six teams that play all over the island. Cubans also enjoy baseball. In America Latina stadium in Havana, crowds cheer their teams energetically, and even dance in the aisles to the sound of bongo drums to celebrate an exceptionally good play.

Answers to ...

CHART STUDY

• northeastern United States; accept any reasonable answer such as family already living there or job availability.

Puerto Ricans in the Mainland United States

Chart Study Many Puerto Ricans have moved to the mainland United States. **Critical Thinking** Which region of the mainland has the most Puerto Ricans? What do you think draws Puerto Ricans to a particular area?

Population	
Total	3,406,178
Northeast	2,074,574
Midwest	325,363
South	759,305
West	246,936

Distribution by Region

7.2%
9.6%
22.3%
60.9%

- Northeast
- Midwest
- South
- West

Source: United States Census Bureau

READ ACTIVELY

Connect What kind of music do you listen to? Does the music you listen to reflect your feelings about your life and your community? Why or why not?

music she loved, they preferred rock music. Most of the time they spoke neither pure Spanish nor English, but a mixture of the two that they called "Spanglish." Although they were Puerto Rican, Esmeralda felt different from them. Eventually, she learned their ways. She became more like them and thought less about her old life on the island.

Most Puerto Ricans who move to the mainland keep connections to Puerto Rico. As people travel back and forth between the mainland and Puerto Rico, they bring customs and products with them. If you visited Puerto Rico, you would see many influences from the U.S. mainland. You would also see that in Puerto Rico, there is a strong cultural connection to the Caribbean. Most people are a mix of Spanish and African ancestry. Some Puerto Ricans like to look even further back into their history by calling themselves "Boricuas" (bohr ee KOO uhs). The name comes from the Boriqueno (bohr ee KAY noh), an indigenous farming people who lived on the island before the Spanish arrived.

More Than the Four Walls

The land of Puerto Rico is a memory no Puerto Rican forgets. Some, like Esmeralda Santiago, never go back to it. But others return, longing for the familiar ways they left behind. Julia de Jesus Chaparro (HOO lee a day HAY soos sha PAHR ro) moved back to a small mountain village in Puerto Rico after more than 14 years in Boston. She is fond of saying that where she lives now there are "more than the four walls of the city." To prove what she means, she takes visitors to her back porch. Outside it, one can see a row of steep mountains. Peeking between them is the bright blue of the Caribbean Sea. The mountain slopes steeply down from her back porch, but she has managed to clear some land. Her garden of mangoes, coconuts, grapefruit, and lemons thrives in the sun. Behind a nearby tree, a hen and six chickens are pecking in the dirt.

On other parts of the island, farmers ride horses through fields of tall sugar cane. Higher in the hills, Puerto Rican cowhands, called *jíbaros* (HEE bahr ohs), hunt, fish, and raise chickens, pigs, and cattle. To the southwest, where the land gets lower, fishing villages dot the coast.

Puerto Rico is an island of cities as well as countryside. Puerto Rican cities show influences of Spanish, Caribbean, and U.S. mainland cultures. About 70 percent of Puerto Ricans live in cities. Many city people work in factories. Others work in the hotels and restaurants that draw many tourists. Puerto Rico's capital, San Juan (san HWAHN), has a large waterfront area known as the Condado (kohn DAH do). It is packed with luxury hotels. Not far away, modern skyscrapers pierce the brilliant sky. In the old section of San Juan, Spanish-style buildings are everywhere. A 450-year-old Catholic church built by the Spanish has been carefully restored. Not far from it sit ancient houses graced with iron balconies in lacy Spanish style.

A Commonwealth in Question

In 1951, Puerto Ricans voted to adopt their own constitution. A **constitution** is a statement of a country's basic laws and values. This gave Puerto Rico its own group of lawmakers. But it was still connected

Visualize What might you see if you looked out the back door of an apartment in the city? What might you see if you looked out the back door of a house in the countryside?

New York City's Spanish Harlem

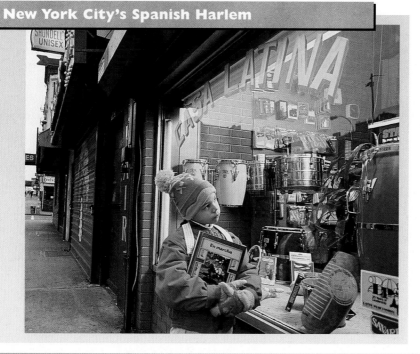

Puerto Ricans are one of the largest ethnic groups in New York City. They make up about 12 percent of the city's total population.

SKILLS MINI LESSON

Identifying Central Issues
To **introduce** the skill, indicate to students that the information in this section has been organized around a central issue, which is a question or problem that Puerto Ricans face. Help students **practice** the skill by asking them to identify this issue. Record their responses on the chalkboard. If students need help, suggest that they review the headings and subheadings of the section for clues. Have students **apply** the skill by finding evidence in the text that supports their answer.

Interdisciplinary Connections

Language Arts Have students use the charts they made for the Teach activity to produce a debate on the central issue of Puerto Rico's future status. Organize students into three groups, directing each group to present arguments for and against one of the three status options. Invite groups to choose spokespersons to present their arguments in a debate. After all arguments have been presented, hold a secret ballot to determine which solution students think should be adopted. *English Language Learners, Auditory*

to the United States. Puerto Rico is bound by many United States laws. Puerto Ricans have many questions about this. Is it good for Puerto Rico? Should Puerto Rico become independent? Or should it become a state of the United States?

READ ACTIVELY

Connect Would people in your area want to become part of another state? Why or why not?

What Direction to Take? Puerto Ricans have many disagreements over the answers to these questions. Many feel that having "one foot" in Puerto Rico and "one foot" in the United States can lead to problems. Others point out how the relationship with the United States has helped Puerto Rico. U.S. businesses on the island have raised the standard of living. Each year, the U.S. government sends millions of dollars to the island to help people in need.

Some people still feel that Puerto Rico has a disadvantage because people there cannot vote in U.S. elections. They say Puerto Rico should try to become a state. But if it does, it will become the poorest state in the union. Puerto Ricans earn more money than people in other Caribbean countries. However, they earn less than people on the U.S. mainland. Also, if Puerto Rico becomes a state, Puerto Ricans will have

San Juan: Old and New

San Juan, Puerto Rico's oldest city, is famous for historic forts and the wrought iron balconies of its oldest neighborhoods. But San Juan is also a vacation spot for tourists, with modern hotels lining its sandy beaches.

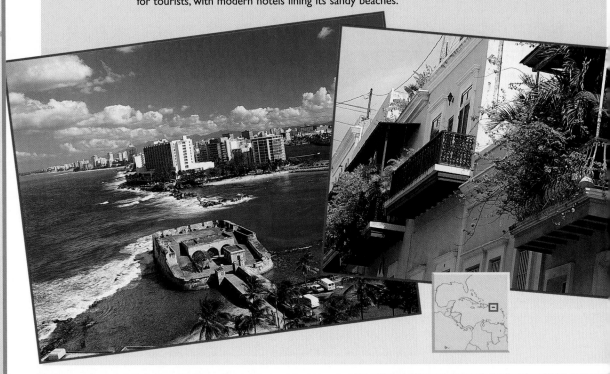

Resource Directory

Teaching Resources

Section Quiz in the Chapter and Section Resources booklet, p. 77, covers the main ideas and key terms in the section. Available in Spanish in the Spanish Chapter and Section Resources booklet, p. 48.

Vocabulary in the Chapter and Section Resources booklet, p. 79, provides a review of key terms in the chapter. Available in Spanish in the Spanish Chapter

and Section Resources booklet, p. 50.

Reteaching in the Chapter and Section Resources booklet, p. 80, provides a structure for students who may need additional help in mastering chapter content.

Enrichment in the Chapter and Section Resources booklet, p. 81, extends chapter content and enriches students' understanding.

Spanish Glossary in the Spanish Chapter and Section Resources, pp. 62–65, provides key terms translated from English to Spanish as well as

▶ These women are celebrating Puerto Rico's Spanish heritage. Puerto Ricans celebrate many holidays with traditional music and dancing.

to pay U.S. taxes. This could lower the earnings of many who have little to spare. For these reasons, in 1993 and again in 1998, Puerto Ricans voted not to become the 51st state of the United States.

The Question of Independence Some people who voted against statehood have even bigger dreams for the country. They want Puerto Rico to become a separate nation. If not, they fear that Puerto Ricans will become confused about their identity, just as Esmeralda Santiago became confused about hers. They stress Puerto Rico's connection to other Caribbean nations. They want to make sure that Puerto Ricans always identify with the Spanish language and Spanish culture. But for now, Puerto Rico will keep its links to the mainland. Many Puerto Ricans hope that their relationship with the United States will lead to a profitable and peaceful future.

SECTION 3 REVIEW

1. **Define** (a) citizen, (b) commonwealth, (c) constitution.

2. **Identify** (a) San Juan, (b) Condado.

3. What is the political connection between Puerto Rico and the United States?

4. Compare life in the mainland United States with life in Puerto Rico.

Critical Thinking

5. **Identifying Central Issues** What are the three options Puerto Ricans consider in terms of their relationship with the United States? What are the benefits and drawbacks of each?

Activity

6. **Writing to Learn** Try to put yourself in Esmeralda Santiago's place. Write a paragraph telling what it was like to move to New York from Puerto Rico.

definitions in Spanish.

📁 **Chapter Summary** in the Chapter and Section Resources booklet, p. 78, provides a summary of chapter content. Available in Spanish in the Spanish Chapter and Section Resources booklet, p. 49.

📁 **Cooperative Learning Activity** in the Activities and Projects booklet, pp. 36–39, provides two student handouts, one page of teacher's directions, and a scoring rubric for a cooperative learning activity on creating a magazine story.

📁 **Critical Thinking Activity** in the Chapter and Section Resources book-

let, p. 82, helps students apply the skill of distinguishing facts from opinions.

Media and Technology

🎧 **Guided Reading Audiotapes** (English and Spanish)

🎧 **Student Edition on Audio CD** The entire text of the Student Edition is available in a series of audio CDs.

Section 3 Review

1. (a) individual with certain rights and responsibilities under a particular government (b) a place that has its own government, but also has strong ties to another country (c) statement of a country's basic laws and values

2. (a) the capital of Puerto Rico (b) a beachfront area of Puerto Rico

3. Puerto Rico is a commonwealth that receives U.S. financial aid and investment.

4. Life on the mainland is a blend of cultures. Many people speak "Spanglish," eat American foods. Life is more traditional in Puerto Rico.

5. Students' answers should address these three options: commonwealth, statehood, and nationhood. Possible benefits and drawbacks follow.

	Benefits	Drawbacks
Common-wealth	U.S. aid, invest-ment; no federal taxes	confused cultural identity, second-class citizenship
State-hood	more U.S. invest-ment, con-gressional represen-tation, more political power	might lose Spanish lan-guage and culture, high federal taxes would lower incomes
Nation-hood	keep sepa-rate identi-ty, Spanish language and cul-ture; stronger cultural ties to Caribbean	weak nation without U.S. defense, might lose U.S. invest-ment and aid

6. Student editorials should contain opinions backed by facts.

Reviewing Main Ideas

1. Cuba lost economic aid and trade with the Soviet Union. The result was economic decline and shortages of food and other necessities.

2. Lydia Martin noticed food and clothing shortages.

3. Haiti is the only nation in the Americas formed from a successful revolt of enslaved Africans.

4. Democracy ended, and Aristide's followers were persecuted by the military government.

5. Among the examples students might cite are the Spanish language, customs, and architecture; American baseball, English language, popular music and culture, and American form of government.

6. Students might mention stronger ties to American culture and weaker identity as Puerto Ricans. They might also state that large numbers have moved permanently to the mainland.

Reviewing Key Terms

Sentences should show the correct meaning of the term through context.

Critical Thinking

1. Answers may vary. Students might cite these similarities: Both groups had to learn English and new ways of life. Both groups include those who wish to return to their homeland and others, especially those born here, who are adopting American culture and language. Differences include: Some Cubans cannot, or do not want to, return while Castro is in power. On the other hand, Puerto Ricans are American citizens and can travel freely between the island and the mainland.

2. Student answers should show understanding of how the slave revolt against the colonial French inspires Haitians with their heritage of victory over oppression.

CHAPTER 5 Review and Activities

Reviewing Main Ideas

1. What happened to Cuba when the communist regime in the Soviet Union fell?

2. What changes did Lydia Martin notice when she visited Cuba in 1995?

3. How is Haiti's history unique?

4. What were two results of Jean-Bertrand Aristide's forced exile from Haiti?

5. How do the cultures of Spain and the United States influence Puerto Rico? Give one example of how each has influenced Puerto Rico.

6. How have frequent trips to the U.S. mainland affected some Puerto Rican families?

Reviewing Key Terms

Use each key term below in a sentence that shows the meaning of the term.

1. communist
2. dictator
3. exile
4. illiterate
5. Creole
6. dialect
7. commonwealth
8. citizen
9. constitution

Critical Thinking

1. Making Comparisons Both Cubans and Puerto Ricans have settled in the United States. How has the experience been similar for both? How has it been different?

2. Drawing Conclusions How do you think Toussaint L'Ouverture's fight for independence inspires Haitians to fight for democracy?

Graphic Organizer

Copy the chart to the right onto a piece of paper, then fill in the empty boxes to complete the chart.

	Cuba	Haiti	Puerto Rico
Form of government			
United States Influence			

Graphic Organizer

	Cuba	Haiti	Puerto Rico
Form of Government	communist	republic	commonwealth of United States
United States Influence	radio, music, clothing styles	United States is helping to restore democracy	bound by U.S. laws, confused cultural identity

Map Activity

For each place listed below, write the letter from the map that shows its location.

The Caribbean: Place Location

1. Port-au-Prince
2. San Juan
3. Havana
4. Miami
5. Gulf of Mexico
6. Guantánamo Bay
7. Dominican Republic

Writing Activity

Writing a Poem
Write a poem describing the culture in your region. Does your region have a blend of cultures, like Haiti? Why or why not? How does the culture in your region affect the way you feel about yourself?

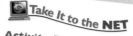

Activity Take a virtual tour of some historic sites in Old San Juan, Puerto Rico. For help in completing this activity, visit www.phschool.com.

Chapter 5 Self-Test To review what you have learned, take the Chapter 5 Self-Test and get instant feedback on your answers. Go to www.phschool.com to take the test.

Skills Review

Turn to the Skill Activity. Review the steps for locating information. Then write a one page biography of Fidel Castro. Make a list of four routes you could take to find information.

How Am I Doing?

Answer these questions to help you check your progress.

1. Do I understand why many Cubans have emigrated to the United States?
2. Can I explain how Haiti's people have struggled for democracy?
3. Do I understand Puerto Rico's relationship with the United States?
4. Can I describe what factors have affected culture in the Caribbean islands?
5. What information from this chapter can I include in my journal?

Students may wish to use the Internet to search for similar topics or activities. Suggest possible search terms, such as "Old San Juan" or "historic Puerto Rico."

Guide students to a search engine. Four of the most useful are Infoseek, AltaVista, Lycos, and Yahoo. For additional suggestions on using the Internet, refer to the Prentice Hall Social Studies' Educator's Handbook "Using the Internet," in the *Prentice Hall World Explorer* Program Resources.

For chapter-by-chapter links to age-appropriate sites in world studies and geography, including Self-Tests, visit the *World Explorer* companion Web site at: **http://www.phschool.com**

How Am I Doing?

Point out to students that this checklist is just a quick reminder for them of what they learned in the chapter. If their answer to any of the questions is *no* or if they are unsure, they may need to review the topic.

Map Activity

1. E		**4.** B		**6.** D	
2. G		**5.** A		**7.** F	
3. C					

Skills Review

Students' routes will vary. Sample resources: library, almanac, encyclopedia, newspaper articles on Cuba and Castro, books on Castro.

Writing Activity

Students' poems will vary, but should reflect their views of the local culture.

Resource Directory

Teaching Resources

📁 **Chapter Tests** Forms A and B are in the Tests booklet, pp. 26–31.

Program Resources

📁 **Writing Process Handbook** includes Proofreading, p. 37, to help students with the Writing Activity.

Media and Technology

📺 **Color Transparencies** Color Transparency 174 (Graphic organizer table template)

💿 **Computer Test Bank CD-ROM**

💿 **Resource Pro® CD-ROM**

⚙ **Prentice Hall Assessment System**

Exploring South America

To help you plan instruction, the chart below shows how teaching resources correspond to chapter content. Use the resources to vary instruction, add activities, or plan block schedules. Where appropriate, resources have **suggested time allotments** for students. Time allotments are approximate.

Managing Time and Instruction

	Latin America Teaching Resources Booklet		World Explorer Program Resources Binder	
	Resource	mins.	Resource	mins.
1 SECTION 1 Brazil Resources of the Rain Forest	**Chapter and Section Support** Reproducible Lesson Plan, p. 84 Ⓢ Guided Reading and Review, p. 85 Ⓢ Section Quiz, p. 86 Critical Thinking Activity, p. 100 ▯ Section Reading Support Transparencies	 20 25 30 15	**Outline Maps** Brazil: Political, p. 10 **Interdisciplinary Explorations** Ⓣ *Fate of the Rain Forest* **Nystrom Desk Atlas** Ⓣ **Primary Sources and Literature Readings** My Friend the Painter, p. 10; Whose Falkland Islands Are They?, p. 22 **Environmental and Global Issues** Topic: Environmental Damage	 20 20 40 40
SKILLS ACTIVITY Using Isolines to Show Elevation	**Social Studies and Geography Skills,** Understanding Isolines, p. 29 Reading a Contour Map, p. 30			
2 SECTION 2 Peru Life in the Altiplano	**Chapter and Section Support** Reproducible Lesson Plan, p. 87 Ⓢ Guided Reading and Review, p. 88 Ⓢ Section Quiz, p. 89 ▯ Section Reading Support Transparencies	 20 25 15	**Outline Maps** South America: Political, p. 11	 20
3 SECTION 3 Chile A Growing Economy Based on Agriculture	**Chapter and Section Support** Reproducible Lesson Plan, p. 90 Ⓢ Guided Reading and Review, p. 91 Ⓢ Section Quiz, p. 92 ▯ Section Reading Support Transparencies	 20 25 15	**Outline Maps** South America: Political, p. 11	 20
4 SECTION 4 Venezuela Oil Powers the Economy	**Chapter and Section Support** Reproducible Lesson Plan, p. 93 Ⓢ Guided Reading and Review, p. 94 Ⓢ Section Quiz, p. 95 Ⓢ Vocabulary, p. 97 Reteaching, p. 98 Enrichment, p. 99 Ⓢ Chapter Summary, p. 96 ▯ Section Reading Support Transparencies **Tests** Forms A and B Chapter Tests, pp. 32–37	 20 25 20 25 25 15 15 40	**Outline Maps** South America: Political, p. 11 **Writing Process Handbook** Locating Information, pp. 17–18	 20 25
ACTIVITY SHOP Interdisciplinary Rain Forest Resources	**Activities and Projects** Ⓣ Activity Shop: Interdisciplinary, p. 7	 30		
LITERATURE *Question Book* by Pablo Neruda				

Block Scheduling Program Support

- Block Scheduling Booklet — PROGRAM RESOURCES BINDER
- Activities and Projects
- Interdisciplinary Links
- Resource Pro® CD-ROM
- Media and Technology
- Pacing Charts Booklet — PROGRAM RESOURCES BINDER

Media and Technology

Resource	mins.
World Video Explorer	20
Color Transparencies 36, 37, 64	20
Resource Pro® CD-ROM	30
Presentation Pro CD-ROM	20
Social Studies Skills Tutor CD-ROM	30
Color Transparencies 19, 69	20
Color Transparencies 34, 35, 64	20
Color Transparency 69	20
Guided Reading Audiotapes	20
Color Transparency 174 (Graphic organizer table template)	20
Computer Test Bank CD-ROM	30
Student Edition on Audio CD	30
Passport to the World CD-ROM	30

T Teaming Opportunity
well-suited for teaching teams

S Spanish
This resource is also in Spanish support.

CD-ROM

Laserdisc

Transparency

Videotape

Audiotape/CD

Assessment Opportunities

From Guiding Questions to Assessment A series of Guiding Questions serves as an organizing framework for this book. The Guiding Questions that relate to this chapter are listed below. Section Reviews and Section Quizzes provide opportunities for assessing students' insights into these Guiding Questions. Additional assessments are listed below.

GUIDING QUESTIONS

- *What factors have affected cultures in Latin America?*
- *How has geography influenced the ways in which Latin Americans make a living?*

ASSESSMENTS

Section 1

Students should be able to write a letter to the editor detailing the rain forest's effect on Brazil's economy.

▶ **RUBRIC** See the Assessment booklet for a rubric on assessing a letter to the editor.

Section 2

Students should be able to write a poem that expresses what life is like for the Uros people on the straw islands of Lake Titicaca.

▶ **RUBRIC** See the Assessment booklet for a rubric on assessing a student poem.

Section 3

Students should be able to describe how Chile's location affects the crops it grows.

▶ **RUBRIC** See the Assessment booklet for a rubric on assessing cause-and-effect statements.

Section 4

Students should be able to give an oral presentation describing Venezuela's economy and its possible future.

▶ **RUBRIC** See the Assessment booklet for a rubric on assessing an oral presentation.

Prentice Hall Assessment System allows you to:
- Diagnose and Prescribe
- Review and Reteach
- Practice and Assess

Activities and Projects

Mental Mapping

Southern Lands Tell students that South America has many notable natural features, including the Amazon River, the Amazon rain forest, Lake Titicaca (the world's highest navigable lake), Angel Falls (the world's highest waterfall), and the Andes Mountains. The South American continent also includes landforms and vegetation areas such as desert, mountains, and grasslands.

Give students outline maps of South America. Ask them to locate and label some of these physical features on the map. Give them just a few minutes to do this. Then have students compare their sense of where these features are with the information on a published map.

Links to Current Events

Fact Cards Have students work in groups of four to create sets of fact cards about each of the four countries covered in this chapter. One member of each group should concentrate on one country.

Using almanacs, an encyclopedia, and other reference sources, students can collect information about the current form of government, political leaders and parties, major products, natural resources, type of currency used, language, religion, and other facts that can give them a picture of the country. Students should put one fact or piece of information on each index card.

After each student has created five to ten cards about his or her country, the members of each group can exchange cards to compare and contrast four countries.

Hands-On Activities

Are We There Yet? The Pan-American Highway is a network of roads connecting North America and South America. The system covers about 30,000 miles of roads. Although parts of the highway have yet to be completed, most of it is finished. The highway has been under construction since 1936.

Display a map of the Americas with countries and their capitals labeled. Suggest to students that the highway might link all these countries. Invite students to take turns coming up to the map to trace routes the Pan-American Highway might take. You may wish to give students push pins and yarn to mark their proposed routes. You may want to challenge students to find possible routes that would connect the capitals of all the countries in North America, Central America, and South America.

Challenge Preconceptions Ask students to brainstorm their associations with South America. Then have each student write down several of their associations on a piece of paper. As students work through this chapter, encourage them to look for information that supports their previously held ideas and information that challenges or disproves their previously held ideas about South America. Have students set up their preconceptions and information that confirms or challenges their preconceptions in chart form. *Average*

Resourceful Reinforce understanding of the economies of some countries of South America by having students make a simple chart with three columns: Rain Forest, Oil, and Agriculture. Under each column, have students list words that illustrate how the resource is used or why it is important. Under Rain Forest, students might list different products as well as the importance of the rain forest to the world's ecology. Under Oil, they may write words that describe how oil is used. Under Agriculture, they may list various agricultural products. Students may use pictures rather than words to illustrate the uses or importance of these resources. *English Language Learners*

Different Countries Help students see that the countries of South America have distinct identities by asking a group of students to put on a skit about an interaction among citizens of three or more South American countries. These people might be portrayed as encountering each other in a major airport, at the United Nations, at a major international conference, or at a tourist attraction in another country such as Disney World or the Eiffel Tower. Encourage students to develop a scenario that emphasizes some of the differences among people from different cultures and countries of South America as well as some of the similarities. *Challenging*

This page can help you extend your own and students' understanding of the concepts in this chapter. You may want to browse through some of the suggestions in the **Bibliography**. **Interdisciplinary Links** can connect social studies understandings to areas elsewhere in the curriculum through the use of other Prentice Hall products. **National Geography Standards** reflected specifically in this chapter are listed for your convenience. Some hints about appropriate Internet access are also provided in **Take It to the Net**. **School to Careers** provides insights into the practical uses of some of the concepts in this chapter as they might pertain to various careers.

BIBLIOGRAPHY

FOR THE TEACHER

Ashford, Moyra. *Brazil.* Steck-Vaughn, 1991.

Beani, Laura, Francesco Dessi, and Massimo Pandolfi. *The Pampas, Andes, and Galapagos.* Steck-Vaughn, 1992.

The Cousteau Society. *An Adventure in the Amazon.* Simon, 1992.

Fox, Geoffrey. *The Land and People of Venezuela.* HarperCollins, 1991.

FOR THE STUDENT

Easy
Peru—In Pictures. Lerner, 1994.

Lewington, Anna, adapter. *Antonio's Rain Forest.* Carolrhoda, 1993.

Average
Schwartz, David. *Yanomami: People of the Amazon.* Lothrop, 1995.

Challenging
Fernandez, Jose B. *José de San Martin: Latin America's Quiet Hero.* Millbrook, 1994.

Roman, Joseph. *Pablo Neruda.* Chelsea, 1992.

LITERATURE CONNECTION

Cohen, Miriam. *Born to Dance Samba.* Harper, 1984.

Kendall, Sarita. *Ransom for a River Dolphin.* Lerner, 1993.

INTERDISCIPLINARY LINKS

Subject	Theme: Interdependence
MATH	Middle Grades Math: Tools for Success *Course 2*, Lesson 11-2, **Graphing Linear Equations**
SCIENCE	Science Explorer *Environmental Science*, Lesson 6-1, **Fossil Fuels** *Chemical Interactions*, Lesson 1-2, **Describing Chemical Reactions**

NATIONAL GEOGRAPHY STANDARDS

Students explore the 18 National Geography Standards throughout Latin America. Chapter 6, however, concentrates on investigating the following: standards 1, 3, 4, 6, 8, 9, 10, 11, 12, 13, 14, 15, 16, 17, 18. For a complete list of the standards, see the *Teacher's Flexible Planning Guide.*

SCHOOL TO CAREERS

In Chapter 6, Exploring South America, students learn about the economies and natural resources of Brazil, Peru, Chile, and Venezuela. Additionally, they address the skill of using isolines. Understanding the balance of economic and environmental issues can help students prepare for careers in economics, science, conservation, business, and geology. Using isolines is useful for civil engineers, forest and park rangers, surveyors, and geologists. The curriculum presented in this book, as in all eight titles of Prentice Hall's *World Explorer* program, is designed to prepare students not only for careers but also for good citizenship—of the world as well as of this country.

Take It to the NET

Many social studies teachers and students use Internet browsers, or search engines, to investigate particular topics. For the best results, use narrow rather than broad topics. Try these for Chapter 6: Yanomamo, Brazilian rain forest, altiplano, Cuzco. Finding age-appropriate sites is an important consideration when using the Internet. For links to age-appropriate sites in world studies and geography, visit the *World Explorer* companion Web site at:

http://www.phschool.com

CHAPTER 6
Exploring South America

CHAPTER 6

Connecting to the Guiding Questions

In this chapter, students will read about the people, economies, and ways of life in Brazil, Peru, Chile, and Venezuela. Content in this chapter thus corresponds to these Guiding Questions:

● What factors have affected cultures in Latin America?

● How has geography influenced the ways in which Latin Americans make a living?

Using the Map Activities

Use a mounted globe, tilted on its axis, to demonstrate that at the Equator, the sun shines directly overhead. As one travels away from the Equator—north or south—the sun is lower in the sky. The sun's rays become more and more slanted and provide less heat.

● cooler, because the sun's rays are slanted

● Mountains form a natural boundary between countries.

Heterogeneous Groups

The following Teacher's Edition strategies are suitable for heterogeneous groups.
Cooperative Learning
Uninvited Pests   p. 146
Critical Thinking
Identifying Central Issues   p. 133
Recognizing Cause and Effect   pp. 133, 144
Interdisciplinary Connections
Science   p. 145

SECTION 1
Brazil
RESOURCES OF THE RAIN FOREST

SECTION 2
Peru
LIFE IN THE ALTIPLANO

SECTION 3
Chile
A GROWING ECONOMY BASED ON AGRICULTURE

SECTION 4
Venezuela
OIL POWERS THE ECONOMY

MAP ACTIVITIES

South America is more than two times as large as the mainland United States. Because it is so large, its geography and cultures are diverse. To learn more about South America, complete the following activities.

Understanding geography
Much of South America is located south of the Equator. If you were to start at the Equator and travel south, how do you think the climate would change? Why?

Study the map
How do you think the Andes Mountains may have affected political boundaries in South America?

Resource Directory

Media and Technology

Daily Life: Life on the Amazon River, from the World Video Explorer, enhances students' understanding of the many ways that people have adapted to living on the banks of the Amazon.

Chapter 9

Brazil
RESOURCES OF THE RAIN FOREST

Reach Into Your Background

In this section, you will learn about the rain forests in Brazil.

List three things you already know or can guess about the rain forests.

Questions to Explore

1. Why are the rain forests in Brazil a global issue?
2. How does what happens to the rain forests affect Brazil's economy?

Key Terms

canopy
photosynthesis

Key People and Places

Rio de Janeiro
Salvador
Yanomamo
Brasília

D eep in the rain forest in Brazil, the light barely penetrates. At the top of the trees, the leaves form a dense mass called a **canopy.** Sun and rain beat down upon the canopy. But on the ground, the air feels almost chilly. The only sounds are the calls of birds, monkeys, and insects.

Brazil and Its Rain Forests

Brazil, the largest country in South America, is nearly as large as the United States. It is also one of the richest countries in the world in land and resources. Until recently, its immense rain forests remained undisturbed. Only the few Native American groups that had lived in them for centuries ever explored them.

Brazil's Geography Brazil's rain forests take up about one half of the country. Look at the map in the Country Profile. In the southeast, the forests give way to a large plateau divided by mountain ranges and river valleys. The plateau reaches Brazil's long coast. Many harbors lie along the coast. Large cities, such as Rio de Janeiro (ree oh day zhuh NER oh), grew up around harbors. Most of Brazil's people live near the coast, far from the rain forests.

▼ The canopy of Brazil's rain forest parts only where rivers slice through it.

2 Explore

Have students read the section. Tell them that as they read, they should look for answers to the following questions: Which groups in Brazil use the rain forests for their livelihood? Why are Brazil's rain forests important to the world? What solutions have been found to the conflict over the use of the rain forest?

3 Teach

Suggest that students work in groups of four to list the rain forest problems and solutions described in this section. Then have them discuss whether or not they feel the solutions are fair. Ask a member of the group to share with the class how the group judged the fairness of the solutions. This activity should take 15 minutes.

COUNTRY · PROFILE

Brazil: People and the Environment

Manaus, Brazil

Brazil: Natural Vegetation KEY
- Tropical rain forest
- Mixed forest
- Tropical savanna

Lambert Azimuthal Equal Area Projection

Urban and Rural Population

78%   22%

Source: Dorling Kindersley World Desk Reference

Geography The map shows information about Brazil's vegetation. The charts show how Brazilians interact with the environment. **Map and Chart Study** (a) In what areas of Brazil are tropical rain forests located? (b) What does the line graph show about deforestation in Brazil?

Total Deforested Area in Amazon Region

Source: Brazilian Embassy

Take It to the NET
Data Update For the most recent data on Brazil, visit **www.phschool.com**.

The People of Brazil

The Native Americans living in the rain forest were some of the first people to live in Brazil. Today, most Brazilians are a mix of Native American, African, and European heritages.

Many parts of African culture still flourish in Brazil. The most African of Brazilian cities, Salvador, lies on the coastal plains. Visitors are surprised by how much Salvador is like a town in Africa. Most of the people who live here descend from the millions of Africans brought to Brazil as slaves.

Resource Directory

Program Resources

Nystrom Desk Atlas
Interdisciplinary Explorations *Fate of the Rainforests*

📁 **Environmental and Global Issues**
Topic: Environmental Damage

Media and Technology

💿 **Social Studies Skills Tutor CD-ROM** builds core social studies skills through interactive lessons and provides skill assessment.

💿 **Passport to the World CD-ROM** This interactive CD-ROM allows students to explore each region of the world. Students view regional videos, take a photo tour, and explore a historical time line. Students record their travels in an Explorer's Journal, and receive passport stamps when they pass regional tests.

Working on Farms and in Factories Many Africans in Brazil were forced to work the coffee plantations. Brazil used their labor to become the world's largest coffee grower. When the slaves were freed in the late 1800s, they became paid but cheap labor.

Coffee prices dropped in the first few years of the 1900s. Brazilians realized that they could not depend on one or two crops to survive. In the 1930s, the government discouraged coffee production and tried to diversify the economy by building more factories. Today, Brazil produces many goods, including iron and steel, cars, and electrical equipment. Since 1960, about 30 million people have left farms and plantations to get jobs in these new industries. They moved into the cities.

A Brazilian City Brazilian cities are home to the rich and the very poor. Rio de Janeiro is a good example of these contrasts. It lies on the coast, surrounded by huge mountains that dip to the sea. If you climbed to the top of one, you could see the whole city. To the south, you would see expensive hotels and shops for tourists. In the downtown area, you would see old palaces and government buildings.

But to the north, you would see clusters of small houses where factory workers live. Below this neighborhood is an even poorer one, crowded with homes that have no electricity or running water. About a quarter of Rio's more than 10 million people live in these neighborhoods known as *favelas* (fuh VEH lus). However, most of Rio's people live in well-built houses with electricity and running water.

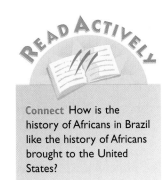

READ ACTIVELY

Connect How is the history of Africans in Brazil like the history of Africans brought to the United States?

Brazil's African Heritage

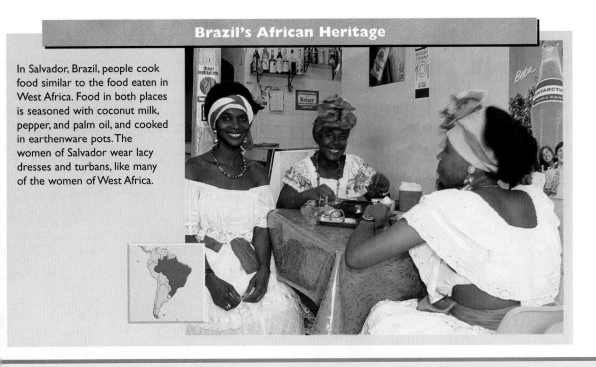

In Salvador, Brazil, people cook food similar to the food eaten in West Africa. Food in both places is seasoned with coconut milk, pepper, and palm oil, and cooked in earthenware pots. The women of Salvador wear lacy dresses and turbans, like many of the women of West Africa.

4 Assess

See the Answers to the Section Review. You may also use the student discussion for assessment.

Acceptable responses include several problems, solutions, and evaluations.

Commendable responses include more and show an understanding of why solutions are fair or unfair.

Outstanding responses include student suggestions of original, practical, and equitable solutions.

Background

Daily Life

Capoeira Capoeira, a Brazilian combination of dance and martial arts, developed in the northeastern part of the country. The dance form was created by enslaved Africans. Forbidden to fight each other, the slaves developed a form of fighting to music that looked like dancing. Music was played on drums and on a *berimbau* made from a bow and a gourd. Today, young men, boys, and some girls study capoeira, just as American young people study karate, judo, and other martial arts.

Global Perspectives

Global Warming The gases in our planet's atmosphere act like the glass in a greenhouse, letting sunlight in to provide warmth, then keeping the heat from escaping. Changing the mix of gases in the atmosphere may change the warmth inside the Earth's "greenhouse." For example, burning fuels such as coal, oil, and natural gas has increased the amount of carbon dioxide in the atmosphere. Trees remove carbon dioxide from the atmosphere, replacing it with oxygen. But as industry spreads, more carbon dioxide is sent into the atmosphere. At the same time, fewer trees are available to remove this gas from the air. As a result, the increased carbon dioxide traps more heat, leading to warmer climates and possibly disastrous results. For instance, if climates warm sufficiently, polar ice caps will melt and ocean levels will rise. Coastal ocean areas, on which large populations now live, will flood.

READ ACTIVELY

Visualize What do you think you would see if you climbed to the top of a tree in the rain forest?

Using the Rain Forest's Resources

On a sunny January in 1994, two boys who lived in the rain forest scrambled up the trees. The boys were Yanomamos. The Yanomamo are a Native American group that lives in the rain forests. The boys pointed to a plane soaring close to the treetops. The plane dipped down and landed on a dirt strip. "Foreign visitors!" the boys called excitedly.

Brazil's New Capital: Brasília The visitors were from Brasília (bruh ZIL yuh), the capital city of Brazil. Brasília is closer to the rain forest than the coastal cities are. On the vast interior plain where Brasília now stands, there used to be nothing but a savanna called the Cerrado (suh RAH doh). The Cerrado was a region 10 times larger than the state of Kansas. The government thought that moving the capital there would attract some people from the coastal areas.

The government wanted to develop Brazil's interior region using the resources of the rain forest. The rain forests are important to Brazil's economy because people cut timber, mine for gold, and farm there. Now, the government hoped to develop industry using the resources of the rain forest.

Worldwide Impact of the Rain Forest The rain forest where the Yanomamo live is very important to life all around the Earth. Scientists estimate that rain forests produce about one third of the world's oxygen. Green plants and trees produce their own food using

▼São Paulo is the largest city in Brazil and all of South America.

Resource Directory

Teaching Resources

📁 **Critical Thinking Activity** in the Chapter and Section Resources booklet, p. 100, helps students apply the skill of assessing your understanding.

Two Cities, Two Climates

Brasília: A City of the Savanna

Manaus: A City of the Rain Forest

Curved lines show temperatures in Fahrenheit degrees. **Bars** show rainfall in inches.

Chart Study A climate graph shows rainfall and temperature in the same space. The bars show rainfall, while the curved lines show temperature. **Critical Thinking** How are the seasons in Brasília and Manaus different from each other?

water, carbon dioxide, and sunlight. This process is called **photosynthesis** (foht oh SIN thuh sis). In the process of photosynthesis, oxygen is given off. All people and animals need oxygen to breathe.

The rain forest also holds about one fifth of the world's fresh water. Many scientists think that when people come to the rain forest, they may upset the delicate balance of nature.

Protecting the Rain Forest Brazil's government is taking care to use the rain forest's resources without upsetting this balance. The government has started using satellites to keep an eye on the rain forest. That way, the government can respond fast to protect the rain forest from the following dangers.

First, if too much timber is cut down, there will not be enough trees to absorb the carbon dioxide in the atmosphere. The carbon dioxide layer may trap heat near the Earth, changing the world's climate. When part of the forest is destroyed, the animals and plants that live there may not survive. When plant life is destroyed, less oxygen is produced.

CITIZEN HEROES

A Voice of Protest Friar Hector Turrini moved from Italy to Brazil more than 45 years ago. At that time, there were so few roads that Turrini had to learn to fly a plane to get around his parish. He dedicated himself to protecting the Native Americans and rubber tappers who depend on the rain forest. Now Turrini is working to protect the rain forest.

SKILLS MINI LESSON

Understanding Special Geography Graphs
To **introduce** the skill, point out that climate graphs can help students decide what kinds of clothes and gear to take on an expedition to a particular place. Direct students' attention to the climate graph of Brasília. Point out the abbreviations for the months at the base of the graph, the temperature scale at the left of the graph, and the rainfall scale at the right of the graph. Ask these questions to help students **practice** the skill: *Which are Brasília's hottest months? How much rain does Brasília usually receive in January? In July?* (August, September, and October; about 10 inches; less than one inch) Encourage students to **apply** the skill by writing three questions that can be answered by using the climate graph of Manaus. Have students share and answer one another's questions.

Critical Thinking

Identifying Central Issues
Suitable for an individual or whole-class activity.
Encourage students to discuss what they think are the most important issues surrounding Brazil's rain forests. Then have students prepare a one-minute news bulletin presenting the issues they feel are most important to the protection of the rain forests. Encourage volunteers to present their bulletins to the class. Ask the class to evaluate the news bulletins, choosing three they feel accurately identify the central issues. *Auditory*

Answers to ...
CHART STUDY

• Brasília has both rainy and dry seasons, Manaus is rainy nearly all year.

1. (a) dense mass of leaves on trees in the rain forest (b) process by which green plants and trees produce their own food using water, carbon dioxide, and sunlight

2. (a) coastal city in Brazil, surrounded by huge mountains that dip to the sea (b) Brazilian city on the coastal plains with a flourishing African culture (c) Native American group that lives in the rain forest (d) the capital of Brazil

3. Answers may vary. Sample answer: The rain forests supply needed oxygen and keep the level of carbon dioxide down. The Brazilian rain forest also holds about one fifth of the world's fresh water.

4. Answers may vary. Sample answer: Wood is cut and sold, gold is mined, and the forest is cleared for farming. The Yanomamo, a Native American group, make their living from hunting and gathering in the rain forest.

5. Students' answers will vary. Answers may include that it is unlikely the Brazilians will completely stop using the rain forests, because of the country's economic needs. However, as time goes on, economic activities in other places may help ease the economic burden and slow the pace of rain forest destruction.

6. Students' writings should reflect section content.

LINKS TO SCIENCE

Amazon Fruit What is green and bumpy, round like a softball, and looks like the sole of a shoe? It is a conde (KON day). Scientists in Brazil have discovered more than 40 types of fruits growing in the Amazon rain forest. Besides being high in vitamins and protein, these fruits taste good. Scientists hope to persuade Amazon farmers to stop clearing rain forest land and begin planting these fruits instead.

Second, there is the problem of smuggling. Each year, Brazil loses about 12 million animals to smugglers. Many of these animals are endangered. Smugglers look for monkeys, parrots, and other animals. One parrot can be sold for $10,000. One woolly monkey can be sold for as much as $50,000. It is illegal to capture or kill these animals, but the smugglers often get away with it.

Third, development can cause pollution. In the late 1980s, the discovery of gold attracted many miners to the rain forest. Mining gold involves mixing the gold with mercury. The mercury polluted streams in the forest. It made people in several Yanomamo villages sick.

The gold mining in the rain forest attracted the attention of the world. The government of Brazil passed strict laws about mining in the rain forest. Sometimes the government insisted that the miners leave. At times, military police had to be called in to make sure they did.

Giving Land to the Poor One of the main reasons that people come to the rain forest is the lack of land to farm. This may seem strange when one considers Brazil's large size. However, most of Brazil's land is owned by a few people who may choose not to farm their land. About one third of Brazil's farmland is unused. This represents about 300 million acres (122 million hectares) of crop and ranch land.

In 1995, Brazil's president gave some of this unused land to poor farmers. The goal is to resettle more than 3,600 poor families who want a new place to live and who want to return to farming. The process is a slow one. However, life for some resettled Brazilians is improving.

People are starting small farms just north of Rio de Janeiro. The farms help people make a living for themselves. On a balmy July day in 1995, farmer Joe Brum showed a reporter his farm. Brum had received the 17-acre plot from the government. Now his tin-roofed house was shaded by the coconut and banana trees he had planted. He had a couple of pigs and had earned enough money to buy a satellite dish and a television.

Brum's eyes gleamed as he pointed to the rows of vegetables. "What I have here," he explained to the reporter, "I made myself."

SECTION 1 REVIEW

1. **Define** (a) canopy, (b) photosynthesis.

2. **Identify** (a) Rio de Janeiro, (b) Salvador, (c) Yanomamo, (d) Brasília.

3. Why are Brazil's rain forests important to the whole world?

4. In what ways does Brazil depend on its rain forest?

Critical Thinking

5. **Expressing Problems Clearly** Some people want Brazil to stop using rain forests completely. Is this reasonable? What do you think it would do to Brazil's economy?

Activity

6. **Writing a Journal Entry** Use what you know about the rain forest to write a journal entry about a visit to it.

Resource Directory

Teaching Resources

Section Quiz in the Chapter and Section Resources booklet, p. 86, covers the main ideas and key terms in the section. Available in Spanish in the Spanish Chapter and Section Resources booklet, p. 53.

Peru
LIFE IN THE ALTIPLANO

BEFORE YOU READ

Reach Into Your Background
Did you choose your clothing according to the weather report this morning? The decision you made was affected by climate. Think of other ways that climate affects your life.

Questions to Explore
1. How has geography affected the lifestyle of Native Americans of the altiplano?
2. How do people on the altiplano survive?

Key Terms
altiplano
sierra
montaña
tundra

Key People and Places
Lake Titicaca
Uros
Quechua
Cuzco

When people on Tribuna, an island in Lake Titicaca, play soccer, they must be careful. That's because the island is made of straw. The ground is uneven, and when they walk on it they can feel the water shifting below. "It seems crazy to play soccer on water," says Luis Colo, who lives on Tribuna. "We don't jump on each other after a goal, or we'd probably fall through the field."

Tribuna is one of about 70 islands made by the Uros (oor OHSS). The Uros have adapted to the geography of Lake Titicaca. The Uros make their islands out of totora reeds. They join the floating roots of totora reeds together and then lay cut reeds on top. This process creates an island that is firm enough to support small communities of people with huts and livestock. When the Uros need more land, they build another island.

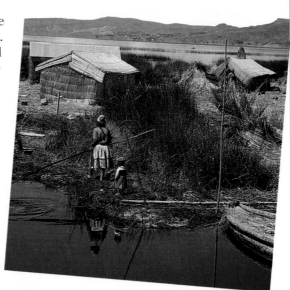
▲ When the wind comes up, the Uros must anchor their islands to keep them from being swept away.

Peru's Three Geographic Regions

The Uros live on Lake Titicaca. Find Lake Titicaca on the map in the Country Profile. Lake Titicaca lies high in Peru's **altiplano** (al tih PLAH noh), a high plateau region in the Andes. The altiplano is about 12,000 feet (3,658 m) above sea level. It lies in the southern part of Peru near the Bolivian border.

Teaching Resources

📁 **Reproducible Lesson Plan** in the Chapter and Section Resources booklet, p. 87, provides a summary of the section lesson.

📁 **Guided Reading and Review** in the Chapter and Section Resources booklet, p. 88, provides a structure for mastering key concepts and reviewing key terms in the section. Available in Spanish in the Spanish Chapter and Section Resources booklet, p. 54.

📖 **Section Reading Support Transparencies** provide answers to the Questions to Explore in a graphic organizer format.

Program Resources

📁 **Outline Maps** South America: Political, p. 11

Section 2

Lesson Objectives

1. Identify the three main geographical regions of Peru.
2. Analyze how geography affects people's way of life in the altiplano.
3. Explain why the traditional way of life of the Native Americans of Peru is changing.

Lesson Plan

1 Engage
Warm-Up Activity
Ask volunteers who have camped outdoors to describe how they lived with only fire for heat. How did they keep warm? How did they cook their food? Involve other students by asking them to imagine what it would be like to have only fire for heating and cooking and no electricity for light or for such appliances as a refrigerator.

Activating Prior Knowledge
Have students read Reach Into Your Background in the Before You Read box. Encourage students to supply other examples of how climate affects their lives.

2 Explore

Have students read the section. Direct them to keep in mind the following questions as they read. What are the three main regions of Peru like? How do people live in Peru's cities? How do the climate and geography of the altiplano affect the lives of people living there? You may wish to write these questions on the chalkboard.

3 Teach

Have pairs make Venn diagrams to compare the similarities and differences between life in a Quechua village and life on an island in Lake Titicaca. Have them draw two overlapping circles, one labeled *A Quechua Village,* the other labeled *Lake Titicaca.* Tell them to include details about food, housing, and livelihood. Then have them use the information in the diagram as a basis for a paragraph describing how the climate and natural resources of the altiplano and lake affect people's lives. This activity should take about 15 minutes.

Background

Links Across Time

Incas The present-day Quechuas are the descendants of the Incas. The Incas ruled the region in the 1400s and 1500s.

Answers to ...

MAP AND CHART STUDY

(a) 0–650 feet
(b) hydro

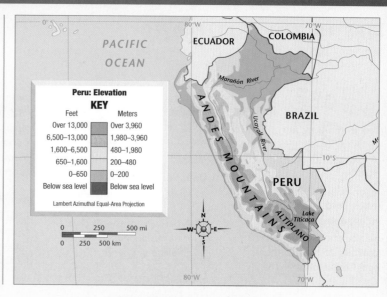

COUNTRY · PROFILE

Peru: People and the Environment

Sources of Electricity

Hydro 82%
Combustion 18%
Nuclear 0%

0   20   40   60   80   100

% of total generation by type

Source: Dorling Kindersley World Desk Reference

Peru: Elevation
KEY

Feet	Meters
Over 13,000	Over 3,960
6,500–13,000	1,980–3,960
1,600–6,500	480–1,980
650–1,600	200–480
0–650	0–200
Below sea level	Below sea level

Lambert Azimuthal Equal-Area Projection

Workers in a Peruvian zinc mine

Urban and Rural Population

72%   28%

Source: Dorling Kindersley World Desk Reference

Geography The map above shows information about the land in Peru. The charts show how Peru's population interacts with the land. **Map and Chart Study** (a) What is the elevation of Peru's coastal lands? (b) What is Peru's main source of electricity?

Take It to the NET
Data Update For the most recent data on Peru, visit **www.phschool.com.**

Peru's mountains divide the country into three geographic regions. The altiplano and Peru's highest mountains are in the sierra, the mountains that run from northwest to southeast Peru. The mountains are so high that the temperature can drop as low as 20°F (–7°C). People who live in this region must sleep under many blankets. They sometimes wear sweaters to bed.

Their life is far different from the lives of those who live on the coastal plain, which is Peru's second geographical region. This dry region is warmed by the sun and cooled by sea breezes. Several cities, including Trujillo (troo HEE yoh), Chimbote (chim BOH tay), and Lima (LEE muh), dot the coast.

The third region is called the montaña. The montaña is made of large stretches of tropical forests on the lower slopes of mountains in northeast Peru. Here the weather is warm and humid all year round.

Resource Directory

Media and Technology

Social Studies Skills Tutor CD-ROM builds core social studies skills through interactive lessons and provides skill assessment.

Passport to the World CD-ROM This interactive CD-ROM allows students to explore each region of the world. Students view regional videos, take a photo tour, and explore a historical time line. Students record their travels in an Explorer's Journal, and receive passport stamps when they pass regional tests.

Peru's People

Native Americans make up more than half of Peru's population. Most Native Americans living in Peru are Quechua. Another 32 percent are mestizo. The remaining Peruvians are of European, African, and Asian descent.

Peru's Cities The altiplano contains cities and isolated towns. City life is very different from village life. Most city dwellers have electricity. The streets are paved, and there are telephones. But in Peru's cities, the old mixes with the new.

One Peruvian city, Cuzco, is the site of the ancient Incan capital. Parts of the old Incan wall that once surrounded the city are still standing. Today's modern houses are made of adobe, with red tile roofs. But their foundations are the remains of Incan stonework. There are buildings from the time of the Spanish colonists as well.

Spanish conquistador Francisco Pizarro founded Peru's largest city and capital, Lima, in 1535. Lima lies on the coastal plain. Like Cuzco, Lima is a mix of old and new. Historic Spanish cathedrals and government buildings from the 1600s and 1700s stand next to modern skyscrapers.

LINKS ACROSS TIME

Bridging Canyons The Incas invented the technology for building suspension bridges. First, they built stone towers on each side of a canyon. They suspended cables woven from plants from the stone towers. Then, they laid wooden slats across the cables to make a bridge. They used smaller cables for railings. People still use Incan-style bridges today. Modern suspension bridges have steel cables and are reinforced with iron beams.

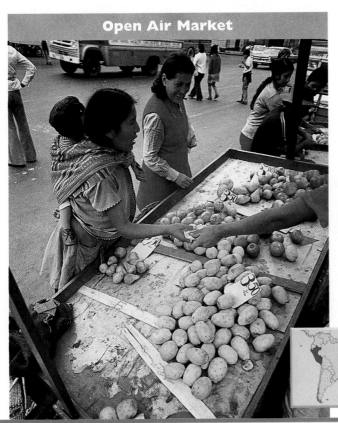

Open Air Market

◄ Lima is the busiest and most modern of Peru's cities. What details in the photo are modern? What details are more traditional?

4 Assess

See the answers to the Section Review. You may also use students' Venn diagrams and paragraphs for assessment.

Acceptable diagrams list three differences and one similarity. They give concrete examples.

Commendable diagrams and paragraphs organize information in the categories provided and point out the effects of climate and resources on lifestyle.

Outstanding diagrams list several differences and similarities. Paragraphs refer to ways in which the two groups benefit from trading products at the market.

Background

Biography

Francisco Pizarro Pizarro (c. 1475–1541) was a Spanish adventurer. When news of a rich Indian empire reached the Spanish colonists, Pizarro led an expedition to find it. His attack on the Peruvian Incas was successful. Pizarro captured the ruler and held him for a huge ransom that the Incas were rich enough to pay. The Spanish executed Atahualpa anyway. By 1535, Pizarro had founded Lima and made it the capital city. Pizarro was killed in 1541 in a power struggle with another Spanish leader.

Answers to . . .
OPEN AIR MARKET

- vehicles; open-air market, people dressed in traditional clothing

Background

Links Across Time

Quechuas When Spain conquered the Incas, the Quechua were forced to work on large farms for Spanish landlords. The Quechua people were treated poorly and barely survived; the Quechua culture was mostly destroyed. Even so, the Quechua are now Peru's largest ethnic group. Quechua and Spanish are the two official languages of Peru.

Background

Daily Life

High-Altitude Living The Quechua have been the subjects of medical studies to understand how they thrive at such high altitudes. It was found that their bodies have adapted to the thin air with larger-than-average lungs and hearts.

Life in Rural Areas In the isolated towns of the altiplano, life is very different from life in the city. There are no telephones to ring. Few buses drive through the villages. Most people are Quechua or Aymara.

READ ACTIVELY

Predict How do you think the Quechuas of the altiplano make a living?

A Day in a Quechua Village Modesto Mamani (moh DES toh muh MAN ee) is a 13-year-old Quechua boy. He wakes before dawn to the freezing mountain air. He eats breakfast as soon as the sun comes up. Breakfast is always the same: a couple of rolls, coffee with sugar, and whole wheat kernels that can be eaten like popcorn. The only other meal may be lunch. It is usually potato and barley soup with chunos—freeze-dried potato skins.

For much of the day, Modesto works in the field with his father and brothers. On other days, he looks after the sheep or goes with his mother to the market. Despite all of these chores, Modesto finds time to play soccer on the tundra in back of his house. A **tundra** is an area where no trees grow because the soil is always cold.

Modesto Mamani at School and at Work

Modesto's life mixes the modern and the traditional. He wants to study to become an engineer so that he can bring technology to the altiplano. But even when he is studying, Modesto is never far from his soccer ball. He also spends a lot of time tending sheep and knitting wool sweaters. Sometimes he even knits when he is playing soccer!

The Straw People Modesto's village is not far from the Uros islands on Lake Titicaca. The people there live on one of the 70 totora reed islands that float on the lake. The islanders use totora reeds for many other purposes besides building islands. They weave it to make boats. They use it as fuel for cooking. They eat the soft inside of the reeds. Most important, though, they use the reeds to repair the islands. Totora reeds last only a few months before they start to rot. A person who slipped through them could die in the lake's icy waters.

On the straw islands, women wake at dawn to get water from the lake for cooking and washing. They spend the rest of the day washing clothes, untangling fishing nets, and making new homes out of reeds. Once or twice a week they go to market to trade fish for rice, potatoes, and sugar. Meanwhile, the men fish and help to repair the straw islands.

A Modern Future Quechuas and other Native Americans living on the altiplano follow traditions that are hundreds of years old. Their communities, however, are slowly changing. Thousands of Native Americans have left for jobs in the city. Life is changing even for those who stay in the village. The future holds a promising mix of old and new ways.

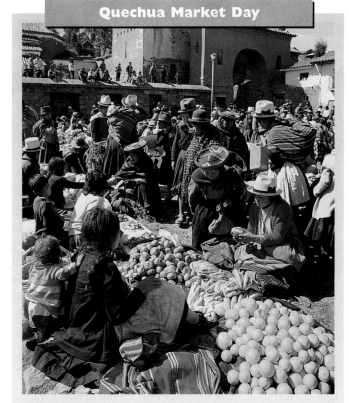

Quechua Market Day

On market days, Quechua from several communities gather together to buy and sell goods. What kinds of goods are being sold at this market?

SECTION 2 REVIEW

1. **Define** (a) altiplano, (b) sierra, (c) montaña, (d) tundra.

2. **Identify** (a) Lake Titicaca, (b) Uros, (c) Quechua, (d) Cuzco.

3. How is the daily life of the Quechua affected by the high altitude of the altiplano?

4. Describe people's lives on the straw islands of Lake Titicaca.

Critical Thinking

5. **Recognizing Bias** Do you think the Quechua see their way of life as outsiders see it? Explain.

Activity

6. **Writing to Learn** Compare life in a Peruvian city with life in a rural Quechua or Uros community.

Resource Directory

Teaching Resources

📁 **Section Quiz** in the Chapter and Section Resources booklet, p. 89, covers the main ideas and key terms in the section. Available in Spanish in the Spanish Chapter and Section Resources booklet, p. 55.

SKILLS ACTIVITY

Using Isolines to Show Elevation

Lesson Objectives

1. Demonstrate how isolines show elevation.
2. Describe how to interpret an isoline map.

Lesson Plan

1 Engage

Warm-Up Activity

To **introduce** the skill, ask volunteers to role-play the scenario in the opening paragraphs. You might point out to students that hikers are not the only people who use maps that show elevation. Engineers also use such maps to figure out the best places to build highways, tunnels, and dams.

Activating Prior Knowledge

Encourage students to think of some of the other advantages of Melissa and José's map. Ask: *How could such a map save time? How would it help them estimate how long their hike would take? How could they use the map to avoid danger?*

2 Explore

Read the paragraphs under the heading Get Ready with students. Review with students what the terms *isoline* and *contour* mean. Assemble materials and organize students into small groups. Then have them read the rest of the skills activity.

Climb straight up, hike over the side, or walk all the way around? That was the question Melissa and José faced.

They stared up at the huge hill in front of them. According to the map, the campsite they were hiking to was exactly on the opposite side of the hill. What was the best route to take?

Melissa spread the map out on a fallen log. "Look," she said, pointing at the map. "This hill is steep on this side, but we can climb it." She traced the route on the map. "But look what we'd run into on the other side!"

"A cliff!" José responded. "We'd never be able to get down. It's way too steep. I guess we'll have to walk around the hill."

"Not so fast. If we head to our left, we can climb up a gentle slope and work our way past the cliff down the hill on the other side. It's kind of steep, but at least we'll be going downhill!"

Get Ready

How could Melissa tell from the map how steep different parts of the hill were? The answer is that the map showed isolines. The word *isolines* comes from the Greek word *iso,* which means "equal," and our word *lines.* Isolines link together equal parts of a map. On the map Melissa and José used, every part of the hill that was the same elevation was linked by an isoline. By studying the pattern of the isolines, Melissa could figure out the best route to take.

Isolines that show elevation are also called contour lines, because their pattern shows the contour, or shape, of the land.

You can make your own contour map. To do this, you will need:

- an irregularly shaped rock, about the size of a cantaloupe
- a pan of water big enough and deep enough to submerge the rock
- a crayon or waterproof marker
- a sheet of blank paper and a pencil

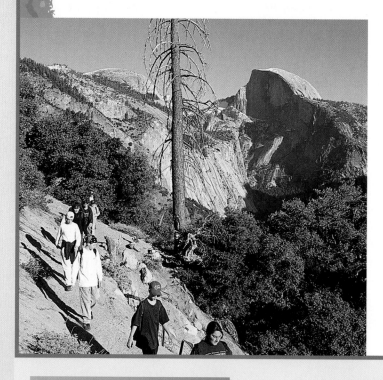

Resource Directory

Teaching Resources

📁 Social Studies and Geography Skills Understanding Isolines, p. 29

Reading a Contour Map, p. 30

Media and Technology

💿 **Social Studies Skills Tutor CD-ROM** builds core social studies skills through interactive lessons and provides skill assessment.

Try It Out

A. Fill the pan with water deep enough to cover the rock.

B. Holding the top of the rock, dip the bottom of it evenly about one inch into the water. Don't drop it! Remove the rock. Use the crayon or marker to trace the waterline all the way around the rock.

C. Dip the rock again, about one inch deeper. The waterline will now be about one inch higher up on the rock. Trace the new waterline with the crayon or marker, all the way around the rock.

D. Continue this process, dipping the rock about one inch deeper each time. Do this until you can go no farther.

E. Now, put the rock on the floor, and look at it from above. Can you see how each crayon or marker line connects the parts of the rock that are the same height? These are isolines. Using a pencil, copy the pattern you see looking down on the rock onto to your piece of paper. Next, label each of your isolines from the outside in. The outside line should be marked "1 inch," the next line "2 inches," and so on.

You have just drawn a map of the top of the rock using isolines.

Apply the Skill

The map on this page shows isolines of a region around the city of Lima, Peru. Use the map to visualize the shape of the land.

1 **Remember that isolines connect places of equal elevation.** Just like the isolines you made on the rock, the isolines on this map connect places of equal elevation. The lines are numbered to show their elevation. What is the lowest elevation shown on the map? What is the highest elevation?

2 **Use the isolines to get useful information from the map.** Remember that where the land is steep, isolines are close together. Where the land is flatter, isolines are farther apart. As you head east from Lima, does the elevation increase or decrease? Now sketch a side view of the map. What is the highest point? What is the lowest? How can you tell?

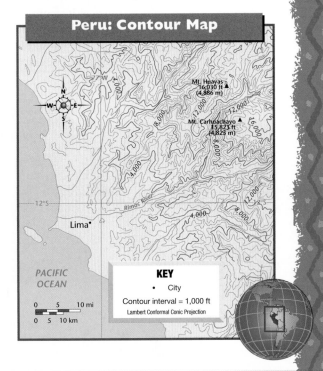

Peru: Contour Map

Mt. Huayas 16,030 ft ▲ (4,886 m)

Mt. Carhuachayo ▲ 15,823 ft (4,823 m)

Rimac River

Lima •

PACIFIC OCEAN

KEY
• City

Contour interval = 1,000 ft
Lambert Conformal Conic Projection

0   5   10 mi
0   5   10 km

3 Teach

Have students **practice** the skill by carrying out the Try It Out demonstration. You might suggest that group members take turns immersing and marking the rock. Display students' rocks and "maps" and discuss how even slight variations in size and shape between different groups' rocks correspond to differences in maps.

For additional reinforcement, students might perform the demonstration again using a much flatter rock. Students should add the pattern of the flat rock to their maps. Ask students to compare the two isoline patterns and explain what the lines reveal about the differences between the two rocks.

4 Assess

Have students **apply** the skill by completing the final part of the activity. To **assess,** evaluate the accuracy of students' answers to the questions and their side-view sketches of the topography shown on the map.

Lesson Objectives

1 Identify the various climates and landscapes of Chile's different regions.

2 Describe how climate affects the products that a region can produce.

3 Explain the relationship between environment and health.

Lesson Plan

1 Engage

Warm-Up Activity

Ask students what they already know about Chile. Have volunteers contribute to a K-W-L chart with these columns: "What We **K**now About Chile," and "What We **W**ant to Find Out." After reading the section, students can fill in a third column, "What We **L**earned About Chile," with the answers to their questions.

Activating Prior Knowledge

Have students read Reach Into Your Background in the Before You Read box. Ask students to speculate on where the peaches they eat in summer come from. Then ask them to speculate on where peaches might come from when it is winter in the United States.

SECTION 3

Chile

A GROWING ECONOMY BASED ON AGRICULTURE

BEFORE YOU READ

Reach Into Your Background

Do you like eating fresh fruit in summer? What if you could have fresh, juicy strawberries and peaches in the middle of winter? Think of ways to make this possible.

Questions to Explore

1. How does Chile's location affect the crops it grows?
2. How does producing more crops help Chile?

Key Terms

pesticide

Key Places

Santiago
Andes
Atacama Desert

It was a fairly quiet day at the airport of Santiago (san tee AH goh), the capital of Chile. Two passengers from Venezuela stepped off a plane. They had their carry-on luggage and a couple of maracas. A maraca is a musical instrument that sounds like a rattle. It is made from a hollow gourd filled with dried-out seeds or pebbles.

There is nothing very surprising about seeing maracas in South America. They are used in many orchestras and bands to play Latin music. So why was the customs officer staring at them suspiciously? Before the travelers had time to pass through customs, the officer grabbed the maracas and X-rayed them. Then he broke them open. Just as he thought, they did not contain dried-up seeds or pebbles. They were full of new seeds that were good for planting.

▼ Maracas are normally used to play music.

Life in Chile

Chile may be the only country in the world that inspects maracas brought into its borders. In recent years, Chile's agriculture has been booming. Chile makes millions of dollars a year by exporting peaches, grapes, cherries, and other

Resource Directory

Teaching Resources

📁 **Reproducible Lesson Plan** in the Chapter and Section Resources booklet, p. 90, provides a summary of the section lesson.

📁 **Guided Reading and Review** in the Chapter and Section Resources booklet, p. 91, provides a structure for mastering key concepts and reviewing key terms in the section. Available in Spanish in the Spanish Chapter and Section Resources booklet, p. 56.

📠 **Section Reading Support Transparencies** provide answers to the Questions to Explore in a graphic organizer format.

Program Resources

📁 **Outline Maps** South America: Political, p. 11

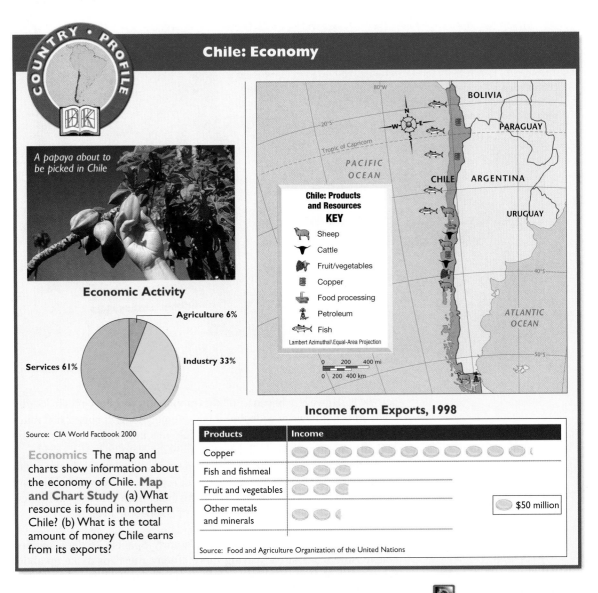

Chile: Economy

A papaya about to be picked in Chile

Economic Activity

Agriculture 6%
Industry 33%
Services 61%

Source: CIA World Factbook 2000

Chile: Products and Resources
KEY

- Sheep
- Cattle
- Fruit/vegetables
- Copper
- Food processing
- Petroleum
- Fish

Lambert Azimuthal\Equal-Area Projection

0 200 400 mi
0 200 400 km

Income from Exports, 1998

Products	Income
Copper	
Fish and fishmeal	
Fruit and vegetables	
Other metals and minerals	

$50 million

Source: Food and Agriculture Organization of the United Nations

Economics The map and charts show information about the economy of Chile. **Map and Chart Study** (a) What resource is found in northern Chile? (b) What is the total amount of money Chile earns from its exports?

fruits and vegetables. Their country is protected by the Andes mountains, so some of the insect pests and animal diseases that plague other countries never reach Chile. That is why the government is so concerned about what enters now. Protecting Chile's crops is very important. No plant or animal matter from foreign places is allowed because it might bring disease to the crops.

The Geography of Chile Look at the physical map of Latin America in the Activity Atlas at the front of your book. Find the Andes Mountains. They run down the whole length of this long country like a giant spine. Chile is narrow. On average, it is about 100 miles (161 km) wide. If Chile were flat, it would take less than two hours to drive

Take It to the NET
Data Update For the most recent data on Chile, visit **www.phschool.com**.

Media and Technology

Social Studies Skills Tutor CD-ROM builds core social studies skills through interactive lessons and provides skill assessment.

2 Explore

Have students read the section. Tell them to think about the following questions as they read. Why do certain crops grow in particular locations? What are the important products of Chile? Why did the government encourage the growth of industry in the early 1980s? Why did industrial growth cause some problems?

3 Teach

Direct student pairs to make a product map of Chile. Indicate that maps should show the country's main regions, important geographical features, and the products grown, manufactured, or mined in each region. This activity should take about 15 minutes.

4 Assess

See the Answers to the Section Review. You may also use students' product maps as assessment.

Acceptable maps show the main regions mentioned in the text and at least one product for each region.

Commendable maps include industrial and mining products as well as agricultural.

Outstanding maps show the major geographical features of each region as well as most of the products mentioned in the text.

Answers to ...

MAP AND CHART STUDY

(a) fish
(b) about $950 million

Critical Thinking

Recognizing Cause and Effect *Suitable as a whole class or an individual activity.* Indicate to students that one way to understand natural events, such as seasons of the year, is to learn what causes them. Have students use a globe and a flashlight to model the sun's rays at the Equator as well as north and south of the Equator. They may want to refer to the diagrams in the Map and Globe Handbook. Have them answer questions such as these: *If you were visiting southern Chile in July, would the temperature be low or high? What clothes would you wear? What sports could you participate in?* Have students place their responses in a cause- and effect-diagram.

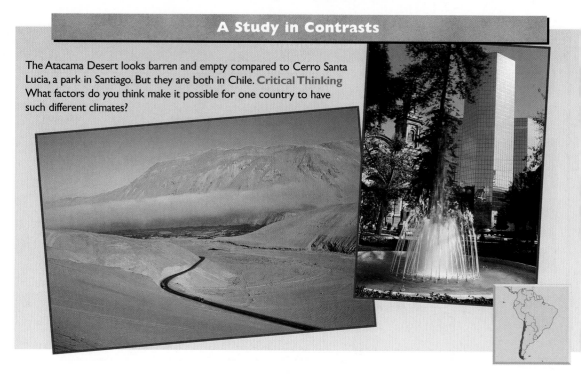

The Atacama Desert looks barren and empty compared to Cerro Santa Lucia, a park in Santiago. But they are both in Chile. **Critical Thinking** What factors do you think make it possible for one country to have such different climates?

LINKS TO LANGUAGE ARTS

What Makes a Poem? What do you think is a proper topic for a poem? Chilean poet Pablo Neruda was willing to write a poem about anything. He wrote many poems about everyday subjects, like dusty wheels, sweat, and his socks. He even wrote a poem about a person wearing out a pair of shoes. He called it "You Flame Foot!"

across it. However, because of the mountains, it takes much longer. Chile may not be very wide, but it is extremely long. It runs 2,650 miles (4,265 km) down the Pacific Coast. Chile reaches all the way to the tip of South America. It is the longest, narrowest country in the world.

Chile contains an amazing variety of lands and climates. In the north is the Atacama Desert, one of the driest regions in the world. The long central valley near the coast has rolling hills, high grasses, and dense forests. This is the region where most of the people live.

The People of Chile Chile's early Spanish settlers married Native Americans already living there. Today, mestizos make up about 95 percent of the population. Only 3 percent of Chileans are Native Americans.

The lifestyles of Chileans vary from region to region. In the far south, sheep herders in heavy wool sweaters brave the strong winds. Farther north in the central valley, farmers grow wheat, potatoes, sugar beets, corn, tomatoes, and many fruits. In the cities, people in business suits hurry in and out of tall skyscrapers. Few people live in the Atacama Desert of the far north. Not many plants or animals can survive here either. But the desert is rich in copper, so the region is dotted with mines. Chile exports more copper than any country in the world.

A Chilean City A visit to Santiago is unforgettable. Old Spanish buildings stand near gleaming skyscrapers. The city is in the valley of the central plain, so the altitude is low enough to produce mild weather.

Answers to ...

A STUDY IN CONTRASTS

- physical features such as mountains, ocean coast, and plains

The sea makes the air humid. Palm trees grow in the public parks. The snowcapped Andes lie to the east.

The beautiful sights of Santiago are sometimes blocked by a thick layer of smog. Pollution has become so bad that it makes many small children and old people sick. The signs of pollution are everywhere. On a bad day, people wear surgical masks in order to breathe, or they press scarves to their faces. Few mothers bring their babies out on a day like this. If they do, the babies may have to be rushed to the hospital to receive oxygen.

The Problems of Industry   How did pollution get to be so bad in Santiago? One cause is the city's location. It is surrounded by the Andes on three sides. The mountains trap the exhaust from vehicles and smoke from factories in the valley. This is especially true during the winter, when there is not much wind.

Another reason for the increase in pollution is the economy. Before the 1980s, Chile's economy depended mostly on its copper exports. Part of the copper industry was owned by the government. The profits went into projects that were supposed to help everyone in the country.

READ ACTIVELY

Connect What cities in the United States have problems with pollution? Which of these cities, like Santiago, are surrounded by mountains?

Activity

Interdisciplinary Connections

Science   Remind students that smog is a major problem in many cities and industrial areas worldwide. Direct students to work in groups of four to research these questions: What is smog? How is it produced? What harm can it do? How can we prevent smog? One member of each group can present a short oral report to the class.
Kinesthetic

▼ German architecture can be found in many parts of southern Chile. German immigrants arrived here more than 100 years ago.

Activity

Cooperative Learning

Uninvited Pests Have students work in groups to find out what measures are taken in our own country to keep out pests that might attack fruit and vegetable crops. Have students find information about damaging insects such as the Mediterranean fruit fly. Students should find out what the pest eats, how it travels to the United States, and what damage it can cause. Allow each group to choose one of the following presentation options: (1) an advertisement for the school paper warning against the pest; 2) a song on the topic; or 3) a demonstration on how customs officers search for the pest. *English Language Learners, Kinesthetic*

In northern Chile, the soil is not very good for farming. Many people here fish for a living. Chile's fishing industry is one of the largest in the world. **Critical Thinking** What difference do you see between people who fish for a living and those who fish for fun?

LINKS ACROSS THE WORLD

Falling Copper Prices Other countries besides Chile suffered when copper prices dropped in the 1980s. The Democratic Republic of Congo, in Central Africa, paid all its trade bills in 1980, mostly from the money it earned selling copper. By 1990, however, Congo was heavily in debt because of the fall in copper prices.

In the early 1980s, world copper prices began to drop. The government tried to solve the problem by encouraging industry. The government relaxed the laws that protected the environment from pollution. Government leaders thought that if the laws were too strict, some private industries would not survive. Encouraging private industry did save Chile's economy. It was easier to mine and process copper. Tons of steel, cement, glass, and electronic equipment were made and sold.

The standard of living rose. But so did pollution levels. Also, more people moved to the cities to get jobs in the new industries. More than 80 percent of Chile's people now live in cities.

During the 1990s, Chile's government took action to reduce the problems of pollution in the city. On days when the wind does not blow, industries are shut down. And only a limited number of cars may enter the city. Further, the government may also require new cars to have special exhaust systems that do not produce much pollution. No one knows how well these solutions will work. But most Chileans are hoping for a cleaner and healthier future.

Answers to ...

NET FISHING OFF CHILE'S COAST

• Responses may vary. Possible response: people who fish for fun use rods and reels, not nets.

Chile's Agricultural Revolution

The drop in copper prices in the early 1980s made it clear that Chile could not depend on copper to survive. Chile decided that one way to improve the economy was to sell more crops.

Pest-Free Produce   Chile's fruits and vegetables are free of many common plant pests. As a result, these products are welcome in many other countries. To supply the demands of these countries, about 15 percent of Chile's people farm. Chilean workers are also employed at packing plants for fruits and vegetables. Modern farming methods help grow even more crops.

By the late 1980s, agriculture was especially important for Chile. It had become a billion dollar industry, providing jobs for about 900,000 Chileans. Chile shipped wheat, potatoes, sugar beets, corn, grapes, melons, apples, peaches, apricots, cherries, and other fruits and vegetables around the world.

The United States, Japan, and Europe are an especially good market for Chilean produce from October through May. These months are winter in the Northern Hemisphere, but summer in the Southern Hemisphere. This means that Chile can provide fruits and vegetables to the United States, for example, during the months when American farmers cannot.

Although the Andes mountains protect Chile from many common plant pests and diseases, Chile has some pests of its own. To prevent them from destroying the fruits and vegetables, Chilean farmers use different kinds of pesticides. A **pesticide** (PES tuh syd) is a chemical used to kill insects and stop diseases that can hurt crops. Pesticides have helped farmers to increase crop production. But some people think that the pesticides may have caused certain kinds of illness in young children. As a result, Chilean scientists and farmers are trying to find ways to control pests without using chemicals. They want to make sure that Chilean fruits and vegetables are the tastiest and healthiest that people can buy.

SECTION 3 REVIEW

1. **Define** pesticide.

2. **Identify** (a) Santiago, (b) Andes, (c) Atacama Desert.

3. What aspect of Chile's location gives it an advantage in agriculture?

4. How has the growth of agriculture helped Chileans?

Critical Thinking

5. **Expressing Problems Clearly** Industries can cause pollution, but when industries close down, people lose their jobs. If you were the mayor of an industrial city with a pollution problem, what would you do?

Activity

6. **Writing to Learn** Like many places around the world, Chile is a popular tourist destination. Think about the reasons why a tourist might like to visit Chile. Describe the country's most interesting features. Present these paragraphs in the form of a tourist brochure.

Section 3 Review

1. a chemical used to kill insects and stop diseases that can hurt crops

2. (a) the capital city of Chile (b) mountains that run along the length of Chile (c) desert in northern Chile that is one of the driest regions in the world

3. Because Chile is protected by the high Andes, some of the agricultural pests and diseases are naturally kept out of the country. This allows Chile to be highly productive in growing fruits and vegetables.

4. The growth of agriculture saved the Chilean economy after the price of its chief export, copper, fell in the 1980s.

5. Answers may vary. Student responses should propose a balance between expansion of jobs and industry, a strong concern for health, and industry responsibility for a livable environment.

6. Students' brochures may vary, but should highlight several of the country's interesting features, such as the Andes, the Atacama Desert, and the beautiful sights of Santiago.

SECTION
4

Venezuela

OIL POWERS THE ECONOMY

1. Relate the oil industry to the economy and way of life of Venezuela.

2. Describe the effects of the oil crisis on the people of Venezuela.

3. Trace the changing economy of Venezuela through the history of one family.

4. Evaluate the efforts of the Venezuelan government to deal with its economy.

Lesson Plan

1 Engage

Warm-Up Activity

Ask students to name common life changes people their age might experience, such as a move, the birth of a sibling, a friend moving away, or a change of schools. Then invite them to do a quick-write about a change they have experienced and how it made them feel.

Activating Prior Knowledge

Have students read Reach Into Your Background in the Before You Read box. Students' lists of things they cannot control may include going to school or getting a new brother or sister; things they can control may include choosing after-school activities.

BEFORE YOU READ

Reach Into Your Background

There are some things in life that people can control and others that they cannot. Think of at least one thing in your life that you can control. Think of another thing that is beyond your control.

Questions to Explore

1. How was Venezuela affected by the oil boom?

2. How is Venezuela trying to change its economy for the future?

Key Terms

boom
privatization

Key Places

Caracas
Lake Maracaibo

▼ Many of Venezuela's largest petroleum deposits lie beneath the floor of Lake Maracaibo.

Welcome to Caracas (kuh RAHK us), population more than 3 million. The view from a high-rise apartment can be breathtaking. At night, thousands of lights dot the surrounding hills. Below, on the street, fashionable-looking people walk by on their way to dinner or a movie.

Outside, the air is balmy. You won't find much pollution in the air, either. The city is in a valley that runs from east to west. Winds blow through it. They sweep the exhaust of the many cars out of the city.

Why not visit one of the cafes? Or if you're lucky, you might find a party for teenagers going on right in the street. They may be listening to American-style rap music. But the words will be in Spanish. If you have the time, take the Caracas subway. It cost the government millions to build, more than any other subway in the world. You can get almost anywhere in the city on it, and the fare is only about 25 cents.

A Land Made Wealthy by Oil

Venezuela's government could pay for the subways because of money it made from the sale of oil. Venezuela has vast supplies of oil. The Country Profile map shows where Venezuela's oil is located. Venezuela's oil has earned millions of dollars on the world market. People migrated from the countryside to work for the oil companies.

Resource Directory

Teaching Resources

📁 **Reproducible Lesson Plan** in the Chapter and Section Resources booklet, p. 93, provides a summary of the section lesson.

📁 **Guided Reading and Review** in the Chapter and Section Resources booklet, p. 94, provides a structure for mastering key concepts and reviewing key terms in the section. Available in Spanish in the Spanish Chapter and Section Resources booklet, p. 58

📁 **Section Reading Support Transparencies** provide answers to the Questions to Explore in a graphic organizer format.

Program Resources

📁 **Outline Maps** South America: Political, p. 11

Venezuela: Economy

Economic Activity

- Agriculture 4%
- Industry 63%
- Services 33%

Source: CIA World Factbook 2000

Sources of Electricity

- Hydro 74%
- Combustion 26%
- Nuclear 0%

0 20 40 60 80 100

% of total generation by type

Source: Dorling Kindersley World Desk Reference

Venezuela: Products and Resources KEY
- Petroleum
- Steel
- Gold
- Cocoa
- Coffee
- Fruit

Lambert Azimuthal Equal-Area Projection

0 250 300 mi
0 250 300 km

Workers select coffee beans

Economics The map and charts show information about Venezuela's economy. **Map and Chart Study** (a) What area of Venezuela contains most of its resources? (b) What is Venezuela's main source of electricity?

They helped maintain the giant oil rigs in Lake Maracaibo. They also worked in oil refineries.

Both the government and individuals own oil companies in Venezuela. They have grown rich mining, processing, and selling oil. By the early 1980s, Venezuela was the richest country in Latin America. Much of the money has gone to Caracas, where most Venezuelans live.

Ups and Downs of Oil Prices Venezuela's oil was discovered about 75 years ago. Since then, Venezuela has pumped about 67 billion barrels of oil. There seemed to be no end to the money that could be made in the oil industry. Except for the Persian Gulf region, Venezuela has some of the biggest oil reserves in the world.

During the 1970s, the price of oil went up. An oil boom began. A **boom** is a period of increased prosperity during which more of a product is produced and sold. The standard of living of many Venezuelans went up, too. That is when the government started spending huge sums

Take It to the NET
Data Update For the most recent data on Venezuela, visit **www.phschool.com**.

2 Explore
Have students read the section. Indicate that they should read to find answers to questions such as: How did the oil boom change Venezuela? What happened to Venezuela when the price of oil fell? How is the government of Venezuela dealing with its economic problems? Once students have read the section, discuss the answers to these questions.

3 Teach
Work with the class to create a time line showing the changes in Venezuela's economy. The time line should include the 1920s: Oil Is Discovered; the 1970s: Oil Prices Go Up; the mid-1980s: Oil Prices Fall; and the late 1980s and 1990s: Government Privatizes Its Industries and Encourages New Industries. Have students work in pairs to supply an *effect* for each *cause* listed on the time line. Have them place the effects in the correct time sequence. Encourage them to add more of the effects that they learned from the text. This activity should take about 20 minutes.

SKILLS MINI LESSON

Interpreting Graphs: Circle Graphs
To **introduce** the skill, tell students that many important facts can be shown in a graph. Help students **practice** the skill by asking them to find the following information in the Venezuela Country Profile: the most common economic activity (industry); the least common economic activity (agriculture). Ask them to predict, then find, the sum of the percentages shown in the Economic Activity graph. Have students explain why the sum is 100 percent. Have students **apply** the skill by forming questions using the circle graph in the Country Profile. Direct students to share and answer one another's questions.

Answers to ...
MAP AND CHART STUDY

(a) the north
(b) hydro

SECTION 4 149

4 Assess

See the answers to the Section Review. You may also use students' time lines as assessment.

Acceptable time lines show one effect for each cause.

Commendable time lines include more than one effect for each cause and show understanding of how the causes and effects are linked.

Outstanding time lines exhibit greater detail and depth of understanding regarding how causes and effects are linked.

Background

Global Perspectives

Oil Cartel Venezuela was a founding member of the Organization of Petroleum Exporting Countries (OPEC). The organization was formed in 1960 so that oil-producing countries could control the price of oil throughout the world. Other members of OPEC include Ecuador in South America; Iran, Iraq, Kuwait, Saudi Arabia, Qatar, Libya, and the United Arab Emirates in the Middle East; Algeria, Nigeria, and Gabon in Africa; and Indonesia in Asia. In late 1973, OPEC raised the price of oil by 200 percent, which greatly affected life in the industrial countries of the world. The costs of heating homes, running factories, and fueling motor vehicles skyrocketed.

Predict Do you think that one resource, such as oil, can support a country forever? Why or why not?

of money. Many people were hired to run government agencies and government-owned businesses. The government built expensive subways and high-quality roads. The government began to borrow money so that it could spend even more.

In the mid-1980s, too much oil was produced in the world. The price of oil started to fall, but millions of people were still employed by the government. They ran the many government offices. Or they worked in government industries. Finally, the government was spending much more than it could earn. As the price of oil continued to drop, many people lost their jobs.

The New Poverty Poor people from the country were hit the hardest by the drop in oil sales. They had come to Caracas and other cities to work in the growing industries. When the oil industries cut back, many of these people were left without jobs.

Venezuelan Culture

During the oil boom, Venezuela changed from a traditional culture based on agriculture to a modern urban country. Now about 80 percent of the population lives in cities.

A Venezuelan Life Juan Varderi (hwahn var DEHR ee) is about 28 years old. He is a good example of the new Venezuelan. Juan grew up in a densely populated coastal area north of Caracas.

▼ Caracas is the largest city in Venezuela. It is also the country's capital.

Resource Directory

Media and Technology

Social Studies Skills Tutor CD-ROM builds core social studies skills through interactive lessons and provides skill assessment.

Chart Study The United States has several major petroleum deposits, but still uses more petroleum than it produces. The United States imports petroleum from Canada, Mexico, Nigeria, Saudi Arabia, and Venezuela. **Critical Thinking** When did the United States import the least amount of petroleum from Venezuela? When did it import the most?

Source: Energy Information Administration

Activity

Journal Writing

Pen Pal Ask students to choose the country of Brazil, Peru, Chile, or Venezuela and consider what it would be like to have a pen pal there. Have students make a list of the things they would like to know about the country they chose. Then direct them to write a letter to their pen pal, introducing themselves, telling about their lives, and asking questions.

Juan's grandfather raised sheep on a ranch east of Lake Maracaibo. He made a fairly good living selling wool and meat to people in Caracas. He fully expected that his son, Juan's father, would work with him, so he never encouraged him to go to school. But in the 1970s, Juan's father was lured by the oil industry, which was beginning to boom.

Varderi's father left the ranch at age 16. He went to work on an oil rig that was owned by the government. By the time Juan was born, the family was living in Caracas in a small apartment. They had a radio but no telephone. Juan Varderi grew up playing baseball on the streets of Caracas. Baseball is very popular in Venezuela.

By the early 1980s, Juan's father was making more money. The family bought a television. Televisions had become popular. Varderi remembers those years as the most exciting time of his life.

> " There were American programs you could watch on television, dubbed into Spanish. My friends and I paid attention to the clothes that the Americans wore. We tried to dress like them. We thought their music was the coolest in the world. We used to watch rock videos and try to learn the words of songs. In the early 1980s, we thought we could live just like rich Americans seemed to live. We didn't understand it was only taking place on TV. We didn't know what was going to happen to us in just a few years. "

LINKS ACROSS THE WORLD

Germany in Venezuela In 1843, the Venezuelan government recruited almost 400 Germans to live in the mountains west of Caracas. For over 100 years their colony, Colonia Tovar, was isolated. The people spoke German, ate German food, and married only Germans. The town is still so different from the rest of the country that it deserves its nickname, "Germany in Venezuela."

Teaching Resources

📁 **Section Quiz** in the Chapter and Section Resources booklet, p. 95, covers the main ideas and key terms in the section. Available in Spanish in the Spanish Chapter and Section Resources booklet, p. 59.

📁 **Vocabulary** in the Chapter and Section Resources booklet, p. 97, provides a review of key terms in the chapter. Available in Spanish in the Spanish Chapter and Section Resources booklet, p. 61.

📁 **Reteaching** in the Chapter and Section Resources booklet, p. 98, provides a structure for students who may need additional help in mastering chapter content.

📁 **Enrichment** in the Chapter and Section Resources booklet, p. 99, extends chapter content and enriches students' understanding.

📁 **Spanish Glossary** in the Spanish Chapter and Section Resources, pp. 62–65, provides key terms translated from English to Spanish as well as definitions in Spanish.

Answers to . . .

CHART STUDY

• 1980, 2000

Links Across Time

Venezuelan Farming
Traditionally, agriculture has played a small role in Venezuela's economy. Less than 5 percent of Venezuelan land is used for farming. During the oil-boom years, there was little interest in developing farmland. The country had enough money to import even basic agricultural goods. Currently, large modernized farms produce sugar cane, cotton, and rice. Smaller, family-run farms produce corn and beans for local markets and coffee and cacao for urban and export markets.

Ask Questions If you had a chance to meet Juan Varderi, what questions would you ask? What questions do you think that Juan would ask you?

A few years later, when Juan Varderi turned 15, oil prices fell. His father lost his job. Three years after that, the family was in danger of losing its apartment. Varderi thought his family would have to move. But his father found another solution.

Government Businesses Go Public The solution Juan's father found lay in a new government policy of privatization. **Privatization** (pry vuh tih ZAY shun) occurs when the government sells its industries to individuals or private companies. In the late 1980s and the 1990s, the government decided to sell some of its businesses to private corporations. It hoped that the corporations would make big profits. The profits would help workers. When the government turned over an oil refinery to a private company, Varderi's father applied for a job there. He was hired. The salary was less than he had earned working for the government, but it was enough to keep his family in their apartment.

Finding Other Ways to Make Money Venezuela started new industries in an attempt to make its economy less dependent on oil. The country is producing goods such as steel, gold, cocoa, coffee, and tropical fruits. Varderi's oldest brother, Julio, received money from the government to start a small fruit orchard. This year he made enough money to support his family and help pay for a ticket for Juan to visit New York City. It was a trip Juan had always dreamed of.

Planting Corn in Venezuela

The Piaroa, one of Venezuela's Native American groups, farm on land they have cleared in Amazonas Territory. **Critical Thinking** What details from this photograph provide clues that these men are planting?

Answers to ...

PLANTING CORN IN VENEZUELA

- People are digging holes with hoes in cleared land.

Resource Directory

Teaching Resources

📁 **Chapter Summary** in the Chapter and Section Resources booklet, p. 96, provides a summary of chapter content. Available in Spanish in the Spanish Chapter and Section Resources booklet, p. 60.

📁 **Cooperative Learning Activity** in the Activities and Projects booklet, pp. 40–43, provides two student handouts, one page of teacher's directions, and a scoring rubric for a cooperative learning activity on making a mural.

Media and Technology

🎧 **Guided Reading Audiotapes** (English and Spanish)

🎧 **Student Edition on Audio CD** The entire text of the Student Edition is available in a series of audio CDs.

Teenagers in Caracas

Many Venezuelans like to wear fashions from the United States, especially jeans. They also like to meet each other in plazas, or public squares. In fact, addresses in Caracas are given by plazas and corners, not streets.

A Changed Venezuela Whatever Venezuela's economic fortune is, one thing is certain. The oil boom brought Venezuela into the modern world. When televisions, cellular phones, and other conveniences came into Venezuelan homes, life changed permanently. Juan Varderi dreams of having these things again in the future. And he is willing to work as hard as necessary to get them.

SECTION 4 REVIEW

1. **Define** (a) boom, (b) privatization.

2. **Identify** (a) Caracas, (b) Lake Maracaibo.

3. (a) What happened to many Venezuelans during the oil boom? (b) What happened to them after?

4. Explain how Venezuela is trying to improve its economy.

Critical Thinking
5. **Drawing Conclusions** (a) Why did the drop in oil prices affect Venezuela so much? (b) What do you think Venezuela should do to avoid economic problems in the future?

Activity
6. **Writing Activity** Juan Varderi learned about United States culture from television programs. Describe America as shown on television.

SKILLS MINI LESSON

Organizing Your Time
Suitable as a whole-class activity. To **introduce** the skill, indicate to students that often the best way to tackle a large task is to divide it into small steps and to set a time to complete each step. Have students **practice** the skill by assigning groups of four a South American country not covered in this chapter. Groups can then create a travel brochure aimed at attracting tourists to that country. Remind students that they can find the information they need in almanacs and encyclopedias. Encourage each group to keep track of the time it spends planning, researching, and composing the travel brochure. Display students' brochures and discuss their findings as a class.

1. (a) a period of increased prosperity during which more of a product is produced and sold (b) the process of a government's selling its industries to individuals and private companies

2. (a) city in Venezuela with a population of about 3.3 million people (b) site of giant oil rigs

3. (a) Many Venezuelans moved from farms to the cities to work in the oil industry and for government agencies and industries. Their standard of living improved. (b) When oil prices fell, many government and oil company workers lost their jobs.

4. Answers may vary. Sample answer: Venezuela's government has privatized some of its industries. It has also encouraged the development of industries other than oil and has made loans to farmers.

5. Students' answers will vary. (a) Students should indicate that the country was too dependent on income from oil, and that when oil prices dropped, the government should have cut its spending. (b) Suggestions for the future might include working within a budget and keeping debt at a minimum.

6. Students' answers should show that they understand that the parts of American culture shown on TV do not reflect the lives of all Americans. Accept reasonable examples of typical TV sitcoms, dramas, music, and sports that show some aspects of our culture. Students might mention how American TV ads might give a false picture of Americans.

Reviewing Main Ideas

1. Through a process called photosynthesis, the trees and plants of the rain forest convert the waste gas carbon dioxide into oxygen that people and animals need to breathe.

2. Timber and gold are natural resources from the rain forest that provide income for the country. Hunters, working illegally, capture exotic animals for pets, food, or for their skins, selling them for personal gain. Farmers clear land for farming. Native American groups depend on the rain forest for their livelihood.

3. (a) The climate of the altiplano is cold, with freezing nights. There is little rain for farming. (b) The Quechua sleep with many sweaters and blankets and are accustomed to the cold climate. Because there is little rain, they plant hardy crops like rice and potatoes.

4. They are moving to the cities for jobs in industry.

5. Chile wants to keep out agricultural products that might contain insect pests that eat crops and spread diseases among Chilean animals.

6. (a) The mountains surrounding Santiago, Chile's capital city, trap the pollution from automobile exhaust and industry smoke. (b) The mountains also keep out insect pests that transmit diseases to plants and animals.

7. Many moved from farms to the cities to take jobs in government, oil, and other industries.

8. Relying on one resource, such as oil, makes a country too dependent on and sensitive to changes in the income from that resource.

Reviewing Key Terms

Sentences should show the correct meaning of a word through context.

CHAPTER 6 Review and Activities

Reviewing Main Ideas

1. Why are the rain forests so important for the environment?
2. In what ways does the Brazilian economy depend upon the rain forest?
3. (a) What challenges does life on the altiplano present?
   (b) How do the people who live there overcome these challenges?
4. Why are many Quechua and Aymara moving to the cities of Peru?
5. Why does Chile have such strict customs laws?
6. (a) How does geography contribute to Chile's pollution problem?
   (b) How does it contribute to its agricultural boom?
7. What type of lifestyle changes did many Venezuelans make during the oil boom of the 1970s?
8. Why is it important for Venezuela to develop new ways to boost its economy?

Reviewing Key Terms

Use each key term below in a sentence that shows the meaning of the term.
1. canopy
2. photosynthesis
3. altiplano
4. sierra
5. montaña
6. tundra
7. pesticide
8. boom
9. privatization

Critical Thinking

1. **Making Comparisons** In what ways have Chile's and Venezuela's economic histories been similar? How have they differed?
2. **Recognizing Cause and Effect** How do you think the coming of modern conveniences like electricity will change life for the Quechua?

Graphic Organizer

Copy the chart onto a piece of paper. Then fill in the empty boxes to complete the chart.

	Brazil	Peru	Chile	Venezuela
Important exports				
Major cities				

Graphic Organizer

	Brazil	Peru	Chile	Venezuela
Important exports	coffee	copper	copper, fruits	oil
Major cities	Rio de Janeiro, Brasília	Cuzco	Santiago	Caracas

Map Activity

For each place listed below, write the letter from the map that shows its location.

1. Amazon River
2. Rio de Janeiro
3. Brasília
4. Cuzco
5. Lake Titicaca
6. Santiago
7. Andes
8. Caracas
9. Orinoco River

South America: Place Location

Writing Activity

Writing a Test
Write your own test about the economies of Chile and Venezuela. You may include multiple choice, true/false, fill in the blank, and essay questions on your test. Ask questions about how natural resources are

important in each country's economy. Ask about benefits and problems that have affected each economy. Write an answer key to go with your test. Then trade tests with a partner. Take each other's tests. How did you do?

Take It to the NET

Activity Learn about life in the rain forest, issues of concern, and actions you can take. For help in completing this activity, visit www.phschool.com.

Chapter 6 Self-Test To review what you have learned, take the Chapter 6 Self-Test and get instant feedback on your answers. Go to www.phschool.com to take the test.

Skills Review

Turn to the Skill Activity.
Review the steps for making a contour map. Then answer the following: (a) What are isolines? (b) Explain in your own words how you can use isolines to get useful information from a map.

How Am I Doing?

Answer these questions to help you check your progress.

1. Can I explain how changes in Brazil's rain forests affect the rest of the world?
2. Do I understand how geography has affected the lifestyles of Native Americans in Peru?
3. Can I explain why agriculture is important to Chile's economy?
4. Do I understand how the oil boom affected Venezuela's economy?
5. What information from this chapter can I include in my journal?

Critical Thinking

1. Both countries depended too much on one industry—Chile on copper and Venezuela on oil. When prices dropped for these products, the economies of both countries suffered. Chile returned to an emphasis on agriculture, which has been very successful. Venezuela has emphasized industry and is still working to recover.

2. Electricity may make their lives easier because of better heating and lighting. It will also connect them to the outside world through radio, TV, and the telephone.

Map Activity

1. D	4. E	7. C
2. H	5. F	8. A
3. G	6. I	9. B

Skills Review

(a) On a contour map, isolines are lines that connect places of equal elevation. (b) If the isolines are close together on a map the land is steep. Where the isolines are far apart, the land is nearly flat.

Writing Activity

Students' tests will vary, but all should cover the main ideas presented about the economies of Chile and Venezuela.

Take It to the NET

Students may wish to use the Internet to search for similar topics or activities. Suggest possible search terms, such as "Latin America rain forest" or "rain forest conservation."

Guide students to a search engine. Four of the most useful are Infoseek, AltaVista, Lycos, and Yahoo. For additional suggestions on using the Internet, refer to the Prentice Hall Social Studies' Educator's Handbook "Using the Internet," in the *Prentice Hall World Explorer* Program Resources.

For chapter-by-chapter links to age-appropriate sites in world studies and geography, including Self-Tests, visit the *World Explorer* companion Web site at: **http://www.phschool.com**

How Am I Doing?

Point out to students that this checklist is just a quick reminder for them of what they learned in the chapter. If their answer to any of the questions is *no* or if they are unsure, they may need to review the topic.

Resource Directory

Teaching Resources

 Chapter Tests Forms A and B are in the Tests booklet, pp. 32–37.

Final Exam Form A and B are in the Tests booklet, pp. 38–43.

Media and Technology

 Computer Test Bank CD-ROM

Resource Pro® CD-ROM

Prentice Hall Assessment System

Rain Forest Resources

Lesson Objectives

1. Identify and describe some of the renewable rain forest resources.

2. Design a product that might be made from renewable rain forest resources.

3. Use interdisciplinary skills to create packaging, advertising, and pricing for the product.

Lesson Plan

1 Engage

Warm-Up Activity

Ask students to write a two- or three-line description of their favorite television commercials. Discuss with the class the qualities that make these commercials effective. Make a class list of the features of effective commercials and advertising.

Activating Prior Knowledge

Talk with students about products made from the rain forest. Ask them whether they have seen any consumer products labeled as coming from the rain forest.

The tropical rain forests of South America are in danger. Lumbering, mining, ranching, and farming are destroying the trees and plants of the rain forests. As you know, some people are trying to save the rain forests by using the renewable, or replaceable, parts of the trees and plants in products for sale. For example, cashews and brazil nuts from rain forest trees can be harvested without harming the trees themselves. Oils from rain forest plants and nuts can be used in lotions and shampoos. If people can make money from a rain forest without cutting or burning it, people will have reasons to preserve the forests.

Purpose

In this activity, you will invent a new rain forest product. As you work on this activity, you will discover how rain forest products can be used without destroying rain forest resources.

Invent a Product

Think of a product that can be made with a renewable rain forest resource. Rain forest nuts are used in candy, ice cream, and cookies. Natural rubber from rubber trees is used to make bath toys. Use encyclopedias and other references to find out about the fruits of the assai tree, the oil of the babacu tree, and the resin of the copaiba tree. Think of something from the rain forest that many people need. Once you decide on your product, give it a name that people will remember.

Resource Directory

Teaching Resources

📁 **Activity Shop: Interdisciplinary** in the Activities and Projects booklet, p. 7, provides a structure that helps students complete the interdisciplinary activity.

Design a Package

When you have a product in mind, decide how it should look in a store. Should it come in a bag, a box, a can, or a bottle? Design the package, including art work and a product description.

Set a Price

Do some research to find out what products like yours cost. Visit or call a store. Then decide on the price for your product that is in the range of similar products. Put the price on your package.

Figure Your Costs

Now figure out how much money is needed to make your product. Assume that your costs are half of the selling price. For example, if your selling price is $6.50, then your manufacturing cost is $3.25. Divide your total manufacturing cost into the categories listed below.

- 50 percent for labor
- 25 percent for materials
- 10 percent for transportation
- 10 percent for advertising
- 5 percent for taxes

Then make a circle graph showing the percentage and dollar amount for each type of expense.

Make a Poster

Make a poster showing the layers of rain forest life: herb layer, shrub layer, understory, canopy, and emergent layer. Use encyclopedias and reference books such as *Usborne Science and Experiments: Ecology* (Usborne Publishing, 1988). Show the different kinds of creatures that live at each level and explain how they survive.

Links to Other Subjects

Designing a package for a new product	**Art**
Making a circle graph	**Math**
Doing research on the layers of the rain forest	**Science**
Writing a script	**Language Arts**
Writing a song	**Music**

Create a Commercial

You can make a commercial to advertise your rain forest product. Use the poster you made as a prop for your commercial. Write a short script that explains why it is important to protect rain forests and how your product helps in that effort. Write and perform an original jingle or music for the commercial. You can produce your commercial on computer or shoot it with a video camera. Or, you can perform your commercial for the rest of the class. Remember that your commercial should make people want to buy your product.

ANALYSIS AND CONCLUSION

Write a summary that describes the process you used to create your product. Be sure to answer the following questions in your summary.

1. What did you learn about using rain forest resources?

2. How can rain forest resources be used without destroying them?

3. Do you think it is possible for people to protect rain forests by using their renewable resources?

2 Explore

Have students read the Activity Shop completely. Then ask students to give an example of a renewable resource from the rain forest. (The fruits and nuts of the trees are renewable.)

3 Teach

You might wish to organize the class into groups to work as "companies" for these activities. Within each company, students may serve as researchers, artists, copywriters, cost analysts, television producers, writers, actors, and so on. Students may serve in more than one role. Groups should prepare a written list of their members and their assignments.

4 Assess

Students or groups may create a display of their package and product description, circle graph, and poster. Students may have a video of their commercial or be ready to perform it. They may include an audiotape of their jingle. Evaluate the circle graph for accuracy and clarity of presentation. Evaluate the other materials for the quality of research about rain forest materials, creativity, attractiveness, and originality.

Answers to...

ANALYSIS AND CONCLUSION

1-3. Students' responses should reflect their understanding of rain forest conservation. Opinions should be supported by facts.

Question Book

BY PABLO NERUDA

LITERATURE

Lesson Objectives

❶ Interpret the meaning of a poem.

❷ Compare information in a poem to geographic information about the country of its origin.

Lesson Plan

1 Engage

Building Vocabulary

Point out that notes in the margin can help students understand certain words and can give helpful hints as students read. Vocabulary defined in the margin includes: *aftermath*, *volatile*, and *role*.

Activating Prior Knowledge

Have students read Reach Into Your Background in the Before You Read box. Tell students that Neruda's poem is about the change of seasons. Discuss why the changing of seasons is a good subject for a poem.

2 Develop Student Reading

Have students read the Questions to Explore and then invite volunteers to read the poem aloud. If you have Spanish-speaking students, first have a volunteer read the poem aloud in Spanish. Then have another volunteer read the poem aloud in English. Suggest that students follow the written poem as they listen to the recitation.

BEFORE YOU READ

Reach Into Your Background

Do you pay close attention to the world around you? Describe a plant, a building, or a person that you saw on your way to school today. Remember as many details as you can. If you saw a tree, try to remember the shape of its leaves and whether its roots were visible above the ground. If you saw a person, try to remember what the person was wearing and how old the person seemed to be.

Many of Pablo Neruda's poems help readers pay more attention to the world around them. Neruda, who lived in Chile, often wrote about subjects that people take for granted. The following poem is from a book of Neruda's poetry called *Question Book*.

Questions to Explore

1. How does this poem help you look more closely at the changes of the seasons?

2. Because Chile is in the Southern Hemisphere, its seasons are the reverse of the seasons in the United States. Does knowing this change your understanding of the poem? Why or why not?

Ask Questions If you were going to write a poem of questions, what questions would you ask?

LXXII

Si todos los ríos son dulces
de dónde saca sal el mar?

Cómo saben las estaciones
que deben cambiar de camisa?

Por qué tan lentas en invierno
y tan palpitantes después?

Y cómo saben las raíces
que deben subir a la luz?

Y luego saludar al aire
con tantas flores y colores?

Siempre es la misma
    primavera
la que repite su papel?

LXXII

If all rivers are sweet
where does the sea get its salt?

How do the seasons discover
it's time to change shirts?

Why are winters so slow
and the aftermaths, volatile?

How do the roots know
they must climb toward the light?

And then greet the air
with such colors and flowers?

Is it always the same spring,
repeating the same role?

aftermath (AF ter math) *n.*:
the period that comes after
an event
volatile (VOL a til) *adj.*:
explosive
role (roll) *n.*: a part played
by an actor

◀ ▲ These photos show
winter and summer in
Chile's Patagonian Andes.
How can you tell which
season is which?

READ ACTIVELY

Visualize What does a
root look like as it pushes
away from a seed and up
toward the sky?

EXPLORING YOUR READING

Look Back

1. What do all the questions
in this poem have in
common?

Think It Over

2. Seasons don't wear shirts.
What does Neruda mean
when he refers to the seasons changing their shirts?

3. How is spring like an actor
playing a role in a play?

4. Based on this poem, does
Neruda seem to think
that nature is friendly or
unfriendly? Explain your
answer.

Go Beyond

5. How can paying attention
to details around you help
you appreciate nature?

Ideas for Writing:
Answer Poem

6. The questions that Neruda
asks all have scientific
explanations. Find out
the scientific answer to
Neruda's questions. Then,
write an answer poem in
response to Neruda's.

Background

About the Author

Pablo Neruda was born
in Parral, Chile, in 1904.
Neruda, whose original name
was Neftalí Ricardo Reyes
Basoalto, began writing
poetry when he was 10. By
the age of 20, Neruda was
already one of Chile's best-
known poets. His interest in
political affairs led to his
appointment as Chilean representative to several different countries. Neruda won
the Nobel Prize for Literature
in 1971. He died in 1973.

About the Selection

"Book of Poems" appears in
a volume of Pablo Neruda's
work titled *Late and
Posthumous Poems,
1968–1974,* published by
Grove Press, 1988.

LATIN AMERICA

PROJECT POSSIBILITIES

As you study Latin America, you will be reading and thinking about these important questions.

☛ **GEOGRAPHY** What are the main physical features of Latin America?

☛ **HISTORY** How has Latin America been shaped by its history?

☛ **CULTURE** What factors have affected cultures in Latin America?

☛ **GOVERNMENT** What types of government exist in Latin America today?

☛ **ECONOMICS** How has geography influenced the ways in which Latin Americans make a living?

Doing a project shows what you know! Are you doing this project? Muy bueno!

GEO LEO

Project Menu

The chapters in this book have some answers to these questions. Now it's time for you to find your own answers by doing projects on your own or with a group. Here are some ways to make your own discoveries about Latin America.

A Latin American Concert As you study Latin America, find out about the music of each region. Find out what kinds of instruments people play and what the instruments are made of. Then try to find examples of each kind of music. You might find some in public libraries, which usually have a music collection. Play the music for your class. You might explain how history and geography had an effect on the development of each kind of music. For example, in the Andes, people make a kind of rattle out of llamas' hooves. Talk about the roles of different types of music. For example, merengue is dance music, and reggae often serves as political protest.

From Questions to Careers

INTERPRETER

When people who speak different languages need to talk to each other, they often need an interpreter. An interpreter is someone who speaks both languages and can translate for both people as they talk.

In the United States, most interpreters work for the government. They translate during meetings between U.S. officials and visitors from other countries. Interpreters are especially important when there is an emergency. For example, when a major earthquake struck San Francisco in 1989, interpreters helped Spanish speakers get medical attention and talk to telephone operators.

Interpreters also work for companies doing business in other countries. Large corporations often have a whole team of interpreters.

Many interpreters have a degree in their second language and additional training in interpreting. However, some bilingual people are able to become interpreters for small companies or agencies without training.

Visions of Latin America Create a diorama showing the effect of geography on the way people live in Latin America. Your diorama can be realistic or it can show a symbol. Work in groups of three or four.

After you finish your diorama, write a short report to explain how the subject of your diorama affects the people of Latin America today. Display the whole set of dioramas with the reports. Invite other students to look at them. You might also display them at parents' night.

Latin America in the News As you read about Latin America, keep a bulletin board display called *Latin America in the News*. Look in magazines and newspapers for articles that describe life in Latin America. For example, when you study Mexico, you can collect articles about Mexican culture, politics, or economics.

When you have finished your study of Latin America, choose the articles that you want to keep. Make a scrapbook to contain the articles. Display the scrapbook in the school library or resource center.

Explorer's Dictionary Many languages are spoken in Latin America. As you work on this book, create a dictionary of important terms. Use a foreign-language dictionary to translate your terms into Spanish or another Latin American language.

Illustrate your dictionary with drawings or pictures cut out from magazines or travel brochures. Bind the pages together with yarn or staples. Display your dictionary so other students can use it.

2 Explore

Have students read the two pages. Talk with them about the careers of interpreters. Invite bilingual students to offer their expertise in translating from one language to another. Then allow students to work in groups interested in one of the project possibilities. Ask the groups to list the steps needed to complete the project.

3 Teach

Ask each student to select a project from those listed or to design a project of his or her own. As an alternative, you might wish to assign projects to students. Work with students to create a project description and a schedule. You may wish to have all students working on a similar project follow the same schedule. Some projects can be carried out by cooperative groups. *Latin America in the News* is a good possibility. Post project schedules in the classroom and monitor student progress by asking for progress reports.

4 Assess

Display projects or allow students to make their presentations.

Acceptable projects provide basic, accurate information about the topic and follow the guidelines in the project description.

Commendable projects show evidence of detailed research and understanding of the geography of Latin America.

Outstanding projects show evidence of detailed research, are of high interest and creativity, and demonstrate a clear understanding of the guiding questions about Latin America.

Reference

TABLE OF CONTENTS

MAP AND GLOBE HANDBOOK

This Map and Globe Handbook is designed to help you develop some of the skills you need to be a world explorer. These can help you whether you explore from the top of an elephant in India or from a computer at school.

You can use the information in this handbook to improve your map and globe skills. But the best way to sharpen your skills is to practice. The more you practice, the better you'll get.

GEO CLEO and GEO LEO

Table of Contents

You may choose to present the Map and Globe Handbook as a special unit of study at the beginning of the year or at another point in the school year. As an alternative, you might prefer to choose among the activities in the Map and Globe Handbook to meet the specific needs of your class or of individual students.

Point out to students that they already know a great deal about maps. Ask them to sketch a quick map of the route from their house to school. Discuss the map elements that students include on their maps.

Read through the page with students.

Lesson Objective

Identify and define the five themes of geography.

Lesson Plan

1 Engage

Warm-Up Activity

Work with students to define the word *theme*. (An underlying idea built into or expanded upon in a work of art or study.)

Activating Prior Knowledge

Have students work in small groups for five minutes to write a definition of *geography*. Discuss their definitions. Then write the five themes on the chalkboard and ask students to break up their definitions, putting phrases under the proper headings. For example, if students wrote "studying where other countries are," that would fall under the theme of location. Add to students' definitions as needed.

2 Explore

Read the first verse of the poem "Midwest Town" by Ruth De Long Peterson to the class:

Farther east it wouldn't be on
    the map—
Too small—but here it rates a
    dot and a name.
In Europe it would wear a
    castle cap
Or have a cathedral rising like
    a flame.

Ask students to identify the geography themes in the verse (location and place).

Five Themes of Geography

Studying the geography of the entire world can be a huge task. You can make that task easier by using the five themes of geography: location, place, human-environment interaction, movement, and regions. The themes are tools you can use to organize information and to answer the where, why, and how of geography.

1 Location answers the question, "Where is it?" You can think of the location of a continent or a country as its address. You might give an absolute location such as "22 South Lake Street" or "40°N and 80°W." You might also use a relative address, telling where one place is by referring to another place. "Between school and the mall" and "eight miles east of Pleasant City" are examples of relative locations.

2 Place identifies the natural and human features that make one place different from every other place. You can identify a specific place by its landforms, climate, plants, animals, people, or cultures. You might even think of place as a geographic signature. Use the signature to help you understand the natural and human features that make one place different from every other place.

1. Location
Chicago, Illinois, occupies one location on the Earth. No other place has exactly the same absolute location.

2. Place
Ancient cultures in Egypt built distinctive pyramids. Use the theme of place to help you remember features that exist only in Egypt.

3 Human-Environment Interaction focuses on the relationship between people and the environment. As people live in an area, they often begin to make changes to it, usually to make their lives easier. For example, they might build a dam to control flooding during rainy seasons. Also, the environment can affect how people live, work, dress, travel, and communicate.

4 Movement answers the question "How do people, goods, and ideas move from place to place?" Remember that, often, what happens in one place can affect what happens in another. Use the theme of movement to help you trace the spread of goods, people, and ideas from one location to the next.

5 Regions is the last geographic theme. A region is a group of places that share common features. Geographers divide the world into many types of regions. For example, countries, states, and cities are political regions. The people in these places live under the same type of government. Other features can be used to define regions. Places that have the same climate belong to a particular climate region. Places that share the same culture belong to a cultural region. The same place can be found in more than one region. The state of Hawaii is in the political region of the United States. Because it has a tropical climate, Hawaii is also part of a tropical climate region.

PRACTICE YOUR WORLD EXPLORER SKILLS

1. What is the absolute location of your school? What is one way to describe its relative location?

2. What might be a "geographic signature" of the town or city you live in?

3. Give an example of human-environment interaction where you live.

4. Name at least one thing that comes into your town or city and one that goes out. How is each moved? Where does it come from? Where does it go?

5. What are several regions you think your town or city belongs in?

3. Human-Environment Interaction
Peruvians have changed steep mountain slopes into terraces suitable for farming. Think how this environment looked before people made changes.

4. Movement
Arab traders brought not only goods to Kuala Lumpur, Malaysia, but also Arab building styles and the Islamic religion.

5. Regions
Wheat farming is an important activity in Kansas. This means that Kansas is part of a farming region.

3 Teach
After students have read the definitions of the themes of geography, begin discussion. Encourage students to relate the themes to what they already know about the Earth and its people. Invite them to provide additional examples for each theme.

4 Assess
Have students work in pairs to create a geographic description of where they live. Descriptions should include one or more items for each of the five themes of geography. Students may need an atlas to find the absolute location of your community. If your community is not in the atlas, accept the absolute location of the nearest city, or other political landmark.

As an alternative, have students complete the Practice Your World Explorer Skills. Assess students' understanding by the accuracy of their answers.

Answers to ...
PRACTICE YOUR WORLD EXPLORER SKILLS

Sample answers are given for Chicago, Illinois.

1. 33 North Green street, between Green Park and the highway
2. It's along the shore of Lake Michigan.
3. The city built bridges over the river.
4. Manufactured goods leave the city on railroads to other parts of the country. Fruits and vegetables from nearby farms come into the city on trucks.
5. the Midwest, the Great Lakes region

Explain how the movement of the Earth causes night and day, as well as the seasons.

1 Engage

Warm-Up Activity

To introduce the skill, remind students that the movement of the Earth accounts for some of the differences between places.

Activating Prior Knowledge

Ask students how we know that the Earth moves.

2 Explore

Read the page with students. Discuss anything they have difficulty understanding.

3 Teach

Darken the room and put a lighted lamp on a table. Hold a globe close to the lamp. Turn the globe to show the movement from day to night. Hold the globe in the positions shown in the diagram to show the seasons. Have students practice manipulating the lamp and the globe.

4 Assess

Ask students to apply the skill by explaining why days are longer in the summer in most places in the world—except around the Equator. (The sun's rays hit the Earth most directly near the Equator year-round.)

You may also assess students' understanding by asking them to complete the Practice Your World Explorer Skills.

1. the Earth's tilt
2. March and September

Planet Earth is part of our solar system. The Earth revolves around the sun in a nearly circular path called an orbit. A revolution, or one complete orbit around the sun, takes 365 1/4 days, or a year. As the Earth revolves around the sun, it is also spinning around in space. This movement is called a rotation. The Earth rotates on its axis—an invisible line through the center of the Earth from the North Pole to the South Pole. The Earth makes one full rotation about every 24 hours. As the Earth rotates, it is daytime on the side facing the sun. It is night on the side away from the sun.

The Earth's axis is tilted at an angle. Because of this tilt, sunlight strikes different parts of the Earth at certain points in the year, creating different seasons.

Earth's Revolution and the Seasons

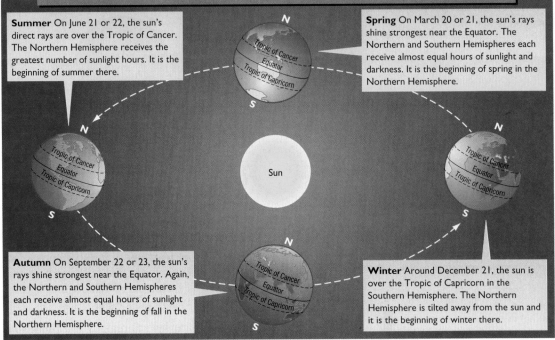

Summer On June 21 or 22, the sun's direct rays are over the Tropic of Cancer. The Northern Hemisphere receives the greatest number of sunlight hours. It is the beginning of summer there.

Spring On March 20 or 21, the sun's rays shine strongest near the Equator. The Northern and Southern Hemispheres each receive almost equal hours of sunlight and darkness. It is the beginning of spring in the Northern Hemisphere.

Autumn On September 22 or 23, the sun's rays shine strongest near the Equator. Again, the Northern and Southern Hemispheres each receive almost equal hours of sunlight and darkness. It is the beginning of fall in the Northern Hemisphere.

Winter Around December 21, the sun is over the Tropic of Capricorn in the Southern Hemisphere. The Northern Hemisphere is tilted away from the sun and it is the beginning of winter there.

▲ **Location** This diagram shows how the Earth's tilt and orbit around the sun combine to create the seasons. Remember, in the Southern Hemisphere the seasons are reversed.

PRACTICE YOUR WORLD EXPLORER SKILLS

1 What causes the seasons in the Northern Hemisphere to be the opposite of those in the Southern Hemisphere?

2 During which two months of the year do the Northern and Southern Hemispheres have about equal hours of daylight and darkness?

Maps and Globes Represent the Earth

Globes

A globe is a scale model of the Earth. It shows the actual shapes, sizes, and locations of all the Earth's landmasses and bodies of water. Features on the surface of the Earth are drawn to scale on a globe. This means a smaller unit of measure on the globe stands for a larger unit of measure on the Earth.

Because a globe is made in the true shape of the Earth, it offers these advantages for studying the Earth.

- The shape of all land and water bodies are accurate.
- Compass directions from one point to any other point are correct.
- The distance from one location to another is always accurately represented.

However, a globe presents some disadvantages for studying the Earth. Because a globe shows the entire Earth, it cannot show small areas in great detail. Also, a globe is not easily folded and carried from one place to another. For these reasons, geographers often use maps to learn about the Earth.

Maps

A map is a drawing or representation, on a flat surface, of a region. A map can show details too small to be seen on a globe. Floor plans, mall directories, and road maps are among the maps we use most often.

While maps solve some of the problems posed by globes, they have some disadvantages of their own. Maps flatten the real round world. Mapmakers cut, stretch, push, and pull some parts of the Earth to get it all flat on paper. As a result, some locations may be distorted. That is, their size, shape, and relative location may not be accurate. For example, on most maps of the entire world, the size and shape of the Antarctic and Arctic regions are not accurate.

PRACTICE YOUR WORLD EXPLORER SKILLS

① What is the main difference between a globe and a map?

② What is one advantage of using a globe instead of a map?

Global Gores

◀ **Location**
When mapmakers flatten the surface of the Earth, curves become straight lines. As a result, size, shape, and distance are distorted.

Teaching Resources

📁 **Comparing Globes and Maps,** in the Social Studies and Geography Skills booklet, p. 12, helps students understand and apply the skill of understanding differences between maps and globes.

Lesson Objective

Compare maps and globes as representations of the Earth.

Lesson Plan

1 Engage
Warm-Up Activity
Ask students what it might be like to see the Earth from space.

Activating Prior Knowledge
Ask students whether they would use a map or a globe to plan a vacation. Discuss how they might use both.

2 Explore
Have students read the page and study the illustrations. Discuss with them similarities and differences between maps and globes.

3 Teach
Roughly sketch the continents on a large grapefruit with a ballpoint pen. Explain that the grapefruit is like the Earth. Carefully peel the grapefruit and then challenge students to reassemble the continents into a flat map.

4 Assess
Assess students' understanding by asking them to complete the Practice Your World Explorer Skills.

Answers to ...
PRACTICE YOUR WORLD EXPLORER SKILLS

1. A globe is a scale model of the Earth; a map is a drawing of the Earth or a region of it.
2. Students should be able to support their choices of either accurate shape, true direction, or accurate distance.

Lesson Objectives

❶ Define the hemispheres of the Earth.

❷ Locate places on a map using the coordinates of latitude and longitude.

Lesson Plan

1 Engage

Warm-Up Activity

Present this challenge to the class. Tell students that they are sailing alone around the world. They have been in a huge storm and have run out of food. They have not seen land for weeks, but when they radio for extra supplies, they can give their exact location. How? (They know their latitude and longitude.)

Activating Prior Knowledge

Draw an unlabeled grid on the chalkboard. Place a large dot somewhere on the grid. Ask students how they could use the grid to describe where the dot is.

The Hemispheres

Another name for a round ball like a globe is a sphere. The Equator, an imaginary line halfway between the North and South Poles, divides the globe into two hemispheres. (The prefix *hemi* means "half.") Land and water south of the Equator are in the Southern Hemisphere. Land and water north of the Equator are in the Northern Hemisphere.

Mapmakers sometimes divide the globe along an imaginary line that runs from North Pole to South Pole. This line, called the Prime Meridian, divides the globe into the Eastern and Western Hemispheres.

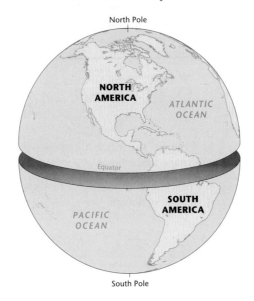

Northern Hemisphere

North Pole

NORTH AMERICA

ATLANTIC OCEAN

Equator

SOUTH AMERICA

PACIFIC OCEAN

South Pole

Southern Hemisphere

▲ The Equator divides the Northern Hemisphere from the Southern Hemisphere.

EUROPE

ATLANTIC OCEAN

Prime Meridian

AFRICA

Western Hemisphere **Eastern Hemisphere**

▲ The Prime Meridian divides the Eastern Hemisphere from the Western Hemisphere.

Resource Directory

Teaching Resources

📁 **Understanding Hemispheres,** in the Social Studies and Geography Skills booklet, p. 7, helps students understand and apply the skill of identifying hemispheres.

Media and Technology

 Color Transparency 98

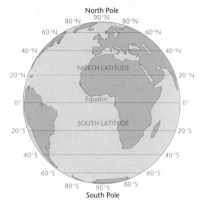

Parallels of Latitude

The Equator, at 0° latitude, is the starting place for measuring latitude or distances north and south. Most globes do not show every parallel of latitude. They may show every 10, 20, or even 30 degrees.

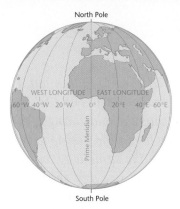

Meridians of Longitude

The Prime Meridian, at 0° longitude, runs from pole to pole through Greenwich, England. It is the starting place for measuring longitude or distances east and west. Each meridian of longitude meets its opposite longitude at the North and South Poles.

The Global Grid

Two sets of lines cover most globes. One set of lines runs parallel to the Equator. These lines, including the Equator, are called *parallels of latitude*. They are measured in degrees (°). One degree of latitude represents a distance of about 70 miles (112 km). The Equator has a location of 0°. The other parallels of latitude tell the direction and distance from the Equator to another location.

The second set of lines runs north and south. These lines are called *meridians of longitude*. Meridians show the degrees of longitude east or west of the Prime Meridian, which is located at 0°. A meridian of longitude tells the direction and distance from the Prime Meridian to another location. Unlike parallels, meridians are not the same distance apart everywhere on the globe.

Together the pattern of parallels of latitude and meridians of longitude is called the global grid. Using the lines of latitude and longitude, you can locate any place on Earth. For example, the location of 30° north latitude and 90° west longitude is usually written as 30°N, 90°W. Only one place on Earth has these coordinates—the city of New Orleans, in the state of Louisiana.

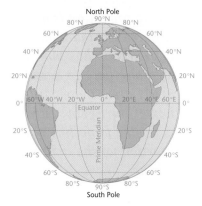

The Global Grid

By using lines of latitude and longitude, you can give the absolute location of any place on the Earth.

① Which continents lie completely in the Northern Hemisphere? The Western Hemisphere?

② Is there land or water at 20°S latitude and the Prime Meridian? At the Equator and 60°W longitude?

Teaching Resources

📁 **Understanding Latitude and Longitude** and **Using Latitude and Longitude,** in the Social Studies and Geography Skills booklet, pp. 10–11, help students understand and apply the skill of reading latitude and longitude lines.

Media and Technology

📽 **Color Transparency** 99

2 Explore

Read through these two pages with students. Using a large map, have students begin at the Prime Meridian and put their fingers on each of the meridians of longitude as they move east and then west. Do the same with the parallels of latitude, moving from the Equator to the North Pole and then to the South Pole. Some students may need help in understanding the definition of *parallel*. (Parallel lines are lines that never meet.)

3 Teach

Ask a volunteer to work with a large map or globe. Have other students name cities around the world. The volunteer must locate them and state their coordinates.

4 Assess

To assess students' understanding, give students coordinates that you have found in an atlas and ask them to locate the city. Have students discuss the process. Use students' discussion to assess their understanding of how to locate places on maps and globes.

Answers to ...

PRACTICE YOUR WORLD EXPLORER SKILLS

1. Asia, North America, Europe; North America, South America
2. water; land

Map Projections

*I*magine trying to flatten out a complete orange peel. The peel would split. The shape would change. You would have to cut the peel to get it to lie flat. In much the same way, maps cannot show the correct size and shape of every landmass or body of water on the Earth's curved surface. Maps shrink some places and stretch others. This shrinking and stretching is called distortion—*a change made to a shape.*

To make up for this disadvantage, mapmakers use different map projections. Each map projection is a way of showing the round Earth on flat paper. Each type of projection has some distortion. No one projection can accurately show the correct area, shape, distance, and direction for the Earth's surface. Mapmakers use the projection that has the least distortion for the information they are studying.

Same-Shape Maps

Some map projections can accurately show the shapes of landmasses. However, these projections often greatly distort the size of landmasses as well as the distance between them.

One of the most common same-shape maps is a Mercator projection, named for the mapmaker who invented it. The Mercator projection accurately shows shape and direction, but it distorts distance and size. In this projection, the northern and southern areas of the globe appear stretched more than areas near the Equator. Because the projection shows true directions, ships' navigators use it to chart a straight line course between two ports.

Mercator Projection

Equal-Area Maps

Some map projections can show the correct size of landmasses. Maps that use these projections are called equal-area maps. In order to show the correct size of landmasses, these maps usually distort shapes. The distortion is usually greater at the edges of the map and less at the center.

Robinson Maps

Many of the maps in this book use the Robinson projection. This is a compromise between the Mercator and equal-area projections. It gives a useful overall picture of the world. The Robinson projection keeps the size and shape relationships of most continents and oceans but does distort size of the polar regions.

Azimuthal Maps

Another kind of projection shows true compass direction. Maps that use this projection are called azimuthal maps. Such maps are easy to recognize—they are usually circular. Azimuthal maps are often used to show the areas of the North and South Poles. However, azimuthal maps distort scale, area, and shape.

Equal-Area Projection

Robinson Projection

Azimuthal Projection

PRACTICE YOUR WORLD EXPLORER SKILLS

1 What feature is distorted on an equal-area map?

2 Would you use a Mercator projection to find the exact distance between two locations? Tell why or why not.

3 Which would be a better choice for studying the Antarctic—an azimuthal projection or a Robinson projection? Explain.

Media and Technology

 Color Transparency 100

2 Explore

After students have read the two pages, have them look up the word *distortion* in a dictionary. Ask them why we use maps that we know are distorted. (All maps are somewhat distorted.)

3 Teach

Students can practice the skill by comparing the maps to a globe. Ask them to note especially the sizes and positions of Greenland and Antarctica.

To apply their understanding of the skill, students can suggest reasons why many maps use the Robinson projection. (It shows the sizes and shapes of the continents with the least amount of distortion.)

4 Assess

Assess students' understanding by the accuracy of their answers.

Answers to...

PRACTICE YOUR WORLD EXPLORER SKILLS

1. shapes
2. No; the Mercator projection distorts distances.
3. An azimuthal projection centered on the South Pole would show all of Antarctica, a Robinson projection would not.

Lesson Objective

Identify and use the parts of a map.

Lesson Plan

1 Engage

Warm-Up Activity

If possible, show students several maps, such as subway or bus route maps and road maps. To introduce the skill, ask students to describe several parts that all of the maps seem to have in common (probably titles, keys, scales, and compasses).

Activating Prior Knowledge

Ask students why they should pay attention to different parts of a map. (They help the user locate places on it.)

2 Explore

Read the page with students. Help them identify the title, compass, scale, and key on several different maps.

3 Teach

Show students several maps, including those in the Atlas of this book. Students can practice and apply using the parts of a map by asking each other questions such as What is this map about? Which city is north of the river? How far apart are these two cities?

4 Assess

Assess students' understanding by the accuracy of their answers.

Answers to ...

PRACTICE YOUR WORLD EXPLORER SKILLS

1. the title
2. key
3. scale

Mapmakers provide several clues to help you understand the information on a map. As an explorer, it is your job to read and interpret these clues.

Compass

Many maps show north at the top of the map. One way to show direction on a map is to use an arrow that points north. There may be an N shown with the arrow. Many maps give more information about direction by displaying a compass showing the directions, north, east, south, and west. The letters N, E, S, and W are placed to indicate these directions.

Title

The title of a map is the most basic clue. It signals what kinds of information you are likely to find on the map. A map titled *West Africa: Population Density* will be most useful for locating information about where people live in West Africa.

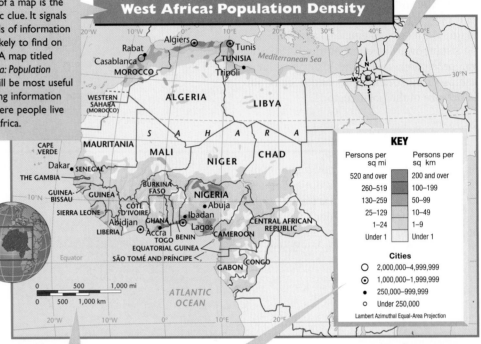

West Africa: Population Density

KEY

Persons per sq mi	Persons per sq km
520 and over	200 and over
260–519	100–199
130–259	50–99
25–129	10–49
1–24	1–9
Under 1	Under 1

Cities

- ◯ 2,000,000–4,999,999
- ◉ 1,000,000–1,999,999
- ● 250,000–999,999
- ○ Under 250,000

Lambert Azimuthal Equal-Area Projection

Scale

A map scale helps you find the actual distances between points shown on the map. You can measure the distance between any two points on the map, compare them to the scale, and find out the actual distance between the points. Most map scales show distances in both miles and kilometers.

Key

Often a map has a key, or legend, that shows the symbols used on the map and what each one means. On some maps, color is used as a symbol. On those maps, the key also tells the meaning of each color.

PRACTICE YOUR WORLD EXPLORER SKILLS

1. What part of a map tells you what the map is about?

2. Where on the map should you look to find out the meaning of this symbol? ●

3. What part of the map can you use to find the distance between two cities?

Resource Directory

Teaching Resources

Using the Map Key, in the Social Studies and Geography Skills booklet, p. 3, helps students understand and apply the skill of using parts of a map. You may also wish to use the following:
Using the Compass Rose on p. 4 and
Using the Map Scale on p. 5.

Comparing Maps of Different Scale

Here are three maps drawn to three different scales. The first map shows Moscow's location in the northeastern portion of Russia. This map shows the greatest area—a large section of northern Europe. It has the smallest scale (1 inch = about 900 miles) and shows the fewest details. This map can tell you what direction to travel to reach Moscow from Finland.

Find the red box on Map 1. It shows the whole area covered by Map 2. Study Map 2. It gives a closer look at the city of Moscow. It shows the features around the city, the city's boundary, and the general shape of the city. This map can help you find your way from the airport to the center of town.

Now find the red box on Map 2. This box shows the area shown on Map 3. This map moves you closer into the city. Like the zoom on a computer or camera, Map 3 shows the smallest area but has the greatest detail. This map has the largest scale (1 inch = about 0.8 miles). This is the map to use to explore downtown Moscow.

Map 1

KEY
— National boundary

0   500   1,000 mi
0   500 1,000 km

One inch = about 900 miles

Map 2

KEY
▢ Built-up area
— Road or street

0   5   10 mi
0   5   10 km

One inch = about 12.5 miles

Map 3

KEY
— Road or street
■ Point of interest

0   .5   1 mi
0   .5   1 km

One inch = about 0.8 miles

PRACTICE YOUR WORLD EXPLORER SKILLS

1. Which map would be best for finding the location of Red Square? Why?

2. Which map best shows Moscow's location relative to Poland? Explain.

3. Which map best shows the area immediately surrounding the city?

Teaching Resources

📁 **Comparing Maps of Different Scale,** in the Social Studies and Geography Skills booklet, p. 6, helps students understand and use maps of different scale.

Lesson Objective

Use political maps.

Lesson Plan

1 Engage

Warm-Up Activity

To introduce the skill, tell students that American writer Mark Twain once wrote about people in a hot-air balloon who were confused because the ground below them was not colored like maps.

Activating Prior Knowledge

Point out that the word *political* comes from a Greek word meaning "citizen." A political map is one that emphasizes the boundaries of an area established by its citizens.

2 Explore

Read through the page with students. Make sure they realize that a political map mainly shows how people have divided and named the land.

3 Teach

Ask students to practice using a political map by locating a boundary between countries, the capital of Russia, and a river that is also a boundary.

4 Assess

Have students complete the Practice Your World Explorer Skills. Assess their understanding by the accuracy of their answers.

Answers to ...

PRACTICE YOUR WORLD EXPLORER SKILLS

1. red line **2.** star in a circle; solid circle **3.** none

Mapmakers create maps to show all kinds of information. The kind of information presented affects the way a map looks. One type of map is called a political map. Its main purpose is to show continents, countries, and divisions within countries such as states or provinces. Usually different colors are used to show different countries or divisions within a country. The colors do not have any special meaning. They are used only to make the map easier to read.

Political maps also show where people have built towns and cities. Symbols can help you tell capital cities from other cities and towns. Even though political maps do not give information that shows what the land looks like, they often include some physical features such as oceans, lakes, and rivers.

Political maps usually have many labels. They give country names, and the names of capital and major cities. Bodies of water such as lakes, rivers, oceans, seas, gulfs, and bays are also labeled.

PRACTICE YOUR WORLD EXPLORER SKILLS

1 What symbol shows the continental boundary?

2 What symbol is used to indicate a capital city? A major city?

3 What kinds of landforms are shown on this map?

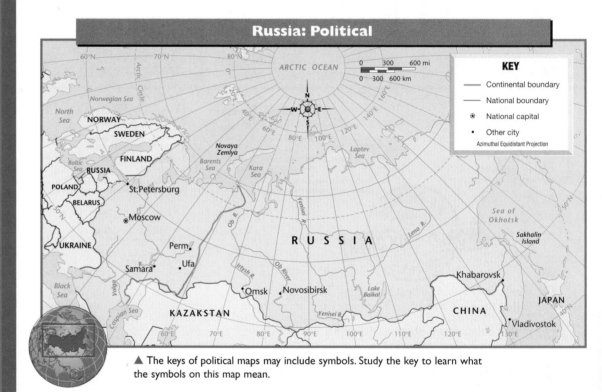

Russia: Political

KEY
— Continental boundary
— National boundary
⊛ National capital
• Other city
Azimuthal Equidistant Projection

▲ The keys of political maps may include symbols. Study the key to learn what the symbols on this map mean.

Resource Directory

Reading a Political Map, in the Social Studies and Geography Skills booklet, p. 19, helps students practice using political maps.

Physical Maps

Like political maps, physical maps show country labels and labels for capital cities. However, physical maps also show what the land of a region looks like by showing the major physical features such as plains, hills, plateaus, or mountains. Labels give the names of features such as mountain peaks, mountains, plateaus, and river basins.

In order to tell one landform from another, physical maps often show elevation and relief.

Elevation is the height of the land above sea level. Physical maps in this book use color to show elevation. Browns and oranges show higher lands while blues and greens show lands that are at or below sea level.

Relief shows how quickly the land rises or falls. Hills, mountains, and plateaus are shown on relief maps using shades of gray. Level or nearly level land is shown without shading. Darkly shaded areas indicate steeper lands.

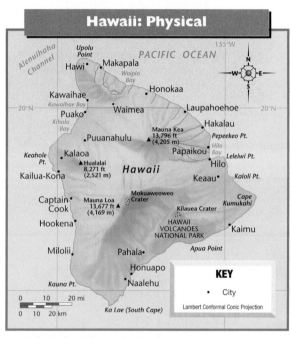

Hawaii: Physical

▲ On a physical map, shading is sometimes used to show relief. Use the shading to locate the mountains in Hawaii.

PRACTICE YOUR WORLD EXPLORER SKILLS

1. How is relief shown on the map to the left?

2. How can you use relief to decide which areas will be the most difficult to climb?

3. What information is given with the name of a mountain peak?

▼ Mauna Kea, an extinct volcano, is the highest peak in the state of Hawaii. Find Mauna Kea on the map.

Teaching Resources

📁 **Elevation on a Map,** in the Social Studies and Geography Skills booklet, p. 20, helps students understand and read physical maps that show elevation of land.

Lesson Objective

Use physical maps.

Lesson Plan

1 Engage
Warm-Up Activity

To introduce the skill, tell students that they are going for a hike in the mountains. Encourage them to consider that a map showing the heights of the mountains might be useful.

Activating Prior Knowledge

Remind students that political maps do not necessarily show features of the landscape.

2 Explore

Have students read the page. Point out that a physical map makes the physical features of a place clearer than a political map does.

3 Teach

Students can practice using a physical map by checking this one for the highest mountain it shows. Have students apply the skill by pointing out other physical features on the map.

4 Assess

Have students complete the Practice Your World Explorer Skills. Assess their understanding by the accuracy of their answers.

Answers to ...

PRACTICE YOUR WORLD EXPLORER SKILLS

1. shading
2. Darkly shaded areas are steep and more difficult to climb.
3. its elevation

Special Purpose Maps

Lesson Plan

1 Engage

Warm-Up Activity

Discuss with students the tools they would need during an archaeological dig in the desert of South Asia. Ask what kinds of maps they would need.

Activating Prior Knowledge

Ask students to think of as many meanings for the word *special* as they can. Have them define special-purpose map, and then read the lesson to check their definitions.

2 Explore

When students have read the page, ask them to offer other examples of special-purpose maps.

3 Teach

Review the importance of the map title and the map legend. Discuss the purposes of the map on the page. How is it different from political maps and physical maps?

4 Assess

Have students complete the Practice Your World Explorer Skills. Assess their understanding by the accuracy of their answers.

Answers to ...

PRACTICE YOUR WORLD EXPLORER SKILLS

1. its title
2. the key

A s you explore the world, you will encounter many different kinds of special purpose maps. For example, a road map is a special purpose map. The title of each special purpose map tells the purpose and content of the map. Usually a special purpose map highlights only one kind of information. Examples of special purpose maps include land use, population distribution, recreation, transportation, natural resources, or weather.

The key on a special purpose map is very important. Even though a special purpose map shows only one kind of information, it may present many different pieces of data. This data can be shown in symbols, colors, or arrows. In this way, the key acts like a dictionary for the map.

Reading a special purpose map is a skill in itself. Look at the map below. First, try to get an overall sense of what it shows. Then, study the map to identify its main ideas. For example, one main idea of this map is that much of the petroleum production in the region takes place around the Persian Gulf.

1 What part of a special purpose map tells what information is contained on the map?

2 What part of a special purpose map acts like a dictionary for the map?

North Africa and the Middle East: Oil Production

KEY
- • Oil fields
- — Pipelines
- → Major sea routes

Mercator Projection

◀ The title on a special purpose map indicates what information can be found on the map. The symbols used on the map are explained in the map's key.

Resource Directory

Teaching Resources

Reading a Time Zone Map, in the Social Studies and Geography Skills booklet, p. 24, helps students understand and use this type of special-purpose map. You may also wish to use the activities on pp. 25–39. Each covers a different type of special-purpose map.

Landforms, Climate Regions, and Natural Vegetation Regions

Maps that show landforms, climate, and vegetation regions are special purpose maps. Unlike the boundary lines on a political map, the boundary lines on these maps do not separate the land into exact divisions. A tropical wet climate gradually changes to a tropical wet and dry climate. A tundra gradually changes to an ice cap. Even though the boundaries between regions may not be exact, the information on these maps can help you understand the region and the lives of people in it.

Landforms

Understanding how people use the land requires an understanding of the shape of the land itself. The four most important landforms are mountains, hills, plateaus, and plains. Human activity in every region in the world is influenced by these landforms.

- **Mountains** are high and steep. Most are wide at the bottom and rise to a narrow peak or ridge. Most geographers classify a mountain as land that rises at least 2,000 feet (610 m) above sea level. A series of mountains is called a mountain range.

- **Hills** rise above surrounding land and have rounded tops. Hills are lower and usually less steep than mountains. The elevation of surrounding land determines whether a landform is called a mountain or a hill.
- A **plateau** is a large, mostly flat area of land that rises above the surrounding land. At least one side of a plateau has a steep slope.
- **Plains** are large areas of flat or gently rolling land. Plains have few changes in elevation. Many plains areas are located along coasts. Others are located in the interior regions of some continents.

▶ A satellite view of the Earth showing North and South America. What landforms are visible in the photograph?

Lesson Plan

1 Engage
Warm-Up Activity

Ask students how they would describe their community to someone moving to their area from Australia. What words would they use to describe the land, the general climate, and the kinds of trees and plants?

Activating Prior Knowledge

Invite volunteers who have moved to your area from a different region to explain how the climate and vegetation are different.

Teaching Resources

📁 **Four Types of Landforms,** in the Social Studies and Geography Skills booklet, p. 21, helps students understand and read maps that show mountains, hills, plateaus, and plains.

2 Explore

Write the terms *landforms, climate regions,* and *natural vegetation regions* on the chalkboard. As students read the material on this page and the following page, have them find examples for each term.

3 Teach

Divide the class into small groups. Ask each group to draw a picture of one of the following landforms: a mountain, a hill, a plateau, a plain. Then ask each group to find the landform on a map in this book or in an atlas.

Direct each student to choose one of the 12 climate types. Ask them to use the maps in this book or in an atlas to find a place in the world with that climate. Then have students use one of the natural vegetation maps in the textbook to figure out which of the 12 natural vegetation regions covers that climate location.

Climate Regions

Another important influence in the ways people live their lives is the climate of their region. Climate is the weather of a given location over a long period of time. Use the descriptions in the table below to help you visualize the climate regions shown on maps.

Climate	Temperatures	Precipitation
Tropical		
Tropical wet	Hot all year round	Heavy all year round
Tropical wet and dry	Hot all year round	Heavy when sun is overhead, dry other times
Dry		
Semiarid	Hot summers, mild to cold winters	Light
Arid	Hot days, cold nights	Very light
Mild		
Mediterranean	Hot summers, cool winters	Dry summers, wet winters
Humid subtropical	Hot summers, cool winters	Year round, heavier in summer than in winter
Marine west coast	Warm summers, cool winters	Year round, heavier in winter than in summer
Continental		
Humid continental	Hot summers, cold winters	Year round, heavier in summer than in winter
Subarctic	Cool summers, cold winters	Light
Polar		
Tundra	Cool summers, very cold winters	Light
Ice cap	Cold all year round	Light
Highlands	Varies, depending on altitude and direction of prevailing winds	Varies, depending on altitude and direction of prevailing winds

Resource Directory

Teaching Resources

Reading a Climate Map, in the Social Studies and Geography Skills booklet, p. 26, helps students understand and read maps that show different climate regions.

Natural Vegetation Regions

Natural vegetation is the plant life that grows wild without the help of humans. A world vegetation map tells what the vegetation in a place would be if people had not cut down forests or cleared grasslands. The table below provides descriptions of natural vegetation regions shown on maps. Comparing climate and vegetation regions can help you see the close relationship between climate and vegetation.

Vegetation	Description
Tropical rain forest	Tall, close-growing trees forming a canopy over smaller trees, dense growth in general
Deciduous forest	Trees and plants that regularly lose their leaves after each growing season
Mixed forest	Both leaf-losing and cone-bearing trees, no type of tree dominant
Coniferous forest	Cone-bearing trees, evergreen trees and plants
Mediterranean vegetation	Evergreen shrubs and small plants
Tropical savanna	Tall grasses with occasional trees and shrubs
Temperate grassland	Tall grasses with occasional stands of trees
Desert scrub	Low shrubs and bushes, hardy plants
Desert	Little or no vegetation
Tundra	Low shrubs, mosses, lichens; no trees
Ice cap	Little or no vegetation
Highlands	Varies, depending on altitude and direction of prevailing winds

PRACTICE YOUR WORLD EXPLORER SKILLS

1. How are mountains and hills similar? How are they different?

2. What is the difference between a plateau and a plain?

Teaching Resources

Reading a Natural Vegetation Map, in the Social Studies and Geography Skills booklet, p. 25, helps students understand and read maps that show natural vegetation regions.

4 Assess

Ask students to complete the Practice Your World Explorer Skills. Assess their understanding of landforms by the accuracy of their answers.

Assess students' understanding of the effect of climate on vegetation by asking them to share the results of their work in finding places with their assigned landform, climate, and vegetation. Have students check one another's work and match appropriate climate and vegetation regions.

Answers to . . .

PRACTICE YOUR WORLD EXPLORER SKILLS

1. Mountains and hills rise above the surrounding land. Hills are usually lower and less steep than mountains.
2. Both plains and plateaus are mostly flat areas. A plateau rises above the surrounding land, and one side may have a steep slope.

Using the Regional Database

The Regional Database can be used in the following ways:

✓ to provide a comprehensive study of all nations in a region

✓ to provide a source of information for student research projects

✓ to provide comparative data for a group of countries under study

Mexico and Central America

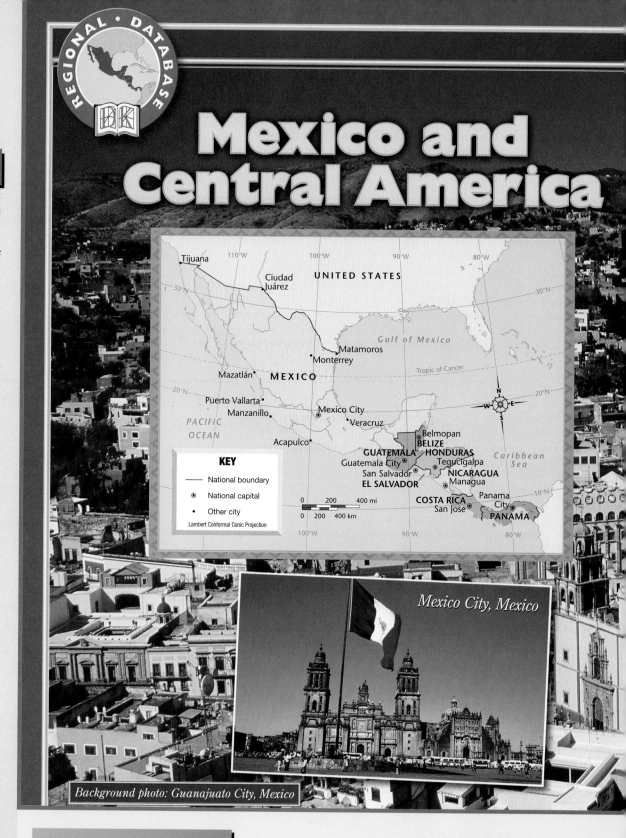

Tijuana
110°W
Ciudad Juárez
100°W
90°W
80°W
UNITED STATES
30°N
30°N
Gulf of Mexico
Matamoros
Monterrey
Tropic of Cancer
Mazatlán MEXICO
20°N
20°N
Puerto Vallarta
Manzanillo
Mexico City
Veracruz
PACIFIC OCEAN
Acapulco
Belmopan
BELIZE
GUATEMALA HONDURAS
Caribbean Sea
Guatemala City
Tegucigalpa
San Salvador
NICARAGUA
EL SALVADOR
Managua
COSTA RICA
Panama City
10°N
San Jose
PANAMA
100°W
90°W
80°W

KEY
— National boundary
⊛ National capital
• Other city

0   200   400 mi
0   200   400 km
Lambert Conformal Conic Projection

Mexico City, Mexico

Background photo: Guanajuato City, Mexico

Resource Directory

Program Resources

Outline Maps Latin America: Physical, p. 5; Latin America: Political, p. 6; Mexico: Political, p. 8; Central America and the Caribbean: Political, p. 9

Nystrom Desk Atlas Political maps, physical maps, and regional maps and charts for Mexico and Central America, pp. 82–87; Country Tables, pp. 145–146

GEOFACTS

Mexico and Central America

Population: 136.8 million

Most Populated City: Mexico City, Mexico (19.8 million)

Largest Country: Mexico (736,945 sq mi/ 1,908,690 sq km)

Smallest Country: Belize (8,803 sq mi/ 22,800 sq km)

Highest Point: Citlatepetl (18,701 ft/5,700 m)

Lowest Point: Near Mexicali, Mexico (33 ft/10 m)

Longest River: Rio Grande, Mexico (1,885 mi/ 3,035 km)

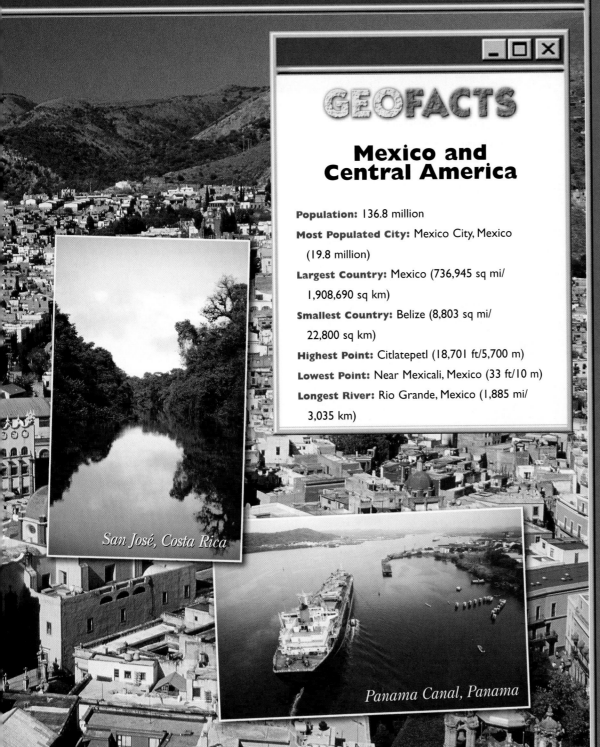

San José, Costa Rica

Panama Canal, Panama

Using Political Maps

Political maps show national boundaries. The opener maps shows every country, and lists information about the region in the following categories of data:

- ✓ **population**
- ✓ **most populated city**
- ✓ **largest country**
- ✓ **smallest country**
- ✓ **highest point**
- ✓ **lowest point**
- ✓ **longest river**

On subsequent pages, countries in the region are listed alphabetically. In addition, information is given in the following categories of data for each country:

- ✓ **capital**
- ✓ **area**
- ✓ **population**
- ✓ **ethnic groups**
- ✓ **religions**
- ✓ **government**
- ✓ **currency**
- ✓ **exports**
- ✓ **official language(s)**

Take It to the NET

Prentice Hall's *World Explorer* companion Web site offers activities for exploring geographical, historical, and cultural resources on the Internet. It also provides online links for key content, data updates, and all chapter review activities.

The **Teacher site** provides teachers with ideas for student research and activities. It also presents *eTeach*, a monthly discussion with Master Teachers.

Students can use the **Student site** to find chapter-by-chapter Internet resource links, data updates, and Self-Tests.

http://www.phschool.com

continued

Lesson Objective

Gather, understand, and apply information about Mexico and the countries of Central America.

Lesson Plan

1 Explore

Refer to the political map of Mexico and Central America. Remind students that this region is part of the continent of North America. Have volunteers list the countries of this region.

2 Teach

Ask volunteers to read some of the descriptions of Mexico and the countries of Central America. Tell students that *mestizo* is a Spanish word used to describe descendants of Spanish settlers and Native Americans. Explain that mestizos make up a majority of the population in most of the countries of this region. Ask students if they think the mestizo population in the region is alike or different from populations of ethnic groups in the United States today.

REGIONAL · DATABASE

Belize (be LEEZ)

Capital: Belmopan
Area: 8,803 sq mi/22,800 sq km
Population: 200,000
Ethnic Groups: mestizo, Creole, Maya, Garifuna, Asian Indian
Religions: Roman Catholic, Protestant, Anglican, Methodist
Government: parliamentary democracy
Currency: Belizean dollar
Exports: sugar, bananas, citrus fruits, clothing, fish products
Official Language: English

El Salvador (el SAHL vah dawr)

Capital: San Salvador
Area: 8,000 sq mi/20,720 sq km
Population: 6.2 million
Ethnic Groups: mestizo, Indian, white
Religions: Roman Catholic, Evangelical
Government: republic
Currency: Salvadorean colón
Exports: offshore assembly exports, coffee, sugar, shrimp, textiles, chemicals, electricity
Official Language: Spanish

Costa Rica (KOHS tah REE kah)

Capital: San José
Area: 19,714 sq mi/51,060 sq km
Population: 3.9 million
Ethnic Groups: mestizo, African, Indian
Religions: Roman Catholic, Protestant
Government: democratic republic
Currency: Costa Rican colón
Exports: coffee, bananas, sugar, textiles, electronic components
Official Language: Spanish

Guatemala (gwah te MAH lah)

Capital: Guatemala City
Area: 41,865 sq mi/108,430 sq km
Population: 11.1 million
Ethnic Groups: indigenous Indian, mestizo
Religions: Roman Catholic, Protestant, indigenous Mayan beliefs
Government: constitutional democratic republic
Currency: Quetzal
Exports: fuels, machinery and transport equipment, construction materials, grain
Official Language: Spanish

Resource Directory

Program Resources

Environmental and Global Issues Topic: Health, p. 10

Media and Technology

Color Transparencies Mexico: Political, 65; Central America and the Caribbean: Political, 66; Middle America: Physical-Political, 85; Mexico: Physical-Political, 87; Fine Art, 154

Capital: Tegucigalpa

Area: 43,201 sq mi/111,890 sq km

Population: 6.3 million

Ethnic Groups: mestizo, black African, Indian, white

Religions: Roman Catholic, Protestant

Government: democratic constitutional republic

Currency: Lempira

Exports: coffee, bananas, shrimp, lobster, meat, zinc, lumber

Official Language: Spanish

Honduras
(hahn DOOR ahs)

Capital: Managua

Area: 45,849 sq mi/118,750 sq km

Population: 4.9 million

Ethnic Groups: mestizo, white, black, indigenous Indian, Zambos

Religions: Roman Catholic, Protestant

Government: republic

Currency: Córdoba oro

Exports: coffee, shrimp and lobster, cotton, tobacco, beef, sugar, bananas, gold

Official Language: Spanish

Nicaragua
(nik ah RAH gwah)

Capital: Mexico City

Area: 736,945 sq mi/1,908,690 sq km

Population: 97.4 million

Ethnic Groups: mestizo, indigenous Indian, European

Religions: Roman Catholic, Protestant

Government: federal republic

Currency: Mexican peso

Exports: manufactured goods, oil and oil products, silver, coffee, cotton

Official Language: Spanish

Mexico
(MEKS i koh)

Capital: Panama City

Area: 29,340 sq mi/75,990 sq km

Population: 2.8 million

Ethnic Groups: mestizo, white, black, Indian, Asian

Religions: Roman Catholic, Protestant

Government: constitutional democracy

Currency: Balboa

Exports: bananas, sugar, shrimp, coffee

Official Language: Spanish

Panama
(PAN ah mah)

3 Assess

Have students look again at the descriptions of Central America. Prompt students to list similarities between these countries and the United States (*large Spanish-speaking populations; large non-white populations; large Roman Catholic populations*). Then ask students to list some differences (*The United States is much larger in population and area, and has different types of exports and currency.*)

Media and Technology

 World Video Explorer See the Mexico case study for an overview of Mexico's history, economy, government, and culture. Discussion questions are included.

Passport to the World CD-ROM This interactive CD-ROM allows students to explore each region of the world. Students view regional videos, take a photo tour, and explore a historical time line. Students record their travels in an Explorer's Journal, and receive passport stamps when they pass regional tests.

Lesson Objective

Gather, understand, and apply information about the countries of the Caribbean.

Lesson Plan

1 Explore

Refer students to the map of the Caribbean. Remind them that Cuba is the largest of the islands of this region. Ask the class to use the map to estimate how many miles away Cuba is from the United States (*about 90 miles*).

2 Teach

Explain that the Caribbean includes many independent nations as well as islands that are affiliated with other countries (*Puerto Rico is a commonwealth of the United States; Martinique is a department of France, etc.*) Ask students why they think many islands of the region have ties to the United States and European nations.

Caribbean

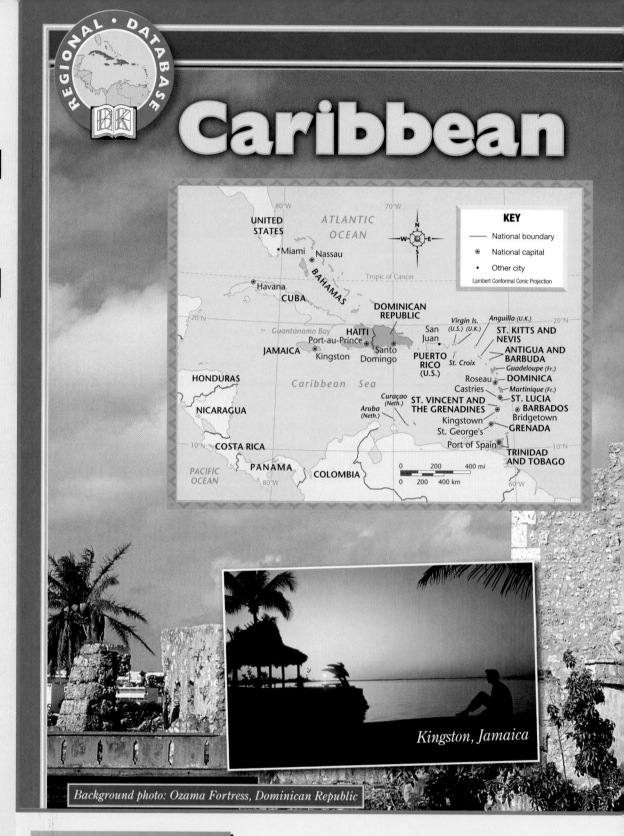

KEY
— National boundary
⊛ National capital
• Other city
Lambert Conformal Conic Projection

UNITED STATES · Miami · Nassau · ATLANTIC OCEAN · Tropic of Cancer · Havana · CUBA · BAHAMAS · DOMINICAN REPUBLIC · Guantánamo Bay · HAITI · Port-au-Prince · San Juan · Virgin Is. (U.S.) (U.K.) · Anguilla (U.K.) · ST. KITTS AND NEVIS · JAMAICA · Kingston · Santo Domingo · PUERTO RICO (U.S.) · St. Croix · ANTIGUA AND BARBUDA · Guadeloupe (Fr.) · HONDURAS · Caribbean Sea · Roseau · DOMINICA · Castries · Martinique (Fr.) · Curaçao (Neth.) · ST. VINCENT AND THE GRENADINES · ST. LUCIA · NICARAGUA · Aruba (Neth.) · Kingstown · BARBADOS · Bridgetown · St. George's · GRENADA · COSTA RICA · Port of Spain · TRINIDAD AND TOBAGO · PACIFIC OCEAN · PANAMA · COLOMBIA

0 200 400 mi
0 200 400 km

Kingston, Jamaica

Background photo: Ozama Fortress, Dominican Republic

Resource Directory

Program Resources

📁 **Outline Maps** Central America and the Caribbean: Political, p. 9

Media and Technology

📺 **Color Transparencies** Central America and the Caribbean: Political, 66

GEOFACTS

Caribbean

Population: 32.7 million

Most Populated City: Havana, Cuba (2.2 million)

Largest Country: Cuba (42,803 sq mi/ 110,860 sq km)

Smallest Country: Saint Vincent and the Grenadines (131 sq mi/340 sq km) and Grenada (131 sq mi/340 sq km)

Highest Point: Duarte Peak (10,417 ft/3,175 m)

Lowest Point: Lake Enriquillo (-144 ft/-44 m)

Longest River: Cauto River (230 mi/370 km)

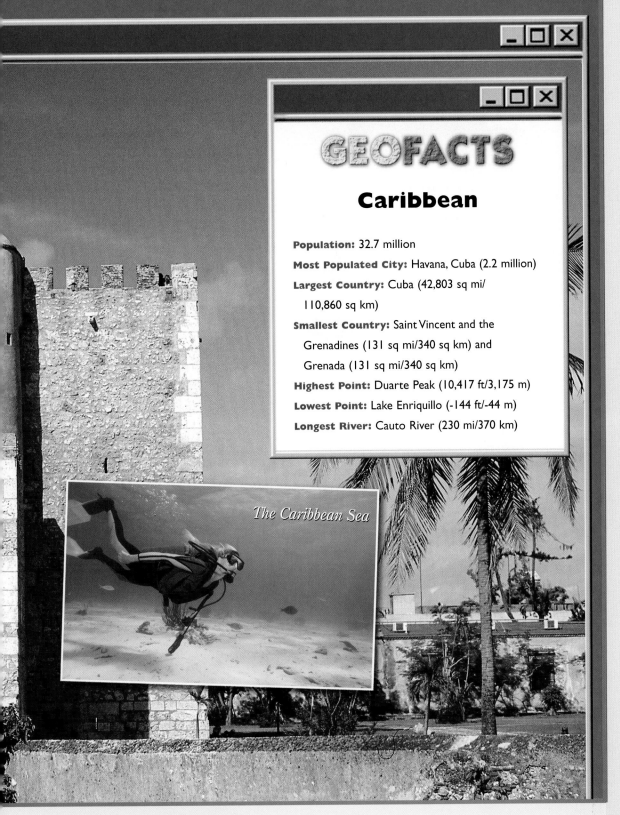

The Caribbean Sea

3 Assess

Have a volunteer read the export entries for several countries. As the volunteer reads, other students should note which kinds of agriculture appear most frequently. Then ask students to guess which climates would best suit the most common products that are grown in the Caribbean (*tropical, subtropical, rainy*).

Resource Directory

Media and Technology

 Prentice Hall Humanities Pack Fine art transparencies, posters, audio CDs and a performing arts video help students explore the arts and cultures of all regions of the world. Includes discussion questions and activities and a correlation to the *World Explorer* program.

Portfolio Assessment

Overview

The following activities help students explore, collect, and arrange the information they find in the Regional Database. You may wish to have students add these activities to a portfolio of information about the countries of the world. To assess student work, refer to the generic rubrics in the Assessment Handbook of the Program Resources.

Main Activity

Explain to students that each of the countries in this region has a unique history shaped by the interaction between native peoples and European settlers or colonizers.

• Have students, working in small groups, choose one country from the Caribbean. Students should use the library or the Internet to do research on the country they chose.

• Ask students to write a report on the history of that country. Their reports should pay special attention to where the people of that country came from, how the culture of the country has evolved, and how people have made a living in the past and today.

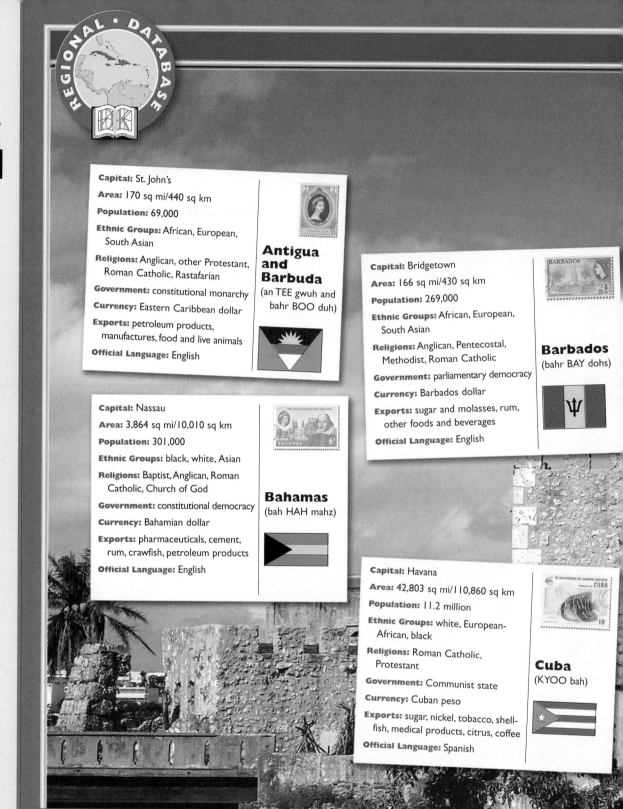

Capital: St. John's
Area: 170 sq mi/440 sq km
Population: 69,000
Ethnic Groups: African, European, South Asian
Religions: Anglican, other Protestant, Roman Catholic, Rastafarian
Government: constitutional monarchy
Currency: Eastern Caribbean dollar
Exports: petroleum products, manufactures, food and live animals
Official Language: English

Antigua and Barbuda
(an TEE gwuh and bahr BOO duh)

Capital: Bridgetown
Area: 166 sq mi/430 sq km
Population: 269,000
Ethnic Groups: African, European, South Asian
Religions: Anglican, Pentecostal, Methodist, Roman Catholic
Government: parliamentary democracy
Currency: Barbados dollar
Exports: sugar and molasses, rum, other foods and beverages
Official Language: English

Barbados
(bahr BAY dohs)

Capital: Nassau
Area: 3,864 sq mi/10,010 sq km
Population: 301,000
Ethnic Groups: black, white, Asian
Religions: Baptist, Anglican, Roman Catholic, Church of God
Government: constitutional democracy
Currency: Bahamian dollar
Exports: pharmaceuticals, cement, rum, crawfish, petroleum products
Official Language: English

Bahamas
(bah HAH mahz)

Capital: Havana
Area: 42,803 sq mi/110,860 sq km
Population: 11.2 million
Ethnic Groups: white, European-African, black
Religions: Roman Catholic, Protestant
Government: Communist state
Currency: Cuban peso
Exports: sugar, nickel, tobacco, shellfish, medical products, citrus, coffee
Official Language: Spanish

Cuba
(KYOO bah)

Resource Directory

Program Resources

Generic Rubrics 9, 19, and 26 in the **Assessment Handbook**

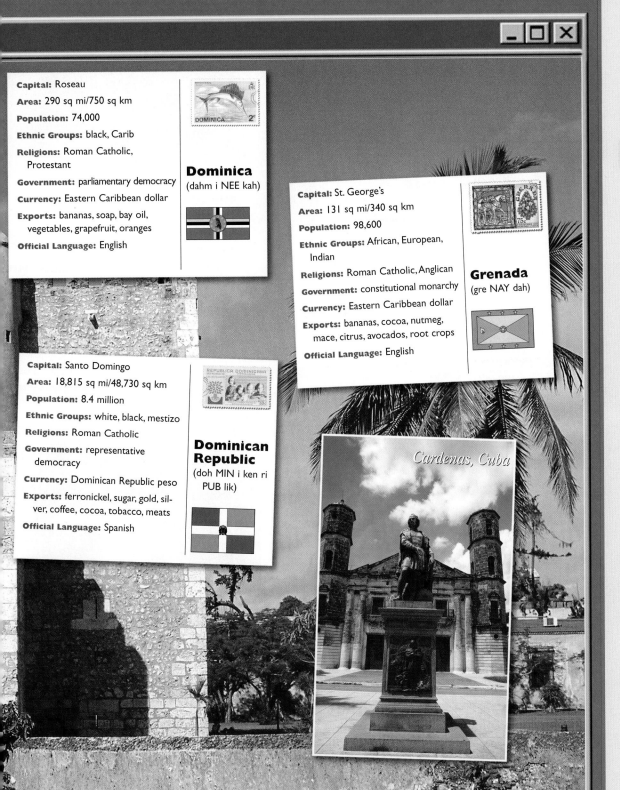

Capital: Roseau

Area: 290 sq mi/750 sq km

Population: 74,000

Ethnic Groups: black, Carib

Religions: Roman Catholic, Protestant

Government: parliamentary democracy

Currency: Eastern Caribbean dollar

Exports: bananas, soap, bay oil, vegetables, grapefruit, oranges

Official Language: English

Dominica
(dahm i NEE kah)

Capital: St. George's

Area: 131 sq mi/340 sq km

Population: 98,600

Ethnic Groups: African, European, Indian

Religions: Roman Catholic, Anglican

Government: constitutional monarchy

Currency: Eastern Caribbean dollar

Exports: bananas, cocoa, nutmeg, mace, citrus, avocados, root crops

Official Language: English

Grenada
(gre NAY dah)

Capital: Santo Domingo

Area: 18,815 sq mi/48,730 sq km

Population: 8.4 million

Ethnic Groups: white, black, mestizo

Religions: Roman Catholic

Government: representative democracy

Currency: Dominican Republic peso

Exports: ferronickel, sugar, gold, silver, coffee, cocoa, tobacco, meats

Official Language: Spanish

Dominican Republic
(doh MIN i ken ri PUB lik)

Cardenas, Cuba

 Take It to the NET

Prentice Hall's *World Explorer* companion Web site offers activities for exploring geographical, historical, and cultural resources on the Internet. It also provides online links for key content, data updates, and all chapter review activities.

The **Teacher site** provides teachers with ideas for student research and activities. It also presents *eTeach*, a monthly discussion with Master Teachers.

Students can use the **Student site** to find chapter-by-chapter Internet resource links, data updates, and Self-Tests.

http://www.phschool.com

Portfolio Assessment

Overview

The following activities help students explore, collect, and arrange the information they find in the Regional Database. You may wish to have students add these activities to a portfolio of information about the countries of the world. To assess student work, refer to the generic rubrics in the Assessment Handbook of the Program Resources.

Main Activity

Explain to students that while the countries of the Caribbean share similar geographic features, there are also variations in climate, vegetation, and terrain throughout the region.

• Group students into pairs and have each group choose two Caribbean nations. Allow the pairs to research the library, Internet, or other sources for information on the geography of the two nations. Students should be encouraged to find information like highest and lowest points, common vegetation, major lakes and rivers, and natural resources.

• Ask groups to draw two maps depicting the information they have found in their research. Students should include a key in their maps with symbols to indicate what information is being presented on the map.

Capital: Port-au-Prince
Area: 10,641 sq mi/27,560 sq km
Population: 8.1 million
Ethnic Groups: black, mulatto, white
Religions: Roman Catholic, Protestant
Government: elected government
Currency: Gourde
Exports: manufactures, coffee, oils, mangoes
Official Languages: French and French Creole

Haiti
(HAYT ee)

Capital: Basseterre
Area: 139 sq mi/360 sq km
Population: 41,000
Ethnic Groups: black, white
Religions: Anglican, Methodist, Moravian, Roman Catholic
Government: constitutional monarchy
Currency: Eastern Caribbean dollar
Exports: machinery, food, electronics, beverages, tobacco
Official Language: English

**Saint Kitt
and Nevi:**
(saynt kits and NEE vis)

Capital: Kingston
Area: 4,181 sq mi/10,830 sq km
Population: 2.6 million
Ethnic Groups: black, East Indian, white, Chinese, mestizo
Religions: Protestant, Church of God, Baptist, Anglican
Government: constitutional parliamentary democracy
Currency: Jamaican dollar
Exports: alumina, bauxite, sugar
Official Language: English

Jamaica
(juh MAY kah)

Kingston, Jamaica

Resource Directory

Program Resources

 Generic Rubrics 7 and 16 in the Assessment Handbook

Media and Technology

Color Transparencies Fine Art, 158

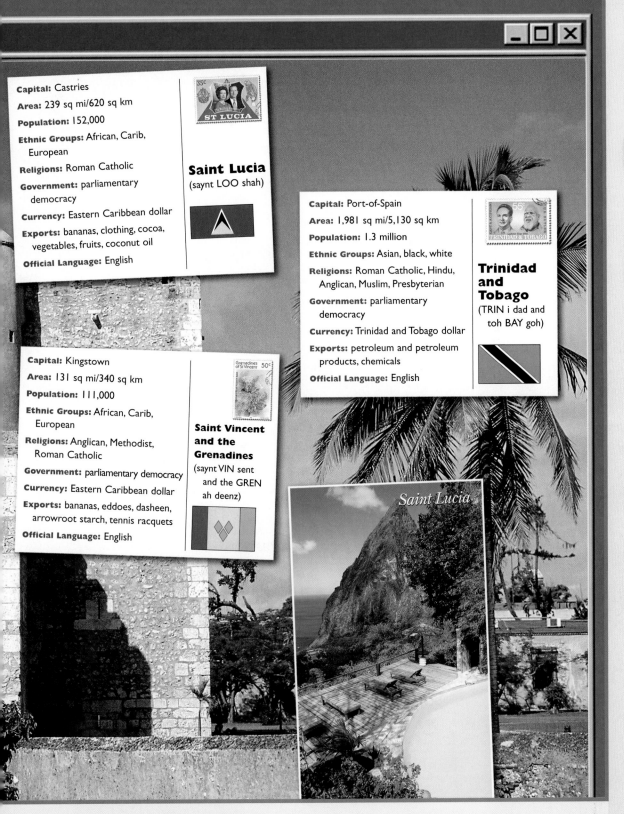

Capital: Castries

Area: 239 sq mi/620 sq km

Population: 152,000

Ethnic Groups: African, Carib, European

Religions: Roman Catholic

Government: parliamentary democracy

Currency: Eastern Caribbean dollar

Exports: bananas, clothing, cocoa, vegetables, fruits, coconut oil

Official Language: English

Saint Lucia
(saynt LOO shah)

Capital: Port-of-Spain

Area: 1,981 sq mi/5,130 sq km

Population: 1.3 million

Ethnic Groups: Asian, black, white

Religions: Roman Catholic, Hindu, Anglican, Muslim, Presbyterian

Government: parliamentary democracy

Currency: Trinidad and Tobago dollar

Exports: petroleum and petroleum products, chemicals

Official Language: English

Trinidad and Tobago
(TRIN i dad and toh BAY goh)

Capital: Kingstown

Area: 131 sq mi/340 sq km

Population: 111,000

Ethnic Groups: African, Carib, European

Religions: Anglican, Methodist, Roman Catholic

Government: parliamentary democracy

Currency: Eastern Caribbean dollar

Exports: bananas, eddoes, dasheen, arrowroot starch, tennis racquets

Official Language: English

Saint Vincent and the Grenadines
(saynt VIN sent and the GREN ah deenz)

Saint Lucia

Resource Directory

Media and Technology

Passport to the World CD-ROM
This interactive CD-ROM allows students to explore each region of the world. Students view regional videos, take a photo tour, and explore a historical time line. Students record their travels in an Explorer's Journal, and receive passport stamps when they pass regional tests.

continued

Lesson Objective

Gather, understand, and apply information about the countries of South America.

Lesson Plan

1 Explore

Explain that South America is the fourth largest continent in area, after Asia, Africa, and North America. It ranks fifth among continents in population, after Asia, Europe, Africa, and North America.

2 Teach

Point out that South America has a wide variety of climates and landscapes. The largest tropical rain forest in the world is located in the Amazon River Basin. South America is also home to many animals that cannot be found naturally in the United States, including many types of monkeys, anacondas, and penguins.

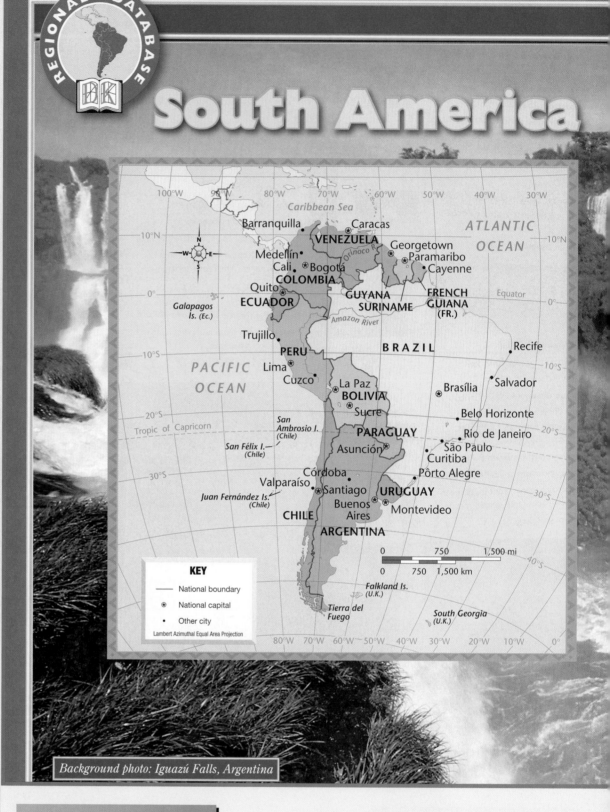

REGIONAL · DATABASE

South America

KEY

— National boundary

⊛ National capital

• Other city

Lambert Azimuthal Equal Area Projection

```
0        750      1,500 mi
0    750  1,500 km
```

Background photo: Iguazú Falls, Argentina

Resource Directory

Program Resources

Nystrom Desk Atlas Political maps, physical maps, and regional maps and charts for South America, pp. 88–93; Country Table, p. 147

Outline Maps South America: Political, p. 11

GEOFACTS

South America

Population: 340.7 million

Most Populated City: São Paulo, Brazil (9.8 million)

Largest Country: Brazil (265,059 sq mi/ 8,456,510 sq km)

Smallest Country: French Guiana (35,100 sq mi/ 91,000 sq km)

Highest Point: Aconcagua (22,835 ft/6,960 m)

Lowest Point: Valdes Peninsula (-131 ft/-40 m)

Longest River: Amazon River (4,000 mi/6,437 km)

3 Assess

Have volunteers read the information in the Geofacts box about South America. Ask students what the categories Most Populated City and Longest River have in common (*both can be found in the largest country, Brazil*).

Easter Island, Chile

Caracas, Venezuela

Take It to the NET

Prentice Hall's *World Explorer* companion Web site offers activities for exploring geographical, historical, and cultural resources on the Internet. It also provides online links for key content, data updates, and all chapter review activities.

The **Teacher site** provides teachers with ideas for student research and activities. It also presents *eTeach*, a monthly discussion with Master Teachers.

Students can use the **Student site** to find chapter-by-chapter Internet resource links, data updates, and Self-Tests.

http://www.phschool.com

Lesson Objective

Gather, understand, and apply information about Brazil.

Lesson Plan

1 Explore

Point out that Brazil occupies almost the entire eastern half of South America, and is much larger than any of the continent's other countries. Ask a volunteer to name the largest river in Brazil (*the Amazon*).

2 Teach

Ask students in which hemisphere most of Brazil is located (*Southern*). Explain that most of Brazil, like other countries south of the Equator, has seasons opposite to those in the Northern Hemisphere. Ask students what season it would be right now in Brazil.

Brazil

REGIONAL · DATABASE

KEY

—— National boundary
⊛ National capital
• Other city

Lambert Azimuthal Equal Area Projection

Background photo: Rio de Janeiro, Brazil

Resource Directory

Program Resources

📁 **Outline Maps** Brazil: Political, p. 10

Media and Technology

📠 **Color Transparencies** Brazil: Physical-Political, 88

Capital: Brasília

Area: 3,265,059 sq mi/8,456,510 sq km

Population: 168 million

Ethnic Groups: African, European, Indian

Religions: Roman Catholic, Protestant, Afro American Spiritist

Government: federative republic

Currency: Real

Exports: manufactures, iron ore, soybeans, footwear, coffee

Official Language: Portuguese

Brazil
(brah ZIL)

Amazon rain forest

Media and Technology

 Passport to the World CD-ROM
This interactive CD-ROM allows students to explore each region of the world. Students view regional videos, take a photo tour, and explore a historical time line. Students record their travels in an Explorer's Journal, and receive passport stamps when they pass regional tests.

continued

3 Assess

Have a volunteer read the items that appear in the export entry. Ask students if they think a small country would be likely to export such a variety of products.

continued

Lesson Objective

Gather, understand, and apply information about the countries of northern South America.

Lesson Plan

1 Explore

Ask a volunteer to name the countries on the map of northern South America (*Colombia, Venezuela, Guyana, Suriname, and French Guiana*). Emphasize that all of these countries have extensive coastlines.

2 Teach

Point out to students that most of the countries of this region share similar characteristics. For example, most have dense forests and central plateaus or highlands. Explain that unlike the other countries of the region, Colombia's terrain includes high mountains, as part of the Andes chain runs through the country.

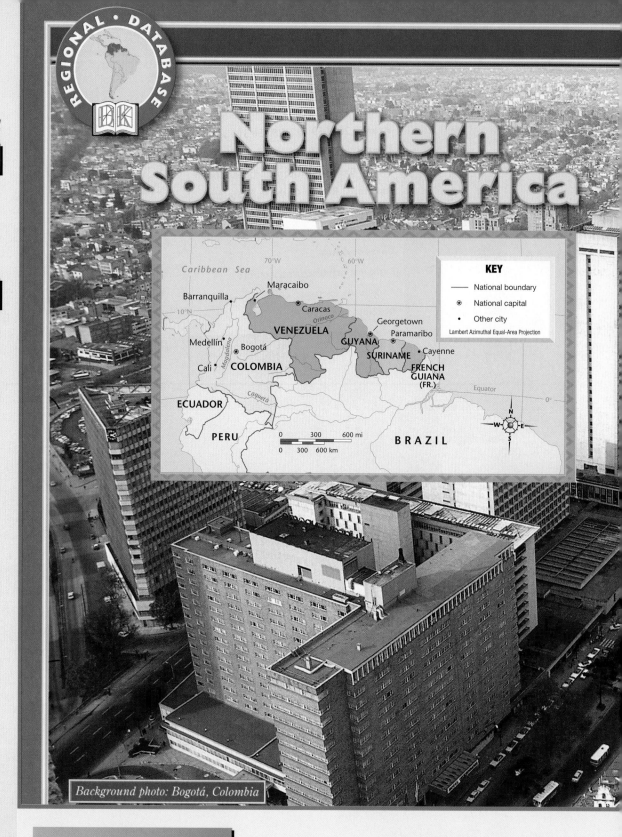

Northern South America

KEY

--- National boundary
⊛ National capital
• Other city

Lambert Azimuthal Equal-Area Projection

Caribbean Sea

Barranquilla
Maracaibo
Caracas
VENEZUELA
Georgetown
Paramaribo
Medellín
Bogotá
GUYANA
SURINAME
Cali
COLOMBIA
Cayenne
FRENCH GUIANA (FR.)
Equator
ECUADOR
0 300 600 mi
0 300 600 km
PERU
BRAZIL

Background photo: Bogotá, Colombia

Resource Directory

Media and Technology

 Color Transparencies Latin America: Physical-Political, 34; Major Crops, 35

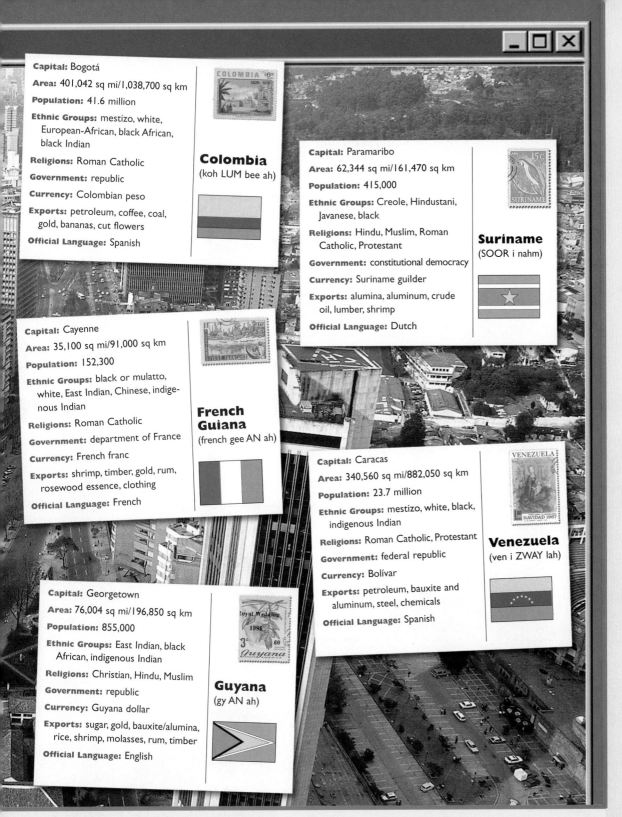

Capital: Bogotá

Area: 401,042 sq mi/1,038,700 sq km

Population: 41.6 million

Ethnic Groups: mestizo, white, European-African, black African, black Indian

Religions: Roman Catholic

Government: republic

Currency: Colombian peso

Exports: petroleum, coffee, coal, gold, bananas, cut flowers

Official Language: Spanish

Colombia
(koh LUM bee ah)

Capital: Cayenne

Area: 35,100 sq mi/91,000 sq km

Population: 152,300

Ethnic Groups: black or mulatto, white, East Indian, Chinese, indigenous Indian

Religions: Roman Catholic

Government: department of France

Currency: French franc

Exports: shrimp, timber, gold, rum, rosewood essence, clothing

Official Language: French

French Guiana
(french gee AN ah)

Capital: Georgetown

Area: 76,004 sq mi/196,850 sq km

Population: 855,000

Ethnic Groups: East Indian, black African, indigenous Indian

Religions: Christian, Hindu, Muslim

Government: republic

Currency: Guyana dollar

Exports: sugar, gold, bauxite/alumina, rice, shrimp, molasses, rum, timber

Official Language: English

Guyana
(gy AN ah)

Capital: Paramaribo

Area: 62,344 sq mi/161,470 sq km

Population: 415,000

Ethnic Groups: Creole, Hindustani, Javanese, black

Religions: Hindu, Muslim, Roman Catholic, Protestant

Government: constitutional democracy

Currency: Suriname guilder

Exports: alumina, aluminum, crude oil, lumber, shrimp

Official Language: Dutch

Suriname
(SOOR i nahm)

Capital: Caracas

Area: 340,560 sq mi/882,050 sq km

Population: 23.7 million

Ethnic Groups: mestizo, white, black, indigenous Indian

Religions: Roman Catholic, Protestant

Government: federal republic

Currency: Bolívar

Exports: petroleum, bauxite and aluminum, steel, chemicals

Official Language: Spanish

Venezuela
(ven i ZWAY lah)

Media and Technology

  Prentice Hall Humanities Pack Fine art transparencies, posters, audio CDs and a performing arts video help students explore the arts and cultures of all regions of the world. Includes discussion questions and activities and a correlation to the *World Explorer* program.

continued

3 Assess

Have a volunteer read the items that appear in the exports category. Ask students what exports would require people to work in mining (*coal, gold, bauxite/alumina and aluminum*) and fishing (*shrimp*).

Lesson Objective

Gather, understand, and apply information about the Andean and Southern countries of South America.

Lesson Plan

1 Explore

Have a volunteer read out the names of the countries on the map. Point out that Argentina is the largest country of the region, and that it occupies almost the entire southern tip of the continent.

2 Teach

Tell students that though much of the terrain of this region is dominated by the Andes mountains, the many fertile valleys between the mountains provide land for crop cultivation. Explain that Argentina, Paraguay, and Uruguay are known for their extensive grasslands, known as *pampas*, and well-developed river systems. Remind students that Peru was the seat of the vast Incan empire, and nearly half of Peru's population today are Incan descendants. Explain that Native American and mestizo groups make up a large population of the region.

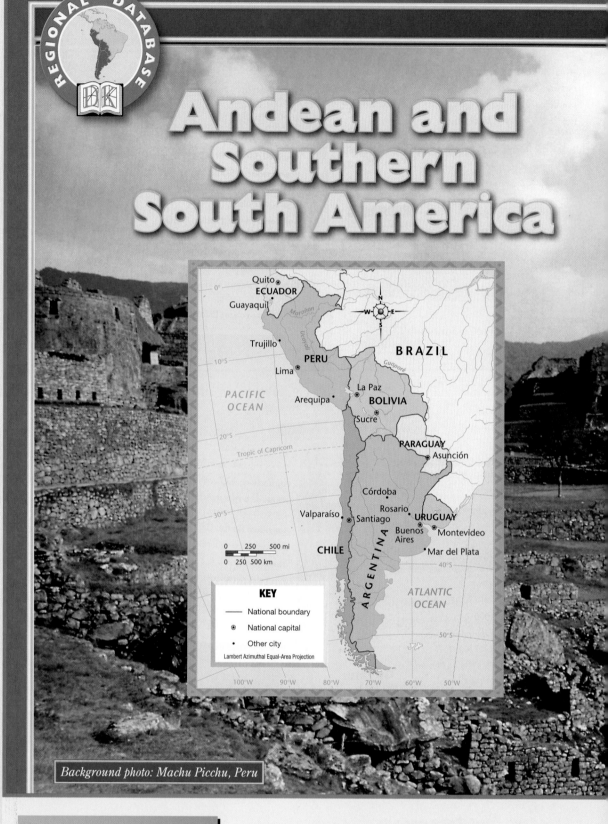

REGIONAL · DATABASE

Andean and Southern South America

KEY
— National boundary
⊛ National capital
• Other city
Lambert Azimuthal Equal-Area Projection

Background photo: Machu Picchu, Peru

Resource Directory

Program Resources

📁 **Outline Maps** South America: Political, p. 11

📁 **Environmental and Global Issues** Topic: Conflict, p. 41

Media and Technology

📠 **Color Transparencies** Student Art, 157

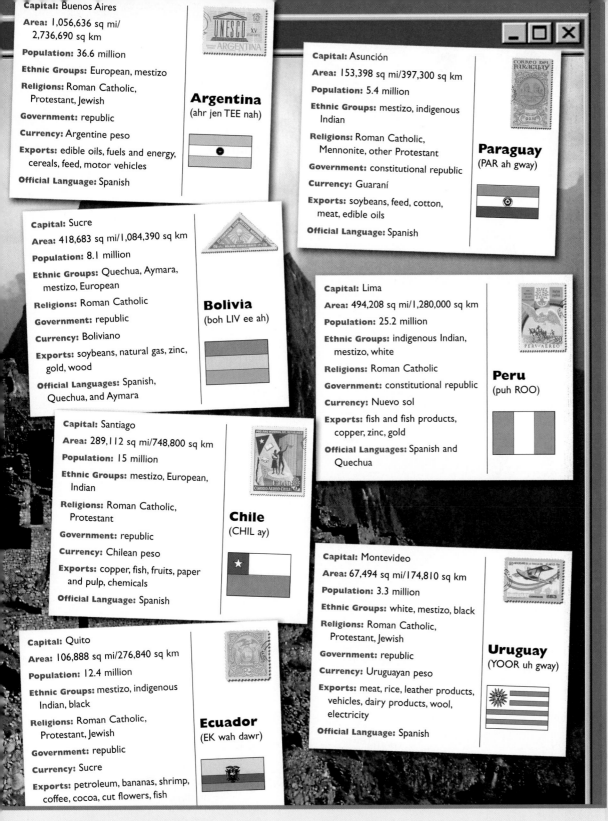

Capital: Buenos Aires

Area: 1,056,636 sq mi/2,736,690 sq km

Population: 36.6 million

Ethnic Groups: European, mestizo

Religions: Roman Catholic, Protestant, Jewish

Government: republic

Currency: Argentine peso

Exports: edible oils, fuels and energy, cereals, feed, motor vehicles

Official Language: Spanish

Argentina
(ahr jen TEE nah)

Capital: Asunción

Area: 153,398 sq mi/397,300 sq km

Population: 5.4 million

Ethnic Groups: mestizo, indigenous Indian

Religions: Roman Catholic, Mennonite, other Protestant

Government: constitutional republic

Currency: Guaraní

Exports: soybeans, feed, cotton, meat, edible oils

Official Language: Spanish

Paraguay
(PAR ah gway)

Capital: Sucre

Area: 418,683 sq mi/1,084,390 sq km

Population: 8.1 million

Ethnic Groups: Quechua, Aymara, mestizo, European

Religions: Roman Catholic

Government: republic

Currency: Boliviano

Exports: soybeans, natural gas, zinc, gold, wood

Official Languages: Spanish, Quechua, and Aymara

Bolivia
(boh LIV ee ah)

Capital: Lima

Area: 494,208 sq mi/1,280,000 sq km

Population: 25.2 million

Ethnic Groups: indigenous Indian, mestizo, white

Religions: Roman Catholic

Government: constitutional republic

Currency: Nuevo sol

Exports: fish and fish products, copper, zinc, gold

Official Languages: Spanish and Quechua

Peru
(puh ROO)

Capital: Santiago

Area: 289,112 sq mi/748,800 sq km

Population: 15 million

Ethnic Groups: mestizo, European, Indian

Religions: Roman Catholic, Protestant

Government: republic

Currency: Chilean peso

Exports: copper, fish, fruits, paper and pulp, chemicals

Official Language: Spanish

Chile
(CHIL ay)

Capital: Montevideo

Area: 67,494 sq mi/174,810 sq km

Population: 3.3 million

Ethnic Groups: white, mestizo, black

Religions: Roman Catholic, Protestant, Jewish

Government: republic

Currency: Uruguayan peso

Exports: meat, rice, leather products, vehicles, dairy products, wool, electricity

Official Language: Spanish

Uruguay
(YOOR uh gway)

Capital: Quito

Area: 106,888 sq mi/276,840 sq km

Population: 12.4 million

Ethnic Groups: mestizo, indigenous Indian, black

Religions: Roman Catholic, Protestant, Jewish

Government: republic

Currency: Sucre

Exports: petroleum, bananas, shrimp, coffee, cocoa, cut flowers, fish

Ecuador
(EK wah dawr)

Media and Technology

Passport to the World CD-ROM
This interactive CD-ROM allows students to explore each region of the world. Students view regional videos, take a photo tour, and explore a historical time line. Students record their travels in an Explorer's Journal, and receive passport stamps when they pass regional tests.

REGIONAL · DATABASE

continued

3 Assess

Have students read the ethnic group entries for all of these countries. Which group is common to all countries? (*mestizo*)

Atlas

The World: Political

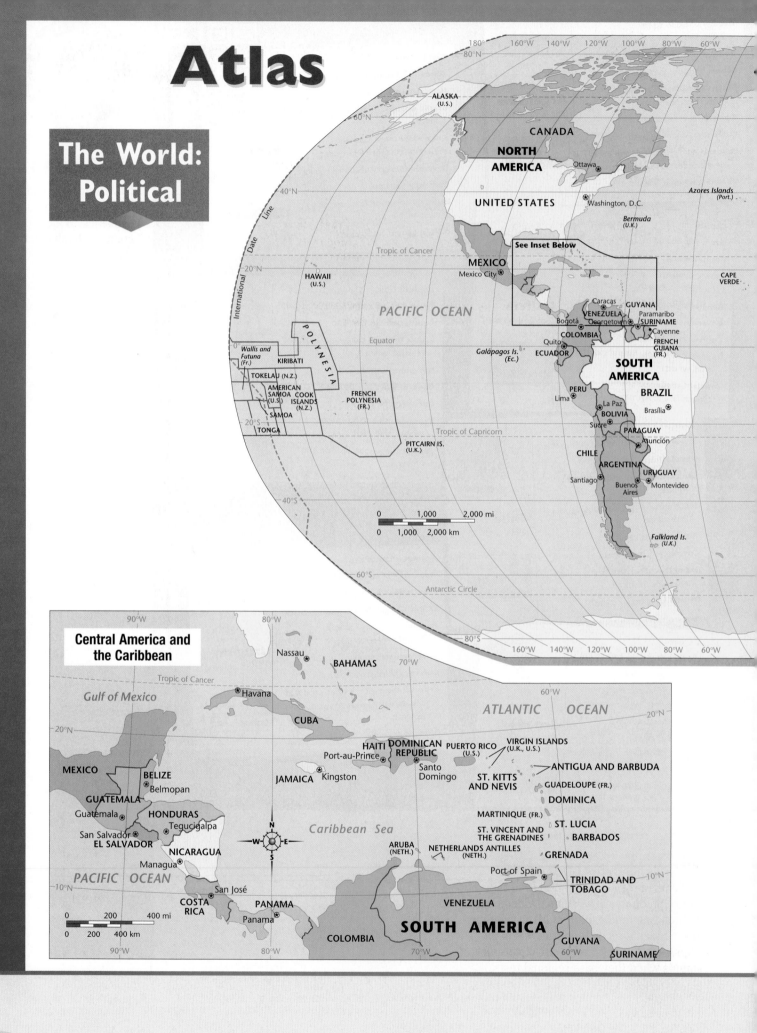

80°N
180° 160°W 140°W 120°W 100°W 80°W 60°W

ALASKA
(U.S.)

60°N

CANADA

**NORTH
AMERICA**

Ottawa

40°N

UNITED STATES

Washington, D.C.

Azores Islands
(Port.)

Bermuda
(U.K.)

Tropic of Cancer

MEXICO

Mexico City

See Inset Below

CAPE
VERDE

20°N

HAWAII
(U.S.)

Caracas GUYANA

VENEZUELA Paramaribo

Bogotá Georgetown SURINAME

COLOMBIA Cayenne

FRENCH
GUIANA
(FR.)

PACIFIC OCEAN

Equator

Quito
Galápagos Is. ECUADOR
(Ec.)

**SOUTH
AMERICA**

POLYNESIA

Wallis and
Futuna
(Fr.)

KIRIBATI

TOKELAU (N.Z.)

AMERICAN
SAMOA COOK
(U.S.) ISLANDS
(N.Z.)

SAMOA

TONGA

FRENCH
POLYNESIA
(FR.)

20°S

PERU
Lima

La Paz
BOLIVIA
Sucre

BRAZIL

Brasília

PARAGUAY
Asunción

PITCAIRN IS.
(U.K.)

Tropic of Capricorn

CHILE
ARGENTINA URUGUAY

Santiago Buenos Montevideo
Aires

0	1,000	2,000 mi
0	1,000	2,000 km

40°S

60°S

Antarctic Circle

Falkland Is.
(U.K.)

80°S
160°W 140°W 120°W 100°W 80°W 60°W

Central America and the Caribbean

90°W 80°W

Nassau 70°W

BAHAMAS

Tropic of Cancer

Gulf of Mexico

Havana 60°W

ATLANTIC OCEAN
20°N

20°N

CUBA

HAITI DOMINICAN
REPUBLIC PUERTO RICO VIRGIN ISLANDS
(U.S.) (U.K., U.S.)

MEXICO

BELIZE

Belmopan

Port-au-Prince Santo
Domingo

ST. KITTS
AND NEVIS

ANTIGUA AND BARBUDA

GUADELOUPE (FR.)

JAMAICA Kingston

DOMINICA

GUATEMALA

Guatemala

HONDURAS
Tegucigalpa

MARTINIQUE (FR.)

ST. VINCENT AND
THE GRENADINES

ST. LUCIA

BARBADOS

San Salvador
EL SALVADOR

NICARAGUA

Caribbean Sea

ARUBA
(NETH.)

NETHERLANDS ANTILLES
(NETH.)

GRENADA

PACIFIC OCEAN

Managua

Port of Spain

TRINIDAD AND
TOBAGO

10°N

10°N

San José

COSTA
RICA

PANAMA

Panama

VENEZUELA

SOUTH AMERICA

0	200	400 mi
0	200	400 km

COLOMBIA

GUYANA

90°W 80°W 70°W 60°W SURINAME

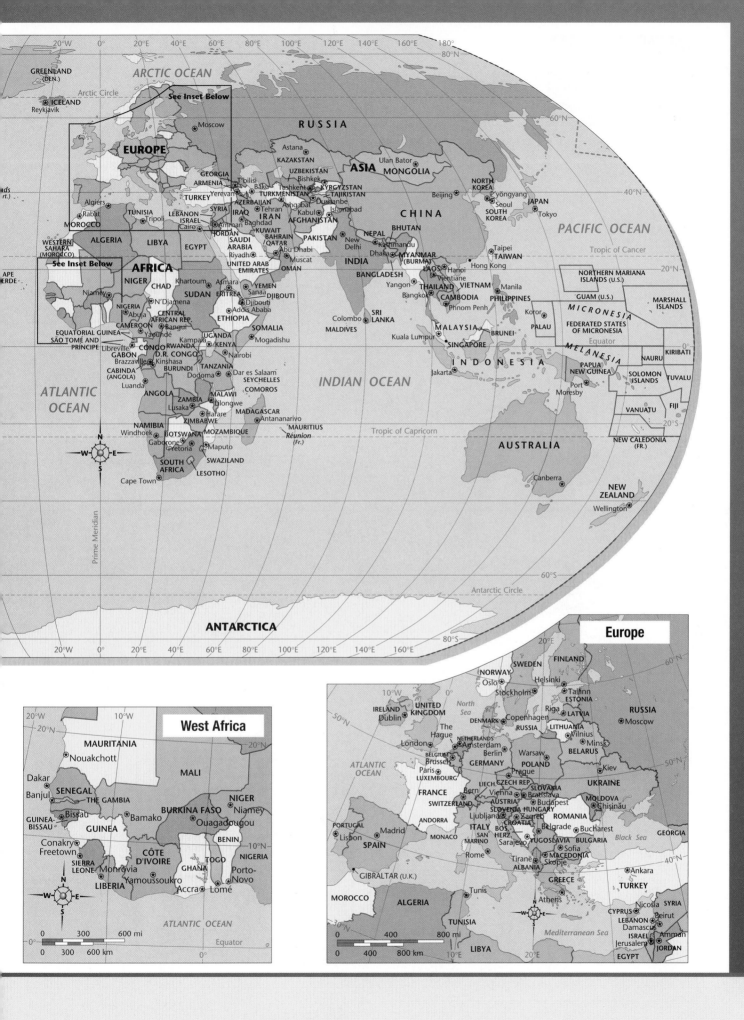

ARCTIC OCEAN

GREENLAND
(DEN.)

Arctic Circle

ICELAND
Reykjavik

Moscow

See Inset Below

RUSSIA

EUROPE

Astana

KAZAKSTAN

Ulan Bator

ASIA

MONGOLIA

60°N

GEORGIA
ARMENIA
T'bilisi
Yerevan
TURKEY
Algiers
Rabat
MOROCCO
TUNISIA
Tripoli
Baku
AZERBAIJAN
Tashkent
Bishkek
UZBEKISTAN
KYRGYZSTAN
TAJIKISTAN
TURKMENISTAN
Ashgabat
Dushanbe
Islamabad
Kabul
AFGHANISTAN
PAKISTAN

Beijing

CHINA

40°N

NORTH
KOREA
P'yongyang
Seoul
SOUTH
KOREA

JAPAN

Tokyo

PACIFIC OCEAN

LEBANON
ISRAEL
Cairo
Amman
JORDAN
SYRIA
IRAQ
Baghdad
Tehran
IRAN
KUWAIT
BAHRAIN
QATAR
Abu Dhabi
UNITED ARAB
EMIRATES
Riyadh
SAUDI
ARABIA
OMAN
Muscat

New
Delhi
NEPAL
Kathmandu
BHUTAN
Dhaka
MYANMAR
(BURMA)

BANGLADESH

INDIA

Yangon

Taipei
TAIWAN

Hong Kong

Hanoi
LAOS
Vientiane
THAILAND
VIETNAM
Bangkok
CAMBODIA
Phnom Penh

Manila

PHILIPPINES

Tropic of Cancer

NORTHERN MARIANA
ISLANDS (U.S.)

20°N

GUAM (U.S.)

MARSHALL
ISLANDS

WESTERN
SAHARA
(MOROCCO)
ALGERIA
LIBYA
EGYPT

AFRICA

See Inset Below

NIGER
CHAD
Khartoum
SUDAN
Asmara
ERITREA
Sanaa
DJIBOUTI
Djibouti

YEMEN

SRI
LANKA
Colombo
MALDIVES

MICRONESIA
Koror
PALAU
FEDERATED STATES
OF MICRONESIA

Niamey
NIGERIA
Abuja
N'Djamena
CENTRAL
AFRICAN REP.
Bangui
Addis Ababa
ETHIOPIA
SOMALIA
Mogadishu

MALAYSIA
BRUNEI

Equator

NAURU
KIRIBATI

CAPE
VERDE

0°

EQUATORIAL GUINEA
SÃO TOMÉ AND
PRÍNCIPE
CAMEROON
Yaoundé
Libreville
GABON
CONGO
Brazzaville
Kinshasa
D.R. CONGO
CABINDA
(ANGOLA)
Luanda

UGANDA
Kampala
RWANDA
BURUNDI
KENYA
Nairobi
TANZANIA
Dodoma
Dar es Salaam
SEYCHELLES

Kuala Lumpur
SINGAPORE

INDONESIA
Jakarta

MELANESIA
PAPUA
NEW GUINEA
Port
Moresby

SOLOMON
ISLANDS
TUVALU

ANGOLA
ZAMBIA
Lusaka
MALAWI
Lilongwe
COMOROS
MADAGASCAR
Antananarivo
MAURITIUS
Réunion
(Fr.)

VANUATU

FIJI

NEW CALEDONIA
(FR.)

20°S

ATLANTIC
OCEAN

NAMIBIA
Windhoek
BOTSWANA
Gaborone
ZIMBABWE
Harare
MOZAMBIQUE
Maputo

ZAMBIA

INDIAN OCEAN

Tropic of Capricorn

AUSTRALIA

SOUTH
AFRICA
Pretoria
SWAZILAND
LESOTHO
Cape Town

Canberra

NEW
ZEALAND
Wellington

60°S

Antarctic Circle

ANTARCTICA

80°S

20°W 0° 20°E 40°E 60°E 80°E 100°E 120°E 140°E 160°E

West Africa

MAURITANIA
Nouakchott

MALI

Dakar
SENEGAL
Banjul
THE GAMBIA
GUINEA-
BISSAU
Bissau
GUINEA
Bamako
BURKINA FASO
Ouagadougou
NIGER
Niamey
BENIN

Conakry
Freetown
SIERRA
LEONE
Monrovia
LIBERIA
CÔTE
D'IVOIRE
GHANA
Yamoussoukro
Accra
TOGO
Lomé
NIGERIA
Porto-
Novo

ATLANTIC OCEAN

Equator

0   300   600 mi
0   300   600 km

Europe

NORWAY
Oslo
SWEDEN
Stockholm
FINLAND
Helsinki
Tallinn
ESTONIA
Riga
LATVIA
RUSSIA
Moscow

IRELAND
Dublin
UNITED
KINGDOM
North
Sea
Copenhagen
DENMARK
LITHUANIA
Vilnius
Minsk
BELARUS

London
The
Hague
NETHERLANDS
Amsterdam
Berlin
Warsaw
POLAND
Kiev

ATLANTIC
OCEAN
BELGIUM
Brussels
GERMANY
Prague
CZECH REP.
UKRAINE

Paris
LUXEMBOURG
LIECH.
Vienna
SLOVAKIA
Bratislava
MOLDOVA
Chișinău

FRANCE
SWITZERLAND
Bern
AUSTRIA
SLOVENIA
HUNGARY
Budapest
ROMANIA
Bucharest
GEORGIA

ANDORRA
Ljubljana
CROATIA
Zagreb
BOS.
HERZ.
Belgrade
YUGOSLAVIA
BULGARIA
Black Sea

PORTUGAL
Lisbon
Madrid
MONACO
ITALY
SAN
MARINO
Rome
Sarajevo
Sofia
Tiranë
MACEDONIA
Skopje

SPAIN
ALBANIA
GREECE
Athens
TURKEY
Ankara

GIBRALTAR (U.K.)
Tunis
CYPRUS
Nicosia
SYRIA
LEBANON
Beirut
Damascus

MOROCCO
ALGERIA
Mediterranean Sea
ISRAEL
Jerusalem
Amman
JORDAN

TUNISIA
LIBYA
EGYPT

0   400   800 mi
0   400   800 km

The World: Physical

ARCTIC OCEAN

Greenland

Beaufort Sea

Bering Sea

Yukon R.

Aleutian Islands

Baffin Island

Hudson Bay

NORTH AMERICA

ROCKY MOUNTAINS

GREAT PLAINS

CANADIAN SHIELD

Missouri R.

Great Lakes

St. Lawrence R.

Mississippi R.

APPALACHIAN MTS.

ATLANTIC OCEAN

Tropic of Cancer

Hawaiian Islands

SIERRA MADRE ORIENTAL

SIERRA MADRE OCCIDENTAL

Gulf of Mexico

West Indies

Caribbean Sea

PACIFIC OCEAN

P O L Y N E S I A

Equator

Orinoco R.

GUIANA HIGHLANDS

AMAZON BASIN

Amazon R.

SOUTH AMERICA

ANDES MTS.

BRAZILIAN HIGHLANDS

Tropic of Capricorn

PAMPAS

Rio de la Plata

PATAGONIA

Cape Horn

Drake Passage

Antarctic Circle

ANTARCTIC PENINSULA

KEY

Elevation

Feet		Meters
14,000		4,270
7,000		2,135
1,500		457
700		213
(sea level) 0		0 (sea level)

Ice pack

Ice shelf

Orthographic Projection

South Pole

SOUTHERN OCEAN

QUEEN MAUD LAND

COATS LAND

ENDERBY LAND

Antarctic Peninsula

Weddell Sea

Amery Ice Shelf

Prime Meridian

Ronne Ice Shelf

ANTARCTICA

South Pole

QUEEN MAUD MTS.

TRANSANTARCTIC MTS.

Ross Ice Shelf

Roosevelt I.

Ross Sea

International Date Line

WILKES LAND

VICTORIA LAND

South Magnetic Pole

0   800 mi

0   800 km

20°W 0° 20°E 40°E 60°E 80°E 100°E 120°E 140°E 160°E 180°

land 80°N

ARCTIC OCEAN

Arctic Circle
Iceland

SCANDINAVIAN PEN.
British Isles

North Sea

URAL MTS.

SIBERIA

60°N

NORTH EUROPEAN PLAIN

WEST SIBERIAN PLAIN

Ob R.

Yenisei R.

Lena R.

KOLYMA MTS.

KAMCHATKA PENINSULA

EUROPE

Volga R.

ASIA

CAUCASUS

Aral Sea

Baikal

Amur R.

Sea of Japan

40°N

IBERIAN PEN.

BALKAN PEN.

Black Sea

Caspian Sea

TIAN SHAN

GOBI DESERT

NORTH CHINA PLAIN

ATLAS MTS.

Mediterranean Sea

ZAGROS MTS.

PLATEAU OF IRAN

HINDU KUSH

KUNLUN SHAN

TIBETAN PLATEAU

Huang He

Yangtze R.

SAHARA

ARABIAN PENINSULA

Persian Gulf

Mt. Everest 29,035 ft (8,848 m)

Tropic of Cancer

AFRICA

Red Sea

Arabian Sea

DECCAN PLATEAU

Ganges R.

Bay of Bengal

Philippine Sea

20°N

SUDAN

Nile R.

ETHIOPIAN PLATEAU

South China Sea

Philippine Islands

MICRONESIA

Congo R.

Lake Victoria

Sumatra

Borneo

Celebes

East Indies

Equator

MELANESIA

0°

ATLANTIC OCEAN

INDIAN OCEAN

New Guinea

Zambezi R.

Madagascar

KALAHARI

AUSTRALIA

20°S

Tropic of Capricorn

Darling R.

GREAT DIVIDING RANGE

North Island

Cape of Good Hope

N
W E
S

0   1,000   2,000 mi
0   1,000   2,000 km

South Island

40°S

60°S

Antarctic Circle

ANTARCTICA

80°S

20°W 0° 20°E 40°E 60°E 80°E 100°E 120°E 140°E 160°E

North Pole

ASIA 90°E

TAIMYR PEN.

Laptev Sea

Severnaya Zemlya

Novaya Zemlya

Kara Sea

Barents Sea

New Siberian Islands

Franz Josef Land

East Siberian Sea

ARCTIC OCEAN
North Pole

Svalbard

International Date Line

Prime Meridian

Chukchi Sea

0   500 mi
0   500 km

North Magnetic Pole

Ellesmere Island

NORTH AMERICA

Queen Elizabeth Islands

Baffin Bay

United States: Political

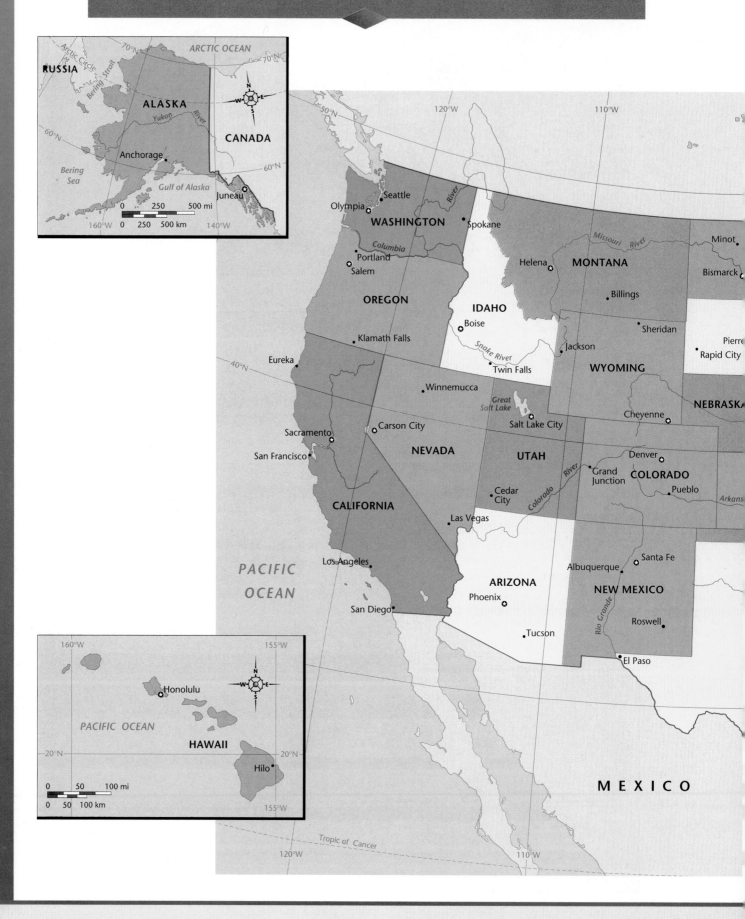

ARCTIC OCEAN

RUSSIA

ALASKA

CANADA

Arctic Circle

70°N
70°N

60°N
60°N

Bering Strait

Yukon River

Anchorage

Bering Sea

Gulf of Alaska

Juneau

160°W

140°W

0   250   500 mi
0   250   500 km

160°W   155°W

Honolulu

PACIFIC OCEAN

HAWAII

20°N   20°N

Hilo

0   50   100 mi
0   50   100 km

155°W

PACIFIC
OCEAN

50°N

120°W   110°W

River

Seattle
Olympia
WASHINGTON   Spokane

Columbia

Portland
Salem

OREGON

Klamath Falls

Eureka

40°N

Missouri River

Helena   MONTANA

Billings

IDAHO
Boise

Snake River

Sheridan

Minot

Bismarck

Pierre
Rapid City

Jackson

Twin Falls

WYOMING

Winnemucca

Great
Salt Lake

NEBRASKA

Carson City

Sacramento

San Francisco

NEVADA

Salt Lake City

UTAH

Cheyenne

Denver

Colorado River

Grand
Junction   COLORADO

Pueblo

Arkans

Cedar
City

Las Vegas

CALIFORNIA

Los Angeles

San Diego

ARIZONA

Phoenix

Albuquerque

Santa Fe

NEW MEXICO

Roswell

Rio Grande

Tucson

El Paso

M E X I C O

Tropic of Cancer

120°W   110°W

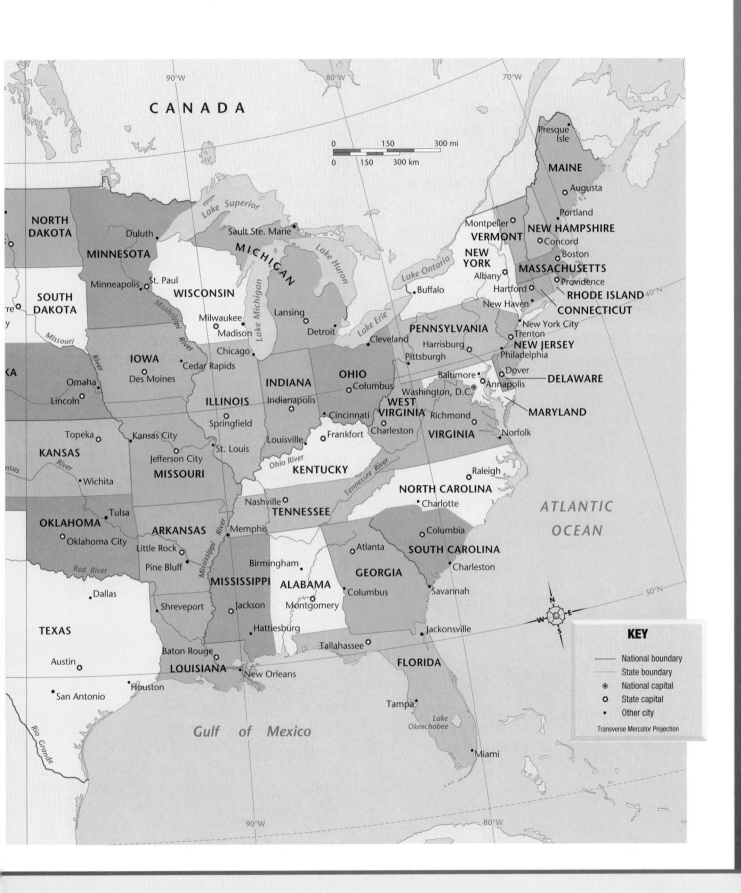

CANADA

0 150 300 mi
0 150 300 km

NORTH DAKOTA

Duluth

Sault Ste. Marie

MINNESOTA

Lake Superior

MICHIGAN

Lake Huron

MAINE

Presque Isle

Augusta

Portland

Montpelier

VERMONT

NEW HAMPSHIRE

Concord

Boston

Minneapolis St. Paul

WISCONSIN

Lake Michigan

Lansing

NEW YORK

Lake Ontario

Albany

MASSACHUSETTS

Providence

SOUTH DAKOTA

Milwaukee

Madison

Detroit

Buffalo

Hartford

New Haven

RHODE ISLAND

CONNECTICUT 40°N

Mississippi River

Chicago

Lake Erie

Cleveland

PENNSYLVANIA

New York City

Missouri River

IOWA

Cedar Rapids

Des Moines

INDIANA

OHIO

Columbus

Harrisburg

Pittsburgh

Trenton

NEW JERSEY

Philadelphia

Dover

DELAWARE

Omaha

Lincoln

ILLINOIS

Indianapolis

Springfield

Cincinnati

WEST VIRGINIA

Washington, D.C.

Baltimore

Annapolis

MARYLAND

Topeka

Kansas City

Louisville

Frankfort

Charleston

Richmond

Norfolk

St. Louis

KANSAS

Jefferson City

Ohio River

KENTUCKY

VIRGINIA

Wichita

MISSOURI

Tennessee River

NORTH CAROLINA

Raleigh

OKLAHOMA

Tulsa

ARKANSAS

Nashville

TENNESSEE

Charlotte

Oklahoma City

Little Rock

Memphis

Columbia

ATLANTIC OCEAN

Red River

Pine Bluff

Mississippi River

Birmingham

Atlanta

SOUTH CAROLINA

Charleston

Dallas

MISSISSIPPI

ALABAMA

GEORGIA

Columbus

Savannah

Shreveport

Jackson

Montgomery

N

TEXAS

Hattiesburg

Jacksonville

30°N

Austin

Baton Rouge

LOUISIANA

Tallahassee

FLORIDA

KEY

San Antonio

Houston

New Orleans

— National boundary

State boundary

National capital

Tampa

Lake Okeechobee

State capital

Other city

Transverse Mercator Projection

Rio Grande

Gulf   of   Mexico

Miami

90°W

80°W

North and South America: Political

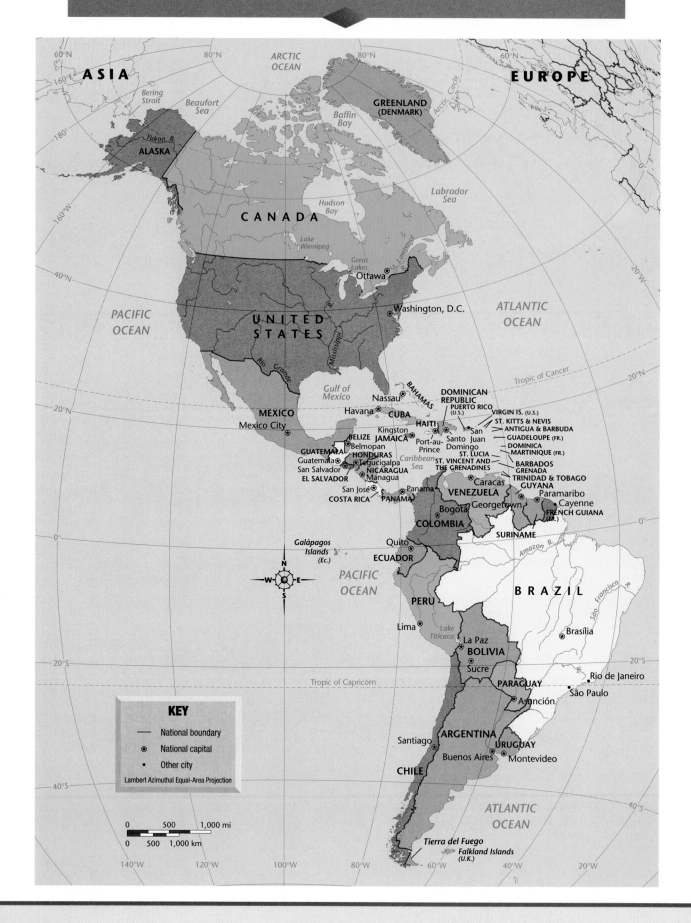

ASIA

ARCTIC OCEAN

EUROPE

Bering Strait

Beaufort Sea

Baffin Bay

GREENLAND (DENMARK)

Yukon R.

ALASKA

Labrador Sea

Hudson Bay

C A N A D A

Lake Winnipeg

Great Lakes

St. Lawrence R.

Ottawa ✪

40°N

PACIFIC OCEAN

ATLANTIC OCEAN

U N I T E D
S T A T E S

Washington, D.C. ✪

Mississippi

Rio Grande

20°N

Gulf of Mexico

Tropic of Cancer

20°N

MEXICO

Nassau

BAHAMAS

DOMINICAN REPUBLIC

Mexico City

Havana ✪

CUBA

PUERTO RICO (U.S.)

VIRGIN IS. (U.S.)

ST. KITTS & NEVIS

Kingston

HAITI

San

ANTIGUA & BARBUDA

BELIZE

JAMAICA ✪

Port-au-Prince

Santo Juan

GUADELOUPE (FR.)

Belmopan

Domingo

DOMINICA

GUATEMALA

HONDURAS

MARTINIQUE (FR.)

Guatemala

Tegucigalpa

Caribbean Sea

ST. LUCIA

San Salvador

NICARAGUA

ST. VINCENT AND

BARBADOS

EL SALVADOR

Managua

THE GRENADINES

GRENADA

TRINIDAD & TOBAGO

San José ✪

Panama

GUYANA

COSTA RICA

PANAMA

VENEZUELA

Caracas ✪

Paramaribo

Bogotá ✪

Georgetown

Cayenne

COLOMBIA

SURINAME

FRENCH GUIANA (FR.)

0°

Galápagos Islands (Ec.)

Quito ✪

Amazon R.

ECUADOR

PACIFIC OCEAN

B R A Z I L

PERU

São Francisco R.

Lima ✪

Lake Titicaca

Brasília ✪

La Paz ✪

BOLIVIA

Sucre ✪

20°S

Tropic of Capricorn

Rio de Janeiro

PARAGUAY

20°S

São Paulo

Asunción ✪

KEY

— National boundary

✪ National capital

• Other city

Lambert Azimuthal Equal-Area Projection

ARGENTINA

Santiago ✪

URUGUAY

Buenos Aires ✪

Montevideo ✪

CHILE

| 0 | 500 | 1,000 mi |
| 0 | 500 | 1,000 km |

40°S

ATLANTIC OCEAN

40°S

Tierra del Fuego

Falkland Islands (U.K.)

140°W 120°W 100°W 80°W 60°W 40°W 20°W

North and South America: Physical

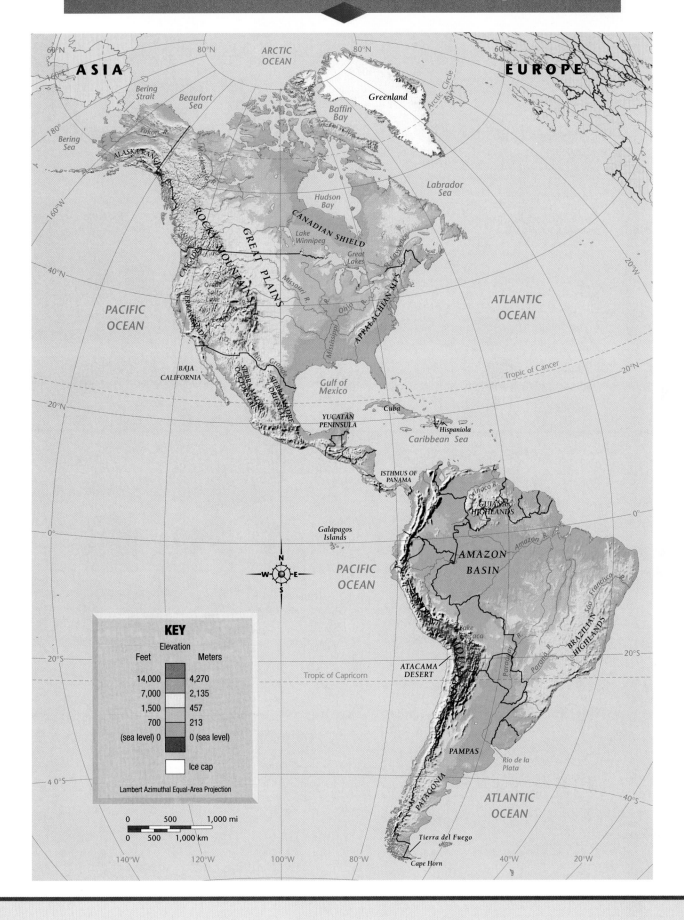

ASIA

EUROPE

ARCTIC OCEAN

Bering Strait

Beaufort Sea

Greenland

Baffin Bay

Arctic Circle

Bering Sea

Yukon R.

ALASKA RANGE

Mackenzie R.

Labrador Sea

Hudson Bay

CANADIAN SHIELD

ROCKY MOUNTAINS

GREAT PLAINS

CASCADES

Lake Winnipeg

Great Lakes

St. Lawrence R.

Missouri R.

Ohio

APPALACHIAN MTS.

PACIFIC OCEAN

SIERRA NEVADA

Great Salt Lake

Mississippi R.

ATLANTIC OCEAN

BAJA CALIFORNIA

SIERRA MADRE OCCIDENTAL

SIERRA MADRE ORIENTAL

Rio Grande

Gulf of Mexico

Tropic of Cancer

YUCATÁN PENINSULA

Cuba

Hispaniola

Caribbean Sea

ISTHMUS OF PANAMA

Orinoco R.

GUIANA HIGHLANDS

Galápagos Islands

N
W · E
S

PACIFIC OCEAN

AMAZON BASIN

Amazon R.

Lake Titicaca

ANDES

São Francisco

BRAZILIAN HIGHLANDS

KEY
Elevation

Feet		Meters
14,000		4,270
7,000		2,135
1,500		457
700		213
(sea level) 0		0 (sea level)

Ice cap

Lambert Azimuthal Equal-Area Projection

ATACAMA DESERT

Tropic of Capricorn

Paraguay R.

Paraná R.

PAMPAS

Rio de la Plata

0	500	1,000 mi
0	500	1,000 km

PATAGONIA

ATLANTIC OCEAN

Tierra del Fuego

Cape Horn

140°W   120°W   100°W   80°W   40°W   20°W

60°N   80°N   80°N   60°N

160°W   180°   160°W

40°N   20°W

20°N

20°N

0°   0°

20°S   20°S

40°S   40°S

Europe: Political

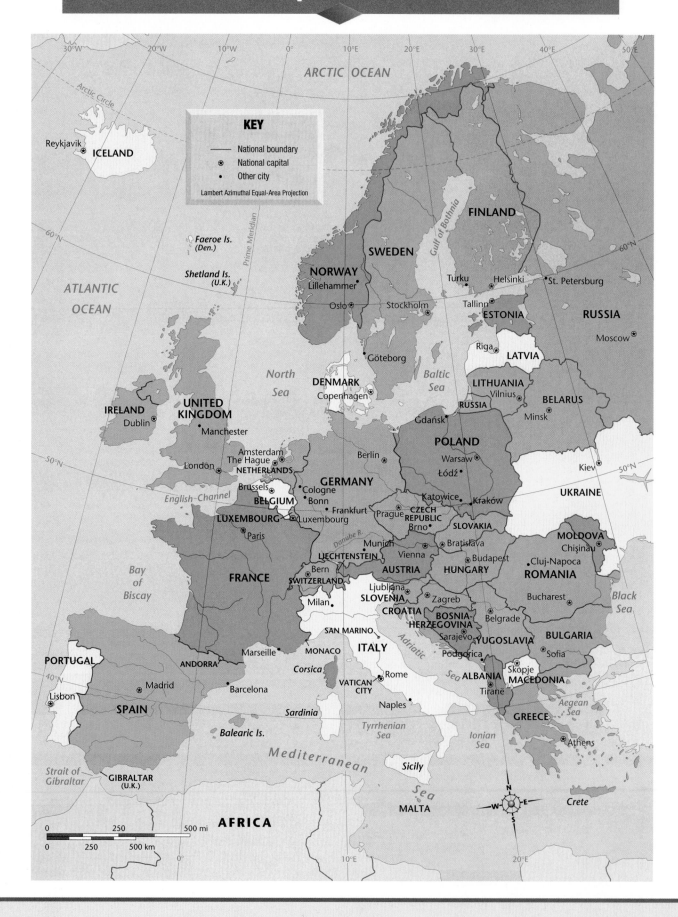

KEY

— National boundary

⊛ National capital

• Other city

Lambert Azimuthal Equal-Area Projection

ARCTIC OCEAN

Arctic Circle

Reykjavik ⊛ **ICELAND**

ATLANTIC OCEAN

Faeroe Is. (Den.)

Shetland Is. (U.K.)

Prime Meridian

FINLAND

SWEDEN

NORWAY
Lillehammer•
Oslo ⊛   Stockholm ⊛

Turku•   Helsinki ⊛   •St. Petersburg

Tallinn ⊛   **ESTONIA**   **RUSSIA**

Moscow ⊛

•Göteborg   Riga ⊛   **LATVIA**

Baltic Sea

North Sea

DENMARK
Copenhagen ⊛

LITHUANIA
Vilnius ⊛   **BELARUS**

Gulf of Bothnia

RUSSIA   Minsk ⊛

IRELAND   **UNITED KINGDOM**
Dublin ⊛

Gdańsk•

•Manchester

POLAND
Warsaw ⊛
Łódź•

Kiev ⊛

London•
Amsterdam ⊛
The Hague ⊛   Berlin•
NETHERLANDS
Brussels•   **GERMANY**
•Cologne
BELGIUM   •Bonn   •Frankfurt
LUXEMBOURG
Luxembourg ⊛

Prague ⊛   Katowice•   Kraków•
CZECH REPUBLIC   **UKRAINE**
Brno•   **SLOVAKIA**

English Channel

MOLDOVA
Chişinău ⊛

•Paris

Danube R.
Munich•   Vienna ⊛   Bratislava ⊛
LIECHTENSTEIN   •Budapest   •Cluj-Napoca

Bay of Biscay

FRANCE
Bern ⊛
SWITZERLAND

AUSTRIA   **HUNGARY**   **ROMANIA**

Ljubljana ⊛
SLOVENIA   Zagreb ⊛

Bucharest ⊛   Black Sea

Milan•
CROATIA
BOSNIA-HERZEGOVINA
Belgrade ⊛

PORTUGAL

ANDORRA

SAN MARINO

Marseille•   **MONACO**

Corsica

ITALY

Adriatic Sea
Sarajevo•   Podgorica•   **YUGOSLAVIA**   **BULGARIA**
⊛Sofia

ALBANIA   Skopje ⊛
Tiranë ⊛   **MACEDONIA**

Lisbon ⊛   Madrid ⊛   •Barcelona

VATICAN CITY ⊛   •Rome

Sardinia

Naples•

Aegean Sea

GREECE

SPAIN

Balearic Is.

Tyrrhenian Sea

Ionian Sea

Athens ⊛

Strait of Gibraltar   **GIBRALTAR** (U.K.)

Mediterranean Sea

Sicily

Crete

AFRICA   **MALTA**

0   250   500 mi

0   250   500 km

Europe: Physical

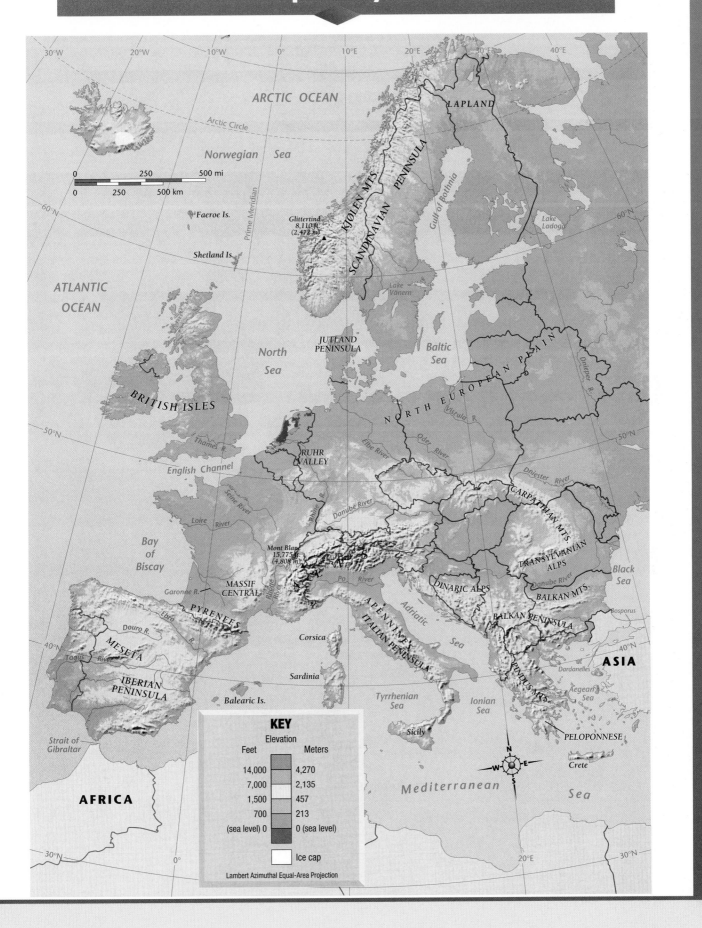

ARCTIC OCEAN

LAPLAND

Norwegian Sea

0   250   500 mi
0   250   500 km

Faeroe Is.

Glittertind
8,110 ft
(2,472 m)

KJØLEN MTS.

SCANDINAVIAN PENINSULA

Gulf of Bothnia

Lake Ladoga

Shetland Is.

ATLANTIC OCEAN

Lake Vänern

JUTLAND PENINSULA

Baltic Sea

North Sea

BRITISH ISLES

NORTH EUROPEAN PLAIN

Dnieper R.

Thames R.

RUHR VALLEY

Elbe River

Oder River

Vistula R.

English Channel

Seine River

Dniester River

CARPATHIAN MTS.

Loire River

Danube River

Bay of Biscay

Mont Blanc
15,775 ft
(4,808 m)

Garonne R.

MASSIF CENTRAL

Rhône River

ALPS

Po River

TRANSYLVANIAN ALPS

Danube River

DINARIC ALPS

BALKAN MTS.

PYRENEES

Ebro R.

Adriatic Sea

BALKAN PENINSULA

Black Sea

Bosporus

Douro R.

MESETA

APENNINES

ITALIAN PENINSULA

ASIA

Tagus River

Corsica

Dardanelles

PINDUS MTS.

Aegean Sea

IBERIAN PENINSULA

Sardinia

Tyrrhenian Sea

Ionian Sea

PELOPONNESE

Crete

Balearic Is.

Strait of Gibraltar

Sicily

AFRICA

Mediterranean Sea

KEY

Elevation

Feet		Meters
14,000		4,270
7,000		2,135
1,500		457
700		213
(sea level) 0		0 (sea level)

Ice cap

Lambert Azimuthal Equal-Area Projection

Africa: Political

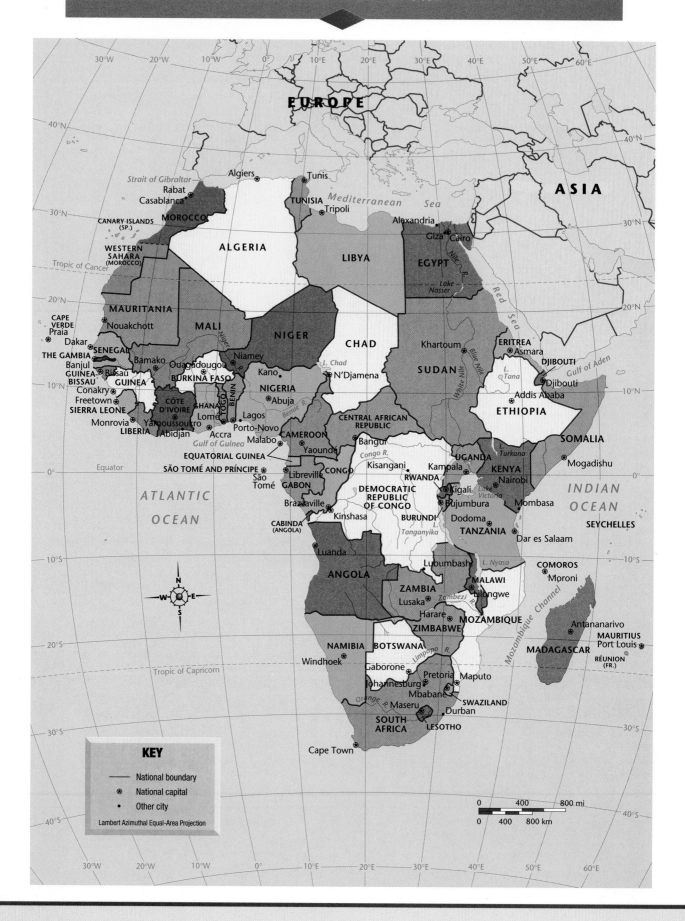

EUROPE

ASIA

Strait of Gibraltar
Algiers
Tunis
Rabat
Casablanca
TUNISIA
Tripoli
Mediterranean Sea
Alexandria
Giza Cairo
CANARY ISLANDS (SP.)
MOROCCO
30°N
WESTERN SAHARA (MOROCCO)
ALGERIA
LIBYA
EGYPT
Nile R.
Lake Nasser
Red Sea
Tropic of Cancer
20°N
MAURITANIA
Nouakchott
MALI
NIGER
CHAD
Khartoum
Blue Nile
ERITREA
Asmara
DJIBOUTI
Gulf of Aden
CAPE VERDE
Praia
Dakar
Niger R.
Niamey
SUDAN
L. Tana
Djibouti
THE GAMBIA
SENEGAL
Bamako
Ouagadougou
Kano
N'Djamena
L. Chad
White Nile
Addis Ababa
Banjul
GUINEA-BISSAU
Bissau
GUINEA
BURKINA FASO
NIGERIA
Abuja
ETHIOPIA
Conakry
Freetown
GHANA
Lomé
Lagos
Benue R.
CENTRAL AFRICAN REPUBLIC
SOMALIA
SIERRA LEONE
CÔTE D'IVOIRE
TOGO
BENIN
Porto-Novo
CAMEROON
Bangui
Mogadishu
Monrovia
Yamoussoukro
Accra
Malabo
Yaoundé
UGANDA
L. Turkana
LIBERIA
Abidjan
Gulf of Guinea
EQUATORIAL GUINEA
Kisangani
Kampala
KENYA
SÃO TOMÉ AND PRÍNCIPE
Libreville
CONGO
RWANDA
Kigali
Nairobi
INDIAN OCEAN
Equator
São Tomé
GABON
Congo R.
Lake Victoria
Mombasa
ATLANTIC OCEAN
Brazzaville
DEMOCRATIC REPUBLIC OF CONGO
Bujumbura
BURUNDI
Dodoma
SEYCHELLES
Kinshasa
CABINDA (ANGOLA)
L. Tanganyika
TANZANIA
Dar es Salaam
Luanda
Lubumbashi
L. Nyasa
COMOROS
Moroni
ANGOLA
ZAMBIA
MALAWI
Lilongwe
Lusaka
Zambezi R.
Antananarivo
Harare
MOZAMBIQUE
MAURITIUS
Port Louis
ZIMBABWE
Mozambique Channel
MADAGASCAR
RÉUNION (FR.)
NAMIBIA
BOTSWANA
Windhoek
Gaborone
Pretoria
Maputo
Limpopo R.
Johannesburg
Mbabane
SWAZILAND
Orange R.
Maseru
Durban
SOUTH AFRICA
LESOTHO
Cape Town

KEY

— National boundary

⊛ National capital

• Other city

Lambert Azimuthal Equal-Area Projection

| 0 | 400 | 800 mi |
| 0 | 400 | 800 km |

Africa: Physical

EUROPE

ASIA

Strait of Gibraltar

Mediterranean Sea

ATLAS MOUNTAINS

Canary Islands

QATTARA DEPRESSION

Suez Canal

ARABIAN DESERT

Nile R.

Tropic of Cancer

AHAGGAR MOUNTAINS

S A H A R A

LIBYAN DESERT

Lake Nasser

Red Sea

20°N

Cape Verde Islands

S A H E L

Senegal R.

Niger R.

White Nile

Blue Nile

L. Tana

Gulf of Aden

FOUTA DJALLON

L. Chad

ETHIOPIAN PLATEAU

10°N

MANDARA MTS.

Benue R.

SUDD

Gulf of Guinea

Ubangi R.

Congo R.

CONGO BASIN

L. Albert

L. Turkana

GREAT RIFT VALLEY

Equator

ATLANTIC OCEAN

L. Edward

Lake Victoria

Kilimanjaro 19,341 ft (5,895 m)

INDIAN OCEAN

L. Mai-Ndombe

SERENGETI PLAIN

Kasai R.

Tanganyika

Zanzibar

Lake Nyasa

Comoros Islands

Zambezi R.

Mozambique Channel

Mauritius

Réunion

Okavango Basin

NAMIB DESERT

Limpopo R.

Tropic of Capricorn

KALAHARI DESERT

Orange R.

Cape of Good Hope

Cape Agulhas

N
W E
S

KEY

Elevation

Feet	Meters
Over 13,000	Over 3,960
6,500–13,000	1,980–3,960
1,600–6,500	480–1,980
650–1,600	200–480
0–650	0–200
Below sea level	Below sea level

Lambert Azimuthal Equal-Area Projection

0   400   800 mi
0 400 800 km

Asia: Political

KEY
European Russia
National boundary
⊛ National capital
• Other city
Two-Point Equidistant Projection

EUROPE

AFRICA

ARCTIC OCEAN

North Pole

PACIFIC OCEAN

INDIAN OCEAN

Arctic Circle

Tropic of Cancer

Equator

RUSSIA

(RUSSIA)

Barents Sea

East Siberian Sea

Bering Sea

Sea of Okhotsk

Kuril Islands (Russia)

Sakhalin Island

Sea of Japan

JAPAN
Tokyo ⊛

Vladivostok

N. KOREA
P'yongyang ⊛
Seoul ⊛
S. KOREA

Yellow Sea

Harbin

Beijing ⊛

Fuzhou

East China Sea

Ryukyu Islands

Hong Kong
Macau

Taipei ⊛
TAIWAN

Philippine Sea

PHILIPPINES
Manila ⊛

South China Sea

Verkhoyansk

Lena R.

Lake Baikal

Irkutsk

Bratsk

Ulan Bator ⊛
MONGOLIA

Xi'an

CHINA

Huang He

Chang Jiang

VIETNAM
Hanoi ⊛

LAOS
Vientiane ⊛
THAILAND
Bangkok ⊛
CAMBODIA
Phnom Penh ⊛

MYANMAR (BURMA)
Yangon

BHUTAN
Thimphu ⊛

NEPAL
Kathmandu ⊛

Dhaka ⊛
BANGLADESH

Bay of Bengal

Chennai (Madras)

SRI LANKA
Colombo ⊛

MALDIVES
Male ⊛

Kuala Lumpur ⊛
MALAYSIA
SINGAPORE
Singapore ⊛

INDONESIA
Bandar Seri Begawan ⊛
BRUNEI
Borneo
Celebes
Java Sea
Jakarta ⊛
Sumatra
Java

Timor

Tanimbar

PALAU
Koror ⊛

PAPUA NEW GUINEA
Port Moresby ⊛
New Guinea

Yenisei R.

Ob R.

Irtysh R.

Ekaterinburg

Omsk

Astana ⊛
KAZAKSTAN
Qaraghandy

Lake Balkhash

Aral Sea

Almaty

Bishkek ⊛
KYRGYZSTAN

TAJIKISTAN
Dushanbe ⊛

UZBEKISTAN
Tashkent ⊛

AFGHANISTAN
Kabul ⊛

Islamabad ⊛
PAKISTAN

INDIA
New Delhi ⊛

Ganges R.

Mumbai (Bombay)

Arabian Sea

St. Petersburg

Moscow ⊛

Volga R.

Samara

Caspian Sea

GEORGIA
Tbilisi ⊛
ARMENIA
Yerevan ⊛
AZERBAIJAN
Baku ⊛

TURKMENISTAN
Ashgabat ⊛

IRAN
Tehran ⊛
Shiraz

Muscat ⊛
OMAN

Socotra (Yemen)

Black Sea

TURKEY
Ankara ⊛
Nicosia ⊛
CYPRUS
LEBANON
Beirut ⊛
ISRAEL
Jerusalem ⊛
JORDAN
Amman ⊛
SYRIA
Damascus ⊛
IRAQ
Baghdad ⊛

Kuwait ⊛
KUWAIT
BAHRAIN
QATAR
Abu Dhabi ⊛
UNITED ARAB EMIRATES

SAUDI ARABIA
Riyadh ⊛

YEMEN
Sanaa ⊛

Mecca

Red Sea

Gulf of Aden

Persian Gulf
Gulf of Oman

Mediterranean Sea

0   500   1,000 mi
0   500   1,000 km

Asia: Physical

Elevation

Feet	Meters
14,000	4,270
7,000	2,135
1,500	457
700	213
(sea level) 0	0 (sea level)

Two-Point Equidistant Projection

ARCTIC OCEAN

North Pole

EUROPE

AFRICA

AUSTRALIA

PACIFIC OCEAN

INDIAN OCEAN

Mediterranean Sea

Black Sea

Caspian Sea

Aral Sea

Barents Sea

East Siberian Sea

Bering Sea

Sea of Okhotsk

Sea of Japan

Yellow Sea

East China Sea

South China Sea

Philippine Sea

Java Sea

Bay of Bengal

Arabian Sea

Red Sea

Gulf of Aden

Persian Gulf

Gulf of Oman

URAL MOUNTAINS

KOLYMA MTS.

KAMCHATKA PENINSULA

STANOVOI RANGE

NORTH SIBERIAN LOWLAND

CENTRAL SIBERIAN PLATEAU

MONGOLIAN PLATEAU

GOBI DESERT

KUNLUN SHAN

PLATEAU OF TIBET

HIMALAYAS

CAUCASUS MTS.

ZAGROS MTS.

PLATEAU OF ANATOLIA

ARABIAN PENINSULA

INDIAN PENINSULA

DECCAN PLATEAU

WESTERN GHATS

EASTERN GHATS

INDOCHINA PENINSULA

MALAY PENINSULA

Lake Balkhash

Lake Baikal

Ob R.

Irtysh R.

Yenisei R.

Lena R.

Amur R.

Huang R.

Yangtze R.

Mekong R.

Ganges R.

Indus R.

Sakhalin Island

Kuril Islands

Hokkaido

Honshu

Shikoku

Kyushu

Ryukyu Islands

Luzon

Mindanao

Celebes

Borneo

Sumatra

Java

New Guinea

Tanimbar

Timor

Socotra

Equator

Tropic of Cancer

Tropic of Capricorn

Arctic Circle

20°N, 30°N, 40°N, 50°N, 60°N, 70°N, 80°N

10°N, 10°S, 20°S

170°W, 180°, 170°E, 160°E, 150°E, 140°E, 130°E, 120°E, 110°E, 100°E, 90°E, 80°E, 70°E, 60°E, 50°E, 40°E, 30°E

N W E S

| 0 | 500 | 1,000 mi |
| 0 | 500 | 1,000 km |

PACIFIC OCEAN

PACIFIC OCEAN

INDIAN OCEAN

Philippine Sea

Arafura Sea

Timor Sea

Coral Sea

Tasman Sea

Line Islands

Gilbert Islands

New Hebrides

Society Islands

Tahiti

Hawaiian Islands (U.S.)

Midway Islands (U.S.)

Wake Island (U.S.)

FRENCH POLYNESIA (FR.)

PITCAIRN ISLAND (U.K.)

COOK ISLANDS (N.Z.)

AMERICAN SAMOA (U.S.)

SAMOA
Apia

TONGA
Nukualofa

FIJI
Suva

TUVALU
Funafuti

KIRIBATI

NAURU
Yaren

VANUATU
Port-Vila

NEW CALEDONIA (FR.)

SOLOMON ISLANDS
Honiara

MARSHALL ISLANDS
Tarawa

FEDERATED STATES OF MICRONESIA
Palikir

CAROLINE ISLANDS

NORTHERN MARIANA ISLANDS (U.S.)

GUAM (U.S.)

NEW ZEALAND
North Island
South Island
Stewart Island
Auckland
Wellington
Christchurch
Dunedin
Cook Strait

AUCKLAND ISLANDS (N.Z.)

AUSTRALIA

WESTERN AUSTRALIA

NORTHERN TERRITORY

SOUTH AUSTRALIA

QUEENSLAND

NEW SOUTH WALES

VICTORIA

TASMANIA

Darwin

Perth

Adelaide

Melbourne

Sydney
Canberra

Brisbane

Hobart

ARNHEM LAND

KIMBERLEY PLATEAU

GREAT SANDY DESERT

GIBSON DESERT

GREAT VICTORIA DESERT

SIMPSON DESERT

BARKLY TABLELAND

CAPE YORK PENINSULA

GREAT DIVIDING RANGE

GREAT ARTESIAN BASIN

NULLARBOR PLAIN

DARLING RANGE

Great Barrier Reef

Great Australian Bight

Lake Eyre

Murray R.

Darling R.

Bass Strait

Tropic of Cancer

Tropic of Capricorn

Equator

International Date Line

20°N

20°S

20°S

20°N

20°S

40°S

120°E 140°E 160°E 180° 160°W 140°W

KEY

Feet	Elevation	Meters
14,000		4,270
7,000		2,135
1,500		457
700		213
(sea level) 0		0 (sea level)

⊛ National capital
✪ State or territorial capital
• Other city

Mercator Projection

Scale:
0 500 1,000 mi
0 500 1,000 km

The Arctic

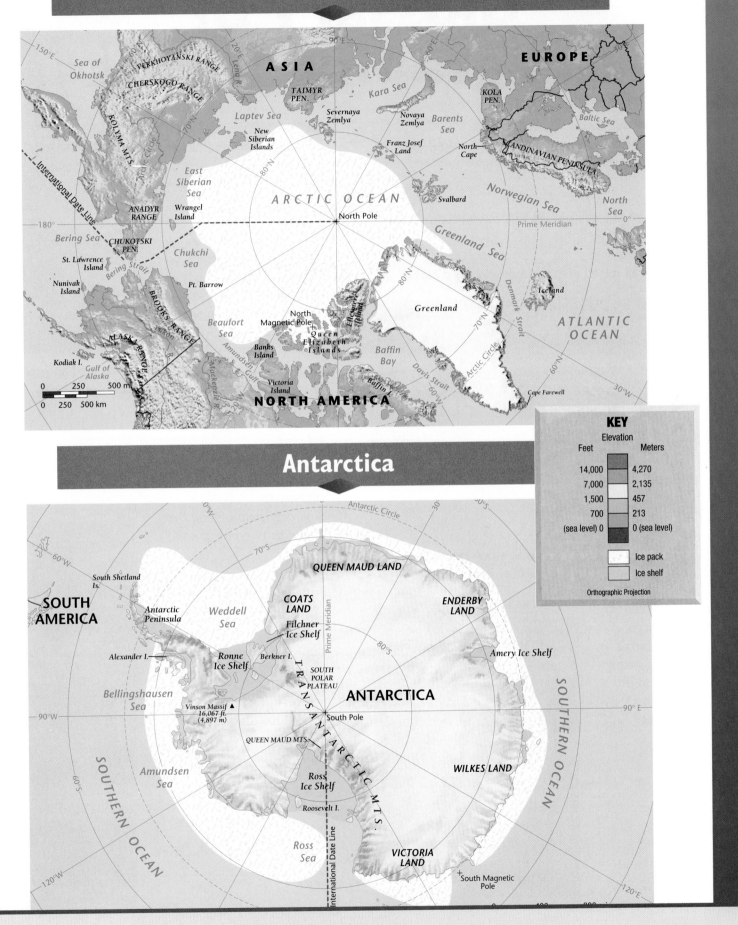

ASIA

Sea of Okhotsk

VERKHOYANSKI RANGE

CHERSKOGO RANGE

KOLYMA MTS.

TAIMYR PEN.

Kara Sea

EUROPE

Laptev Sea

Severnaya Zemlya

Novaya Zemlya

Barents Sea

KOLA PEN.

New Siberian Islands

Franz Josef Land

Baltic Sea

North Cape

SCANDINAVIAN PENINSULA

East Siberian Sea

ARCTIC OCEAN

Svalbard

Norwegian Sea

North Sea

ANADYR RANGE

Wrangel Island

North Pole

Prime Meridian

International Date Line

Chukchi Sea

Greenland Sea

Bering Sea

CHUKOTSKI PEN.

Bering Strait

Denmark Strait

Iceland

St. Lawrence Island

Pt. Barrow

BROOKS RANGE

Greenland

ATLANTIC OCEAN

Nunivak Island

Beaufort Sea

North Magnetic Pole

Ellesmere Island

Kodiak I.

ALASKA RANGE

Yukon R.

Banks Island

Queen Elizabeth Islands

Baffin Bay

Arctic Circle

Gulf of Alaska

Amundsen Gulf

Mackenzie R.

Victoria Island

Davis Strait

Baffin I.

Cape Farewell

NORTH AMERICA

0 250 500 mi
0 250 500 km

Antarctica

Antarctic Circle

QUEEN MAUD LAND

South Shetland Is.

SOUTH AMERICA

Antarctic Peninsula

Weddell Sea

COATS LAND

ENDERBY LAND

Filchner Ice Shelf

Alexander I.

Ronne Ice Shelf

Berkner I.

Prime Meridian

Amery Ice Shelf

Bellingshausen Sea

TRANSANTARCTIC MTS.

SOUTH POLAR PLATEAU

ANTARCTICA

SOUTHERN OCEAN

Vinson Massif ▲ 16,067 ft. (4,897 m)

South Pole

SOUTHERN OCEAN

QUEEN MAUD MTS.

WILKES LAND

Amundsen Sea

Ross Ice Shelf

Roosevelt I.

Ross Sea

VICTORIA LAND

International Date Line

South Magnetic Pole

KEY

Elevation

Feet		Meters
14,000		4,270
7,000		2,135
1,500		457
700		213
(sea level) 0		0 (sea level)

Ice pack

Ice shelf

Orthographic Projection

Glossary of Geographic Terms

basin
a depression in the surface of the land; some basins are filled with water

bay
a part of a sea or lake that extends into the land

butte
a small raised area of land with steep sides

▲ butte

canyon
a deep, narrow valley with steep sides; often has a stream flowing through it

cataract
a large waterfall; any strong flood or rush of water

delta
a triangular-shaped plain at the mouth of a river, formed when sediment is deposited by flowing water

flood plain
a broad plain on either side of a river, formed when sediment settles on the riverbanks

glacier
a huge, slow-moving mass of snow and ice

hill
an area that rises above surrounding land and has a rounded top; lower and usually less steep than a mountain

island
an area of land completely surrounded by water

isthmus
a narrow strip of land that connects two larger areas of land

mesa
a high, flat-topped landform with cliff-like sides; larger than a butte

mountain
an area that rises steeply at least 2,000 feet (610 m) above surrounding land; usually wide at the bottom and rising to a narrow peak or ridge

▶ glacier

 ◀ cataract

◀ delta

mountain pass
a gap between mountains

peninsula
an area of land almost completely surrounded by water and connected to the mainland by an isthmus

plain
a large area of flat or gently rolling land

plateau
a large, flat area that rises above the surrounding land; at least one side has a steep slope

river mouth
the point where a river enters a lake or sea

strait
a narrow stretch of water that connects two larger bodies of water

tributary
a river or stream that flows into a larger river

volcano
an opening in the Earth's surface through which molten rock, ashes, and gasses from the Earth's interior escape

▶ volcano

Gazetteer

A

Amazon Rain Forest a large tropical rain forest occupying the drainage basin of the Amazon River in northern South America and covering an area of 2,700,000 square miles, p. 19

Andes Mountains (13°S, 75°W) a mountain system extending along the western coast of South America, p. 8

Argentina (35.3°S, 67°W) a country in South America, p. 12

Atacama Desert (23.5°S, 69°W) a desert in Chile, South America; the driest place on the Earth, p. 14

B

Bolivia (17°S, 64°W) a country in South America, p. 3

Brasília (15.49°S, 47.39°W) the capital city of Brazil, p. 76

Brazil (9°S, 53°W) the largest country in South America, p. 12

C

Canal Zone a 10-mile strip of land along the Panama Canal, stretching from the Atlantic Ocean to the Pacific Ocean, p. 101

Caracas (10.3°N, 66.58°W) the capital city of Venezuela, p. 148

Caribbean (14.3°N, 75.3°W) a part of the southern Atlantic Ocean, p. 9

Central America (10.45°N, 87.15°W) the part of Latin America that includes the seven republics of Guatemala, Honduras, El Salvador, Nicaragua, Costa Rica, Panama, and Belize, p. 9

Chile (35°S, 72°W) a country in South America, p. 14

Colombia (3.3°N, 72.3°W) a country in South America, p. 25

Condado a waterfront area of San Juan, Puerto Rico, p. 123

Copán (14.5°N, 89.1°W) a ruined ancient Mayan city in western Honduras, p. 36

Cuba (22°N, 79°W) an island country, the largest of the Caribbean islands, p. 11

Cuzco (13.36°S, 71.52°W) a city in Peru; capital of the Incan empire, p. 39

G

Guatemala (15.45°N, 91.45°W) a country in Central America, p. 36

H

Haiti (19°N, 72.15°W) a country in the Caribbean Sea, on the island of Hispaniola, p. 50

Hispaniola (17.3°N, 73.15°W) an island in the Caribbean Sea, divided between Haiti in the west and the Dominican Republic in the east, p. 11

J

Jamaica (17.45°N, 78°W) an island country in the Caribbean Sea, p. 11

L

Lake Maracaibo (9.55°N, 72.13°W) a lake in northwestern Venezuela, p. 13

Lake Titicaca (16.12° S, 70.33° W) the world's largest lake, in the Andes Mountains in South America, p. 13

M

Mexico (23.45°N, 104°W) a country in North America, p. 9

Mexico City (19.28°N, 99.09°W) the capital of and largest city in Mexico; one of the largest urban areas in the world, p. 36

Miami (25.45°N, 80.11°W) a city in southeastern Florida, p. 107

P

Panama (9°N, 80°W) a country in Central America, p. 53

Panama Canal (9.2°N, 79.55°W) an important shipping canal across the Isthmus of Panama, linking the Caribbean Sea (and the Atlantic Ocean) to the Pacific Ocean, p. 96

Paraguay (24°S, 57°W) a country in South America, p. 3

Patagonia (46.45°S, 69.3°W) a desert in southern Argentina; the largest desert in the Americas, p. 17

Peru (10°S, 75°W) a country in South America, p. 13

Port-au-Prince (18.35°N, 72.2°W) the capital city and chief port of Haiti, p. 113

Puerto Rico (18.16°N, 66.5°W) an island commonwealth of the United States in the Caribbean Sea, p. 11

R

Rio de Janeiro (22.5°S, 43.2°W) a major city in Brazil, p. 129

S

Salvador (12.59°S, 38.27°W) the capital city and major port of Bahia state, in northeastern Brazil, p. 130

San Juan (18.3°N, 66.10°W) the capital and largest city in Puerto Rico, p. 123

Santiago (33.26°S, 70.4°W) the capital city of Chile, p. 142

São Paulo (23.34°S, 46.38°W) the largest city in Brazil, p. 74

South America (15°S, 60°W) the world's fourth-largest continent, bounded by the Caribbean Sea, the Atlantic Ocean, and the Pacific Ocean, and linked to North America by the Isthmus of Panama, p. 9

T

Tenochtitlán Aztec metropolis covering more than five square miles near modern Mexico City; originally located on two small islands in Lake Texcoco, it gradually grew; one of two Aztec capitals, its name means "stone rising in the water," p. 37

Tikal (17.16°N, 89.49°W) the largest Mayan city in the northern part of Guatemala, p. 36

Trinidad and Tobago (11°N, 61°W) republic of the West Indies, on the two islands called Trinidad and Tobago, p. 3

V

Valley of Mexico the area in Mexico where Lake Texcoco, Tenochtitlán, and modern Mexico City are located, p. 36

Venezuela (8°N, 65°W) a country in South America, p. 12

W

West Indies (19°N, 78°W) the islands of the Caribbean, p. 3

Glossary

This glossary lists key terms and other useful terms from the book.

A

altiplano [al tih PLAH noh] a high plateau region; a region of high plateaus in the Andes, p. 135

aqueduct a pipe or channel used to carry water from a distant source to dry areas, p. 41

B

bauxite a mixture of minerals that is the main ore aluminum is made of; looks like clay, p. 23

boom a period of increased prosperity during which more of a product is produced and sold, p. 149

C

cacao a tree that grows in the American tropics and produces seeds used to make chocolate and cocoa, p. 23

campesino [kahm pe SEE noh] a poor Latin American farmer, p. 58

canopy a dense mass of leaves forming the top layer of a forest, p.129

Carnival an annual celebration in Latin America with music, dances, and parades, p. 72

caudillo [kow DEE yoh] a military officer who rules strictly, p. 54

citizen an individual with certain rights and responsibilities under a particular government, p. 121

commonwealth a self-governing political unit with strong ties to a particular country, p. 121

communist having an economic system in which the government owns all large businesses and most of a country's land, p. 109

conquistador [kon KEES ta dor] 16th-century conquerors working for the Spanish government who were in charge of gaining land and wealth in the Americas, p. 44

constitution a statement of a country's basic laws and values, p. 123

coral a rock-like substance formed from the skeletons of tiny sea animals, p. 11

Creole a person, often of European and African descent, born in the Caribbean or other parts of the Americas, whose culture has strong French and African influence; a dialect spoken by Creoles, p. 115

criollo [kree OH yoh] a person born of Spanish parents born outside Spain; often among the best-educated and wealthiest people in the Spanish colonies, p. 50

D

dialect a version of a language that is spoken in a particular region, p. 115

dictator a ruler of a country who has complete power, p. 109

diversify to add variety; to expand, p. 27

diversity variety, p. 64

E

economy the ways that goods and services are produced and made available to people, p. 55

elevation height of land above sea level, p. 17

El Niño [el NEEN yoh] a warm ocean current that flows along the western coast of South America; this current influences global weather patterns, p. 14

emigrate move out of one country into another, p. 67

encomienda [en KOH mee en duh] the right to demand taxes or labor from Native Americans; this right was granted to American settlers by the Spanish government, p. 47

ethnic group a group of people who share the same ancestors, culture, language, or religion, p. 70

exile a person who leaves or is forced to leave his or her homeland for another country, p. 110

H

hacienda [hah see EN duh] plantation owned by the Spanish settlers or the Catholic Church in Spanish America, p. 47

hieroglyphics [hy ur oh GLIF iks] a system of writing using signs and symbols, used by the Maya and other cultures, p. 36

hydroelectricity [hy droh ee lek TRIS ih tee] electricity produced by rushing water, p. 23

I

illiterate unable to read or write, p. 112

immigrant a person who has moved into one country from another, p. 67

import to bring products into one country from another to sell, p. 76

indigenous [in DIJ uh nus] describes people who are descendants of the people who first lived in a region, p. 64

injustice lack of fairness, p. 65

invest to spend money to earn more money, p. 55

isthmus narrow strip of land that has water on both sides and joins two larger bodies of land, p. 11

L

ladino [luh DEE noh] in Guatemala, a mestizo, p. 90

Line of Demarcation an imaginary line from the North Pole to the South Pole (at about 50° longitude) set forth in the 1494 Treaty of Tordesillas; Spain had the right to settle and trade west of the line and Portugal had the right to settle and trade east of the line, p. 44

lock a section of waterway in which ships are raised or lowered by adjusting the water level, p. 96

M

maize both the plant and the kernel of corn, p. 36

maquiladora [ma kee la DOR a] a U.S.-owned factory in Mexico that is located close to the U.S.-Mexico border, p. 66

mestizo a person of mixed Spanish and Native American ancestry, p. 46

migrant farmworker a laborer who travels from one area to another, picking crops that are in season, p. 86

moderate a climate that is mild and without extremes in temperature or weather; also known as temperate, p. 178

montaña in northeast Peru, large stretches of tropical forests on the lower slopes of mountains, p. 136

P

pampas [PAHM puhs] flat grassland regions in the southern part of South America; a region similar to the Great Plains in the United States, p. 12

pesticide [PES tuh syd] a chemical used to kill insects and diseases that can attack crops, p. 147

photosynthesis [foht oh SIN thuh sis] the process by which green plants and trees produce their own food using water, carbon dioxide, and sunlight; oxygen is released as a result of photosynthesis, p. 133

plateau [pla TOH] large raised area of mostly level land, p. 11

plaza public square at the center of a village, town, or city, p. 85

political movement a large group of people who work together to defend their rights or to change the leaders in power, p. 93

privatization [pry vuh tih ZAY shun] a policy by a government to sell its industries to individuals or private companies, p. 152

Q

quipu [KEE poo] a knotted string used by Incan government officials and traders for record keeping, p. 41

R

revolution a political movement in which people overthrow the existing government and set up another, p. 50

rural having to do with the countryside, p. 59

S

sierra a group of mountains, such as the one that runs from northwest to southeast Peru, p. 136

squatter a person who settles on someone else's land without permission, p. 84

strike work stoppage; a refusal to continue to work until certain demands of workers are met, p. 93

subsistence farming the practice of growing only as much food as a group of people needs to survive, p. 75

subtropical a climate that occurs in regions next to the Tropics, and is hot and humid although less so than in tropical climates, p. 178

T

treaty an agreement in writing made between two or more countries, p. 44

Treaty of Tordesillas [tor day SEE yas] the 1494 treaty setting up the Line of Demarcation, giving Spain the right to settle and trade west of the line and Portugal the same rights east of the line, p. 44

tributary [TRIB yoo tehr ee] river or stream that flows into a main river, p. 13

tropical a climate that is very hot and humid, p. 20

tundra a cold region with little vegetation; in mountains, the area above the tree line, p. 138

U

urban having to do with cities, p. 59

Index

The *italicized* page numbers refer to illustrations. The *m, c,* or *p* preceding the number refers to maps (*m*), charts, tables, or graphs (*c*), or pictures (*p*).

Acknowledgments

Cover Design

Bruce Bond, Suzanne Schineller, and Olena Serbyn

Cover Photo

Jon Chomitz

Maps

MapQuest.com, Inc.
Map information sources: Columbia Encyclopedia, Encyclopaedia Britannica, Microsoft® Encarta®, National Geographic Atlas of the World, Rand McNally Commercial Atlas, The Times Atlas of the World.

Staff Credits

The people who made up the *World Explorer* team—representing editorial, editorial services, design services, on-line services/multimedia development, product marketing, production services, project office, and publishing processes—are listed below. Bold type denotes core team members.

Joyce Barisano, Margaret Broucek, **Paul Gagnon, Mary Hanisco, Dotti Marshall,** Kirsten Richert, Susan Swan, and Carol Signorino.

Additional Credits

Art and Design: Emily Soltanoff. Editorial: Debra Reardon, Nancy Rogier. Market Research: Marilyn Leitao. Publishing Processes: Wendy Bohannan.

Program Development and Production

Editorial and Project Management: Summer Street Press
Production: Pronk&Associates

Text

30, "Where the Flame Trees Bloom," by Alma Flor Ada. Text © 1994 Alma Flor Ada. Reprinted with the permission of Atheneum Books for Young Readers, an imprint of Simon & Schuster Children's Publishing Division. **110,** Excerpt from "Finding My Father," by Lydia Martin, *The Miami Herald,* June 18, 1995. Reprinted with permission of *The Miami Herald.* **158,** Poem LXXII (Question Book) by Pablo Neruda. Spanish original reprinted from *Libros de las Preguntas,* by Pablo Neruda. © Pablo Neruda and Fundación Pablo Neruda, 1974. English translation from *Late and Posthumous Poems 1968–1974,* by Pablo Neruda, translated by Ben Belitt. © 1988 by Ben Belitt. Used by permission of Grove/Atlantic, Inc.

Photos

v TR, © SuperStock International, **v BR,** © Robert Frerck/Odyssey Productions, **iv TL,** © Chip & Rosa María de la Cueva Peterson, **v BL,** © Doug Armand/Tony Stone Images, **1** background, Artbase Inc., **1 TL,** © Chip & Rosa María de la Cueva Peterson, **1 TR,** © Stock Montage, **1 CL,** © Corbis-Bettmann, **1 BR,** © Ed Simpson/Tony Stone Images, **5 BL,** © Mark Thayer, Boston, **7 CL,** © Photri, **8 CR,** © Chip & Rosa María de la Cueva Peterson, **11 BR,** © Chip & Rosa María de la Cueva Peterson, **12 BR,** © Bryan Parsley/Tony Stone Images, **13 TR,** © Will & Deni McIntyre/Tony Stone Images, **14 BL,** © Robert Frerck/Odyssey Productions, **16 TR,** © Martin Rogers/Tony Stone Images, **19 CR,** © Wolfgang Kaehler/Wolfgang Kaehler Photography, **21 B,** Credit Unavailable, **22 BL,** © Chip & Rosa María de la Cueva Peterson, **23 BR,** © Robert Frerck/Odyssey Productions, **25 TR,** © Robert Frerck/Odyssey Productions, **26 TL,** © Erik Svenson/Tony Stone Images, **26 TR,** © Chip & Rosa María de la Cueva Peterson, **31 TL,** © Photri, **32 TR,** © Chip & Rosa María de la Cueva Peterson, **35 BR,** © Chip & Rosa María de la Cueva Peterson, **36 C,** © Robert Frerck/Odyssey Productions, **36 TC,** © Robert Frerck/Odyssey Productions, **36 TL,** © Robert Frerck/Odyssey Productions, **38 TL,** © Chip & Rosa María de la Cueva Peterson, **38 TR,** © Robert Frerck/Odyssey Productions, **39 BR,** © Chip & Rosa María de la Cueva Peterson, **40 B,** © Ed Simpson/Tony Stone Images, **41 C,** © Robert Frerck/Odyssey Productions, **42 TR,** © Wolfgang Kaehler/Wolfgang Kaehler Photography, **43 BR,** © Daniel Aubry/Odyssey Productions, **45 TR,** © Stock Montage, **49 B,** © David Young-Wolff/PhotoEdit, **50 BR,** © North Wind Picture Archives, **51 BR,** © Robert Frerck/Odyssey Productions, **53 BL,** © Chip & Rosa María de la Cueva Peterson, **55 BR,** © Robert Frerck/Odyssey Productions, **57 BR,** © Mark Segal/Tony Stone Images, **58 TR,** © Elizabeth Harris/Tony Stone Images, **59 TR,** © Chip & Rosa María de la Cueva Peterson, **62 CR,** © Robert Frerck/Odyssey Productions, **64 BC,** © Sheryl McNee/Tony Stone Images, **66 CL,** © Tom Benoit/Tony Stone Images, **66 TR,** © Robert E. Daemmrich/Tony Stone Images, **68 BL,** © Jason Laure'/Laure' Communications, **70 BR,** © SuperStock International, **71 TL,** © Corbis-Bettmann, **71 TR,** © Photri, **72 TR,** © Doug Armand/Tony Stone Images, **73 BR,** © Alex Irvin/Alex Irvin Photography, **74 BR,** © Ed Simpson/Tony Stone Images, **75 TL,** Untitled, by Yhaninc Puelles Enriquez, age 12, Peru. Courtesy of the International Children's Art Museum, **85 BL,** © Demetrio Carrasco/Tony Stone Images, **87 CR,** © David R. Frazier/Tony Stone Images, **88 TR,** © Robert Frerck/Odyssey Productions, **89 BR,** © Robert Frerck/Odyssey Productions, **90 CL,** © Bonnie Kamin/PhotoEdit, **91 CL,** © James Nelson/Tony Stone Images, **92 TR,** © Chip & Rosa María de la Cueva Peterson, **94–95 TR,** © David Young-Wolff/PhotoEdit, **97 CL,** ©Michael P.L. Fogden/Bruce Coleman Inc/Picture Quest, **99 TL,** © Chip & Rosa María de la Cueva Peterson, **100 CL,** © Odyssey Productions, **100 CR,** © Odyssey Productions, **107 BR,** © Shepard Sherbell/SABA Press Photos, **108 TL,** © Nick Sapieha/Stock Boston/Picture Quest, **109 TC,** © Corbis-Bettmann, **110 TR,** © Alyx Kellington/D.D. Bryant Stock Photo, **111 BL,** © Miami Herald/Miami Herald Publishing Co., **112 TL,** © Mary Altier/Mary Altier Photography, **113 BR,** © Corbis-Bettman, **114 CL,** © Alon Reininger/Contact Press Images/Picture Quest, **115 CL,** © Corbis-Bettman, **115 BR,** © Corbis-Bettman, **116 BR,** Untitled, by Cange Walthe, age 12, Haiti. Courtesy of the International Children's Art Museum, **117 TR,** © Corbis-Bettman, **120 BL,** © Benno Friedman, **121 CL,** Dorling Kindersley, **123 BR,** © Lawrence Migdale/Tony Stone Images, **124 BL,** © Robert Frerck/Odyssey Productions, **124 BR,** © Wolfgang Kaehler/ Wolfgang Kaehler Photography, **125 TC,** © Suzanne L. Murphy/D.D. Bryant Stock Photo, **129 BR,** © Jacques Jangoux/Tony Stone Images, **130 CL,** © Bill Gallery/Stock Boston/Picture Quest, **131 BR,** © Sylvain Grandadam/Tony Stone Images, **132 B,** © Ary Diesendruck/Tony Stone Images, **135 BR,** © Wolfgang Kaehler/Wolfgang Kaehler Photography, **136 CL,** © Paul Franklin/Latin Focus, **137 BL,** © D.E. Cox/Tony Stone Images, **138 BR,** © David Mangurian/David Mangurian Photography, **138 BL,** © David Mangurian/David Mangurian Photography, **139 TR,** © Robert Frerck/Odyssey Productions, **140 BR,** © David Young-Wolff/ PhotoEdit, **142 BL,** © Photography by S.R.H. Spicer, Vermillion, South Dakota, U.S.A., **143 TL,** © Richard T. Nowitz/CORBIS/MAGMA, **144 TL,** © Rhonda Klevansky/Tony Stone Images, **144 TR,** © Robert Frerck/ Odyssey Productions, **145 B,** © Chip & Rosa María de la Cueva Peterson, **146 TR,** © Charles Philip/Photri, **148 BL,** © Photri, **149 C,** © Richard T. Nowitz/CORBIS/MAGMA, **150 B,** © Chip & Rosa María de la Cueva Peterson, **152 BR,** © Jacques Jangoux/Tony Stone Images, **153 TL,** © Julie Marcotte/Tony Stone Images, **156 B,** © David Young-Wolff/ PhotoEdit, **159 CL,** © Francois Gohier/Francois Gohier Pictures, **159 CR,** © Francois Gohier/Francois Gohier Pictures, **160 BL,** © Mark Thayer, Boston, **163 BL,** © Mark Thayer, Boston, **164 CL,** © Steve Leonard/Tony Stone Images, **164 B,** © Robert Frerck/Odyssey Productions, **165 CL,** © Wolfgang Kaehler/Wolfgang Kaehler Photography, **165 BL,** © John Elk/Tony Stone Images, **165 BC,** © Will & Deni McIntyre/Tony Stone Images, **175 B,** © G. Brad Lewis/Tony Stone Images, **177 BR,** © Nigel Press/Tony Stone Images, **180 B,** Artbase Inc., **180–183** background, Artbase Inc., **181 CL,** Artbase Inc., **181 BR,** Artbase Inc., **184–188** background, Artbase Inc., **184 B,** Artbase Inc., **185 CL,** Artbase Inc., **187 BR,** Artbase Inc., **188 BR,** Artbase Inc., **189 BR,** Artbase Inc., **190–191** background, Artbase Inc., **191 BL,** Artbase Inc., **191 CR,** Artbase Inc., **192–193** background, Artbase Inc., **193 C,** Artbase Inc., **194–195** background, Artbase Inc., **196–197** background, Artbase Inc., **214–215 B,** © Spencer Swanger/Tom Stack & Associates, **214 BL,** © John Beatty/Tony Stone Images, **214 CL,** © A.&L. Sinibaldi/ Tony Stone Images, **215 CR,** © Hans Strand/Tony Stone Images, **215 TL,** © Paul Chesley/Tony Stone Images.